Walking Shadows

Walking Shadows

Archetype and Psyche in Crisis and Growth

Dr Tim Read

muswell hill press

London • New York

First published by Muswell Hill Press, London, 2014

www.muswellhillpress.co.uk.

British Library CIP Data available
ISBN: 978-1-908995-09-4
Printed in Great Britain

For the children:
Becky, Jenny, Thomas, Phoebe and Nicholas.

Contents

Acknowledgments

Who knows when a book really starts to take its shape, when is the point of conception? I remember my surge of curiosity and excitement when I read the words 'archetype' and 'collective unconscious' for the first time, but I suppose my interest in these ideas and the germ of this book was already formed by then. The final birthing of this book is a process of completion – but within the bigger picture of incompleteness. I will continue to learn and some of the future learning will probably modify some of the views that I have expressed here. I look forward to the on-going process.

This book represents a distillation of what I think I have learned so far. The learning comes in many forms of course, but much of it has come in the context of my work in psychiatry. It is a wonderful gift to work with people and to learn something new every day. Some days teach us more than others; sometimes the learning comes easily but sometimes the fruit lies on the higher branches and is harder to acquire. Such learning requires some stretching and a degree of risk – one can pick up some bruises in the process. The bruises are to ego rather than tissue and I think they are necessary and ultimately helpful.

For me, this learning could not happened without my colleagues, the patients, and the sprawling mass of the hospitals and clinics that we all served. I have drawn heavily on this experience but have disguised all clinical material. Thus the cases I discuss are composites and do not belong to any one person. There are five main groupings of people in this shared journey through psychiatry.

- The patients who trust themselves to our care.
- Jenny Bunker, Eugene Clerkin, Deborah Goodes and the Crisis Service.
- Gareth Richards, Matt Callaghan, Peter Martin and the Liaison Service.
- My psychiatrist colleagues in the London Borough of Tower Hamlets. My brothers in arms in the gritty 1990s, Jan Falkowski, Dave Curtis and Nick Bass and the second generation of deeply committed, skilled and compassionate psychiatrists who joined us after 2000, such as Frankie Connell and Karl Marlowe. Comrades I salute you.

- The 150 or so psychiatrists in training that have joined me over the years with their freshness and enthusiasm, I hope you enjoy this book and that it gives you something of value.

Thank you also to all my fellow retreatants over the years and those who have shared their stories with me. A special thank you to Meg Sharpe, Stanislav Grof, Tav Sparks, Diana Medina, Simon Buxton and Zoe Bran who have been my teachers and mentors as well as Kate Midmore, John Schlapobersky, Louise O'Reilly and Phoebe Read for their assistance with this book.

My gratitude to my colleagues at Muswell Hill Press, Mark Chaloner and Keiron Le Grice, for their expertise and their friendship. I greatly appreciate Keiron's wise and skilful editing, the rigour of his scholarship and his unerring eye for the passages where further work was required.

Most of all, my deep and eternal love to Jo for our sharing together of life's rich journey.

TR. Rye. East Sussex. May 2014.

Preface

Its psychiatry, Jim, but not as we know it

This book rests on four pillars. The first is my professional life as a psychiatrist. The second is my personal journey as a human being, ever learning and sharing my life with family and friends. The third is one of ideas, of theories—of Jung, Plato and Bohm. The fourth is my interest in highly charged and meaning-filled states of mind, both challenging and sublime.

I was probably always destined to be a psychiatrist. My father intended to follow his father into medicine but was of the generation called to fight in the Second World War and the opportunity for a medical career passed him by. My mother planned to become a psychologist but she developed a mild form of tuberculosis that prevented her from taking the necessary exams. So in becoming a psychiatrist I was fulfilling both of my parent's unrealized ambitions. This was not a conscious decision but came from a far deeper, unconscious place; indeed, at medical school it became completely clear to me when I sat in my first psychiatry clinic that the subject was utterly fascinating and I had found my vocation.

This book includes an unconventional take on psychiatry, but my practice as a psychiatrist was conventional. I prescribe medication when I think it will help—although, in practice, I probably stop unnecessary medication as often as I start necessary medication. My primary interest has been in the use of psychological techniques and treatments, and I am very aware, working in London's East End, of the social deprivation and disadvantage of many of our fellow human beings. For me psychiatry is not just about treating illness but about recovery, about nurture, learning, growing and developing. It is about maximising someone's potential as a human being.

The question that interests me most is the issue of growth. What is growth and how can we find it? What is the growth-orientated option? How can we learn, and how can we most fully achieve our human potential? Growth is difficult to define, and the passage towards it may have hazards. What indeed may the side effects of growth? There is stasis that masquerades as growth. As there is fool's gold, there is fool's growth.

There are many barriers to growth, with one such barrier being mental illness. There are also certain unusual mental states that have an extraordinary intensity that can predispose to illness but, if carefully negotiated, can bring enormous potential for growth. This book is about these high intensity mental states.

I conform to the bio-psycho-social perspective in that I hold great respect for the insights derived from neuroscience, cognitive science and psychoanalysis and I use these models every day of my professional life. However, I believe there is another layer of psyche that I refer to as archetypal, and that this archetypal layer is inextricably entwined with our biological hardware and our psycho-social programming. This book articulates a bio-psycho-social-archetypal model that I term BPSA for short. The first section of the book addresses the concept of the archetype, the second section explores how archetypal forces may affect us in various ways, while the third section looks at some possible ways of harnessing these forces in a useful, growth-orientated manner.

Upstairs and Downstairs

British psychiatry is generally multidisciplinary, comprising people from a number of different professional backgrounds—whether medical, nursing, psychology, social work or occupational therapy. A good team is greater than the sum of its parts, with people learning from each other, supporting each other and honing skills together over time. For over twenty years, I was the Consultant Psychiatrist at the Royal London Hospital with responsibility for two remarkable teams, both working with psychiatric emergencies. The first was the Crisis Intervention Service and the second the Liaison Psychiatry service. These teams will be referred to throughout the book in abbreviated form as the Crisis team and the Liaison team. The Crisis team was situated on the third floor of the Hospital and the Liaison team office was in the emergency room on the ground floor so we often referred to the teams as 'upstairs' and 'downstairs'.

The role of the Crisis team was to see people in acute psycho-social crisis. Something so traumatic had happened to these people that it had overwhelmed their capacity to cope and they had become suicidal. They did not usually have the type of psychiatric condition for which medication was required; rather, they needed expert psychological help in making sense of their life crisis. These crisis states are fraught with difficulty but present a valuable opportunity for growth. The crisis invariably involves a re-enactment of a previous trauma, usually of loss or abuse. There is the opportunity to not only help a person to recover from the current crisis, but also to more completely resolve the previous trauma and strengthen some of the fault lines that the original trauma created in their personality structure. If this process is supported, they will be less vulnerable to events with a similar emotional resonance in the future. If the crisis is unresolved, there is potential for matters to become much worse with disruption of relationships, the development of harmful patterns of behaviour and possibly suicide.

The questions we ask ourselves and our patients in the crisis service are simple. How can we fully understand the crisis, what is the meaning of it, and how can we work together towards resolution of the crisis so that life can be enhanced? This third consideration applies not only the life of the person who comes to see us, but the people who are close to them, such as their partner, their children, and perhaps even their grandchildren. How, we ask ourselves, can something difficult, which feels so bad, eventually be turned to something that is potentially life enhancing?

For the people who came to the crisis service, this would usually be the only time in their lives that they would see a psychiatrist or psychotherapist. These patients do not usually have a recurrent mood disorder or any other mental illness, and they are not usually people who have much interest in personal exploration or longer-term psychotherapy. The crisis allows an opportunity to do some work on themselves that is unlikely to be repeated. The trigger that caused the crisis had induced a mental state of such dreadfulness, of such intensity, that they considered ending their lives. They had either harmed themselves or sought help through their doctor. This intense mental state did not last for long but provided the impetus to seek treatment. The nature of the triggering crisis had highlighted the key traumas in their biographical history, their formative relationships and their personality structure. Because of the shock of the crisis, their defences were lowered and they were more amenable to the possibility of change. As the intensity of the crisis waned, the defences and characteristic personality patterns tended to reassert themselves but maybe, just maybe, something had shifted and a life could be more richly lived.

Downstairs was different. Downstairs was the place where people had become overwhelmed by the intensity of their mental life. They were in an unusual and highly charged mental state and had often harmed themselves. There are not many more dramatic things that a human can do than jumping from a high building or falling under a train. These incidents are not a 'cry for help' and most psychiatrists do not often encounter someone who has really, really tried to kill themselves in this way. The Royal London Hospital is a regional trauma centre and the base for the helicopter emergency service. Thus, many of the survivors of such violent suicide attempts within the greater London area were ferried into the Royal London where they were referred to me and the Liaison team. So, over the course of years, I have worked with hundreds of survivors of extraordinarily intense mental states that caused them to make determined attempts to end their lives. The majority of these patients had jumped from high places. The technical term for this act is *autokabalesis*, but we called them 'jumpers' and I will discuss them further in chapter 13.

Mapping the Psyche

When I was a very new psychiatry trainee, I quickly realised that the drugs were often highly effective for people who had severe forms of mental illness, but I had very little idea how to work with people whose issues were more related to emotions and personality. The biological model of psychiatry held little relevance for them and, in order to be of assistance to them, I needed to find out about psychotherapy and how it worked. So I duly signed up for an introductory course in group therapy at the Institute of Group Analysis. The attraction for me was that, as well as a series of lectures, there was an experiential group where we would sit around in a circle, look each other in the eye—and talk. I am not going into psychotherapy, I reassured myself, but this is a taste of what it might be like. The first group session was an epiphany for me in that, although nothing much seemed to happen, it was clear that something very powerful had been triggered. I found it very hard to sleep that night; a swirling torrent of thoughts, feelings and emotions had been unleashed, but again it was very unclear to me what forces were operating in my perturbed psyche. I really wanted a better understanding; I needed a much more detailed map of the mind than I was going to find in my general psychiatry training. So, over the next ten years, in addition to my 'day job', I saw as many psychotherapy patients under supervision as I could and trained in psychoanalytic psychotherapy, qualifying finally as a group analyst. Eventually I felt as though I had acquired some understanding of how the psyche worked and how to use psychotherapy to help people grow. But it was difficult, and as soon as I thought I had acquired some knowledge of the territory, something would happen that would show me how much I still had to learn.

People find it hard to change; the fundamental patterns of relating to the world about us are very difficult to shift. The mutative moments in psychotherapy, the moments that really cause change, often emerge from high-intensity mental states. Freud understood this well and used various techniques to amplify the intensity of the encounter, such as avoiding face-to-face contact and having the patient lie on a couch to encourage the development of the transference. Psychotherapists these days rarely use the couch and generally believe that the crucial factor in psychotherapy is the quality of the relationship rather than the actual method used. For the psychotherapy to be therapeutic there has to be a safe, reliable environment, the patient has to be motivated to do the work rather than be a passive recipient and this requires the ability to be reflective. I will refer to these factors—the setting, the mindset and the integration—throughout the book as the most important factors influencing the outcome of intense mental states.

My first psychotherapy training provided a map of personal unconscious, the Freudian territory of the psychodynamic world. My second training, some years afterwards, sought a map of archetypal or psychospiritual experience. It was certainly a less conventional and more eclectic training than the first. For around ten years, I periodically attended workshops and retreats with the intention of experiencing and understanding the deeper layers of the unconscious, including a layer of mind that could be described as transpersonal – extending beyond the personal psyche. I sought out retreats that were high quality and run by reputable organisations but which offered a particular intensity of experience, often with a spiritual component. The core discipline was the Grof Transpersonal Training, which extended over five years and which I consider provides an excellent model for the induction and integration of high intensity archetypal experience. I have described some of these retreat experiences in the last four chapters.

I use the term *archetype* in the Jungian tradition to describe an underlying or deeper order of mind involving a heightened intensity of meaning. This is different to the use of the term *stereotype*, which does not refer to an underlying order but a superficial order and which does not have the amplification of meaning. Stereotypes reduce us to nothing but static types, often clichéd, while archetypes are fundamentally beyond definition. A stereotype has meaning but an archetype has Meaning. The concept of concentrated meaning is fundamental to an understanding of archetypes. An archetypal experience will have a meaning tone that evokes a sense of awe or the uncanny. This sense of awe, which we may call numinous experience, may be deeply positive or deeply negative. Attending retreats taught me much about the variety of numinous experience, the beautiful spiritual moments, the value of the darker, challenging experience of the shadow and how to bring the insights usefully back into conscious everyday life.

I came across the works of Jung as a student and found the concepts of archetypes and the collective unconscious both fascinating and impenetrable. I wondered what these terms mean and if they have validity. I still ask myself the same questions and this book is an attempt to reach some tentative conclusions about the range of archetypal experience. For me the concept of archetypes makes most sense when considered with the theories of Plato and David Bohm, the Greek philosopher and the quantum physicist separated by nearly two-and-half-thousand years. Indeed, this book is written with a Platonic perspective in mind. This strategy puts me at odds with the prevailing scientific paradigm, which subscribes to the belief that all mental activity is reducible to neural activity, that all of mind is in the brain and of the brain. It also puts me at odds with the psychoanalytic world, which holds that unusual experiences flow from the vicissitudes of infantile or childhood relationships. We are the first culture that has held this view. Previous cultures, which we may consider primitive, thought that there was an external, extra psychic element of conscious experience —and they generally used religious terminology to describe it. I will discuss some evidence that mind is not entirely reducible to the brain and that there may be a component of consciousness that is not derived from our brain cells. I do not believe it is necessary to adopt a religious perspective about this, but I certainly do not think that it is acceptable to dismiss all unusual mental experience as a sign of mental illness or brain dysfunction.

The more that I learn, the less I find that I know. I don't know for certain that these ideas are valid, but my view is that they are worthy of serious consideration. I believe that ideas should be vulnerable, that ideas should be creative, carefully considered and made available for discussion. Psychology and psychiatry can have an overly narrow focus and, while this may be entirely appropriate if this focus is in the patient's interest, I believe that exploring ideas and the creative tension between them is infinitely more interesting than the collapse into a belief system. However, there is one belief that I do hold with something approaching certainty—that the domain of mind is more complicated than we imagine.

I believe it likely that our current limited understanding of the psyche and consciousness can be likened to the era in physical science at the beginning of the twentieth century when it seemed as though everything that was important had been discovered. There followed the paradigm changing discoveries of quantum physics that showed that the structures that we thought were solid and immutable, such as atoms, had non-physical wave-like components. From this revelation, a whole new era was born. Perhaps inner space, like outer space, has immeasurable depth and potential. I believe that a fuller understanding of the psyche could enable us to lead lives that are richer and more whole, both individually and collectively. Of course, there is much to be gained from studying the hardware of the brain, neuroscience, imaging techniques and burgeoning technology, but this may be only part of the story.

My aim is to share my passion for these ideas in a way that is digestible for those who are familiar with them and those who are not. This is my 'best guess' based on available information from my four pillars. There is some repetition in the expectation that readers like to dip into books rather than read from start to finish. It is not intended to be a balanced review of argument and counter argument and I have not provided a comprehensive list of references. The references provided are merely to point readers to texts that may be of further interest. In my attempt to build bridges between two paradigms, the materialist and the transpersonal, I am aware of the risk of alienating both camps. My psychiatric colleagues, who I hold in great affection and respect, may consider this book an eccentric perspective while my transpersonally orientated colleagues who I hold in similar affection and respect may consider that I am being too cautious in my arguments and too tentative in my conclusions.[1] So be it. Goethe famously said that the only matter worth addressing was the tension between faith and scepticism. While I try to speak to this tension, it is not my intention to persuade sceptics, indeed those who are firmly unsympathetic to a Platonic perspective should probably not read this book.

Finally, this is a personal book. I am always interested in the provenance of ideas. What is the nature of the psyche that is generating them, what is the personal story behind them and how does it influence a view point? So I have added something of my personal perspective and how it came to be shaped. It is not autobiographical but uses my own experience of being a curious human to illustrate certain points. It is not possible to learn about or write about the numinous layers of psyche without some personal exploration of the territory. Of course, learning is lifelong and inevitably this is work in progress.

SECTION ONE

Intense States of Meaning

Reality is what we take to be true.

What we take to be true is what we believe.

What we believe is based upon our perceptions.

What we perceive depends upon what we look for.

What we look for depends upon what we think.

What we think depends upon what we perceive.

What we perceive determines what we believe.

What we believe determines what we take to be true.

What we take to be true is our reality.

—Gary Zukav

CHAPTER 1

Visiting Heaven and Hell

In ordinary perception, the senses send an overwhelming flood of information to the brain, which the brain then filters down to a trickle so it can manage the task of survival in a highly competitive world. Man has become so rational, so utilitarian, that the trickle has become most pale and thin. It is efficient, for mere survival, but it screens out the most wondrous part of man's potential experience without us even knowing it. We are shut off from our own world.

—Tom Wolfe[2]

Adam's Visit to Hell

Adam was in a serious condition on the trauma ward at the Royal London Hospital.[3] He had been found unconscious in a public park, partially clothed, with serious stab wounds. The paramedics reported that his blood pressure had been unrecordable due to blood loss. He was taken straight to the operating theatre to repair his torn arteries and save his life. The police found no evidence that any other person had been involved in the incident and as Adam regained consciousness after surgery, he admitted that the wounds were self-inflicted. The surgeons called me straight away for an emergency psychiatric assessment. They were concerned, of course, that he would try to end his life again.

When I first met him Adam was still in a very bad way. The surgeon who had operated on him told me that he had not just cut his wrists, but he had sliced into his arm as though he was trying to scrape the flesh off his bone. Muscles and tendons had been severed and there was nerve damage. His arm was functionally useless and it was unlikely to regain much useful function. These were life-changing injuries. He had also stabbed his leg repeatedly and there was a wound to his penis. He was 24 years old.

Adam was friendly and smiling when I saw him, although his eyes filled with tears when I asked him what had happened. He said that he just didn't know, he couldn't remember anything. He wasn't sure if he had harmed himself but agreed that this seemed to be the only explanation for his injuries. He told me that the last thing that he could clearly remember was going into the park to kill some time before starting work. He had been feeling perfectly normal and didn't think that he had been troubled in any particular way. He was shocked at his injuries and couldn't think of any reason why he would do such a thing to himself. He wanted to recover, spend some time with his family, return to his flat that he shared with his girlfriend and carry on with his job.

The nurse in charge of the ward told me that he seemed like a 'drug case' in that he seemed confused and sometimes suspicious when he was recovering from surgery, but had rapidly become more normal and the nurses had not noticed anything abnormal about his mental state today. A burly psychiatric nurse sitting by his bed was closely supervising him. This nurse thought that Adam was upset, which was to be expected considering the circumstances, but otherwise he was interacting normally and did not seem to be psychotic.

Adam was still drowsy and a little confused, which was not surprising given his recent surgery and powerful medication. His mother had just arrived from the north of England and his girlfriend, Anna, was waiting to speak to me. Anna told me that he had seemed stressed about having to do a night shift at his workplace over the last month and he was worried about money but otherwise she hadn't noticed any difference in him. He liked to smoke a little cannabis to relax in the evenings and she thought he was drinking more than previously, but the quantity of alcohol consumption did not seem high or problematic and she had no reason to think that he was upset or distressed. On reflection, she observed, perhaps he had been a little quieter, less of a joker than he normally was. She had known him for five years and described him as a sensible, hard-working fellow who did not seem prone to depression or moodiness and she had never known him do anything impulsive. His mother told me that no one in his family had ever been psychiatrically unwell. Adam had always been a steady lad and there had been no particular problems in his childhood or adolescence, except perhaps a tendency to worry. He kept in regular contact with his family and they had not noticed that he was anything other than his normal self.

I saw Adam every day that week and each time he seemed a little more grounded, articulate and shocked as the extent of his injuries and the implications for his future became clearer. His mental state was consistent with someone who had suffered a severe and unexpected trauma. He was not suspicious, he didn't feel in any danger from anyone and he was not having any unusual perceptions such as hallucinatory voices. His mood was up and down but he was not clinically depressed.[4] He enjoyed his visitors when they were there and he enjoyed listening to music when they were not. He was able to concentrate, he was sleeping as well as any one does on a busy trauma ward and he was looking forward to the future. He most definitely was not suicidal and could not understand why he had wanted to hurt himself so badly. In short, his mental state seemed entirely normal.

We tried to piece together what had happened. He told me that he was not enjoying his shift work and did not like working nights. He felt frustrated that his career was not progressing as he hoped and he thought the night manager was turning against him. There was nothing specific about the night manager to indicate that Adam might be developing paranoid ideas about him. It was more a feeling that the manager was not very interested in him and did not appreciate his hard work in the way that the daytime managers did. Adam had been a little worried about money and wanted to buy his girlfriend an expensive present for Christmas and he missed his family. He described to me a sense of developing tension and mild 'persecutory anxiety' in that as his anxiety became more intense he developed feelings that something bad might happen and that people might behave towards him in a rejecting way. These feelings didn't develop into paranoid delusions and he had not experienced any other symptoms suggestive of a serious mood disorder or developing schizophrenia.

He remembered going to the park to walk for a couple of hours before going to work. He was adamant that he had not smoked any cannabis, taken any other drugs or drunk any alcohol. 'Why would I?', he commented, 'I was getting ready for work'. Adam found it very difficult to describe what happened in the park. He would start by saying 'it was like this . . .', and his words would trail off. He just didn't have the words and anyway his memory for what had happened seemed very patchy. But it seemed that a very bad feeling came over him very quickly and he felt compelled to destroy himself and cause himself pain to match what he was feeling inside. He tried to explain to me how principles of good and evil, light and dark had developed an extraordinary significance for him. He thought that his penis suddenly seemed like an evil thing to him but couldn't remember any more of the thoughts he was having. He thought that he was in Hell, the worst place imaginable and he had to get out of it even if it meant dying. He remembers climbing a tree 'to get higher', and thinks he may have fallen. He thought he had climbed the tree for a 'spiritual' reason but couldn't describe it, 'maybe to get closer to God'. This puzzled him as he wasn't in the slightest bit religious, but he felt that he'd been taken over by something enormous and pregnant with meaning, which totally over-whelmed him. He said it felt like it had happened to a different person in a different time and bore no relation to how he felt at the moment. That was about all he could say.

Brief Psychotic Episode?

The job of a psychiatrist is to understand the nature of a person's psycho-logical distress and to help him or her recover in a way that gives the best possible platform for the future—a growthful recovery. As psychiatrists, our most important tool is a careful and detailed enquiry. Blood tests and brain scans are part of a comprehensive assessment but it is the patient's story that is crucial, together with information from other sources. We ask a lot of questions to clarify the nature of the current problem and how the symptoms developed. We enquire into the family background. We are interested in the nature of family relationships and the development of the personality. We want to know if any one else in the extended family has had contact with a psychiatrist to establish whether there is any obvious genetic vulnerability to serious mental illness such as schizophrenia, bipo-lar disorder or recurrent depression. We try to get an understanding of the current life situation, the strains and stresses, the support systems and cop-ing mechanisms. Being trained in the medical model, this usually leads to a diagnosis, which in turn informs the treatment plan.

So with Adam, I duly interview as many people as I can who know him well to get a picture of his development. I am particularly interested in any recent changes in behaviour or personality. The psychiatric nurses looking after him will be able to tell me how he behaves over any 24-hour period. Eventually, I felt that I had been able to assess Adam in a compre-hensive and thorough way. The problem was that I still didn't really under-stand what had happened to him. He was a young man who had undergone a sudden and devastating psychological crisis, for no obvious reason and had very nearly died. He had been relatively normal until shortly before the crisis and he returned to his normal self shortly afterwards. There was no evidence that he was developing a serious mental illness such as schizo-phrenia or bipolar disorder. He was not clinically depressed. Most psychia-trists would give him a diagnostic label of 'brief psychotic episode'. This is a descriptive label that is not particularly useful, except in distinguishing it from a psychotic episode of longer duration, which we would be more likely to call schizophrenia. There would be a concern that a brief psychotic episode could be the beginning of a process that would develop into classical schizophrenia and ideally, he would be followed up in a clinic to see how matters developed over the next year or so.

I continued to see Adam over the next few months as he recovered in hospital and after his discharge. He wasn't able to go back to work because of his injuries and I lost contact with him after he and Anna returned to the north of England. During this period Adam was focussed on his physical recovery and regaining as much function in his arm as he could. He came dutifully to his appointments with me, but he was never able to remember anything more about his crisis and suicide attempt. He was unable to describe what had happened or discuss what it had meant to him. He didn't really want to think about it. It frightened him.

Martin's Visit to Heaven

Martin considered himself to be a regular guy. He worked, he liked watching sport, he enjoyed his friends and family, and he liked a glass of wine. He wasn't particularly religious but he tried to live a moral life and be kind to people. He had felt drawn to meditation earlier in his adult life but hadn't been able to develop a regular practice. He could think of no reason why he had the experience that he described to me.

He had always enjoyed nature and sitting in old churches and on the day that his life changed he had done both of these things. It was one of those perfect English late summer days with blue sky and soft wind rustling the trees. Martin was in the second week of his holiday, far away from thoughts of work and the demands of practical life. He was on a country walk through well marked footpaths and there was no risk of losing his way. The countryside was safe, benign and gorgeous. He stopped to sit in a church and enjoyed the cool sense of space under the old stone and the stained windows. He wandered outside and found a bench with a view of the meadows and the orchards. The birds were singing, the sun was warm and it just looked perfect. He had a brief moment of realising that he was happy.

Then his perceptions started to change. The first thing that he noticed was that the colours were becoming more intense. The blue sky was becoming even bluer and the grass and the leaves of the trees were the most intense green that he had ever seen. The light was getting brighter and had a shimmering quality. The singing of the birds seemed to be the most beautiful sound that he had ever heard. He was feeling more than good. He was probably feeling better than he had ever felt in his entire life.

Thus far Martin could describe what seemed to be happening to him but from this point words seemed to fail him. He could use his vocabulary to point in the right general direction but his experience was entirely beyond description. He felt as though he was in another place, a place beyond time and a place that was not of this physical world. He felt as though he was merged with something that was so vast that it felt like the entire universe—and it was all made of love. He felt the most exquisite beautiful feelings. Time passed; probably only 15 minutes or so before Martin began to move back towards his normal state. The light started to fade and the colours around him seemed to be returning to their normal level. He felt tears streaming down his face. He was weeping with the sheer intensity and beauty of his experience. He remembers a realisation that the message of the great religions was essentially true although his experience had nothing to do with religion. He knew that this was the most important event of his life.

By the time I met Martin, about 3 years had passed since his experience. He had just turned 40. Nothing like it had happened before or since. He told me that his experience still seemed real and vivid to him and permeated his life in a profound way. The most obvious life change that he had made was to give up his job as a corporate lawyer to work in a position that he felt was more compatible with his changed perspective. He wanted to do something more helpful and he especially wanted to avoid being exploitative. His moral compass had become more finely tuned. The changes he had made were not always easy and he told me that he had been a little depressed for a while. He thought that this was partly because of life changes that he needed to make. Perhaps more importantly, he felt he had been given a taste of heaven and it was dispiriting to find himself back on imperfect planet Earth. He had been to his local Buddhist centre where he found some people who could listen gently to him if needed and one or two people there seemed to know something about the place that he had visited. He had found that a regular meditation practice had helped him to become less agitated and to gradually rediscover something of the serenity and beauty of his experience.

Through the Filmiest of Screens

I met Adam in a hospital and I met Martin on a meditation retreat. Both had life-changing experiences and were permanently marked in very different ways. Because of the nature of my working life, I have met many more Adams than Martins. Indeed Martin's type of experience is rare, although well documented since the Canadian psychiatrist Richard Bucke described fifty similar cases in his book *Cosmic Consciousness* published in 1901.[5] People who are unfortunate enough to have Adam's type of experience are extraordinarily vulnerable, will often injure themselves or worse, and are likely to see a psychiatrist on the trauma ward. People who are fortunate enough to have the type of experience that Martin enjoyed do not generally see a psychiatrist but may gravitate instead towards a spiritual or religious community who are likely to have a language and a model to help them make some sense of their experience and a method to enable a continuing spiritual practice.

Although the quality of their experiences was very different, Martin and Adam had something in common in that their normal state of being in the world became flooded by psychological material of extraordinary power and intensity. Much has been written about the common ground between psychosis and spiritual experience.[6] Why is it that the experiences of some of the saints sound so similar to those of lunatics?[7] We have long suspected that there are mental states that do not conform to the usual patterns of mental illness. The father of modern psychology, William James published his seminal book *The Varieties of Religious Experience* in 1902. This was around the same time that Max Planck discovered quanta and Freud published *The Interpretation of Dreams* so this was a period in history where old models and certainties were being challenged. William James's authoritative quote sets the scene by telling us that these unusual mental experiences are valid and important although we do not understand them:

> Our normal waking consciousness, rational consciousness as we call it, is but one special type of consciousness, whilst all around, parted from it by the filmiest of screens, there lie potential forms of consciousness entirely different. We may go through life without suspecting their existence but apply the requisite stimulus and at a touch they are there in all their completeness. No account of the universe in its totality can be final which leaves these other forms of consciousness disregarded. How to regard them is the question, for they are so discontinuous with ordinary consciousness. Yet they may determine attitudes although they cannot furnish formulas, and open a region although they fail to give a map. At any rate they forbid a premature closing of accounts with reality.[8]

Both Martin and Adam had been precipitated into a form of consciousness that was entirely different from consensus reality. They had, in their different ways, entered a 'non-ordinary' state of consciousness—NOSC. The term *non-ordinary* is used here to differentiate from the 'ordinary' consciousness of everyday life and the 'altered' consciousness associated with brain pathology.[9] We can discern that Adam was in a troubled mood and Martin was in an excellent mood before their experiences, but both of their moods at this stage would be regarded as within the normal range. There is no obvious explanation for why they both passed through this 'filmiest of screens' and why their experiences unfolded in such different ways. Their experiences both involved an extraordinary intensity of meaning that was far outside the normal range and which they found very difficult to put into words. They both felt overwhelmed by the enormity of the moment; it was bigger than anything they had experienced before. They were helpless in its grasp. For both of them in their separate ways, the moment was mutative and changed their lives.

The Psyche as a Sense Organ

It seemed that both Adam and Martin has had an overdose of *meaning*. Martin's experience was more digestible, having a form and impact that he was able to incorporate into his life while Adam's was much more primitive, chaotic and indigestible. In both cases, the function of their psyche had been temporarily disabled. I use the term psyche here in its classical Freudian sense with the ego mediating between the animal instincts of id and the regulatory super ego. The psyche is the psychological apparatus for making sense of the environment and could be understood as a sixth sense organ that is used to discern meaning. Used in conjunction with other senses, meaning adds a texture and nuance to our world and further organises our consciousness. One of the key tasks of our meaning apparatus is to distinguish danger and we have mechanisms of mind and brain that have evolved to this end. Research has shed some light on some possible brain mechanisms underpinning the attribution of significance to bits of information captured by the sensory system.[10] This information is given a positive or negative meaning that influences goal directed behaviour because of its association with reward or punishment. If this system malfunctions it may lead to inappropriate levels of significance being connected to external events. This is what we think occurs in the endogenous psychoses.

The role of the brain and ego structures that contribute to our psyche is to keep our perception of meaning within a useful range. Our psyche needs to be sensitive enough but not oversensitive. It needs to be in tune to the demands of our everyday life. It would not be useful to be flooded with meaning in a way that would undermine our ability to survive. All our other senses exist within certain useful ranges. Our eyes respond to a small part of the electromagnetic spectrum. In the same way that there are frequencies that we cannot hear, and smells that are beyond the resources of our olfactory system, there are ranges of meaning that we cannot usually comprehend.

The writer Aldous Huxley proposed a model of the brain as a 'reducing valve', which reduces the intensity of meaning to an acceptable range to stop us being overwhelmed with information that is irrelevant to our everyday task. For Huxley there was a much greater range of meaning that he termed 'mind at large', which our reducing valve filtered to a 'measly trickle'. Huxley continues:

> To formulate and express the contents of this reduced awareness, man has invented and endlessly elaborated those symbol-systems and implicit philosophies, which we call languages. Every individual is at once the beneficiary and the victim of the linguistic tradition into which he has been born . . . the victim in so far as it confirms him in the belief that reduced awareness is the only awareness and as it bedevils his sense of reality, so that he is all too apt to take his concepts for data, his words for actual things. That which, in the language of religion, is called 'this world' is the universe of reduced awareness, expressed, and, as it were, petrified by language. . . . Most people, most of the time, know only what comes through the reducing valve and is consecrated as genuinely real by the local language. Certain persons, however, seem to be born with a kind of by-pass that circumvents the reducing valve.[11]

There are a number of ways in which this hypothetical reducing valve can be bypassed to bring a greater intensity of meaning into our consciousness. We know that this occurs in various abnormal mental states that we classify as psychiatric illness. We know that there are various techniques developed over millennia that have been prized for the ability to induce heightened meaning. These techniques include ritual, the use of sound, meditation, fasting and psychoactive substances. Sometimes, as with both Adam and Martin, these intense meaning states may come upon us spontaneously.

An Overplus of Meaning

Adam's and Martin's experiences both involved a flooding with meaning. Using Huxley's model, their reducing valves were bypassed and they lost their ability to interact with the everyday world in a normal way. The quality of their separate meaning states and the consequences of them were at the opposite ends of the spectrum. Intense meaning states come in a variety of flavours or tones which we call *archetypes*. Archetypes are the weather systems of the mind, holding an extraordinary concentration and intensity of meaning and significance. For Adam, the meaning tone of his state was utterly terrible and for Martin it was wonderful beyond belief. The quantity and quality of the meaning overwhelmed their normal balance of mind and I am suggesting that they each developed an *archetypal crisis*.

Archetypal material has a number of different qualities. It is ineffable in that words just cannot capture the nuance and intensity, although poets may come close. The concentration of meaning holds a 'numinous' quality, imbued with overwhelming power. Indeed, it is this numinous quality that is the characteristic hallmark of an archetypal crisis. The term *numinous* is derived from the Latin word *numen*, which is usually translated as 'divine presence', it implies a strong religious or spiritual quality.[12] The German theologian Rudolf Otto described 'the numinous' as the principle that underlies all religion, a mystery that both terrified (*mysterium tremendum*) and a mystery that fascinated (*mysterium fascinans*) at the same time.[13] By definition, a numinous experience always involves a sense of the sacred.

Otto tells us that the term *sacred* or *holy* is not synonymous with goodness but means 'an *overplus* of meaning'.[14] Meaning is amplified so that the tone and resonance of meaning becomes overwhelming and magnetic. Otto describes how incomplete or partial forms of numinous experience can have a nightmarish primitive quality with an abrupt and capricious character, but this crude stage with its ominous tone has the potential to be transcended as the numen reveals itself and the process unfolds eventually becoming integrated by the more rational elements of consciousness. The crucial point about the idea of the numinous is its bivalence having both dark and light manifestations. It can be beautiful or dreadful; the literature of religious experience abounds in references to the pains and terrors overwhelming those who have come, too suddenly, face to face with some manifestation of the *mysterium tremendum*.

Otto's attempts to describe numinous experience can be summarized as follows:[15]

- It can sweep in like a gentle tide or can burst in a sudden eruption
- It is beyond conception or understanding, extraordinary and unfamiliar
- There are elements of awe-fullness, the blood runs cold and we shudder
- Joy and exaltation—impossible to describe, ineffable
- A majesty that overpowers and consumes us absolutely. Our sense of self is annihilated
- Wholly other—supernatural
- Huge—too vast for our faculties

CHAPTER 2

Is There an Underlying Reality?

The safest general characterization of the European philosophical tradition is that it consists of a series of footnotes to Plato.

—Alfred North Whitehead[16]

Any discussion of archetypes needs to attempt to define what an archetype may be and what it is not. An archetype represents a deeper organising system rather than the superficial pattern of a stereotype. Archetypes invariably bring an intensification of meaning, a concentration of essence, but there is a spectrum of this intensification. There are the extreme experiences of Adam and Martin and there are the lighter intensifications of meaning mediated through everyday life, drama, the arts and the senses. A chef can go to extraordinary lengths to intensify flavours, as an example of 'archetypal cuisine', onions can be sealed in a vacuum bag and cooked at low temperature in water bath for 72 hours to create a concentration of Onion ness.

Attempts to define archetype present us with some difficulties if they are inherently unknowable and impossible to adequately describe. The ancient civilisations used to personalise the archetypes as their gods. The classical Greece of Homer, who wrote the Iliad and the Odyssey, brings archetypes to life, showing how gods such as Zeus, Athena, Apollo, Aphrodite, Poseidon and many more exerted their influence over the world of men. But here we will focus our attention on another Greek who, through a parable, gives us a working definition of the archetypal domain. His name was Plato.

Plato's Search for Truth

The 4th and 5th centuries BCE in Greece were a critical point in the development of Western thought. During the same era, in other parts of the world, teachers such as the Buddha, Lao Tzu, Jeremiah and Confucius

were developing ideas that would give a distinctive flavour to the civilisations that followed them. This defining historical period is termed the
'axial age'.[17] In classical Greece, Socrates was the teacher of Plato, who in
turn was the teacher of Aristotle. Socrates did not leave a written legacy but
we can assume that Plato, who wrote extensively and founded the Acad-
emy, assimilated much of his teaching. Plato reached similar conclusions
to the Buddha about the endless and futile attempts that we make as human
beings to reduce our suffering. People graze like cattle seeking to avoid
pain and gain pleasure, according to Plato, but the pleasure and pain are
illusory and they do not ever experience steady, pure pleasure.[18] We label
pleasure as such because it forms a contrast from that which we label as
painful. But this pleasure is a leaky vessel, it does not endure and we are
seeking satisfaction in unreal things for a part of ourselves that is also
unreal. So what is real asks Plato? How can we be guided by something
that is true?

We can perhaps understand why Plato sought something that was permanent, pure and incorruptible. He was born into an aristocratic family in
the Athenian democratic age and was educated by the best teachers available. As a young man he served in the disastrous war against Sparta and
witnessed the demise of democracy when Athens was taken over by the
oligarchs. When he was in his mid twenties, his mentor Socrates was sentenced to death for questioning conventional wisdom in a way that the
rulers clearly found threatening. Socrates seems to have accepted his
scapegoat role without rancour and perhaps relished the opportunity to
show that a true philosopher does not fear death.

Plato had lost his own father when he was very young and it seems
likely that he was particularly sensitive to the loss of the father figure that
Socrates represented for him. After Socrates' execution, Plato abandoned
his political ambitions, left Athens and travelled for 12 years, assimilating
the best ideas of his time involving mathematics, geometry, astronomy,
religion and philosophy. Not surprisingly, he was preoccupied with the
theme of good governance and justice. How can rulers rule according to
the best possible principles? What are the most important ideas that are not
tainted by politics and personal interests? Above all what is the nature of
goodness?

Socrates and Plato believed that there was an underlying order of
timeless fundamental 'forms' or archetypes that governed our everyday
reality giving it form and meaning. I will substitute the word archetype
where Plato used 'forms' as the terms are essentially interchangeable.
These fundamental structures that we call archetypes include the mathematical forms of geometry and arithmetic, light and dark, male and female

as well as the templates of the primary emotions, patterns and physical structures of our everyday life.[19] Plato's primary interest lay in defining moral qualities, the Good, the True and the Beautiful. He was deeply impressed by the Pythagoreans who found mathematical rules that ordered and governed our material world. Mathematics was an underlying structure that was pristine, timeless and incorruptible and, for Plato, mathematical structures did indeed hold a numinous quality. In nature there are no perfect circles, no perfect right-angled triangles, but these imperfect circles and right-angled triangles are images of impossibly perfect archetypal Circles and Triangles.

Plato's Cave

Plato's theory of archetypes is best understood in his allegory of the cave, which sheds some light on the relationship between the archetypal forms of the fundamental reality and the archetypal images that we perceive.[20] The parable also shows us some of the ways in which we may be affected by turning away from consensus reality and by the encounter with the numinous.

Plato uses Socrates as the narrator of this story. Socrates is teaching a young student called Glaucon using the Socratic method of dialogue to stimulate ideas and creative debate. The purpose of the story is to teach Glaucon how to be a philosopher, how to seek a deeper truth and how to

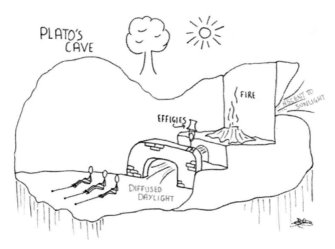

Figure 1. Plato's Cave.

manage that knowledge wisely for the benefit of his fellow men. This is a story that challenges our imagination and requires some perseverance. It is an allegorical story, a device to prove a point and not to be taken too literally.

Plato begins by asking us to imagine a situation where people are chained in a cave so that they are facing the back of the cave and cannot move their heads.[21] Their gaze is fixed. They have been there since childhood and know no other reality.[22] There are two sources of light in the cave: one is from the sun outside which filters into the cave, just taking the edge off the darkness; the other source of light is from a fire at the entrance of the cave. In between the fire and the back of the cave, which serves as a viewing screen, there is a passage where various objects or effigies are paraded. The people parading the objects sometimes talk amongst themselves, the images and sounds are projected onto the back of the cave and the chained people take these projections to be their primary and sole reality. They think that the shadows are real and that the totality of their perceptual experience emanates from these flickering shadows. How could they know any different?

'What a strange picture you paint' says Glaucon. But Plato answers that the people chained to the wall are no different from ourselves, they believe, as we also believe, the version of reality that is presented to them by their senses.

There are two distinct phases to the story. In the first part Plato asks us to consider what it would be like if one of the prisoners is set free of his bonds. It would take some courage for this person to leave his or her peers, to turn away from what is familiar. It would be difficult to get up into a different position, to use unfamiliar muscles and creaky limbs as he or she turns away from the back of the cave and tentatively starts to explore an unfamiliar environment. The light of the fire and the seepage of daylight from the sun would dazzle him. His senses are over stimulated; it is certainly frightening but also fascinating (*tremendum et fascinans*). Eventually he gets to the passageway and discovers the objects that are making the shadows. Suppose somebody tells him that the images that he has been watching all of this time, facing the back of the cave, have no substance but are just shadows? Suppose he is told that what he now sees and touches is a truer version of reality? Plato suggests that this would be intolerable for him; the three dimensional forms and complexity of the images would bewilder him and he would be partially blinded by the firelight. He would most likely run back to where he came from and persuade himself that the shadows were more real than the objects that he had been shown. He returns to the safety of his two-dimensional world.

Ascent and Return

In the second phase, we are asked to imagine the man being taken all the way out of the cave to the sunlight. Of course, he is completely dazzled and his eyes can't make out very much at all. As his eyes become more accustomed, he would gradually be able to make out the shadows cast by the sun first of all, then his vision would discern actual 'things' themselves, three dimensional objects with colour and texture. Then he would cast his eyes upwards and would see the heavens, the stars, the moon and the sun. Plato suggests that after a while the man would come to realise the primary importance of the sun and understand that the sun is absolutely central to everything. The sun is responsible for the light, the heat, the seasons; indeed, everything flows from the sun. Without the sun there is nothing.

Imagine the man going back into the cave, suggests Plato, feeling sorry for those poor people chained up in the dark. They have built up an elaborate value system around the two-dimensional shadows rewarding and giving status to those who are quickest at recognising shadows and the order in which they follow each other. Do you think, says Plato, that our former prisoner would covet those honours and envy those people who had status and power at the back of the cave? The answer is that he would not, that he would probably put up with anything rather than go back to the value system of the two-dimensional world.

Furthermore, suggests Plato, our man who has been outside and seen the sun needs some time for his eyes to readjust to the gloom of the cave and he has become slow and backward at recognising the shadows. If he had to compete with the prisoners in identifying the shadows wouldn't he make a fool of himself? Wouldn't his comrades pour scorn on him for having come back with his eyes ruined? Wouldn't they be deeply unimpressed by anything that he had to tell them about where he had been and what he had discovered? It is unlikely that they would want to follow in his footsteps and it is unlikely that they would be receptive to his telling them that they are wrong to value the shadows so much, that there may be something deeper and richer.

Plato goes on to discuss the meaning of the story. He likens our everyday world to the prison cell of the cave and the firelight to our visible sun in our solar system. The firelight is of the physical world while the sunlight in his allegory is a more nebulous, non physical, spiritual ideal. Plato's allegorical sun is his 'form of the Good' his God term, the source and provider of all truth and knowledge. Plato admits that he doesn't know whether or not this is true, but states that the ideal of goodness is the last thing to be seen in the sphere of knowledge. It is the pinnacle of what we can know.

The shadows on our wall are cast by objects that are effigies of the real objects, which lie a further step beyond, outside of the cave altogether.

Plato's Archetypes

For Plato, the world that we feel, see and hear, the world of our senses, is nothing more than the reflected shadow of a deeper reality of forms, ideals or archetypes. Plato's archetypes are permanent and unchanging whereas anything in the physical world that we see is transient. Physical forms degrade while archetypes do not degrade. An archetype is a universal principle, an essence, an idea that gives the visible world its form and meaning. Everything in our material world has an eternal unchanging form, courage, lust, evil, weather, a tree, even a chair. As Tarnas puts it in his history of Western philosophy: 'Something is beautiful precisely to the extent that it participates in the archetype of Beauty'.[23] A beautiful person is informed by beauty but does not possess it. Physical beauty will fade but Beauty itself persists. Our idea of beauty is interpreted through the lens of our sensory system and cognitive apparatus but Beauty is independent of the physical domain. All the major themes of our human existence, the feelings, the yearnings, the totality of our emotional world could be understood in this way. The archetype is the unknowable form with a dimension that we cannot really comprehend, but we can see the images with varying degrees of intensity.

For Plato, the pinnacle of the archetypal world and the source of all archetypes is the form of the Good. This is the energy that is primary; without it nothing exists, and the archetypes and their images all flow from this primary source. There is some daylight permeating the cave so we are never entirely separate from it; the numinous is always present in small doses intermingled with the imagery from the firelight. Plato links the allegorical sunlight to his ideal of governance by suggesting that knowledge of this primary reality is a prerequisite for the intelligent conduct of either one's private affairs or public business. Thus a relationship between the personal ego with this highest archetype of the Good is a mark of the high-functioning person. For Plato, the big issue was how to integrate this real and unshakable virtue, a moral compass, the archetype of Goodness into the body politic?

Of course, this is a perpetual human theme in our journey together as a species—how to reconcile morality with political and socioeconomic imperatives. Plato's story is an articulation of a theme that predated him and has persisted since in various forms. The idea behind the story is an archetypal image in its own right, it presents us a question, a personal challenge perhaps. Have we lost sight of the form of the Good? Is there too little of Plato's sunlight filtering into our cave? How can we, as individuals and collectively, form a more coherent relationship with the deepest and most nourishing archetypal Self?

Endarkenment and Enlightenment

Plato's allegory identifies four levels:

- The wall of the cave—our consensus reality, the world of illusion and projections.
- The effigies—the archetypal images of our physical world, manipulated by society.
- The pure archetypal forms of the outside world.
- The primary energy source from which everything emanates.

As human beings, living in consensus reality and constrained by our cognitive apparatus, we see the pale and two-dimensional projections of a more complex reality. These projections come from two sources: our physical material world represented by firelight and the nebulous primary energy represented by the sunlight. Both of these light sources are interpreted through our conditioning and our cognitive structures represented by the effigies. The effigies are a complex twilight zone of archetypal imagery; they represent the 'reducing valve' of the brain, our sensory apparatus and our social conditioning. Plato implies that the purpose of the effigies and the people who manipulate them is to keep us transfixed and immobile. We could call this the process of endarkenment.[24] But some of the shadow from the effigies will emanate from the weak sunlight that diffuses in from the outside. The implication is that we are never entirely cut off from the primary reality, from a faint sense of the numinous.

Perhaps it is intrinsic to our human condition to stay enchained. Perhaps it is only for a dissident minority to differentiate sunlight from firelight, to seek an escape from the version of reality that serves most us adequately. The chains represent the state of endarkenment where we are completely invested in the world of illusion and the competitive pursuit of shadows. We oscillate between the twin poles of appetite and fear; we seek the things that we think make us happy and we push away anything that threatens us. In endarkenment, we have entirely lost any notion of a greater scheme of things; we are disconnected, perhaps from our true nature. For Plato, the process of enlightenment would involve not only the ascent from the cave, but an assimilation and integration of the higher form of reality to be used wisely and with compassion and humility for the benefit of the cave dwellers.

The first stage of the journey towards enlightenment is to disengage from our attachments that prevent us from making our ascent. We would need to move beyond our preoccupations, our anxieties and our hungers. We would need to learn to see and to hear in a different way. We will undergo an encounter with the shadow world and the effigies that form them and this is likely to be an uncomfortable encounter. The ascent out of the cave towards primary reality should be gradual and carefully judged. When we emerge from the cave we are overwhelmed and dazzled. This is an encounter with the numinous, it fills us with awe and it takes some time to become acclimatised. The person who has journeyed into the sunlight should then descend back into the cave with great compassion and care, being mindful of people's attachment to their shadow realm and their likely resistance to any challenge to their version of reality.

Archetypal Crisis

Plato introduces the idea of an archetypal or psychospiritual crisis. He describes how a person may be dazzled by the sunlight and his function may be impaired back in the world of the cave, were he to return there. 'Imagine someone returning to the human world and all it's misery after contemplating the divine realm. Do you think it's surprising if he seems awkward and ridiculous while he's not seeing well?'

The potential for confusion is great—we could call this a 'confusion of levels'. This can happen in two ways: firstly in the transition from the darkness to the light and secondly in the transition from light back to the darkness of the cave. Confusion may arise after returning from a place of greater understanding and insight back to normal waking reality or a person may be disorientated by the inrush of insight as they turn away from the two-dimensional shadow world and discover a richer interior. Despite the difficulties of the return from the higher levels back into the cave, Plato felt, in common with Buddha and Confucius, those other sages of the axial age, that, after achieving a passage into the sunlit world, the enlightened person should return and work with the cave dwellers to their benefit.

The parable of Plato's cave holds true for us today. Although our modern technological world is very different to Plato's time, the archetypal currents that animate us remain the same. We have the same appetites for love, lust, status, glory, structure, knowledge and beauty. We muse about good and evil, we seek transcendence in its various forms, and we search endlessly for meaning. Mostly we are transfixed by the flickering images of the shadows, we may be aware of the diffuse presence of the allegorical sunlight, or we may not. Both eras found ways of making the flames flare to produce more intense archetypal images. Music and the arts often act as archetypal amplifiers to bring more metaphorical sunlight into our cave. The two-dimensional screen of television and cinema is more widely available than the theatre of the Athenians and shows us a greater range of archetypal imagery. The Greeks and Romans of the classical world, who wanted a guided ascent from the cave, had the mysteries of Eleusis to help them and in modern times there are some psychospiritual techniques, as we shall see, that serve the same purpose and achieve a similar opening.

CHAPTER 3

Jung's Archetypal Voyage

I loved it and hated it but it was my greatest wealth

All my works, all my creative activity came from those initial fantasies and dreams.[25]

—Carl Jung

Carl's Story

Carl was in his late thirties. His career as a psychiatrist had been meteoric. He was developing an international reputation and delivering papers at prestigious conferences. But there was a difficulty. He had developed a major disagreement over a theoretical issue with his mentor—the Professor. The Professor had developed a major advance with radical new ideas that had the potential to revolutionise treatment. The Professor felt that the psychological distress in adults could be largely understood by considering the development of sexuality in children. Carl accepted these theories but felt that there was an additional dimension of the psyche relating to a more spiritual or religious context. The Professor was adamantly opposed to this and feared that his work would lose scientific credibility by association with 'the black tide of mud of occultism'. After years of collaboration, they had fallen out badly and it seemed that Carl's career had stalled.

Carl had two remarkable grandfathers: one was a professor of medicine, also famous for his flamboyant personality; the other was a theologian with an interest in spiritualism and mediums. Carl's parents were both the youngest of sibships of 13. His father Paul was a brilliant student who became a mildly depressed village priest. His mother was allegedly psychic. His parents did not have a happy marriage and apparently had a disastrous sexual relationship. Carl was brought up in the country parsonage. He was separated from his mother for a while when she was in a mental hospital, and he found her unpredictable mood swings difficult when she returned home. He developed a strong attachment to the family maid who became more of a mother figure for him.

Carl was a solitary child. He seemed to have some odd experiences, claiming to see spirits and having intense visions and dreams. He recalls a dream of God defecating on a cathedral, which would have been sacrilegious in the extreme in those days. He was clever but didn't like school and he developed fainting fits that served the purpose of avoiding school for some months as a teenager. Despite these difficulties he passed his exams and gained a place at medical school. There were two significant events around this time. The first was his father's death from cancer, giving Carl the impression of a disappointed, half-lived life and the second was that he started attending séances with his cousin Helen. Although he later caught Helen cheating, the séances interested him in the existence of the unconscious mind and influenced his decision to become a psychiatrist.

By now he had developed a fine physique and ebullient personality. He was an extrovert medical student; drinking a lot of beer and kissing a number of girls, but he still came top of the class list when he qualified as a doctor. Despite his mother's wish that he become a surgeon and his Principle's wish that he become a physician, he persisted in his eccentric wish to do psychiatry and moved away from his home city to study at a famous psychiatric institution. Psychiatry was not considered a prestigious career in those days, but his first boss Eugen Bleuler had an international reputation and Jung was determined to shine.

Carl threw himself into his work. He wrote academic papers on schizophrenia and developed a correspondence with the Professor who was developing his radical new ideas about the roots of psychiatric disorder arising in the unconscious mind. When they eventually met, they developed an intense chemistry and they talked for 13 hours without stopping. They fascinated each other. Carl spoke about his dreams and fantasies. He told the Professor about his personal life, his marriage and his troubling involvement with a female patient Sabina Spielrein, who had also become his lover.[26]

Over the next few years the Professor developed his theories and trained a coterie of talented young men to transmit the message and deliver the treatment. Carl was his heir apparent, the Crown Prince, and he protected his position fiercely. There is no suggestion of a physical relationship between Carl and the Professor but it was certainly a passionate collaboration.

Carl, of course, was the Swiss psychiatrist Carl Jung (1975–1961) and the Professor was Sigmund Freud, the pioneer of psychoanalysis. Jung was an explorer but rather than mapping the physical world, the wastes of the

Antarctic or the jungles of Africa, he ventured into the deep interior of the psyche. The story so far takes us up to the critical point in Jung's life. After his break with Freud, he entered a serious but eventually fruitful mid-life crisis where he willingly submitted himself to a prolonged immersion in the subterranean depths of his psyche. This was a sustained and challenging archetypal crisis. The ideas that he developed out of this crisis have stood the test of time and continue to fascinate. His work can be difficult to penetrate, as he often seems to lack the clarity and precision of Freud in his writing, but this also reflects the ambiguous and mysterious nature of the territory he was trying to describe.

After steadfastly refusing to write his autobiography, he finally agreed in 1957 to collaborate with his long-time assistant Aniela Jaffe and the result is his book *Memories, Dreams, Reflections*. The most revealing chapter of his autobiography is 'Confrontation with the Unconscious' in which he describes the crisis that followed his break with Freud. Although this material will be familiar to anyone with more than a passing acquaintance with Jung's work, it is worth describing in some detail as a example of how to fully engage in the archetypal process, how to survive it and how to integrate the experience so that it is, after all, of some use. Jung gives us a model of the would-be philosopher who ascends with great difficulty from Plato's cave. He begins by making a descent into the underworld of the psyche, he survives the encounter with the shadows and the dazzling archetypes before returning home eventually to the back of the cave to sensibly communicate to us what he found.

Jung's Crisis

The crisis began around 1912 to 1913 and was triggered by the rupture in his relationship with Freud and the disruption of his career path. Although his crisis was resolving in 1917, the events and memories were clearly still very fresh to him some 40 years later.

Jung begins by describing a state of disorientation. The break with Freud was a devastating blow for him; their relationship was close and complex. Freud was his father figure, mentor and confidante. Ostensibly the rift developed out of theoretical differences. Freud demanded loyalty to his ideas and considered the psychological vicissitudes of childhood sexuality to be the pillar of his theoretical edifice. Jung considered that Freud's theories, while important, were by no means all that could be said about the psyche, that there was a numinous dimension rich in symbolism, which Freud could not grasp or would not entertain. Jung describes a sense of great trepidation as he struggled to finish a chapter, which he knew would spell the end of his friendship with Freud.[27] He reports a growing awareness of Freud's neurosis and describes him as being similar to an Old Testament prophet.[28] There is a sense of the young bull deciding to take on the old bull.

So the stage was set. Jung was staking his professional and academic future on the existence and importance of archetypes—although he did not use that term at that stage. He was in mid-life; he remained hugely ambitious but his career was at a crossroads and his important relationships were in turmoil. He was in a state of psycho-social crisis.

The Descent into the Unconscious

In order to develop his ideas, Jung changed his technique with his patients, becoming decidedly more explorative and investigative while trying to rid himself of any preconceived ideas or theories. As he did this he became aware of 'an unusual activation' of his own unconscious mind accompanied by a number of vivid and profound dreams with a mythic and highly symbolic component. He describes a tension, a constant inner pressure and a feeling of disorientation.

He suspected that he was suffering from an intrinsic psychological disturbance, perhaps emanating from some childhood trauma, so he attempted a Freudian style self-analysis. This did not reveal any obvious cause for his disturbance and so he resolved to consciously submit himself to the impulses of the unconscious. The difficulty was that he knew of no technique to help him. He paid attention to his dreams, which had a rich and mythic content but this did not seem to offer him symptomatic relief and he continued to feel tense and disturbed. The one activity that did seem to help him was building a toy village out of stones gathered from the lake. He had to overcome his reluctance to return to playing this game, which felt childish, but it rapidly grew into an activity that took much of his time. It gave some structure to his inner turmoil and seemed to encourage a further torrent of inner material, which he carefully wrote down.

His descent intensified in autumn 1913 when he records 'the pressure which I felt in me seemed to be moving outwards, as though there was something in the air. The atmosphere actually seemed darker than it had been. It was as though the sense of oppression no longer sprang exclusively from a psychic situation but from concrete reality. This feeling grew more and more intense'. He began having visions and felt that he was 'menaced by psychosis'.

This was clearly a most difficult and frightening time for him; an incessant stream of fantasies had been released:

> I stood helpless before an alien world; everything in it seemed difficult and incomprehensible. I was living in a constant state of tension . . . One thunderstorm followed another. My enduring these storms was a question of brute strength and from the beginning there was no doubt in my mind that I must find the meaning of what I was experiencing in these fantasies. When I endured these assaults from the unconscious I had the unswerving conviction that I was obeying a higher will and that feeling continued to uphold me until I had mastered the task.[29]

Jung found himself a very difficult position. He had committed himself to thoroughly submerging himself in the material that was emerging from his psyche. He knew that he had to write it down, listen to it and understand it. But much of it was very difficult to tolerate; he likened it to someone drawing his nails down a plaster wall or scraping a knife against a dinner plate. This was not a pleasant experience. He found that yoga exercises calmed him down and held his emotions in check to the point where he could write. There followed two specific periods of intensification of his process; both held the potential for great psychological danger but both proved eventually helpful for resolution. The first was his use of 'journey-ing' that led him to Philemon and the second was his channelling of a com-munication from a mysterious part of psyche that he eventually published as a book, *Septem Sermones.*

Philemon and Basilides

Jung was committed to his journey. He understood that attempting to back away from his journey would leave him deeply diminished. He realised that he had to go deeper into his seething turbulent psyche, not just for his sake, but also for his patients. How could he safely guide his patients unless he understood their fantasy material from his own direct experi-ence? He kept his metaphorical foot firmly pressed down on the accelerator pedal. On December 12 1913, Jung let himself drop. He was sitting at his desk when:

> Suddenly it was as though the ground gave way beneath my feet, and I plunged down into dark depths. I could not fend off a feeling of panic. But then, abruptly, at not too great a depth, I landed on my feet in a soft sticky mass.

Jung had landed. These days we would tend to understand Jung's subsequent experiences as being very similar to shamanic journeying.[30] But Jung would not have had this point of reference. He developed a habit of journeying into this abyss and encountered a series of beings, the most important being was Philemon. Philemon is an enormously important figure. Jung describes him as a pagan gentleman of Hellenic Egyptian origin. The extraordinary significance of Philemon is that Jung came to see him not as simply an expression of his own imagination, but as also having a separate existence altogether. Essentially Philemon was a spirit.

Jung considered that he had made a crucial discovery that 'there are things in the psyche which I do not produce, but which produce themselves and have their own life. Philemon represented a force which was not myself'. Philemon seemed like a superior being, a guru. Jung had discovered a tool that was of great help to him.

There was one more crisis to weather before his storm started to expend its energy. This occurred in 1916 after around 3 years of conversations with Philemon. He reports a building restlessness accompanied by an ominous feeling. He describes a growing sense of a haunting and the air being full of ghostly presences. Strange things began to happen, the front door bell rang frantically although there was no one there. It felt as though the house was filling up with spirits. He asked them what they wanted and they replied 'we have come back from Jerusalem where we found not what we sought'. This became the first line of the book that Jung wrote over the course of the next three days, an extraordinary book which is almost impenetrable and completely different to any thing else that he wrote – *Septem Sermones Ad Mortuous*.[31] Jung thought that this experience was archetypal in origin and seemed convinced that he had transcribed the thoughts of a first-century Gnostic from Alexandria called Basilides.[32] The fascination with matters relating to Gnosticism lasted for the rest of his life.[33]

Set, Setting and Integration

Jung not only survived his archetypal crisis, but eventually he flourished. His experiences enriched and nourished him, helping him to mature into the wise elder statesman of the inner world. The key to his safe passage was his adherence to three fundamental principles: set, setting and integration.

The set is the psychological mindset that is brought to the adventure. Jung was fully committed to his deep inner process. He was committed to exploring the depths of his psyche—working, understanding and doing whatever was necessary to navigate his inner process.

Jung enjoyed an unusually supportive setting. He did not function very well in his professional capacity for much of this period. He continued to see some patients but resigned from his academic post as he felt he had lost his competence. His wife came from one of the richest families in Switzerland, so he was absolved from financial worries. He took great comfort from his family and had a number of devoted followers who would comfort him and sit with him when he was in the slough of despond. According to his biographer Frank McLynn, it was the dedication and commitment of his mistress Toni Wolff who pulled him through—at considerable cost to herself.[34] Thus the setting must not only be supportive in a material sense, it must also be supportive to the natural process unfolding in the psyche, particularly with regard to integration. Toni Wolff was his muse, his sounding board and his therapist.

Jung was particularly impressive in his development of creative methods of integration. He was determined to lose no opportunity to mine the rich seam of unconscious material and use whatever means at his disposal to bring it slowly into his consciousness. He talked, he made models, he wrote and he drew. Where his autobiography gives a brief overview of Jung's crisis, the publication of the *Red Book* in 2009 made available for the first time the extraordinary detail of Jung's thought processes and fantasies during his crisis.[35] This is a huge book, reminiscent of a medieval illustrated bible. Jung's deeply symbolic artwork sits alongside his evocative prose, poetry and incantations charting his heroic labours to be reborn. As the book progresses, there is an ecstatic outpouring to the figure of Phanes, who represents the divine child (Puer Aeternus) and the immortal Self. It shows clearly that this is above all a spiritual journey. Jung prided himself in his scientific approach and took great care to try to understand to classify every image, every item of his psychic inventory and classify them. He warns us that just allowing images to rise up without working on them and taking the trouble to understand them conjures the negative effects of the unconscious.[36] This is a serious warning that we will return to later.

So What Was the Matter with Jung?

How can we understand Jung's crisis from a modern perspective, attempting a balance between the standard bio-psycho-social model and the archetypal perspective?

Most psycho-social crises are triggered by life events, particularly those involving loss. The obvious trigger for Jung was the devastating loss of his relationship with Freud. We can easily understand the significance of Freud as a father figure. Freud provided the strong ebullient appreciative fathering that Jung probably yearned for, but never received from his depressed and wan father, Paul. The loss of Freud may well have triggered some unresolved grief over his father's death. This was accompanied by the loss of his role as heir apparent in the psychoanalytic movement and the guarantee of international reputation and renown. This was the first major setback in Jung's meteoric career. He was disowned; he was an outcast from the movement. This rejection may have resonated with previous experiences of rejection, of being the outcast, the boy who was bullied, who couldn't belong.

Going a little deeper, we know that Jung was having marital difficulties related to his adultery. His relationship with Sabina Spielrein had been intense. We know that Sabina was a deeply disturbed young woman with whom Jung engaged with great depth and commitment on a psychological level before their relationship became intimate. Jung was a particularly masculine man whose relationships with the women in his family, notably his mother, were turbulent and unfulfilling. While Emma provided the role of stable, sane wife, it seems likely that Jung was disturbed at a much deeper level by Sabina. His ego, his persona, his sense of how he carried himself in the world was shaken to its core.

But this does not explain the nature of Jung's experiences and the shape and content of his unfolding crisis. Of course there were professional considerations. Jung was profoundly ambitious. He wanted to develop his own understanding of the deep psyche and his exploration was partly driven by research interests. His family background of religion, spirits and the occult would have lent a potential context for his unfolding experiences. This may also point to a possible genetic predisposition towards instability and Jung may have inherited more that the average amount of genes that predispose to mental illness or schizotypy. But genes persist for a reason, they must sometimes confer a genetic advantage, otherwise they tend to fade from the gene pool. Could it be that Jung was also genetically predisposed in some way so that his crisis when it arrived, would be accompanied by an increased exposure to archetypal material?

Did Jung have a form of schizophrenia? The respected British psychoanalyst and paediatrician Donald Winnicott suggested in 1964 that Jung suffered from childhood schizophrenia aged 3 caused by his parent's separation. This is an extreme view that would not be shared by consensus psychiatric opinion today, but it held some weight at the time and served to undermine Jung's perspective while enhancing the position of the Freudians. The classical symptoms of schizophrenia include delusions (fixed false beliefs) as well as hallucinatory voices that are typically derogatory and say very unpleasant things. These voices tend to talk about you in the third person or perform a running commentary. Sometimes they give commands. In schizophrenia, there is usually a disorder of the flow of thinking (thought disorder) that is reflected in disorganised, sometimes incoherent speech. There may be delusions of being controlled by an external force. There may be a belief that thoughts are being withdrawn from or inserted into one's mind or that thoughts are being transmitted or broadcast to other people.

There is no doubt that Jung had experiences that were outside of consensus reality and that for a long period of time he was in some distress and not functioning well in his everyday life. But was he deluded? The definition of delusion is one of the basic problems of psychopathology. Most definitions hold that a delusion is a fixed belief held with extraordinary intensity that is not part of a shared belief system. Clearly, there could be a debate over whether or not Jung was deluded with regard to Philemon.

For me, potentially the most dangerous symptom that Jung describes was the ominous feeling, the haunting prior to the rapid writing of his book *Septem Sermones*—the seven sermons of the dead. This developing sense of the ominous is typical of delusional mood, one of the most dangerous symptoms of acute psychosis. This is a dawning uncertainty that something of great import and probably danger is about to happen. It involves a sense of dread that has an awe-inspiring quality. The very sense of self, the ego is threatened. In clinical practice, delusional mood is a time when people are at maximum risk; the mood often crystalizes into a sudden fixed delusion, usually of a paranoid or grandiose nature. Sometimes this leads to actions that are damaging or self injurious.

I believe that a consensus of modern psychiatric opinion would hold that Jung did not suffer from the usual symptoms of schizophrenia and that it would be an error of diagnosis to describe him as schizophrenic.[37] However, I believe that the same consensus of psychiatrists would consider that he could very easily have declined into a chronic delusional disorder. In this scenario, he could have deteriorated into a withdrawn, rambling and inconsequential figure preoccupied with his spirits. Did Jung suffer from bipolar disorder or a depressive illness? No, there is no evidence of the sustained depression of mood or the typical biological or cognitive symptoms of depression – and he never developed suicidal thought. Thus Jung's 'creative illness' still defies diagnosis according to the accepted classification of psychiatric disorders.[38]

From an archetypal perspective, the position is more straightforward. Jung suffered an archetypal crisis. For Plato, there was an ascent from a cave, for Jung there was a descent into a cave, but they are both describing aspects of the same territory. Jung was, above all, a navigator and map-maker. He had travelled to a place that was beyond consensus reality and he spent the rest of his life trying to understand and transmit to us what he had learned. In time he developed a secular interpretation of archetype, identifying the psychological principles behind the gods of the ancients, such as Anima, Shadow and the Self.

CHAPTER 4

Archetypal Crisis

There are many trails in life and the best trail a man can follow is the trail of becoming a human being.

—Ten Bears, *Dances with Wolves*

Jung was a powerful factor influencing my choice of career, but I was interested in just about every aspect of psychiatry: the science, the psychopharmacology and the social milieu of the patients. Most of all, I relished the opportunity to sit down and engage with a human being, exploring together the mystery of their life experience, puzzling out the issues underlying their distress, and working towards a way of moving that person forward in a positive and growth-orientated way.

I imagined that I would come across people who were having similar experiences to Jung, people who were going through an archetypal crisis that did not conform to the usual pattern of mental illness, who wanted to work on themselves and who needed help and support in order to find their way through it. To my surprise, I did not come across such cases in my clinical psychiatric practice, but I did come across a considerable number among my fellows when attending meditation retreats and similar. Indeed, often these people had either avoided psychiatry or had felt misunderstood by psychiatrists in a way that was not only unhelpful, but often wounding. It seemed to me that these people had often undergone a crisis with a marked archetypal component. Usually the archetypal crisis was in the distant past, but the integration process had not been completed and the issues that had arisen were still being worked with. Indeed, the continuing search for meaning and integration was often what had brought the person to the retreat.

Ruth's Story

Ruth gave me a very detailed account of her crisis that had happened over 25 years before our paths crossed. She is a wise and impressive woman in her sixties who radiates humility and kindness, strength and balance. These are her words.

I am 36 years old and married with three children. They are 7, 5 and 2; two girls and a boy. We moved to a small house in a tiny village in the Welsh countryside just before my youngest daughter was born. It has been a hectic few years, involving divorce, remarriage, studying for a degree and three pregnancies, two with complications. We are leading a very unsettled lifestyle with frequent changes of accommodation and we have moved again to be near my husband's job as he has been offered some lecturing work while working on his Ph.D. This had involved letting someone down with whom we had planned to buy a house in a different part of the country. I am deeply unhappy, but trying to make the best of it. I had begun to make friends and we had set up a playgroup. I worked one night a week in an old peoples' home as we are desperately short of money.

Strangely, the village we had landed in had two committed Buddhists in it, albeit of very different traditions. I had always had strong spiritual inclinations and, when living in Oxford some years before, had starting practicing meditation and yoga. Since that time we had been to hear Krishnamurti speak at Brockwood Park.

One couple in the village, Rory and Helen, had both been on weekend retreats led by Percival Clement who was a psychologist and Buddhist practitioner at his retreat center not far away. They were also deeply dissatisfied with their lives and both of them at different times told me of their unhappiness. I know that I felt their pain very keenly. Rory had a tragic beauty about him that I found strongly attractive. He reminded me of my first husband, who had died a few years previously. They both suggested to me that I go on one of Percival's retreats, Helen saying to me, 'It'll really clean you out'. So I went, totally unprepared.

I had not spent more than half an hour or so away from the children for a long time and I put at least 120% into all the practices. I gave it my all. I remember the exercise 'Tell me who you are?' In pairs we would sit opposite each other, very close, almost touching. Percival rings a bell. One person asks the question 'Tell me who you are?' The other starts to speak. After five minutes he rings the bell again and the roles reverse. I remember the person sitting opposite me with tears running down her face as I responded to her question and feeling puzzled and surprised at her reaction.

I remember a strong experience of joy, rhythmic contractions moving through my body, as though I was giving birth and being born at the same time. I remember us dancing out on the hillside. I remember an early morning meditation practice, our palms cupped together at the heart and moving them out towards the rising sun, humming as we did so. We ran up a hill every morning on rising. We sat in meditation outside beside a fast-running stream. We raked hay, which reminded me of combing my daughter's hair. We installed and dedicated a statue of Green Tara.

Meals were in silence and we chanted together before eating—'The first bite is to discard evil . . .'. I threw myself wholeheartedly into everything, finding it all deeply meaningful and significant. I went for a walk up the stream and came across a cloud of vivid azure dragon-flies. I found a badger's skull and collected some of the teeth. We had individual interviews with Percival from time to time and he asked me 'Well, tell me who you are?' and I answer something like 'I am eating, I am sitting, I am walking, I am breathing . . .' and he said 'Now change the question to "How is life fulfilled?"'. I couldn't remember the question and kept going back to him to be reminded, 'how is life fulfilled?'. He asked us to pay attention to our dreams and on the last night I dreamed I was sitting by a pond and a goldfish leaped out and said to me 'Discover'.

I woke in the middle of the night and there was a loud crash from downstairs. I go down to investigate and find a piece of wood that had been leaning against the wall had fallen down. I go and sit by the fire-place, now just glowing ash, and it springs into flame. I hear the stone walls of the old farmhouse speaking Welsh to me. I go outside and walk down the long twisting lane to the gate by the main road and turn round and walk back up in the dawning light, feeling I am walking the path of my life.

As far as I am aware, no one else on that retreat was as profoundly affected as me. They seemed to be taking it as a kind of holiday. I don't remember any preparation for leaving given us by Percival. Helen comes to meet me at the end of the retreat. I don't remember what I said but I must have been babbling to her. When we got home there was a large sow by the back door and we had to chase her back up the road. The next day a rose that had never bloomed was in full flower. A friend's husband started reading books about Buddhism. When my daughter peed on the floor it sounded like a bell, the conclu-sion of something. I went into a kind of trance, moving in patterns in the house, across the garden and into the building at the back where the playgroup met. Images of elephants came alive for me and were strongly significant in some way. I couldn't sleep. I was seeing spinning circles everywhere. I held a chunk of ice in my hand and it was my life melting. It was as if flowers and plants were speaking to me although I do not hear them. Sometimes words would break open in my head, showering their inner meanings in upon me.

My husband has had experience of taking large amounts of LSD from some years before and he recognizes the kind of state I am in. I ask him not to call the doctor as I know reality has slipped away from me and that I was in danger of being put in hospital. He puts me to bed. I call myself Ruth Ardent. I read about Tibetan Buddhism, write down fragments of sutras and create some kind of altar. I'm trying to work something out. I want to function better but I don't want to return simply to my old unhappy self. I phone Percival asking for help, but he was just about to lead another retreat and wasn't able to speak to me. He seemed to take my attempt to contact him as my wish to make a personal connection, perhaps of a romantic nature. He recommended I speak to someone else who lived locally, but I didn't know them very well and didn't feel I could follow it up.

Meanwhile, Rory and I kept bumping into each other. He worked as a gardener on a nearby estate and if I went for a walk he would be sure to be working outside just nearby. When I went out of the house he would drive by. He called round one day when I was alone in the house and we fell into each other. All the repressed emotion just poured out all over him. I knew somehow that the feelings weren't real, but the attraction was very strong.

It was my youngest daughter's birthday and we had a party for her down by the river. I had a big thing about telling the truth and being honest and felt I had to tell Helen about my feelings for Rory. She says 'Enjoy it' and I feel trusted and relieved. The next day she comes to the house, angry and upset saying that she has told Rory that if he is ever unfaithful to her, she will divorce him immediately. The subsequent events are a bit hazy but we all seem to be tied up in some kind of dance. For some reason, Helen and my husband are away at the same time. I remember picking loads and loads of blackcurrants and then making jam. The children have all fallen asleep and Rory and I are kissing. My husband arrives and there is a big scene, but no one wants to fall out. My husband thinks it will all blow over. Rory then tells Helen. She packs a suitcase for him, throws him out and he goes to stay with friends. My husband moves out.

I really want to hear bells and chanting and remember seeing a sign beside the road on the way to town, 'To the Temple'. I ask my sister-in-law to look after the children for the day, borrow her car and drive down there. There is no one around. I see a sign with an elephant's head on it, pointing up a track. I follow it up through ancient oak woods and at the top is a farmhouse with various enclosures housing chickens, ducks and different birds, and in the yard is an ELEPHANT. I talk to the keeper and went back to the Temple several times. On one big festival day I get hold of the Sri Lankan guru who lives there and ask him the significance of elephants. He tells me that they are the remover of obstacles and bringer of wisdom.

I don't remember very well the actual trajectory of what happened next. My husband came back and I moved out. I remember getting on my bike with a black plastic bag on the back and feeling very reluctant, but I went anyway. I stayed with friends for a while. I used to walk and walk and walk, up the railway line, across country to home and back. I remember coming across peacocks in the snow. I was with Rory for a while in the top floor of an old mansion. At this time I talked and talked, the sex was incredibly powerful. I felt myself shift into different beings, and we would just gaze into each other's eyes for long periods of time.

My husband stopped me seeing the children and I then went to live in a shared house to try and ease things, and then into a caravan just down the road. I used to go home during the day to be with the children and then back to the caravan at night. I carried on walking and walking. Flowers and plants were still very significant and imbued with a high intensity of meaning for me. I described it as feeling the earth energy, more than feeling, hearing, sensing, being moved by. The 'Discover . . .' from my dream became 'Discover flowering expression and the power of healing the earth'.

I had a strong dream at around this time of a bomb going off and the fall-out ash was gently raining down on us all, covering everything in a soft grey blanket. Someone I met gave me a drawing he had done of a volcano erupting with a tiger and an elephant at the base and this was a very clear depiction of what was happening for me. I went to spiritualist meetings sometimes and the room would become filled with pink light and frequently the messages would be for me, which caused me acute embarrassment.

I remember books almost falling into my hands in the bookshop or the library. I read a lot of Jung, William Blake, books about Buddhism, herbalism and flower remedies. There was one about bird migration and the magnetism of different symbols. I remember learning some chants from a book about the Medicine Buddha and sitting on an island in the middle of the river, chanting.

I went to the Buddhist society in London to try and find someone who could make some sense of what was going on for me. I went to Amaravati, to the Manjushri Centre up in Cumbria, to Throssel Hole in Yorkshire, and later Samye Ling in Scotland. I went on a retreat at Gaia House in Devon with a Japanese Zen master called Hogan and during Dokusan, the one-to-one interview, I tried to explain some of experiences to him but couldn't get it across very well and his command of English wasn't very good at that time. When I looked into his eyes I could see right down a long line of vision and into the eyes of the Buddha himself. I continued going on retreats with him for some time and later on with an American Zen teacher, Genpo. I took the children to the Amaravati summer camp for quite a few years.

I made contact with people from my past to try and get some help. I wanted to feel more normal and less disturbed but I didn't want to relinquish the riches that have been bestowed on me; that would be the most terrible loss. I knew that I was having some kind of spiritual opening but I wanted to move on to the next stage of it. An American psychiatrist who I had known years before came over to visit me, but was not able to offer any help or understanding. Rory, myself and the children moved into an apartment in a large house that I had admired on my long country walks and his children used to visit at weekends. We had a meditation group there and monks from Amaravati came to stay for a weekend and gave teachings in the nearby town.

My personal life and relationships were difficult. I wanted people to live in harmony but everything became so complicated. I try to find a path that nourishes my spiritual yearning while attending properly to my children. My husband and I have been for some counseling over responsibility for childcare. My relationship with Rory is breaking up. Things are difficult between us and he has already started seeing someone else. I find somewhere to live with the children where I think I can provide the children with some stability. I met a leading aromatherapist. I trained with her and practiced in a small way. I also worked with elderly people and did domestic work. I became involved with a man and his complex family and with him continued on the Zen path. I did some training as a healer and different Celtic and pagan type workshops.

I wanted to train as a counselor to try and better understand myself as well as the people I was treating. This brought me into training as a psychiatric nurse. The most valuable experience of my training was a placement at an Emotional Recovery Centre, which used the 12-step method, or the Minnesota Model. This gave me some very useful insights into my own behavior patterns and recovery as well as the tools for subsequent work with clients. On qualifying, I started counseling training. Through this, I then came across a Centre for Mindfulness and with this practice slowly began to integrate my spiritual and my everyday life.

It has been 26 years since that first eruption, and I would say that it is only now that I am resolving and bringing to earth what was started then. I went back to Percival's retreat center once, about eight years after my crisis began, and I remember saying then that I was still very much actively unpacking what I had first found there. I think Buddhism and the ongoing practice of mindfulness have given me a solid foundation. The responsibility of professional work has helped too. I have been dancing Five Rhythms for about four years, which in turn has led me towards shamanic workshops and practices. I feel I can embody Spirit more fully now. My journey continues.

Managing Turbulence

Ruth told me that she still suffered shame and confusion when recalling the events of 25 years ago. She regretted the pain that she had caused her children and the other people involved, but it is the nature of numinous experience to override other considerations; the tide is too strong to resist. Her experience had much in common with Jung's crisis, although her support systems and integrative methods were much less developed. Like Jung she was entering midlife while undergoing a psycho-social crisis with a number of stresses. There was a strong background of interest in the spiritual and her crisis was triggered by the intensity of a workshop designed to heighten meaning and degrade ego structures. There was a failure of integration so that she left the workshop in a profoundly non-ordinary state of consciousness and in a very vulnerable condition.

Her archetypal crisis was characterized by a strong sense of the sacred, encountering synchronicities, being in an enchanted world with an enhanced intensity of meaning, including an enhancement of sex. She had some perceptions that would not have been available to other people and, like Jung, she struggled to manage her physical energy. In such an aroused state, it is difficult to use meditative techniques as the mind is simply too agitated. Jung found that the more physical discipline of yoga was useful; Ruth grounded some of her energy by walking.

The setting for Ruth was less than ideal. A well-judged workshop of this nature would manage a gradual decrease of intensity as the workshop approaches its conclusion with a careful integration and grounding of the experience so that everybody leaves with their feet firmly on planet Earth. The leader and attendants need to be highly attuned to anyone who is in a heightened mental state. Of course, it may not be obvious at the time, but there should be recourse to some expert help over the next week or so if the heightened state continues. This should be part of the duty of care.

Ruth had some support from her husband and decided to avoid psychiatric help, fearing that she would be detained against her will in hospital.[39] She sought out organizations and methods to try to integrate her experience and limit the potential for damage. She was trying to find someone who could help her find a path through the crisis. It was a slow process and there was an unfolding incoherence in her personal life but she kept her family together and emerged to give a valuable service to her community as a skilled mental health professional. Like Jung, she treasured her experiences as riches that she was still processing many years later.

I asked Ruth what she thought would have been most helpful to her at the time. Her words again:

> I experienced a shift in consciousness, so being with people or a community who have been through similar experience or are familiar with different levels of consciousness would have been very helpful. It's interesting, because I would say that I am going through a similar experience now after the recent retreat in Dorset, but with the years of experience and practice I can manage and flow with it.[40] I have also built up an excellent support network over the years of friends and like-minded people. Looking back at the account of my experience then, I can see how alone I was. How long was I not functioning? It is very hard to say as my experience of time was non-existent and I probably didn't know I wasn't functioning. I would guess, with hindsight after that retreat so many years ago, that I probably needed intense practical support for about a month, further support for three months and then helpful points of reference for some time to come.

Charles and the Disappearing Dot

After the Second World War had finally ended, my father decided not to go to medical school. Ostensibly this was because he didn't want to be a financial burden to his parents but also, at 23, having been involved in a great undertaking and seen something of the world, I don't think he wanted to go back to exhausted, austere, post-war England with its grey skies and grey prospects. So he found himself working in Kuwait for an oil company at a time when the oil industry was in its adolescence, Kuwait was undeveloped and the extent of Western civilisation there was a series of tin huts in the desert. Kuwait in those days was full of young adventurers, who had survived the war relatively unscathed, who worked hard and tended to play hard too. Like my father, many of them had spent their lives in conservative institutions, passing seamlessly from boarding school to the military and then to the Oil Company.

One of those young men was Charles, a little older and wiser than the others. He had been in the army in India but he had not been in combat and did not seem scarred by the war. He had developed more than a passing interest in Indian religion and spirituality. He hadn't taken it further; he hadn't engaged with a guru or meditated in the Himalayas—he was, after all, an officer in the British army—but it seemed to have resonated with something important within him. In those days, people stayed in overseas postings for long periods. My father was in Kuwait for 10 years, where he met my mother. They married and his job required a move to Iran, where my sister and I were born. Sometimes wives and children returned to Britain while the man remained in post abroad. This was the case with Charles; he married, his first child was born and then his family returned home, leaving Charles in the desert in Kuwait.

Most of the young men seemed to occupy themselves with sport, an endless round of parties, camping trips to the desert and swimming in the sea, but Charles decided to concentrate on an internal journey. He decided to emulate the yogis of India and he started reading Jung. He was entranced by Jung's ideas and wanted to gain first-hand experience of the psychological territory that Jung described; he wanted to go to the deep interior. Charles began a series of mental exercises designed to take himself into the recesses of the psyche. He told me many years later that he wanted to transcend the everyday world entirely. He had read about the collective unconscious, he knew that the Yogis tried to travel to an area of psyche beyond ego by concentration exercises, he wanted to raise his Kundalini and he wanted to explore the Hindu concept of Atman. From my parents I gleaned that he had spent hours concentrating on a dot on a piece of paper, trying to make it disappear. He had been meditating for long periods and he had been recording his dreams. Charles had kept these practices from his friends and colleagues, as they would have been frowned upon. My mother, who did know a little about Buddhism, was very clear that these practices should not be done alone—you need a guide.

Charles ended up having a devastating 'nervous breakdown', as it was called in those days. I never found out the details but he was apparently flown back to the UK in a straitjacket. He told me once that he had been looking forward to seeing a psychiatrist when he returned to Britain as he assumed this would lead to a Jungian analysis, which would provide him with a creative, growth-orientated way forward. But psychoanalysis wasn't offered to him; these were the days before useful antipsychotics or antidepressants had been developed and he was treated with the only biological treatment that sometimes worked. He was treated with ECT.[41] He was medically retired from the big oil company and never worked again.

Charles was my godfather and he took his responsibilities seriously as a spiritual mentor. He was never religious; indeed, he cordially detested the Church. He was the first person that I knew who had read Jung and he awakened my interest in looking at what may lie underneath the everyday world. Charles was a man who seemed to know that we lived in a world that was illusory and he hinted at something profound and true that lay at a deeper level. He spoke to me sometimes of the Tibetan gods and goddesses, for whom he felt special reverence and affection. He had a well-stocked library on Eastern religion, esotericism and Jung. His relationship with his books was a fundamental structure for him, although his wife claimed that he did not actually read any of them. He loved his library; it was an important internal object for him that reinforced his new place in the world.

From the usual perspective, Charles could have been seen as a broken man. He had had his mental illness and had made a partial recovery. His family just about managed on his small pension and he did some tutoring. His wife ran the house as he wasn't much concerned with the practicalities of daily living, although he had a garden with trees that he gave names to and there were chicken coops and rabbit hutches. One could say that his ego function was diminished but his family were fed and clothed, and Charles just could not see the point in many material possessions. Children, of course, see people through a different lens and for me Charles was special; he had a glow about him. He had a quality of humanity and genuineness and he listened to what people said. He liked people and he had a curiosity that was infectious. He was my favourite adult when I was a child.

From my current perspective as a psychiatrist, I know that in the 30 or so years that I knew him, he was always cheerful, beautifully mannered and sane. There were no further brushes with psychiatry for him, whereas severe psychiatric disorder such as bipolar disorder or unipolar depression tends to be recurrent. I do not know what psychiatric diagnosis he was given at the time but I believe that he suffered a classical archetypal crisis. He absorbed himself in prolonged and unsupervised intense spiritual practice. Like Icarus, he flew too close to the sun. There was no mentor, no

Daedalus to give him guidance. His ego structures dissolved and never quite returned. He never returned to spiritual practice. He spent the rest of his life being fascinated by the transpersonal but was never able to engage with it except at a distance, perhaps like a moth fluttering around the flame. I think this represented his need to integrate his experience but he was never quite able to do this. His archetypal crisis remained essentially un integrated, perhaps the ECT, with it's memory-deleting side effect contributed to this or perhaps the intensity of his crisis was just too powerful. It is perhaps a shame that he never progressed to his Jungian analysis, as that would have been the best available tool available in those days to integrate and metabolise his crisis.

Seeking Shiva

My own archetypal crisis happened during my first visit to India as a medical student. In the final year before qualification, we were supposed to find a three-month placement in a hospital of our choice to gain some extra experience. I thought that this would be the last opportunity to satisfy some wanderlust and curiosity before the constraints and long hours of the junior doctor lifestyle. I travelled to Peshawar in the northeast frontier of Pakistan with the intention of working with 'Medicins sans Frontiers', a French group of doctors that were doing good work in Soviet occupied Afghanistan. But this didn't work out; they needed doctors rather than medical students and they told me that it was too dangerous. So I made my way through Pakistan, across the heavily armed border with India. I spent some time at the Golden Temple of the Sikhs before heading slowly eastwards towards the Himalayas. I was travelling alone and tried to keep away from the places that were frequented by other westerners. I wanted to fully immerse myself in India.

It had become something of a cliché that people went to India to 'find themselves' before returning with long hair, beads and a new found spirituality. I was very clear that nothing like that was going to happen to me. I was interested in the history and culture of the peoples and the monuments. I wanted to see the holy cities of Amritsar and Varanasi before doing some treks in the mountains, but spirituality was not something that held any interest or attraction for me.

I soon discovered that India held an extraordinary power. As well as the density of the population, the noise, the smells and colours, there was something else that I now recognise to be a heightened archetypal intensity. Having been brought up on stories of the myths and gods of ancient Greece, it was fascinating to see such a flourishing pantheistic society in India. At the holy places and the temples, I was struck by the devotion shown by people from the many layers of society to the Hindu gods in all their variety. I didn't really understand what I thought I was seeing and experiencing. The holy places clearly possessed a certain power and I was aware of a faint but numinous experience that seemed to be cumulative after repeated exposure. The more time I spent at the holy places, the greater the impression that I had of this power. It also seemed to me that if the Hindus believed in their gods to such an extent then, on some level they existed. Their lives and their world seemed defined by their religious and spiritual life, which related to these distinct archetypes represented by their gods.

I reached the mountains and I did some trekking. I had conversations with holy men, I smoked some charas and I hung around the temples.[42] I started having fantasies that perhaps I would join the sadhus[1] and walk with them the long pilgrimage route up to the source of the Ganges high in the Himalayas. I was feeling the pull of something that I had never felt before, a yearning for the sacred. I felt drawn to and increasingly fascinated by Shiva, the Hindu god of death and rebirth. It felt as though my old self was dissolving. My life in London as a medical student was beginning to seem very far away—almost as though it belonged to a different person. I couldn't articulate what I was feeling, but the vague and enticing lure of the mystical was getting stronger. Hours sitting in a shrine to Shiva with the sadhus, bells and incense amplified the otherworldly atmosphere. Come on in. Join us, the mountains seemed to say.

With hindsight, this was a dangerous archetypal crisis. I was increasingly gripped by a vague but powerful numinous feeling, a sense of the sacred that I could not really articulate or understand; I was alone, without a peer group and a long way from home. My ego structures, my sense of who I was, were becoming fragile and nebulous. I was in some danger of losing them altogether. My vigour and focus seemed to be leaving me. I was having some difficulty expressing myself and I wondered if I might be developing schizophrenia. Shiva is the god that destroys ego to go beyond the illusory, but I didn't feel ready for that. I decided to decline the invitation.

I was identifying with a Hindu god, but the archetype traditionally associated with the yearning to go beyond the separate self and become part of something greater is represented in the Western esoteric tradition by Neptune, the Roman god of the sea. Neptune speaks to that tantalising pull to the numinous, the spiritual ache and hunger for the sacred. The Neptune archetype tends to dissolve our ego boundaries and pull us towards an

---

[1] Religious ascetics

oceanic state of fusion. High-intensity archetypal experiences with a Neptunian flavour have a numinous component that may help the ego function achieve a higher octave but there is also a high risk of spiritual confusion, delusion or ego inflation if the archetype is poorly integrated. The shadow side of the Neptune archetype is associated with alcoholism, substance abuse, codependence and other forms of escapism.

Indeed, I could see that I was becoming captivated by something that was not good for me. The archetypal wind was too strong, I needed to reef my sail or find shelter before I capsized. At the very bottom of my backpack, I found my textbook of medicine. This became my ladder, my rescue structure, as I used it to restore my focus and concentration. I left the mountains and temples and travelled to Goa for a beach holiday. I was battered by the giant waves and the surf seemed to be knocking some sense back into me. The vicious undertow of the Indian Ocean reminded me to keep my feet firmly planted and not get swept away. I lay in the sun and tried to memorize my medical textbook. It seemed to be working and the yearning for the mystical was fading. I went back to London and focused on passing my final medical examinations. Six months after my close encounter with Shiva, I was walking the hospital wards as a newly qualified doctor. So I survived without injury but there was some failure of integration. Any spiritual leanings, any craving for the numinous had been firmly locked away. It would twenty years before they surfaced again.

CHAPTER 5

Archetypal Penetrance

Man is not by any means of fixed and enduring form.

He is much more an experiment and a transition.

He is nothing else than the narrow and perilous bridge between nature and spirit.

—Herman Hesse

The Bio-psycho-social-archetypal (BPSA) Model of the Psyche

Although they cannot be known directly, archetypes permeate our daily lives. They are the hidden forces that shape our conscious experience and patterns of thought; they leave their traces and images in the fantasy material that flows through our dreams and our daydreams. But they cannot be separated from the physical world. Archetypes are inextricably linked with the bio-psycho-social unit that we usually consider constitutes yourself as an individual person. They are expressed through the hardware that is our body, our nervous system and our sense organs.

We are living, breathing units of tissue with our genes directing the flow of our development in association with the extraordinary complexity of our environment. Thus there is the biological influence of 'nature' combined with the psychological and social influences representing 'nurture'. According to the bio-psycho-socio-archetypal (BPSA) perspective, there is another more subtle layer with an archetypal influence being mediated through our environment, our psyche and our sensory apparatus in varying degrees.

Penetrance is a term used in genetics to describe the likelihood of an underlying genetic predisposition (genotype) being translated into a characteristic of the organism (phenotype). Some genes have complete penetrance in that anyone with that gene will show the physical trait associated with it. Most physical traits are polygenic, associated with a variety of genes that are expressed in variable degrees and subject to environmental influences. I suggest that we can apply the concept of penetrance to describe a similar effect with archetypes. If we are indeed influenced by an archetypal ocean with tides, currents, waves and undertows, then this may be more active – or penetrant – in some people than others and each person may be more receptive to different archetypal flavors at different times.

The degree of archetypal penetrance is highly variable. Sometimes the degree of archetypal penetrance is overwhelming for the psyche and the 'overplus of meaning' may cause a crisis. From this perspective, acute psychiatric disorders occur when there is a failure of the homeostatic mechanisms that normally maintain archetypal penetrance within a comfortable range. The morbid fear associated with paranoid states, the excitement and amplification of manic states, the loathing and constriction of severe depression, the imminence of catastrophe found in post traumatic stress disorder all have an awe-filled quality, that could be called numinous.

There are states with high archetypal penetrance (HAP) in which the individual experiences a numinous state without developing an archetypal crisis. This may be a life enhancing HAP state or it may be unintegrated and problematic. Some conditions lead to a depleted range of archetypal sensitivity with low archetypal penetrance (LAP) and the person endures a dull and grey world with a low intensity of meaning. Sometimes there is a unstable state with low archetypal penetrance interspersed with archetypal crisis. Most of us exist in a comfortable and tolerable level of archetypal intensity state mediated by our brain and our psyche. There are some peaks and troughs of meaning that add some spice and richness and which are usually tolerated without much difficulty. We could call this the normative range of archetypal penetrance (NAP) that represents consensus reality. It would not take much imagination to classify psychotropic medication to match an archetypal classification of psychiatric disorders. Antidepressants and stimulants are 'psychup' drugs that increase archetypal penetrance, antipsychotics are 'psyless' that decrease penetrance, while mood stabilisers could be termed 'psynorms' to keep penetrance in a mid range.[43]

Let us imagine the normal state of a functional human being. Historically the human animal would be engaged primarily in tasks of survival of the self, the family unit and the tribe. The work of daily life would be to avoid predators, to be a homemaker, a provider, a hunter, a social animal and a parent. In primitive societies, once the day's duties were done, there may have been a state of awe as the tribe sat by the fire at the end of a day, told stories and wondered at the stars. As societies developed, archetypal themes would coalesce into the mythic and religious elements of daily life that would become a crucial part of the developing social fabric and body politic.

Joseph Campbell, the world's greatest expert on comparative mythology, suggested that myths were the conduit for archetypal energies emanating from the cosmos. 'It would not be too much to say that myth is the secret opening through which the inexhaustible energies of the cosmos pour into human cultural manifestation'.[44]

The contemporary Jungian and archetypal scholar, Keiron Le Grice defines myths as follows:

> The word *myth* refers to the stories and sets of symbolic images that have informed human lives across the ages, shaping tribal societies, local cultures, and the world's civilisations alike. Myths are stories that provide perspective and meaning to help individuals and cultures orientate themselves to the requirements of living. They serve as a record of humanity's spiritual heritage and they have inspired all the great religions and cultural world views.[45]

These days our mythic life is most commonly expressed in film, literature and even computer games. Le Grice's book *The Rebirth of the Hero* systematically explores the archetypal hero's journey in cinema and film as a symbolic portrayal of our individual struggle for a greater range of consciousness and psychological wholeness. Films such as *The Lord of the Rings* are particularly high in mythic and archetypal themes. Horror films have a particular capacity to induce archetypal experience with a dark numinosity of the *mysterium tremendum et fascinans* variety. Judging by the preponderance of such films, we appear to need them. Indeed this may be one of the most accessible ways in which we can gain a numinous experience.

We find the archetypal flavours particularly in nature, in music, in going to our holy places, both religious and secular, the festivals, the arenas, the temples and the mountain peaks. We seek out our everyday experiences of the archetypal. We have an innate disposition for numinosity seeking behaviour. It is part of our fabric.

Martial Risings

Usually we are exposed to a range of archetypes, but sometimes one specific archetypal flavour stands out and becomes dominant.[46] This is particularly clear at sporting events with the qualities of rivalry, aggression, assertion, courage and power that are traditionally associated with the warlike Roman God Mars. The Olympic flame epitomises that which is imperishable, shared by many and symbolises the very best of humanity. Every four years the flame becomes the centrepiece of the sporting world and to be an Olympian is to transcend, for a moment, the confines of humanity. We may be moved to tears when an athlete crosses the line and wins an Olympic medal. The tears have nothing to do with sadness but are an expression of intensity of feeling as we participate briefly in a higher penetrance archetypal state.

Many of us will relish the atavistic passions of the sporting encounter with the thrill of conquest and the tribal quality of supporting our team. For me, the annual Six Nations rugby union championship between England, Scotland, Ireland, Wales, France and Italy has a perfection of mythic and martial quality being enhanced by the complex historical rivalries of the countries involved. On match day the stadiums are full of people wearing their tribal colours, backing their champions. We see the teams of players, the warriors emerging from the changing rooms. This is their moment on the great stage, the time of the hero, as they flow through the tunnels into the arena to the roar of the crowd. The music, the cheering and the intensity reaches a crescendo. The commentator, who was a famous player in his day, says that this is the best of days, as a player there is nothing quite like it. It is one of those great moments that raises you to a place above everyday life. It can be remembered but it may not be repeated.

It takes courage to be exposed in this way. It is one of the most intense ways in which one can walk the human stage. They line up, these young men who represent us, arms around each other's shoulders as the national anthems play. The music fans the archetypal flames, this is the tribal energy with all its the historic and cultural resonance. Some of the players shed a tear as the camera pans down their line, others are visibly moved, their faces contorted with emotion. This is a concentrated and potent meaning state, the moment of maximum numinosity. Then the match begins and the archetype plays itself out in a game of ritual violence, but with strict rules so that it cleanses and lifts rather than destroys. This is the refined version of Mars in harmony with the biological structures of our bodies and the psycho-social imperatives of our times. There will be no sacking of cities, no rape and murder, no maimed heroes, no emptying of treasuries today.

The darker side of the Mars archetype can be seen most obviously in situations such as Nazi Germany. There were the psycho-social issues of economic collapse and deprivation, the splitting into the good Aryans and the bad non Aryans and the projection of the undesired qualities into these others. The nationalism of the young and humiliated German State was fanned into an archetypal crescendo by the Nazi performances and especially the great rallies that produced communal high archetypal penetrance states. The theologian James Alison tells us that the organisers of these events knew exactly what they were doing. As he puts it:

> You bring people together and you unite them in worship. You provide regular, rhythmic music and marching. You enable them to see many people in uniform, people who have already lost a certain individuality and become symbols. You give them songs to sing. You build them up with the reason for their togetherness, a reason based on common racial heritage. You inflame them with tales of past woe and reminders of past confusion when they were caused to suffer by some shame being imposed on them, the tail end of which woe is still in their midst. You keep them waiting and the pressure building up. All this gradually serves to bring people out of themselves; the normally restrained becoming passionate, unfriendly neighbors find themselves looking at each other anew in the light of the growing 'Bruderschaft.' Then after the build up, the Fuhrer appears...and, before long, the apotheosis takes place and he is in their midst. With a few deft gestures he conjures up the mood of those present.[47]

High Archetypal Penetrance (HAP) States

In 1989, having finished my basic training in psychiatry, I joined a research team at University College London studying the genetics of mental illness under the energetic leadership of Professor Hugh Gurling. The team had published a paper a year earlier finding some evidence of an association between a segment of chromosome 5 and schizophrenia. We hoped that we would identify a major gene defect that predisposed to schizophrenia which would allow the identification of the biological pathways by which the condition became manifest. We hoped that this would lead to new treatments, perhaps specifically tailored to genetic variants. Treatment need not be restricted to medication, perhaps genetically vulnerable people could be identified and given psychological treatments so that full-blown schizophrenia would not develop and medication would not be required. These were heady days full of therapeutic optimism. We thought we were on the threshold of a new neurobiology and that there was a real prospect of curing mental illness.

My role in the research effort was to find extended families that had a high incidence of either bipolar disorder or schizophrenia. I would then meet the various relatives, take a blood sample and interview them to establish whether or not they suffered from any psychiatric disorder. The blood sample would be subjected to a complex linkage analysis to examine any relationship with gene segments and a particular illness. Some 25 years later, we now know that there are many genes that predispose to schizophrenia, at least 60 by time of writing. Each single gene effect is small and so far this research has not led to any advances in treatment.

For me this was a welcome opportunity to travel around the country, go to obscure places and meet some interesting people. I came to know some of these families well. On one occasion, I was invited to a wedding reception, as this seemed the best opportunity to meet and bleed the required quantity of family members. In a typical family of this type there may be three people with schizophrenia, usually of the severe variety. There could also be one or two family members who did not have schizophrenia, had never been psychotic or seen a mental health professional, but who had never worked, did not have relationships and depended on the support of the family to enable them to function. Some of these people had a *schizotypal* personality organisation, with eccentric ideas and speech, and some were more solitary and inward looking, perhaps having a more *schizoid* personality.

This was not a surprise as it was recognised that that there were milder expressions of the schizophrenia genotype, a 'forme fruste' of the condition where psychosis did not develop but the genetic load was expressed in a problematic manner, affecting a person's relationship with their environment in a way that seemed insurmountable. Although bipolar disorder and schizophrenia were supposed to be separate and distinct, it was also clear that there were a number of families where both conditions were represented. I became increasingly aware as my research year progressed that there seemed to be a disproportionate number of unusually talented and energetic people in these families. There was one family that seemed to produce explorers and sailors, another that produced artists and another that seemed to specialise in theatre and literature. I had no way of knowing whether this was statistically significant but I was impressed by the coincidence.

I now consider that these were families with a tendency towards higher archetypal penetrance. With hindsight, I suspect that I was hunting for the 'archetype genes' — those genes that affect the brain structures that influence archetypal penetrance. We have long known that the incidence of schizophrenia is around 1 per cent, and this seems to be a stable finding through different peoples and eras. Given the disadvantages of a chronic illness and that most people with chronic schizophrenia are less likely to have children, it has been a puzzle as to why the genes have survived so successfully.[48] Theories have included the advantage of a schizoid personality in tolerating the solitude required to live and farm in remote places, and the advantage of paranoid person in surviving in troubled times.

Perhaps this is so, but I think far more persuasive is the idea that mental illness is just one of a number of high archetypal penetrance states that can result from this genetic variability.

Some people may have such a genetic load that they are at very high risk of developing a serious psychiatric disorder; for others their tendency to high archetypal penetrance could have an altogether different outcome. Other HAP states would include the experiences of holy men and women, the shamans, the priests, the visionary artists and all those who can pierce these filmy veils described by William James to access non-ordinary states of consciousness. The term *non*-ordinary used in this context differentiates it from the ordinary state of consciousness that is our everyday consensus reality or altered state of consciousness that implies a medical state of impaired consciousness. Sometimes these non-ordinary states can be highly productive for the individual and the community but at other times individuals in such states may fall off the tightrope. Those who enter an archetypal crisis may emerge as a saint or as a lunatic. Jung was probably genetically predisposed to archetypal sensitivity, but he underwent his archetypal crisis and emerged into a mature state of high archetypal penetrance, which was life enhancing for him and for his patients, his colleagues and his students.

Archetypal penetrance may wax and wane; the flow of archetypes is dynamic and changeable. HAP states can be immature or mature, emerging or emerged. The emerging states range from something akin to schizotypy, which is often a chronic dysfunctional state, to the fertile creative state following a numinous experience or the successful navigation of an archetypal crisis. Many people enter such states without guides and end up confusing inner and outer realities, unfortunately running the risk of losing their capacity to function in the everyday world. This needn't be so, but perhaps reflects the way in which contemporary society is so rooted in the practical world that we have lost the knack of navigating between the two worlds.

The proper task of the psychotherapist or psychiatrist is to offer skilled guidance through these critical periods. The Scottish psychoanalyst Ronald Laing saw the ego as a tool to enable us to live in the everyday external world and that the Western world is ego-dominated to the point where losing the boundaries and structure provided by the ego now entails grave risk. He noted the artists and thinkers who have become shipwrecked on these reefs, such as Rimbaud, Van Gogh, Nietzsche and Munch, and suggested that those who survive have to be streetwise needing exceptional qualities, including a capacity for secrecy, slyness, and cunning as well as a thoroughly realistic appraisal of the risks they run—not only from the spiritual realms they frequent, but also from the hatred of their fellows for anyone engaged in this pursuit.[49]

Mature HAP states may arise without going through a crisis but after a gradual and sustained process of development with a succession of more easily digestible experiences. These mature and stable HAP states are comparable with Abraham Maslow's concept of the 'self actualised person'. Maslow, an American psychologist who was interested in the positive qualities of humanity, used this term to describe people who seem to be realising their full potential, being comfortable with themselves and others, feeling alive and fulfilled and engaging in useful tasks. Typically they have an appreciation of beauty as found in nature and the fruits of life, they are resourceful and independent, they feel comfortable with their own company but this is rooted in a deep fellowship with others and with humanity. They are humble and most certainly not egocentric. All of the people that Maslow described reported peak experiences marked by feelings of ecstasy, harmony, and an intense and positive amplification of meaning. They often reported experiences of being at one with the universe, feeling stronger and calmer than ever before, filled with light and feeling beautiful and good.[50]

Luisa and the Dog Mess

Luisa spent her life in a high-archetypal-penetrance state. She saw and felt intensity of meaning that other people didn't feel. She lived in an ever changing, highly charged numinous world. At times this was overwhelming. She knew what it was like to be psychotic and had been diagnosed as having *schizoaffective disorder*.[51] Luisa didn't like this label; she saw herself as gifted but vulnerable, and I agreed with her.

Luisa was an artist. She drew, she painted, she did performance art and she wrote. She made a good living and had built up something of an international reputation. A low dose of a modern antipsychotic often gives helpful protection when high archetypal penetrance threatens to break through into psychosis but Luisa knew from past experience that medication dulled the source of her inspiration and killed her art. We agreed that, in emergency, she could try a low dose for a few days but as it turned out, I never needed to prescribe for her, she had developed her own methods that seemed much more effective.

She had come to the Crisis Service at the Royal London Hospital when she was suicidal after a relationship failure. It transpired that her Argentine father had been executed by the military regime when she was a baby. It had been a frightening time for her mother and eventually they had ended up in London. Her progress through childhood and adolescence had been unremarkable. She tried to avoid anything Argentine and she struggled with romantic relationships. It seemed that she had internalised an idea of her father as a perfect man and, of course, none of her boyfriends could approach meeting her expectations. When relationships ended it was as though her father was dead and lost to her all over again; she felt it very deeply—the pain was almost unbearable for her and she sometimes felt suicidal. Her father had been killed by being thrown from a military plane over the Atlantic and Luisa was clear that if she were to end her life, she too would jump from a high place.

The main focus of her therapy was to be her father's death and its consequences. Luisa worked well with her therapist in the Crisis Service and she enjoyed the newfound feeling of progression and resolution. When we discussed her in the clinical meetings, it seemed clear that she did not have the pervasive interpersonal difficulties found in borderline type personalities. In many ways, she was well adjusted and high functioning. But she did have this tendency towards intense and disturbing mental states, so we agreed that I would follow her up with infrequent regular appointments and that she should arrange an urgent appointment with me should the need arise.

It was an early summer day. Luisa was in a relationship and for the first time in her life, it really felt as though it was going well. He wasn't perfect and they had their differences but she was no longer devastated by small abandonments—her therapy had helped with that. Perhaps she could have a relationship after all. She was walking her little dog in the park and the sun was shining. It was a gorgeous day and she had that delicious feeling that all was well with the world. The world is just so beautiful, she thought and she realised that she was happy.

Then she heard somebody shout and she realised that the shout was directed at her. Her dog had just soiled the path and she hadn't noticed. As a responsible dog owner, Luisa always had bags for such occasions. She searched her pockets but there were no bags and she had no means of disposing of the dog mess. She walked on and the man shouted again for her to attend to the dog mess. It was not a friendly shout. Suddenly the mood switched. The world had become a deeply threatening place; it was as though the sun had been extinguished and it was getting dark. She felt confused and panicky. She stumbled off the path, running up a bank into the woods with her dog. She ran into the trees until she could run no more. In the distance she could see other people. She suddenly realised that they were tracking her and she moved through the trees trying to find an exit. She heard someone talking on a phone and she thought that they were planning to block the entrances. A cyclist came past and she hid knowing that he was looking for her. The world had become charged with threat. Everywhere she looked she saw danger. It was a dark, red, pulsing, visceral danger. Even the trees looked menacing. She had done something that was so terribly bad and she was going to be punished. She walked through the back streets hoping she wasn't being followed. A police car drove past and she hid. Later, much later, she arrived home. She locked the door and she turned off her phones. She drew the curtains and she drank a bottle of wine. Perhaps she drank two.

The next day she wished she hadn't drunk so much. She wanted to draw and paint and write. The hangover slowed her down for a while but the wine had done its job and the paranoia of the day before had faded. She worked her way through the day, slowly expressing herself, painting the dark red pulsing danger. She painted the shout, she painted the dog turd and she painted her flight through the forest with the trees reaching to trap her. At night she had a dream of drowning in dog mess and suffocating in the stink but then it turned into earth that tasted like chocolate with an abundance of flowers. So she painted that too. She called her boyfriend who cooked her some food and kept her company. He admired her art and asked her some gentle questions about what she was trying to express. By the time she saw me a couple of days later, she was leaving her home without fear again. She had painted herself back to sanity and the crisis had passed. She had brought some of her art with her to show me. It made it easier to explain where her mind had been, she said.

For psychoanalysts, such psychotic states would represent the uncovering of primitive, infantile modes of psychic function. An overwhelming state of persecutory anxiety is generally understood as a failure of maternal containment of infantile anxiety. A fragile mother may panic if her baby becomes distressed so that the infant receives back its own projection with the implicit message that its state of mind is not tolerable. This inflames the infant's anxiety, which expands to fill its universe. It suffers a 'nameless dread'.[52] Luisa's paranoia was a projection of her bad and shame-filled feelings onto the world around her. Indeed, Luisa had painted an image of herself as a baby who had soiled herself while her mother was recoiling in horror and her father was falling through the sky. Luisa had an understanding of how her mother's grief had affected her ability to manage a squalling, shitting baby. The dog turd had raised a powerful complex around Luisa's own archaic shame from her own potty training, her sense of her mother's anger and her sense of mental disintegration in the face of her mother's response. All of this had become very clear to her as she painted.

She told me that, as she painted the angry shout and the pulsing red, the images developed into war with armies and implacable men filled with hate. For the first time she felt angry herself. How she would like to punish them, these stupid men with their stupid fighting. Then she realised that she was hating them in the same way that they hated their fellow men. She cried and grieved for how much they must be hurting and for the pain they inflict on each other. She drew an image of a bleeding, weeping dictator in a big peaked military cap suckling on a goddess figure of huge breasts and infinite compassion. She understood that love was a much bigger feeling than hate and she forgave the angry shouting man. Finally, she showed me the chocolate turd covered in flowers that symbolised how her nightmare in the park had turned into something fragrant and nutritious.

Luisa had responded to the immediacy of the archetypal crisis by using a sedative, in her case alcohol, to decrease the intensity of her mental experience. The next day, free of any psychoactive substance, she was able to begin the work that she needed to do to process and integrate her experience. She was in a safe place and organised some support before diving into her internal world using all the tools at her disposal. She emoted, she wept and she dreamt. The images, thoughts and feelings flooded out of her and gathered substance as she painted them into a state of emergence. She felt that hidden wounded parts of herself were being healed, and that she was growing into someone who was more substantial, more whole than before. She felt increasingly confident that she had found the tools and the skills to manage her archetypal sensitivity.

High penetrance archetypal states can change their tone very quickly. Her state of near ecstasy in the park was changed abruptly to a very dangerous paranoid state. Her positive numinous experience, with its association of being in love in the summer sunshine, was triggered by the shout to a negative numinous experience. In this sensitive state, her perception of aggression was the most powerful factor causing this shift. We can imagine that, for vulnerable people in a HAP state, the exposure to any perception of aggression in psychiatric wards, hostels or crowded places would drive a paranoid process. It is one of the great tragedies of psychiatry that our most vulnerable people are often placed in the most unsuitable settings.

Low Archetypal Penetrance (LAP) States

Low archetypal penetrance (LAP) involves an impoverishment of psychic contents. Some people may be habituated to such a state and some may arrive in such a state through illness or depression. Some people in LAP states will medicate or stimulate themselves in an attempt to find some intensity and meaning, so that they may then become vulnerable to archetypal crisis. Schizophrenia is a condition where the acute phases involve high archetypal penetrance but the chronic 'burnt out' phase, with its negative symptoms of apathy and anhedonia, is very much a low archetypal penetrance state. As a psychiatrist on the wards and in the community clinics, I spent a lot of time trying to persuade people with schizophrenia to cut down their cannabis, stop using crack cocaine and take their antipsy-chotics. But they generally didn't. It is perhaps not surprising that people in LAP states are often eager for any opportunity to increase their arche-typal penetrance, even if this involves a strong possibility of a frightening experience.

Bill was a man in his forties who I interviewed in the emergency room at the Royal London Hospital. He had cut his wrists. One of his wrists required the attention of the plastic surgeons to re-attach the ends of ten-dons, and he would need to be in hospital for a few days. Bill was cheer-fully looking forward to the prospect of a few days in hospital. I had seen Bill before and so had some of my colleagues. Bill was a regular.

Bill had not been fortunate in his life. He was not blessed with high intelligence or good looks. His path through life had not held many pleas-ant surprises or opportunities. His family had not been nourishing. He had some contact with his mother who he saw as often as he could, but her main interest was always more in satisfying her own needs and ablating any of her uncomfortable feelings with alcohol. Bill had grown up in cha-otic circumstances and had been sexually abused on more than one occa-sion by various drinking companions of his mother. He was literate and numerate but had left school without any qualifications.

Bill had tried some jobs as a teenager but had never held down perma-nent employment. He had last worked some 20 years ago and had never had a relationship. He lived alone in social housing. He tried not to go out after dark as his neighbourhood was dangerous. He had no friends, no activities that allowed him social contact and he had no possessions apart an old television and a dvd player. There are many people like Bill. They often live in the inner city areas, in the ghettos. They live on welfare and nobody notices them much unless they do something to bring themselves to attention.

Generally, Bill described that his life was 'nothing'. He didn't do very much because he had nothing to do. He stayed in his small, filthy flat and looked at the walls. I asked him the usual questions that a psychiatrist would ask about his mood state and found that he wasn't clinically depressed or suicidal. He told me that he had cut his wrist because he felt bored. In fact I knew, and Bill knew that I knew, that in the past his appar-ent suicide attempts were his ticket to a stay in a mental hospital where he enjoyed the company, the attention and even the food. He had learned what to say to arouse the concern of the psychiatrist in charge of his case. He knew that claiming to hear hallucinatory voices telling him to kill himself would generally extend his hospital stay. After a few days of assessment it always became clear that he was cheerful and sociable on the ward and there was never any objective evidence of disturbed behaviour or psychosis. Attempts were made to improve his social condition, help him towards training or employment but nothing ever seemed to come of it. Bill wasn't very interested in being trained or employed. All he really wanted was to be looked after. Bill was very vulnerable, he clearly had a damaged personality—but he certainly wasn't mad.

The only activity that Bill would stir himself for was watching horror films. He told me that he enjoyed them but hated them at the same time, 'if you know what I mean doctor'. I asked him to tell me a little more. Bill would watch the horror films and becoming increasingly identified with the unfolding horror of the film. He would experience a dawning horror and dread. His skin would tingle with fear. He would start at shadows and any noises coming from outside his room. He was having an experience of *mysterium tremendum et fascinans,* a numinosity of the darker kind. It was terrifying, but it made him feel alive.

The problem was that the feeling of awe and dread, the feeling of being in the presence of a terrifying and mysterious 'other' did not always go away when the film ended. Sometimes it lingered and Bill found himself living out scenes from the film. There had been times, often on noisy crowded buses, when he had seen terrifying images or heard sounds from the films. Sometimes he started screaming and people became alarmed. There had been times in the past when this had led to a suicide attempt. The trouble was, he told me, he just couldn't stop watching the films.

Bill was living in an impoverished world, deriving very little sustenance from his environment. There were normally no sources of pleasure, of stimulation or interests. One could understand how it was that his life had developed in this way but there seemed little that he would or could do to change matters. He was stuck in a state of psycho-social desolation. His default position was a low archetypal penetrance state, but he was demonstrating numinosity-seeking behaviour. His experiences of the terrifying held a magnetic attraction for him. They added colour to a colourless life.

CHAPTER 6

Synchronicity

We thus arrive at the image of a world mosaic or cosmic kaleidoscope, which in spite of constant shufflings and rearrangements, also takes care of bringing like and like together.

—Paul Kammerer[53]

As a psychiatrist, I get to spend a lot of time hearing people's stories. Everyone's story is different, having that unique signature that marks the individual. Often, it is the first time that someone has properly and fully told the story of his or her passage through life. We begin by discussing the current crisis before exploring the background; the nature of the family and the shaping of the important relationships. What was the quality of the nurturing, the attachment? What were the events that were difficult? What were the things that happened to them that shouldn't have happened and what were the things that didn't happen that should have happened?

Often the story is familiar; it may fit a pattern that I recognize very well. Sometimes, it is harder to understand. The interview may flow easily and with fluency or it may be difficult, painful and hesitant. Sometimes a story may evoke strong feelings in me, which I carefully consider as my emotional reaction, my countertransference is a useful clinical tool that will give me useful information about the person with whom I am interacting. If someone's story does not induce strong feelings in me, then I consider that carefully too. Sometimes I know that I can be of help; sometimes I know it will be harder to make a difference. Sometimes the interview is difficult or challenging but on every occasion I am wondering how I might help the person to find a passage towards growth. Occasionally, I hear something unusual, something that really surprises me and pushes the boundaries of my understanding of who we are.

Sally's Story

I met Sally for the first time on the hospital ward where she was having treatment for cancer. The surgeon told me that the cancer that had been blocking her colon had been removed and the quality of her life should be good for a while, but the cancer had advanced with metastatic spread to the liver and her life expectancy was limited. She was 57. The surgical team thought that she was depressed and hoped that some psychiatric treatment might help her. She had been neglecting herself before she came in to hospital, her diabetes was poorly controlled and she hadn't been sleeping well. She had been undecided whether or not to go through with the surgery and had indicated to the surgeon that she didn't really care if she lived or died.

Sally was attached to various tubes when I met her and couldn't leave her bed. She was in the middle of a dormitory type ward in the old Royal London Hospital building. There were twelve beds, each separated by a curtain. It was noisy, the usual ward hubbub of the doctors and nurses doing their rounds, the patients talking, some patients in pain, the physiotherapist working to try to mobilize someone. It was certainly not the ideal setting to have a sensitive conversation about matters of life and death.

I drew the curtain around Sally's bed to give us a little privacy, but the ward suddenly seemed quieter and she didn't particularly want to talk to me about anything personal. It was hot day, the ward had a powerful aroma of faeces and the nurses were harassed and busy. The noise around the ward had a sharp-edged, irritable quality. It was not a great environment in which to recover from a major operation, especially if one were feeling depressed. So we had a brief conversation about the state in which she found herself. It was a process of mutual evaluation. I needed to make a basic assessment of her mental state to establish how depressed she was. Did she feel suicidal? Was there anything that I needed to discuss with her straight away? But Sally was able to smile at me, she was looking forward to her niece's visit and she indicated that she wanted to make the best possible recovery and go home. She felt safe on the ward and her brain was working perfectly well. There was no sign of confusion or mental illness. She told me that there was something that she wanted to talk about, but it was very private and she didn't want to discuss it while she was lying in a bed in a public place. We agreed that I would visit her again in a few days time when she was well enough to sit in a side room.

The second time I met Sally she was looking much better. The various tubes had been removed from her body. She walked slowly and needed a stick but she had a direct gaze and firm handshake. She was tall woman, whose frame hinted at considerable strength before the debilitating effects of her illness. The defining event in her life had happened nearly 40 years ago and it had been brought powerfully back to her by the recent death of a younger brother after a long decline. Sally had looked after him and helped him through his terminal illness. She told me that she had been there when her little brother was born and she had been there when he had died. Sally was well aware of the implications of her own diagnosis of cancer with liver metastases, and knew that she was embarking on the same journey. She told me that there was a part of her that welcomed death as a relief from a difficult life, that she felt familiar with death and had lived all of her life in it's shadow. But there was something that she needed to talk about before she died.

She told me her story with care and precision. She had always lived in the East End of London. Her father was a docker who was in and out of prison. Sally said that her father was not a nice man; he spent his time at the pub and his money on beer. He spoke with his fists and he didn't seem to like the increasing amount of children who cluttered up their small and crowded home. Her mother tried to keep the family together and put food on the table but she had been killed, probably murdered, when Sally was 10. She thought that associates of her father were probably responsible for her mother's death. Her father had about 15 children with a variety of part-ners and after her mother's death, Sally found herself looking after her younger brothers and sisters. Sally and her siblings went to live with an uncle and aunt and occasionally her father visited them. Her aunt was a gentle woman who tried her best and there were some quite happy times. Her uncle was not a kind man who couldn't tolerate noisy children and they were beaten and sometimes locked in the cellar. The cellar did not have lighting, it was cold, there were rats and the aunt didn't have the key. The children lived in fear of the cellar. The cellar was the place of dark-ness, fear and the extinction of hope. When Sally was in her early teens, her aunt died. Her uncle sexually abused her, raping her on at least one occasion. Sally felt that her priority was to look after her younger siblings and make sure they were together. She put up with the uncle, but at some stage he was imprisoned and the family were relocated to a grandmother. Life had become a little better; she had survived.

The most important event of her life happened when she was 19. It had been a normal sort of day. She'd been to work, come home, some people were in the house but her younger sister was out. It was around 11.30 in the evening and Sally was in her room, awake and resting. She had not been drinking or taking drugs. Maybe she was in that hypnogogic state, on the cusp of sleep. Suddenly she was wide awake, more awake than she had ever been before – she told me. She had a sudden searing vision of a face with an expression of concentrated evil and venom. The face was of indeterminate gender, had long red hair and an air of extraordinary menace. She knew that it was not alive but was not dead. There was an intensity about the image that she had not experienced before and has not experienced since. She remembers being shaken to the core of her being by the image and she was unable to sleep. A few hours later, the doorbell rang—it was the police. They told her that her 17 year old sister had been killed in a car crash. Sally was taken to the police station and thence to identify the body. She was told that the crash had happened at around 11.30. Sally knew that her vision with the demonic entity had taken place at the same time that her sister had lost her life. She knew that something extraordinary had happened; somehow the two events were connected.

Encounter with the Numinous

This is a most unusual story. The two outstanding features are, firstly, the extraordinary intensity of her vision and, secondly, the coincidence of this vision with her sister's death – a synchronicity. The image has haunted her and she has never forgotten it, although the intensity of the memory has decreased with the passage of time. She describes her experience as 'more real than everyday reality'. She had never spoken of it and struggled to find words to capture it. She told me that it was like watching the scariest horror film that you ever saw. It seemed to her like a being that had come from Hell. Nearly 40 years later she could still feel the searing intensity of the image and she was shivering as she told me the story. It had a timeless quality; she estimates that it lasted about one second in real time but while it was happening, time had stopped. It was a profoundly numinous experience, an archetypal image, of the terrifying kind and it was really very difficult for Sally to describe.

One of the features of Sally's life was the amount of violence, trauma and evil that she suffered. Sadly, this is not an uncommon story in London's East End, and no doubt there have been dysfunctional, violent and abusive families since humanity began its journey. It makes sense that her experience was heavily influenced by her personal background and her previous experience of evil, although images of this nature with such a concentration of meaning are rare indeed. But the most striking aspect, the life-defining implication, was the synchronicity of the vision with her sister's death. Sally associated the image as a representative from a hell-like place. It seemed very clear to her that this dreadful being had taken her sister's life in some way that she could not begin to understand. She said that the image was a major factor in keeping her alive through all the times in her life when she felt that life was too hard and painful. There was a part of her that had always been deeply drawn to death but she was very frightened that in dying she would meet this being again.

She had thought about this hellish being on a daily basis, although she wished that she could have forgotten it. She had eventually come to an understanding that the concentrated evil was a part of human experience and that there was the capacity for such evil within herself as in everyone else. She came to feel over the years that this had even been a helpful experience and one that had determined her life course to a major degree, although she wished she could have found this insight in a different way. She told me that she had such a clear notion of evil that had crystallized in this image, that she spent her life avoiding any expression of evil in her own behaviour as far as she could manage. She tried to be as good and decent and clean in her dealings with people as she possibly could. The truth was, she told me, that she wasn't very good with people; she didn't 'do relationships'. She supposed that everything that had happened to her as a child had made her not want to have an intimate relationship with anyone or have children herself, but she loved her family, her many nephews and nieces, and she had developed some solid and enduring friendships through her working life.

Synchronicity

The Austrian biologist Paul Kammerer was the first person to systematically study coincidences, classifying them according to the number of chance occurrences they show. He gives an example of a six-order coincidence with two soldiers both named Franz Richter who found themselves in the same hospital ward. They were both 19, they both came from Silesia, they both had pneumonia and they were both volunteers in the transport corps.[54] Most of these coincidences are just that, a chance occurrence, whereas a synchronicity is a *meaningful coincidence*. The term synchronicity was coined by Jung to describe the concurrence of an event and an inner experience, which are connected by a sense of meaning for the individual experiencing them. It is a coming together in time of something of the inner world and something from the outer world. It is something that defies rational belief—an 'ah-ha moment'; it takes the breath away. A synchronicity always has a numinous quality to a greater or lesser degree. A powerful synchronicity can define a life.

Jung's thinking was profoundly influenced by synchronicity. During his early and middle career, he believed that archetypes were patterns in our brain and mind that were derived from our cumulative genetic inheritance all the way from our reptilian ancestors in the evolutionary chain.

However, his experience of synchronicity led him to the conclusion that there was an acausal order that linked the inner world of the mental with the outer world of the physical. It meant that the internal world of mind and the external world of matter were joined together in some way.

For Jung's colleague Marie-Louise von Franz:

> The most essential and certainly the most impressive thing about synchronistic occurrences, the thing that really constitutes their numinosity, is that in them the duality of soul and matter seems to be eliminated. They are therefore an empirical indication of the ultimate unity of all existence.[55]

Archetypes are transgressive and teleological. They transgress in that they cross the boundaries between the physical and the non-physical. They are teleological in that they pull towards a definite end. A powerful synchronicity demonstrates to the person who has experienced it that there is an underlying order that is not normally apparent to us and this can have demonstrable effects. For Tarnas, a synchronicity serves a definite purpose, impelling the psyche toward a more complete psychological and spiritual realization of the individual personality.[56] This is a crucial distinction; a synchronicity is growth orientated although to achieve this growth requires care, thought and integration. In psychiatric practice it is not uncommon for people in excited pathological states to over attribute meaning to unconnected events. It may seem to them as though there are synchronicities everywhere. This may amount to *delusions of reference,* a pathological state where, for example, a person may feel that every passing car registration number is imbued with a personal meaning. Clearly such states are dysfunctional and do not have integrative or growth potential, but psychiatrists do need to be able to distinguish between a genuine synchronicity and psychosis and avoid treating all unusual phenomena as mental illness.

A true synchronicity has inherent integrative power. There are many well-known accounts of how synchronistic experiences at the crucial times in the lives of great men have influenced them profoundly. Jung famously found a scarab beetle at his window just as a patient was recounting a dream of an Egyptian scarab beetle.[57] Joseph Campbell had a similar experience with a praying mantis at the window of his New York apartment.[58] St. Augustine describes a crucial synchronicity in his conversion from psychological agony to spiritual certainty in 386: he heard a child repeating the phrase 'pick up and read' and at random picked up a passage from St. Paul's epistles, which identified and resolved his core conflict.[59] Nearly one thousand years later, Petrarch had a synchronicity after opening St. Augustine's *Confessions* at the top of a mountain and being stunned at the coincidence between Augustine's words and the time and place that he was reading them.[60] This impressed Petrarch deeply, proving a turning point in his life and triggering the symbolic beginning of the renaissance.[61]

Arthur Koestler thought that synchronicities were natural and universal phenomena springing from a higher level of cosmic organization with which we occasionally participate.[62] Synchronicities are reported as occurring particularly at times of psychological crisis, life transitions or in association with spiritual practice such as extended meditation retreats.[63] As Archbishop Temple once said: 'When I pray coincidences start to happen. When I don't pray they don't happen'.[64] Synchronicities are often deeply personal or difficult to translate into understandable terms. Although they can provide dramatic evidence of a deeper order of structure, this is personal evidence and will usually not convince anyone else but the person who experiences them. They do not necessarily have extraordinary import but can point helpfully in a certain direction as I describe below.

To give an example from my own experience of a life transition, this is what I wrote on returning home at the end of my relationship with the hospital where I spent much of my working life.

My Last Day at the Royal London Hospital

It is a big transition. I've worked here in the Royal London Hospital for over twenty years, working with my two teams as the consultant psychiatrist in this large and complex hospital. There have been some difficult days and some good days, but every single day has been stimulating. I feel very close to some of the people I work with. It's been intense and now it has gone. It's entirely my choice, it is the right thing to do and I'm looking forward to the next phase.

The last few weeks have been a little emotional. On the one hand, I perform my clinical duties as normal. On the other hand, there are the complex dynamics of the goodbyes, managing the transition for the services and coping with organizational issues while trying to process and integrate the moment. Each meeting that I go to, each professional interaction, each and every aspect of my job, I am aware that this is the last time. I feel a great sense of affection and gratitude towards my colleagues and I take enormous pleasure in their company. I am aware that I have been drawn into a high archetypal penetrance state and I am enjoying it. There is a certain intensity and amplification of meaning. The sun looks a little brighter and the colours a little sharper. With hindsight, I was in exactly the right state of mind for a synchronicity.

It is the end of my last day. I have cleared my office, handed over my key and said goodbye to everyone. I walk out of the team office in the A&E

department (ER) for the last time. I take the lift up to the 14th floor of the hospital, just to say goodbye and have a quiet reflective moment. I take a last look at the panoramic view on either side seeing the gleaming towers of the financial district, the blocks of social housing, the river and the mass of humanity. I know that when I go down to the ground floor again, that I will walk away from this place forever. It is okay. It's all good. But it is certainly a moment to mark.

I get back into the lift and down we go. 13th floor, the door opens, no one is there. The door shuts. I am the only person in the lift. But the door doesn't quite shut. It jams so there is a gap between the closing doors about 3 inches apart. It sticks and doesn't shift. I do the usual things with the buttons but to no effect. I try to prize the doors apart with my hands. It still doesn't shift. So I am stuck in this metal cage, very high in the hospital. I can see freedom through the gap in the lift door but I cannot get out. The hospital will not let me go.

I am aware of a rising feeling that is quite difficult to describe. Certainly, there was a little frisson of anxiety but it was more than that. I had a sense that I was involved in something that was greater than the everyday. I would say that it had a mild numinous quality. I do not mean that it was a religious or spiritual experience but I had a soft sense of awe. I thought to myself that this would not be a good situation for some of my patients who would perhaps ascribe delusional meanings to such an occurrence. I had seen a patient that morning who felt that the hospital staff were controlling him, surreptitiously filming him and wanted to experiment on him and being stuck in a lift would be a dreadful thing to happen to him.

Then the door opened and somebody else got in. The crisis was suddenly resolved by the entrance of a young female doctor, who I didn't know.[65] The lift went down a couple more floors and then exactly the same thing happened again. We got stuck. There was a gap of a few inches between the lift doors, not wide enough to squeeze out and the doors did not shift. I could see freedom but this hospital did not want to release me. As before, someone entered the lift from the outside and the doors opened. This time I scuttled out and went down the stairs, all 10 flights of them. I was chuckling as I scuttled. It's always a treat to have a little help from the cosmos.

Just a coincidence perhaps; mishaps in lifts are not uncommon after all. But this was a profound experience for me and something seemed to decisively shift in my psyche as a result. I felt less conflicted and some of my ambivalence about my departure had been nudged towards resolution. It was a helpful push towards the next phase of my life. I didn't look back as I passed through the hospital entrance for the last time.

CHAPTER 7

A Meaning-Filled Mind Field

Modern physics has definitely decided for Plato.

For the smallest units of matter are not physical effects in the ordinary sense of the word; they are forms, structures, or in Plato's sense – Ideas, which can be unambiguously spoken of only in the language of mathematics.[66]

—Werner Heisenberg.

In this chapter I briefly introduce some theories and evidence supporting two notions that may be unfamiliar; firstly that meaning may be inherent in the cosmos and secondly that mind has a field effect. I will briefly discuss the role of meaning as the organising factor of the developing mind and how the 'respiratory process' of projection and introjection shapes not only our individual minds but perhaps collective mind too. This is a theoretical chapter and some readers may choose to pass rapidly through it.

Mind or Machine

There is no objective scientific evidence that can reliably and consistently demonstrate that archetypes exist. They are presumably not of the physical world; they cannot be seen under microscopes nor in the hadron collider. The philosophical argument concerning the ontological nature of archetypes has traditionally been polarized between the *nominalists* and the *realists*. The realists follow Plato's position accepting that the archetypal domain is ontologically real although largely denied to us through our perceptual apparatus. Western science, including psychiatry and psychoanalysis, would take the nominalist position holding that consciousness is mediated by neurochemical process alone and that so-called archetypal experiences are the product of an abnormal brain. There may be nominalists who become realists after a subjective experience such as a synchronicity, but this is probably quite an unusual event.

We generally look to physicists to explain to us the characteristics of the cosmos. The insights of quantum physics have demonstrated how matter is essentially an interconnected web of vibrating energy but we do not have an understanding of how meaning fits into the scheme of things. The transpersonal theorist Ken Wilber, in his study of the writings of eight great scientists of the quantum era, describes how the advent of the quantum physics era forced an awareness that physics was indeed dealing with the illusory shadow world rather than reality.[67] Some of these leading quantum physicists did develop a profoundly mystical worldview. Sir James Jeans famously described God as a mathematician and that 'The Universe begins to look more like great thought than a great machine'.[68] For Sir Arthur Eddington, 'The stuff of the universe is mind stuff'.

But it seems that physics cannot take us further than this; the study of form cannot yet account for the formless and quantum physics does not explain intense mental states or mystical experience no matter how appealing some of the parallels to the quantum world may be.[69]

David Bohm and the Implicate Order

The physicist who best articulated a possible relationship between meaning and the material world was David Bohm who came to believe that meaning was a primary and integral component of our physical universe. In his model, meaning was not separate from matter but came from the same fundamental stuff from which matter emerged.[70] For Bohm, the universe is not a mechanical object but a multi layered, multidimensional thought form of infinite complexity.

Bohm was a protégé of Einstein and was nominated for the Nobel prize. He was a man of deep moral principle whose search for the ultimate nature of reality took him far beyond our current understanding of quantum theory. He was deeply influenced by the Indian writer and mystic Krishnamurti, with whom he co authored a book.[71] Bohm understood the physical universe as web of energy that had a deeper structure. He termed our observable physical universe, located in space-time as the 'explicate' order, but he believed that there was a deeper level organised around meaning, that he called the 'implicate' order.

The implicate order is not made of physical material; it is not dependent on space-time but is structured in an entirely different way. Meaning, which Bohm calls 'significance' is an integral dimension of the implicate order which permeates and informs the space-time environment which we inhabit.[72] The term implicate is derived from the Latin verb 'plicare' which means to fold and the implicate order is something which unfolds to become explicate and manifest. We could understand this unfolded meaning or 'significance' as a fifth dimension of our traditional four-dimensional space-time structure. Bohm used the analogy of a dynamic hologram, a holomovement or holoflux to emphasise the fluid nature of this unfolding process. The term flux refers to the movement between different states of meaning and being, rather than movement from place to place.

Bohm emphasized that the usual dualism and separation between mind and matter was out dated and introduced a term *soma-significance* to highlight the unity between the two. Thus soma, which is physical, and significance which is mental, are not separate but are two aspects of an all embracing, undivided reality. For Bohm the primary structure is a flow of energy in which meaning is carried inward and outward between the aspects of soma and significance. Bohm used the term 'subtle' to describe the more intense and concentrated forms of meaning. Meaning states of archetypal intensity, using Bohm's terminology, are more subtle and finely woven than our everyday range of significance.

Bohm suggested that as we access the implicate order, meaning and significance could be infinitely extended to ever greater levels of subtlety and complexity. There is a spectrum of intensity of meaning from the highly concentrated to very low concentrations of meaning found in inanimate matter but, as humans, our sensory apparatus limits our perception of meaning to a certain range, like Huxley's metaphorical valve. The brain, being a finite structure, would not usually be able to grasp the more subtle levels or the very dilute forms of significance. The philosopher Immanuel Kant described a zone of reality which he called 'The Noumenon' which resembles the implicate order or the land outside Plato's cave. Kant held that direct access to the Noumenon is not possible because of the constraints provided by our sensory and cognitive apparatus. Bohm's answer to this conundrum was that we are 'of the Noumenon' so we can participate in the Noumenon – it is not denied to us.[73]

Using Bohm's model we can imagine that we may be able to participate in progressively more subtle, 'meaning-filled' states. The flavours of these meaning states equate to archetypes and our translation and understanding of these states will be limited and coloured by our cognitive apparatus. We may perhaps be genetically predisposed to enter these states, they may come upon us spontaneously or we may seek to purposefully induce them.[74]

Meaning and the Evolution of Consciousness

Bohm's work adds a modern twist to Plato's ideas of eternal forms by introducing the important idea that the men in the shadow world can contribute to the land outside the cave. For Bohm, the men in the cave have a purpose after all. In Plato's cave, the archetypal energy flows in a one-way direction from the sun, there is no reverse process but Bohm's model is a two way evolutionary process. According to Bohm, archetypal form is unfolded from the implicate order into matter, which then evolves and grows using the experiential knowledge of the material world which is re introjected by enfoldment into the implicate order again. Thus there is a continuing process of mutual enrichment so that this introject becomes available to be re projected from the implicate order.[75] So man and cosmos interact. Perhaps we are building mind stuff together in a participatory universe.[76]

There is an intriguing parallel here with the psychoanalytic model of the development of the infantile ego, which relies on a similar respiratory process of projection and introjection. The broad brushstrokes of the development of personality are thought to be the early intense relationships, charged with meaning, that the new born baby builds with the breast as the primary attachment object giving warmth, comfort and nourishment. This primary meaning state is profoundly positive so that pain and discomfort do not exist. It is not just the breast that gives these good feelings, there is something about the sound of the mother, the smell, the warmth, the holding in the arms, but it is the nourishing breast or it's substitute that is primary.

Any bad feelings, whether colic, hunger or irritability are projected out on to the external world, typically onto the breast, which then becomes experienced as profoundly negative and persecutory.[77] These two early states of meaning hold great intensity and fill the baby's view of the world; psychoanalysts call this the *paranoid position.* Most of us can access the heightened meaning state of the paranoid position in our adult lives from time to time and for a few of us it continues to dominate our relationship with the world about us.

The new-born is not aware of other aspects of the mother at this stage and there is no sense of her as a separate object. The mother contains the baby's persecutory anxiety by processing the baby's difficult projections and returning these feelings to the baby who can take them in (introject) in a form that is less disturbing. Thus the baby re introjects an anxiety that has been modified by having been contained by the mother. With good parenting, mother and baby both learn and develop together with this symbiotic respiratory process of projection and introjection. The baby also has to learn to withstand pain and frustration and organise its inner object world so that loving and hateful impulses can co-exist. This is called the *depressive position* and is considered to be the template for the balanced psyche of the normal adult. The infant goes on to build a sense of 'attachment', a more mature meaning state that forms another crucial structure in the developing psyche.

Psychoanalysis tends to understand numinous experiences as projections of this primary object relationship. So an experience of nameless dread would be seen as an expression of the failure of the mother to adequately contain infantile anxiety so that this infantile state of terror forms the template from which the challenging experience of the numinous arises. Similarly, ecstatic mystical states would be understood as projections from the blissful state of fusion with the primary object at the breast. For many, this is overly reductionist, an extrapolation of infantile suckling behaviour is unlikely to represent a complete explanation for numinous experience. But it does illustrate how there may be elements of numinous experience that may be *prepersonal*, related to early development compared to what may be *transpersonal* and related to more mature development.[78]

Transmissive Mind

The psychoanalyst and pioneer of Group Analysis, Michael Foulkes found that phenomena occurred in groups that were not explicable by conventional theory and seemed to involve a field effect of mind, which he called the 'matrix'. In addition to the strong communal and cultural bonds that developed within a group of people meeting regularly with the aim of growing together, there seemed to develop a powerful and mysterious group mind. Foulkes described the matrix as follows:

'its lines of force may be conceived of as passing right through the individual members and may therefore be called a transpersonal network, comparable to a magnetic field'.[79]

The concept of the matrix is mysterious and much debated by group analysts. Many of us feel that there is a telepathic element that operates sometimes at special moments in these intense psychoanalytic groups. According to the prevailing model of mind, this should not be possible. However there is some good evidence supporting the existence of a transmissive aspect of mind, although it is usually ignored. This evidence belongs to the field of 'psi' or parapsychology.

Psi denotes anomalous processes of information or energy transfer; an interaction between consciousness and the physical world. Psi includes processes such as telepathy or other forms of extrasensory perception that are currently unexplained in terms of known physical or biological mechanisms. The term is purely descriptive, it does not imply that such phenomena are paranormal and it does not make conclusions about their underlying mechanisms.[80] Indeed biologists such as Rupert Sheldrake point out that psi is a perfectly natural phenomenon as demonstrated by animals who seem to have a presentiment of natural disasters, dogs who know that their owners are coming home, people with a sense of being stared at and telepathic experiences between people with strong emotional bonds.[81]

To cut a complicated story rather short, I do not believe that any reasonable person, who takes the trouble to study the extensive evidence, would deny that there is robust evidence for a psi effect. The research findings have been comprehensively outlined by courageous and brilliant men such as Sheldrake, Dean Radin, Darryl Bem and Charles Tart. The field is complex and there are conflicting results that cause some confusion, but there is enough evidence to allow a conclusion that there is a transmissive element to consciousness—the brain can function as a transmitter and receiver being able to transfer energy, at least to some extent. Charles Tart describes the 'big five' of telepathy, clairvoyance, precognition, psychokinesis and psychic healing as the psychic phenomena for which we have so much experimental evidence that we can regard them as basic innate possibilities for humans.[82] This is a minority view. There still exists a wide schism between the defenders of the classical paradigm (sceptics) and those who believe that the existence of psi has been proven beyond reasonable doubt.[83]

To give just one brief example—telepathy experiments seek to demonstrate transmission of information from one mind to another. The classical telepathy experiment involves a state of sensory deprivation or 'Ganzfeld' to eliminate distractions. The person who is to receive information is seated on a chair with halved table tennis balls over the eyes in front of a red light bulb while headphones play a soft whooshing noise like the surf on a beach. The effect is dreamy and relaxing. The person who is trying to transmit information concentrates on a randomly generated image or a video for a period of time. In some designs the recipient speaks aloud anything that comes to mind (mentates) while the transmitter hears what she is saying and tries to influence the content of her train of thought. Eventually the recipient is asked to choose between 4 images or video clips giving a 25% chance of selecting the image in the transmitter's mind. The statistical analysis of over 3000 Ganzfeld studies of telepathy (metanalysis) shows a hit rate of 32 – 34%, which greatly exceeds chance. Dean Radin reports that in special populations, pairs of people with strong bonds, people with personality traits of openness or people who report previous psi experiences, that the hit rate rises to around 65%.[84]

Psi research is not easy. Studies are difficult to replicate and the results seem to depend on the mindset of the researcher. For example if a person does not believe in psi, then the results of the experiment will tend to give negative results which are in excess of chance and if a person does believe in psi, the results are more likely to be positive. Thus the meaning state or mindset of the people involved seems to have a material effect. Psi does not fall away with distance, as occurs with electro magnetic radiation, which invites comparison with the non-locality effect found in quantum physics.

Models and Belief Systems

Psi does not really tell us very much apart from that the crucial fact that mind is likely to exert a field effect—although our current understanding of this is very limited. The generation of people growing up today will be utterly familiar with the concept of uploads, downloads, the internet, servers and the cloud. They are natives of the online world but until the 1990s most of us could not imagine such a thing as the World Wide Web or the concept of the download. Nowadays we can grasp the obvious analogies between the web and the collective unconscious. It is not such a step for us to conceptualise the downloading of 'mind stuff' from the collective servers and clouds of mental energy into to our living, breathing hardware systems. We can perhaps understand more easily how our consciousness could derive both from brain and from beyond the brain.

Science has an innate conservatism. There is a dynamic tension between the proponents and opponent of theories. Good science tests hypotheses and forms a perspective based on evidence. It is inherent to the march of science that debate is rigorous especially when new ideas are contentious and challenge existing paradigms. Science is not perfect and is vulnerable to the way in which it is used and interpreted. We know that science does not always tell the truth and we know that pharmaceutical companies are not the only culprits who manipulate data, suppress negative studies and falsify results.[85] Bad science or scientism occurs when new evidence is jettisoned without due consideration as the defenders, or high priests of the existing paradigms cannot bring themselves to give new evidence a fair hearing. Sheldrake gives three examples of debates with eminent sceptics of psi who have not considered it necessary to read the evidence before dismissing psi as inherently impossible.[86] Why read the evidence when you have already decided that it cannot be true?

Worldviews determine our perspectives, how we relate to each other and the world about us. The dominant worldview or paradigm for the last few centuries has been scientific materialism where the universe is a big machine that is devoid of any innate intelligence or meaning. This paradigm includes a reaction to the irrational beliefs of the previous worldview that was over determined by religion. The archetypal (or BPSA) perspective offers a third way; it inclines to a participation between the brain and an external component of consciousness, a meeting of the two forms of mind. Thus archetype mingles inextricably with the bio psycho social and we exist on the cusp of that mingling.

Thomas Kuhn, some 50 years ago described how the advancement of science does not progress in a smooth and linear way but by periodic 'paradigm shifts'. Moreover, these paradigm shifts open up new approaches that scientists would never have considered valid before. Thus the concept of scientific truth, at any given moment, cannot be established solely by objective criteria but is defined by a consensus of a scientific community. Kuhn described three stages of change of scientific paradigms. The first stage is one of denial, where any data that does not fit the prevailing model is ignored or attacked. Then as evidence mounts that cannot easily be ignored, the existing model is modified. This is the second stage, where the model is stretched to fit. It is only when this adaptation fails to work that a radically new model, the third stage, is devised.[87]

It seems inevitable that our models of our mind and the structures that serve them are still in a relatively primitive state of understanding. People have been confidently predicting a paradigm shift related to psi and consciousness research for many years—but it has failed to materialise and we remain in Kuhn's denial phase. Why then do we cling so tenaciously to our existing models and turn our faces so firmly away from new ideas? The British mathematician and wartime code breaker Alan Turing summed it up as follows:

> I assume the reader is familiar with the idea of extrasensory perception and the meaning of four items of it; telepathy, clairvoyance, precognition and psychokinesis. These disturbing phenomena seem to deny all our usual scientific ideas. How we should like to discredit them! Unfortunately the statistical evidence, at least for telepathy is overwhelming. It is very difficult to rearrange one's ideas so as to fit these new facts in. Once one has accepted them it does not seem a very big step to believe in ghosts and bogies.[88]

And here we have it. Perhaps we still have an anxiety about the bad old days when religion and spirits were thought to account for natural phenomena; we became ill because we had sinned or failed to propitiate the Gods. We feel that this nonsense has been swept away by the clear voice of reason and the march of science. Perhaps we feel as concerned as Freud did about the 'black tide of mud of occultism'. Psi evokes primitive fears in us about unseen forces with the threat of erosion of the structures and values of our modern life. Here lies madness we fear; better to stay with what we think we know.

CHAPTER 8

Transcendent Nature

My first memories of encounters with transcendent spirit occurred in nature—in Yosemite Valley, . . . I still have vivid memories of staring up at the massive cliff walls of the valley in silent stupefaction . . . . I was just looking into space, into vastness, into majesty . . . . There was no way to measure or relate to the size and scale of those vertical spans of light and shadow, cut by angles of rocky overhang, tree line, waterfall. And the space that opened up inside me somewhere during all this cliff gazing was equally immeasurable. It was infinite, timeless and captivating.

—Ross Robertson[89]

Our current relationship with nature is defined by the challenge of climate change. We have developed a rapacious attitude towards the natural world that is damaging our planet, and we know that we have to develop a more responsible, sustainable relationship. We must stop biting the breast that feeds us. If we cannot rise to this developmental challenge, if we cannot address our destructiveness, there will be consequences. If we cannot find a way of living in harmony with the natural world, we may perish as a species.[90]

For our ancestors, there was no separation between themselves and their environment. They were completely entwined with natural world. They found in nature their physical and emotional sustenance, their food, their shelter and their gods. Nature was the visible face of spirit, the focus of man's search for meaning and occasionally a contact point for profound numinous experience. Nature gives us a full range of archetypal flavours, from the deepest dread to the most sublime. Even in our busy modern world, we can reach out from behind our chattering minds to engage with something in nature that is greater and deeper than ourselves. Sometimes we can encounter moods and meanings, fragrances and essences of thought that would not otherwise be available for us. We may have our sacred places where we can feel a little closer to the numinous and be enriched.

The Heath

Hampstead Heath is such a touchstone for me. It is a microcosm of a perfect little England on the northern edge of London. From Parliament Hill
you can see the great city laid out beneath; there is parkland and gardens
and swimming lakes; there are prams and joggers, and plenty of dogs.
Move away from the main thoroughfares and there is a silent and empty
hinterland of old oaks and chestnut trees, complex undulating ground,
shimmering light and barely discernable tracks leading through the dense
undergrowth of the forest floor. There is a subtly different heath every time
I visit, with the nuance of the woods, the winds, the birdsong, the changing
of the seasons and the moods of weather.

I was there with my Josephine on our first evening together. I played
football in the mud with our children. My youngest son took his first totter-
ing steps by a fallen tree in a valley there. I have stood by the viaduct pond
that is cradled in the roots of the old oak tree, softly grieving my parents. I
swim with the swans in the lake at the end of a long day at the hospital and
feel cleansed and rejuvenated. I have loved the heath for many years. I have
a relationship with it; it is my life partner of the natural world.

If my mind is agitated by the demands of everyday life, it settles as I
walk and new more interesting notions arise in my mind. For me, the heath
is a barometer of my psycho–spiritual health. There are times when the
heath is especially magical, as if transfused by an inner richness and light—
dancing, creative, inspiring. There have been a few times, just a few, when
the heath becomes just a bunch of trees in the English gloom, when I cannot
lift my mind from its chatter and find some beauty and solace. Then I know
that I am depleted and need nourishment.

The heath is a safe place and it feels that nothing bad will happen
there. In the winter, it is not too cold; in the summer, not too hot. If you get
lost it won't be for long. It feels entirely benign but of course, nature has
other facets. There are other places in our natural world where the numinous experiences become more condensed either towards a heavenly place
or towards a place of awe and dread.

Heavenly Gardens

Christopher Lloyd who died in 2006 is sometimes described as the greatest gardener of the twentieth century. He was the pioneer of the heavily
planted, labour intensive, prairie garden. His biographer indicates that he
was emotionally repressed as a result of his mother's domination.[91] They
had a shared love of gardening but he could not set himself free physically.

He was gay at a time when homosexuality was a criminal offence.[92] His education, upbringing, and his shy, eccentric, gentlemanly behavior made it unlikely that he ever had an intimate relationship with any of the people he fell in love with. His primary relationship was probably with his garden at Great Dixter in Sussex in the south of England.

The garden at Great Dixter has an extraordinary, luminous intensity. The flowerbeds are huge and dense, packed full of colour and shape and fragrance. It is designed so that every sense is stimulated. It is a stepping into a different world—a sharpening, a deepening of nature, a movement to a higher octave. Tribal banks of plants raise the intensity further. You find yourself in a world not of dahlias but Dahlia, not of sunflowers but Sunflower. In the high summer, the blooms are full, the air is warm and hazy. The wind soughs through the trees, the temperature feels just right. The sky is a perfection of blue, but being England, there are some clouds, giving contours and depth. It is a late strutting, summer throb of life before autumn's gentle decay and winter's death. We know that will come but for now this is beauty, it holds the archetypal quality of Venus. This is luxuriant nature at its soft, warm, gorgeous and most rapturous extent.[93]

For me the height of Venusian nature is the garden show with the displays created to magnify and amplify the primal form of the plant world. I find myself walking around in a pleasant, mild non-ordinary state of consciousness as I become immersed in the displays of shrubs, flowers, ferns and heather. There is no need to keep a sense of direction or maintain much of a handle on the practicalities of life. Nature is vibrant and sexy. The organs of the flowers with their abundance of colour and complexity of form represent an exuberant bursting life force. It is almost too intense; there should be conjugal tents for those who resonate with the fruitiness, we muse. The other option is to sedate with carbohydrates in the cake and coffee tent. Most of the other people seem to be gentle elderly folk. I wonder if it helps to be older to cope with the intensity. Leaving, I feel invigorated. My mind is swirling and productive. I try to remember the insights and thoughts. The colours seem a little brighter for a while after. One feels as D. H. Lawrence must have felt when he wrote in *The Apocalypse*: 'For man, as for flower and beast and bird, the supreme triumph is to be most vividly, most perfectly alive'.

Scafell Pike and the Dissolving Map

Many of us seek the aspect of nature that thrills us with its power and destructiveness. This is the side of nature that not only gives life, but can take it away. When we seek to be physically challenged, perhaps it is less obvious to us that we also seek a numinous experience, sometimes of the darker kind. Often this takes us to the wild places of height and depth. There is something about mountaintops that holds a particular resonance with the numinous.

A walk in the mountains of Britain, with its rapidly changing weather and small scale, can take one through different archetypal territories in a rapid and intense manner. One autumnal morning, while ascending Scafell Pike, England's highest hill, I encountered three distinct zones. The lower slopes are bubbling streams, hedgerows, birdsong and some sunshine. This is a safe and familiar version of nature, delighting the senses. The everyday world is still present to begin with, perhaps some traffic noise and the sight of other people. The mind may be preoccupied with the physical effort of walking up a steep slope; there is some catching of the breath and the thoughts may still be full of the normal chatter of everyday life.

The second zone is barren moorland, with some sheep but no other life or shelter. There is a developing bleakness, a pointing towards the challenge ahead. The mind chatter is faltering. It's colder and the wind is picking up, we are far away from the everyday.

The third zone is the summit, reached by a scramble up some rocks to a plateau at the top. At this point, the weather changes abruptly. Dark cloud comes sweeping in and I am enveloped. The wind strengthens again and it starts to rain, hard and horizontal.

Suddenly, the world has become charged and dangerous. I cannot see, I am on my own and no one else is around. I have lost my bearings and cannot find the path from which I came. There is a real risk of taking the wrong route, a peril of taking a step onto the rocks below. I feel that sense of awe and dread. There is a part of me that delights in the situation, for it is what I sought, but there is also a part of me that regrets my foolishness and feels like a trembling and paltry human who dared to challenge the gods. I take out my map; my fingers are stiff and cold. I don't have a map case and the rain smudges the map so that I cannot make out the contour lines. As the map starts to fragment in the deluge, it is as though my ego structures are dissolving too. I feel more than a frisson of anxiety. Time to regroup, gather the ego, accept the challenge to a greater level of competence and return to ground. I had been reminded that, when going to the upper zones of the physical and the non-physical, to ensure means of return, take care of the tools and don't get over-confident.

Being England, the cloud moved on, the rain softened and I found my way down easily enough. Back through the moorland, back to the bubbling brook, down towards the land of people, a pub and a rehydrating beer. It was a minor event in the range of man's brushes with the fiercer

face of nature, but the different octaves of nature had resonated somewhere deep within me. I had been able to leave my everyday self behind,
just for a while, and engage with a more archetypal layer of consciousness. It was a brush with the numinous and I had an enhanced sense of
being alive.

The Forest of Arden

One of the secrets of Shakespeare's greatness was his ability to weave
archetypal themes into the lives of men in a way that transcends time,
geography and culture. Shakespeare has a truly bio-psycho-socio-archetypal perspective. He was not interested in lofty spirituality, but in the
tumultuous currents that play out in our little lives, affecting our animal
bodies, the paths we weave and the journeys we make on the great stage
of life between our entrance and our exit. Shakespeare was interested in
mutative change and the process of transformation. He shows us how lives
can sometimes make a quantum leap from one orbit to another, and how
these perspectival changes cannot be predicted but seem to be brought on
the wind.

There is a special and enchanted symbol of transformative change in
his play *As You Like It*. The Forest of Arden is a primary character in this
play symbolising the place of intensification of meaning, the place where
synchronicities occur, and where deep healing of psychological wounds
can take place. It has some menace and is not without its danger, but there
is a bedrock of kindness and love held by the beating green heart of the
forest itself.

As You Like It begins at Court. The Court could be understood as
standing for the world of the ego. It has developed rules and structures with
problematic envy, injustice, rivalry and hatred. Rosalind and Orlando are
the star-crossed lovers who meet at Court. Orlando has been disinherited,
and he has a crisis and a near death experience when he challenges the
Court wrestler. He is expected to die and indeed, his abusive brother Oliver
wants to be rid of him. But Orlando does not get the life squeezed out of
him by the wrestler—which is perhaps a metaphor for the constriction of
the Court—he prevails.[94]

This sets the scene for their transformative journey as Orlando and
Rosalind are banished separately from the Court, each with their companion. Rosalind disguises herself as a boy, calling herself Ganymede for
safety. As they continue their journey away from Court and the realm of
ego, they come to a wild place. They are entering the Forest of Arden.
There is an intensification of significance as their archetypal threshold

becomes lowered and the forest becomes pregnant with meaning. They are frightened at first, as the forest seems bleak and uncouth. Their crisis is deepening and there is a real threat of death.

Rosalind, a feisty girl who most certainly does not believe in expressing vulnerability, has a dark night of the soul on entering the forest. 'Oh Jupiter, how weary are my spirits', she says; 'I could find it in my heart to disgrace my apparel and cry like a girl'. In another part of the forest Orlando's trusty servant Adam says 'Dear Master, I can go no further. I die for food. Here I lie down and measure my grave'. It is a desperate situation, it is a breakdown—but assistance is at hand. They ask for assistance separately and in very different ways. Rosalind is straightforward in her manner of seeking help and, together with her companion Celia, they are taken in by a shepherd.

Orlando's manner of seeking help is violent and aggressive; he is frightened and desperate to save his servant. He surprises a stranger in the forest and demands food at the point of his sword. This stranger is a man of wisdom and he contains Orlando's aggression with calm and equanimity. This man turns out to be the exiled Duke, a mindful, gentle man, full of peace and love. He symbolises, I would suggest, the aspect of the personality that is forced into exile by the ego's dominance in the world of Court. The Duke lives in harmony in the forest, with his companions, hunting the deer for sustenance rather than sport and even enjoying the harsh winters, which he regards as his teacher. Their meeting is a mutative moment: the Duke greets Orlando with such grace and balance that all the aggression simply melts away, food and succour is provided and the faithful old servant is saved.

Rosalind/Ganymede and Orlando meet by chance and Shakespeare takes us through a complicated gender-bending scenario as they woo each other. Orlando has no idea that the youth Ganymede was in fact the Rosalind who had so entranced him. Indeed, he spends his time carving her name on the trees, thinking that he would never see her again. He told Ganymede of his love for Rosalind who said that he / she would pretend to be Rosalind. They agree that Orlando would visit every day and pour out his heart to her as a remedy for his love sickness. One interpretation of the gender swapping of Shakespeare's characters is to demonstrate the encounter with the archetypal qualities of the opposite sex, the anima and animus, which is a crucial stepping-stone on the way to individuation.

The magic of the forest is deepening. Another synchronicity occurs when Orlando finds a man asleep on the ground with a snake around his neck. It turns out to be Oliver, his murderous brother. Orlando's personality is being radically changed by the forest. His natural anger and aggression is over come by something deeper. He saves his brother who, in turn, is overcome with a deep and genuine penitence. The brothers find themselves in a completely new emotional space that transcends all their previous rivalries. They forgive each other and embrace. Henceforth, they love each other with a true brotherly affection.

The Forest of Arden is earthy and sexy, playful but serious. Meaning is ever amplified. There are synchronicities, chance encounters and the most beautiful and fortunate coincidences. This is a happy place governed essentially by love so that historic conflicts are effortlessly healed and peace fills the territory vacated by strife. There is something about the power of nature—gentle, forceful, strong and essentially kind. Not a soft kindness but a strong, fierce power that melts the piffling concerns that used to preoccupy the ego.

The forest has a shadow, of course. This is epitomised by a depressive, Jacques. Jacques has a particular grounding perspective, a balance that is not unwelcome. He is the character who reminds us that the world is a stage, we are all actors who have our entrances and our exits. We are born, we strut our little stage and we perish. He reminds us that we have our seven stages as we pass through from infancy to senility. Jacques is not someone who will let himself get carried away by overly identifying with the lush surroundings of fertile forest and young people awash with hormones. Jacques is a voice of maturity who feels the pain of the hunted deer. He is the true hermit, the eco-warrior, the one who will not return to Court, the one who stays in the forest.

There is another transformation right at the end of the play. It occupies just a few lines but has a crucial message. The original villain, the Duke who usurped the throne, ran the corrupt Court and represents the stale trappings of ego, is coming to the forest at the head of an army. He stands for the repressive forces of ego; he wants to root out the revolutionaries who threaten his status. He wants to kill them. At the edge of the forest, Shakespeare has him meet an old religious man, a hermit, with whom he 'had much talk' and who in the end completely turned his heart from his wicked design. He became a true penitent. He had a moment of epiphany, a transformation of the spiritual variety, to the extent that Shakespeare has him spending the rest of his days in a religious house. Shakespeare was not particularly interested in religion and the monastic life but he knew that sudden spiritual epiphany and monastic retreat was one possible outcome of the transformative journey. The first act of the Duke's newly conceived penitence is to restore the throne to the banished Duke in the forest, which paves the way for the happy ending with much coming together in marriage and a return to peace and prosperity in the kingdom. Thus, the Court completes its transformative journey by its passage through the Forest of Arden. In Jungian terms, the ego undergoes a crisis and symbolic death before being replenished by its rejected aspects and a higher transformative power to form a new structure.

We all have access to the Forest of Arden. It lies, of course, within ourselves. There are ways in which we stay at Court and keep ourselves removed from the transformative zone. There are ways in which we can enter the transformative forest, although this often happens by chance. The forest is a place of power, holding danger and opportunity. There are ways in which we can perish in it and ways in which we can navigate it safely and with benefit. I believe that anyone working with people in intense mental states should carry something of the Forest of Arden within. Not all day or every day, but one should have a relationship with Arden, being replenished by it and being able to transmute at least a little of its mutative quality.

SECTION TWO

Archetype, the Shadow and Us

A deep experiential encounter with birth and death is regularly associated with an existential crisis of extraordinary proportions, during which the individual seriously questions the meaning of existence, as well as his or her basic values and life strategies.

This crisis can be resolved only by connecting with deep, intrinsic spiritual dimensions of the psyche and elements of the collective unconscious.

—Stanislav Grof

CHAPTER 9

Crisis – Danger and Opportunity

When written in Chinese the word crisis *is composed of two characters.*

One represents danger, and the other represents opportunity.

—John F. Kennedy, 1959

The Disillusioned Psychiatrist

In the early 1990s, I was coming to the end of my training and was eligible to apply for a consultant psychiatrist post but I was not entirely comfortable in my chosen career and the prospect of a permanent post did not seem an attractive prospect.[95] As well as my formal training in clinical psychiatry, I had developed my interest in psychotherapy, which I found endlessly fascinating. I had learned that the times when it felt as though I was making progress were quickly followed by a realisation of how little I knew and how far I had to go. But I had started a more intensive training at the Institute of Group Analysis and at last it seemed that my progress was being reflected in my clinical work.

But—and this was a very big but—the other part of the clinical work was often brutal and lacking in compassion, and there were times when I did not see how I could remain in such a system. I was working in a psychiatric intensive care unit serving an inner city region of London. People were brought in to this unit, usually on a 'section' of the mental health act. They were given very high doses of drugs and there was no meaningful attempt to help these people through recovery towards a more coherent life. When they were discharged, they were offered a follow-up appointment in the clinic but they hardly ever attended and very little effort was made to engage them in treatment. The professor in charge of the service only seemed to see the more fragrant and compliant patients and the community nurses seemed burned out and demoralised.[96]

Medication often works well for people with more severe forms of illness. It still seemed miraculous to me how the hostile, mute, paranoid patient tormented by unpleasant hallucinatory voices could be transformed by antipsychotics. Their personalities would reappear and often their lives and relationships were restored. But this approach lacked any nuance and sensitivity, and a very basic version of the medical model was often used as the only option rather than one of a range of therapeutic strategies. Drugs with powerful toxic side effects were often given to those for whom medication simply was not required. Sometimes people were treated in ways that I thought were wrong.[97]

I vividly remember one young person who came into hospital in crisis and made a rapid recovery. I felt that I had developed a good rapport with him and some understanding of his issues. I thought he could do well with psychotherapy but the important first step was to discharge him from hospital; he was frightened and there was no reason why he could not go home. When he was brought into the weekly ward round, where the decisions are made, he was overawed by the number of people sitting in the room. The professor barked questions at him, he became inarticulate with anxiety and the professor refused to discharge him on the grounds that he might be psychotic and needed more observation. The nurses and I protested in vain. When he was finally discharged, he was too frightened to come and see me in the clinic and I feared that real damage was done to his development. There were many other such stories.

I had become disillusioned. Perhaps this would have been time to find a new direction but I still had faith in good psychiatry and there were many of us who felt we could improve psychiatric services once we got into positions of influence. Besides, I was getting married and needed a job. So when the post with the Crisis Intervention Service at the Royal London Hospital became available, I jumped at it. The Crisis Service was an innovative team that had been set up as an alternative to the traditional mental hospital model for selected patients. The central tenet of the Crisis Service was not just to treat symptoms but also to address the underlying psychological issues to promote healthy development and growth. The intention was that patients would not only recover from their crisis but would emerge stronger and more resilient.

The quality of the team depends on the quality of the people in it and the Crisis Service over the years has attracted and retained people with a deep commitment to the therapeutic task. The work has its challenges, of course. How do people work at the psychiatric coalface day after day, walking with their patients into the darkest areas? It requires skill, courage and honesty, but most of all it requires cohesive team work. A good team is greater than the sum of its parts. The work requires the highest standards but also camaraderie and mutual support to replenish the compassion, rigour and vitality that is fundamental to the therapeutic effort. The Crisis Service restored my faith. In the twenty years that we worked together I came to appreciate that the Crisis Service was our very own Forest of Arden, a nurturing and healing place of transformative power.

Crisis and Suicidal Thought

The Crisis Intervention Service worked with people who fulfilled four criteria: they had either attempted or were considering attempting suicide, the suicide attempt was in response to a crisis rather than a long-term state of mind, they wanted a talking treatment, and they lived in the borough of Tower Hamlets in London's East End.

Most of us will not have experienced serious suicidal thought, although many of us will know what it is like to have transient ideas of feeling as though life is no longer worth living. There is a degree of intensity about serious suicidal thought that is difficult to imagine and difficult for people to communicate. It is often most forbidding and dangerous in the small hours of the morning, when sleep is elusive and our mood is at its most bleak. Suicidal thought usually flows from a feeling of hopelessness and despair that has a numinous quality of dreadfulness. By numinous, I do not mean that it has a sense of the sacred, but that it is both terrifying and fascinating – it cannot simply be put aside. It is a feeling outside of the normal range of human experience and it often the first time that a person has felt something of this intensity. At its most intense it has a compelling quality that is very difficult to withstand. This acts as a powerful driver of behaviour either towards death or towards change. The darkest hour is the most dangerous but also the point where people sometimes have a moment of insight—'I cannot go on like this', 'something needs to shift'. The extraordinary power of this numinous moment means that it is less likely to be a passing impulse but is more likely to persist and drive the hard work that is usually required for proper lasting change. So the darkest hour can also be the mutative moment.

People who have experienced this will usually tell someone about it, either directly through their doctor or their family or less directly by harming themselves and being brought to hospital. Either way, they were often referred to the Crisis service. The emotional shock of this numinous experience tends to influence behaviour for some weeks afterwards in an important way. People who have been through this type of experience are often actively seeking help for the first time and their characteristic psychological defences are more permeable. They are usually more open to examine themselves and explore the possibility of change than they have ever been before.

This newfound openness does not last very long, usually fading within a few weeks once the immediacy of the crisis is over and the difficult feelings begin to fade. So it is crucial to engage and work with these people very quickly to capture the momentum. The aim is not only to help them through the crisis, but also to resolve some of the underlying fault lines and vulnerabilities in their emotional make up, so that they are better adapted to life's challenges and less likely to encounter such difficulties again in the future.

Our emphasis was always on personal growth. How, we asked ourselves, can we help this person to become a little more free, to live the life that they wish to lead, to develop their relationships and their range of activities? How can they live more mindfully, being aware of some of their psychological processes, their vulnerabilities and the dramas they enact? How can they avoid the repetition of hurting other people and being hurt themselves? We believed that any promotion of growth in an individual would probably be reflected in their crucial relationships, so we hoped that their children and their extended family would also come to benefit from the work that we did together. Any lasting change, any significant maturation is worth striving for as it may bring larger rewards and a wider trajectory of change over time.

The nature of the crisis that brought a person to the Crisis Service gave us valuable information about his or her main areas of emotional and personality vulnerability. Usually the presenting crisis is a re-enactment of a previous unresolved trauma. The trauma typically concerns themes of loss or abuse; sometimes this is gross and obvious and sometimes it is more subtle and complex. A careful exploration of the person's personal and family history will almost always provide us with an understanding of why this person has become overwhelmed and suicidal at this point in time. We share our understanding with the person involved and agree a treatment plan. The treatment may range from a few sessions of support to a more sophisticated brief psychodynamic psychotherapy.

Dan's Darkest Night

Dan was a man in his mid thirties when he came to the Crisis Service. He was a tough resilient man. He had never seen a psychiatrist before—the very idea would have seemed ludicrous to him. He had been hit by a car while driving his motorbike three weeks previously. It was not a serious accident. No bones were broken but he suffered heavy bruising and stiffness and he was kept in hospital for observation for a couple of days. The accident seemed to affect him very deeply on an emotional level and after he was discharged from hospital he went to his doctor to enquire how he could best donate his organs when he died. The doctor asked the appropriate questions and Dan admitted that he was having thoughts of ending his life. However he was interested in the idea that there might be some help available for him in his depressed state and he agreed to attend the Crisis Service.

The story that emerged from Dan was that this was the first time he had been in a hospital since his mother had treatment for cancer when he was a child. She died when he was eleven. He had tried to be brave for his little brother and didn't want his friends to think he was soft, so he didn't grieve at all. His parents had divorced and his father had remarried. He went to live with his father's new family, but his father wasn't very interested in him, nor was stepmother and his two older stepbrothers were violent to him. Dan was a steady boy. He did well at school, he had some friends and didn't get into trouble. He left home as soon as he could and slept rough on the streets of London for a while before finding a place in a hostel for homeless teenagers. He found work on building sites and eventually he went to college.

So far his progress had been impressive. The protracted dying and death of his mother, who he loved, followed by an emotional vacuum and violence would often be followed by significant emotional disturbance causing impediment to normal psycho-social development. So many traumatised teenagers anaesthetize their feelings with drink and drugs or express their sadness as anger. But Dan seemed to have avoided these perils. He got a job in a hotel, earned enough money to buy a motorbike and supplemented his income as a motorbike courier while training for a career in the hotel industry. He didn't think much about his past. He rarely saw his father, and he lost contact with his younger brother who had become an addict and stolen money from him. Dan saw himself as a mobile, independent self-contained unit. He liked company, he had some friends and girlfriends but his relationships were transient and he certainly did not intend to get seriously involved with anyone.

Dan transferred to a hotel in America. He loved the sense of a new start, a big brave country where anything seemed possible. He bought a Harley Davidson and he travelled the wide-open spaces. Then he met Maggie. Maggie was an English woman who had been travelling but she'd run out of money and ended up staying with Dan and his friends in a house they were renting. Maggie was not the easiest person to be around, with a tendency to be stormy and divisive. Dan's friend thought she was trouble but Dan was smitten. There was something about Maggie that he found irresistible—she was a troubled and vulnerable person who needed him, a sexual woman who wanted him and a twin soul on a shared journey. He fell deeply in love with her. He sided with her against his friends, he shared his life and his income with her and he supported her art career. He gradually invested everything that he had in her. They developed their life in America, and they spent 6 months travelling on his motor bike from Alaska to Guatemala. They had adventures. They hiked in Yosemite and they dived in the Caribbean. They decided they were life partners and planned their future. Eventually they returned to Europe, found a property in Spain and prepared to run a small hotel.

The change happened just as they were about to put down some roots and advance the transition from adolescence to adulthood. Dan had noticed a change in Maggie, a growing remoteness, a developing iciness. He went to New York to make a business arrangement and when he came back she had gone. He found out that she had rekindled contact with an old lover via the internet and had gone traveling with him. She had cleared out their bank account. Dan managed to talk to her and she told him that she didn't want to settle down. She laughed at him: 'Its over—get over it', she said.

Dan tried to get over it but it was difficult. He was alone again. He didn't have much of a social network to fall back on and he had no money. He really did have to start over again. He returned penniless to East London where he was offered a bedsit in a property awaiting demolition. It would be his for 18 months at half rent. He borrowed enough to buy another motorbike and started to earn some money. He decorated his bedsit, bought a washing machine with his first pay cheque and started to make it into a home. He had made contact with his brother again, and he'd been thinking about his mother.

Then he got knocked off his motorbike. He saw the driver of the car and she was a young woman with dark hair like Maggie. She didn't seem to care when he was lying on the road and she didn't make any effort to help him. During his brief stay in hospital he didn't understand why it seemed to affect him so much. He kept feeling tearful but he hid it and no one noticed. Then his landlord told him that the timetable for the demolition of the property had been brought forward and he had one month to find somewhere else to live. Meanwhile, there had been a problem with his bank and a standing order had apparently been duplicated, cleaning out his account again. He was in pain after the accident. His motorbike was written off. How was he going to make a living? How was he going to manage?

Dan had an attractive personality and everyone seemed to like him. He had a pleasant open face, a wiry build and he had a competent and self-sufficient manner. He was embarrassed that a psychiatrist had been asked to see him and he was not accustomed to talking about himself. He shed some tears as he slowly told his story. Dan told me that he'd had some very dark nights recently. It was difficult to explain he said, but it was as though all the pain of his life that he had been keeping away for as long as he could remember had come back to haunt him. It was very difficult for him to bear. He felt that his life was essentially meaningless and that the world held nothing good for him. It was as though all the world were laughing at his pathetic attempts to have a life. There was one night in particular when something horrible and ghastly seemed to be engulfing him, beckoning him, whispering to him. It was difficult to describe but very frightening and awful, he said. It was more than he could stand. If he could have pressed a button to end his life at that point, he would have pressed it. He would do anything not to feel like that ever again.

The nature of the circumstances leading to his referral to me encapsulated so much of his story. The defining themes in Dan's life were not difficult to identify, with prominent themes of loss and trauma. The immediate trigger was the road accident. He felt assaulted by an uncaring woman in the car, who did him damage. This had a powerful resonance for him just as he was emerging from the emotional assault of Maggie's betrayal and loss, which, in turn, had awakened the unresolved feelings of grief, loss and abandonment relating to his mother's early death. It was almost as though he was that child again—bereft, alone and beaten up. The therapy was obviously going to focus on grief and loss.

Dan worked hard on his recovery. He could see that some of his unresolved childhood traumas had been bottled up in a way that made him vulnerable. He turned up to every session with a smile and mostly left with a smile too, but in the sessions he grieved. The first few sessions had passing mention of Maggie but he spoke at length of his childhood. He had blocked out his childhood memories for so long that it surprised him to find that they had such power. He spoke of his slow realisation that his mother was ill, visiting her in hospital and being frightened by it. He was not aware that his mother was dying, but she became less emotionally available for him as she became more ill and more in pain. He could see that Maggie's distancing from him resonated with his mother's dying. He could see the link between his recent treatment in hospital and the triggering of associations with his mother being in hospital and the imminence of something awful happening.

Dan's normal ego defences had been broken down and at last he was able to allow the normal healing process of grief to flow. He talked of how he had developed his life to make sure that he was never hurt like this again—until he met Maggie. It transpired that Maggie had had a troubled childhood after her own mother became mentally ill and Maggie had been taken into care. He felt, after some reflection, that he chose Maggie not only because they had similar backgrounds, but also because there was a part of him that recognised that Maggie was fundamentally unavailable. He saw eventually that it was beyond Maggie's capabilities to make the transition to the next stage of life, and that on some level that was what had attracted him to her. He could see that on an unconscious level he was setting up a re-enactment of his early loss of his mother.

As the grief began to lose its intensity after the first few sessions, he started to feel lighter, as though the darkness was lifting. He was getting stronger, his natural resilience was kicking in and he had found somewhere else to live. He wasn't going to ride a motorbike again but he had contacted some hotels and was looking for work. As the grief faded, the focus shifted to tracking the effects of his childhood traumas on his adult personality, its effects on his relationships and his worldview. He spoke of how he really wanted a family of his own one day.

There was one last pitfall to negotiate: the ending. Especially for people with issues around loss, the end of therapy, even in brief treatment, can bring an unexpected undertow of pain and feelings of abandonment. This is not so much related to the attachment to the therapist, more a transference of feelings from the bigger losses that have happened before. So the impending end of therapy becomes a focus in its own right. It is a crucial opportunity to resolve another layer of the abandonment and loss complex. Of course, the enormous issue of loss is never fully resolved, it is always work in progress. The end of therapy is a partial completion within the bigger picture of incompleteness.

I don't know what happened to Dan. I don't know if he found a life partner and had the family of his own that he craved. I don't know how the wounds caused by his family of origin played themselves out. Perhaps they will continue to resonate down further generations of Dan's family. I don't know if he was able to flourish and grow, but I did know that he had a chance.

Working with the Mindset

Crisis holds the germ of growth. Minor crises are the stuff and gristle of everyday life giving us some developmental friction. Major crises rock our foundations in a way that holds both danger and opportunity to reorganise and re-orientate. We can be overwhelmed or we can use it as a platform to move up an octave. The main determinants of outcome of any crisis are the mindset, the setting and the integration. The mindset is the mental state that a person brings to any experience—the thoughts, the mood and especially the intention. The setting is the physical, the social and the emotional environment. Integration refers to the process of understanding, incorporating and making use of the whole experience. I suggest that the greater the vulnerability of the mental state, the greater the numinous or archetypal component; the greater is the importance of set, setting and integration.

The first step towards treatment after anyone is referred to the Crisis Service is a phone call from our referrals coordinator. This has a number of purposes: to establish that a person is willing and able to attend, to assess the mental state in case more urgent action is required, to gather some information ahead of the interview and to do some preparatory work on the mindset. The person is told that treatment is not a passive process like taking a tablet, but some work will be involved. The first stage of the preparation of the mindset is to encourage a spirit of joint effort and enquiry.

Dan's mindset, at first sight, looked distinctly unpromising. He had never been very interested in his psychological processes. He was a lifelong expert at the psychological defense of repression, but his dark night and the sheer awfulness of his experience had led him to seek help. His contact with his doctor and the triage phone call with the crisis service had led him a little way towards the idea that there might be a treatment for him that would help him, that there might be a way forward. He was interested in that idea and rolled it around in his mind a little. He thought about the appointment, he wondered what it would be like, what would happen, what he would say. He began thinking a little more about himself. He was developing a psychological mindset of enquiry.

The night before he came to the Crisis Service, he didn't sleep very well. On the day of the meeting, he walked to the Royal London Hospital, through busy streets and the bustle of Whitechapel market focusing his mind on the appointment that he was about to keep. There was some anxiety, of course. Questions raced through his mind: What would he say? Would he be tearful? Would the psychiatrist try to force him into hospital? He remembered that he had heard stories of people being given electric shock treatment for depression. He considered turning back. But there was the other part of him that yearned for someone to hear him, understand him and help him, so he decided to keep the appointment. Eventually he navigated his way through the hospital, he found the Crisis Service waiting room and the receptionist seemed to be expecting him. She smiled, called him by his first name and told him to take a seat. Someone would meet him shortly, she said. He waited.

Throughout this process there was a steady increase in emotional intensity. Dan was gathering himself. It had taken a lot to come to the hospital. It would have been easier not to have come and he had to make sure that he wanted to. The slow ritual of the journey to the hospital and the escalating anxiety while sitting in the waiting room makes him feel that this is a serious business. He is being taken seriously. He is met by the psychiatrist, who greets him formally, but sympathetically. He is taken down the corridor and we sit down in my office. I introduce myself briefly and ask him where he would like to start. To his surprise, he finds himself talking about his mother and within a few minutes, he is in tears. He is embarrassed but the psychiatrist doesn't seem to mind. It is such a relief. We gently go through his life story and by the end of the session, he is beginning to understand how it all seems to fit together.

It is early days for Dan but already we can see how for the first time in his life, he had a certain mental set, an intention to look inside, to find some meaning and to work on himself. The nature of the setting intensified the mindset. The setting was formal but supportive, encouraging him and helping him to feel safe. He felt able to look at the hidden recesses of his psyche and work with his demons, as he put it. He thought about the session some more on the way home and the more he thought about it, the more it seemed to make sense. He felt that he could use the insights and knowledge that he was acquiring. He was beginning to integrate.

The triad of mindset, setting and integration plays a role in every encounter but sometimes this occurs in a manner that is negative. In psychiatry, some of our patients have no interest in their psychological processes, they are not interested in growth and they have no intention to change. Often, the setting of hospital and psychiatric wards is disturbing and does not support the process. Too frequently, there is no attempt to integrate high-intensity experiences as a way of preparation for the onward journey.

Transference and Countertransference

Transference occurs to a greater or lesser extent in every clinical encounter and is an important part of the mindset and setting. Transference refers to the projection of an internalised relationship pattern onto an external object, such as expecting people to mother you, reject you or abuse you; based on past experience. This is an unconscious process and usually people do not know they are doing this. There are certain techniques that amplify transference such as the use of silence and certain rituals such as 'seeing the doctor'.

A doctor has a powerful psychological position, of course. Traditionally, the doctor was the respected village figure or the hospital expert.

Doctors were trusted to have your interests at heart and some power to influence matters. They had a certain parental position. If your internalised relationship with authority or parental figures is straightforward and positive, then generally the doctor will be the recipient of a positive transference of this nature. The doctor in turn will have the emotional reaction or countertransference, that this is a delightful patient and it is a pleasant task to be of help.

The opposite situation may arise with a patient who has had a poor relationship with caregivers. There may be traumas of commission or omission. If physical abuse of whatever nature is committed, this is a trauma of commission, and if essential emotional or physical care is withheld, this is a trauma of omission. It is not surprising that such people, when they see doctors, have a much more complicated unconscious agenda and often generate a more complicated response.

If a patient has an uncomplicated positive transference, I know that the placebo response is likely to be enhanced and that they are likely to respond well to my suggestions. This can affect decisions about prescribing medication. So if I am not sure whether or not to prescribe an antidepressant (if, for example, it is not a severe depressive illness but, because of the crisis, sleep is very disturbed), I am more likely to prescribe a sedative antidepressant for a short period. I may make a strong suggestion that he will find the next few weeks uncomfortable as he grapples with his issues in therapy but after three weeks or so he will start feeling a lot better and he should be ready to return to work in a month or so.

If I have a patient whose history suggests that they will have deep reservations about trusting people in positions of authority, I know that, if I prescribe for them, the medication is likely to be toxic for them by causing side effects, or it will 'not work', or they will not take it. On the other hand, if I have developed a therapeutic alliance with them after a few sessions and we have explored some of these issues, then, if they do need some medication, they will be more likely to accept it and more likely to benefit from it.

The countertransference becomes a very important clinical assessment tool in that one can often deduce important information about the patient's way of relating to the world and his or her internal objects from the feelings aroused in oneself. This is the patient's way of communicating a flavour of their internalised relationship patterns that he or she is unable to put into words. For this to work effectively, you do have to have familiarity with your own psyche to know what feelings belong to the patient and what belongs to you. In psychiatry, and for psychiatrists, the unexamined psyche is a dangerous thing. It is common for doctors to take decisions, sometimes far-reaching decisions, influenced by a complex and misunderstood countertransference. The psychoanalyst Donald Winnicott spoke to this theme in his classic paper 'Hate in the Countertransference':

> The countertransference needs to be understood by the psychiatrist. . . . However much he loves his patients, he cannot avoid hating them and fearing them. The better he knows this, the less will hate and fear be the motive determining what he does to his patients.[98]

The examination of the countertransference works best within a team. If a patient evokes in me a powerful feeling, a feeling that I do not entirely understand, it is invariably helpful to discuss this with the Crisis Service in a clinical team meeting. It doesn't need to be a major discussion, but it increases the reliability and safety of the examination of the countertransference to have it checked out by trusted colleagues.

Issues of transference complicate the set and setting. For example, the classical 'heart sink patient' will have a complex mindset that typically involves the expression of dependency and a need to communicate a deep sense of distress but will have no interest in doing anything constructive to alter the situation.[99] The onus of responsibility is put firmly on other people to alleviate the distress. There are some patients who come to see psychiatrists for depression, who have a chronic misery that is never going to respond to anti-depressants and who develop a dependent relationship with the doctor. This doctor may have a biological perspective and enjoy prescribing, so a certain equilibrium is reached where the unwritten contract is that the patient receives a version of the relationship he is seeking and the doctor has the illusion that he is doing something useful by prescribing. It is much easier to prescribe for low mood than to consider the more nebulous task of exploring and understanding the underlying issues. The problem with these co-dependent relationships is that the patient is much less likely to address the developmental challenges of building living skills, working on relationship patterns or perhaps reducing consumption of food, alcohol or drugs. Antidepressants have side effects, the patient will often have enhanced appetite and weight gain, and the risk of diabetes is increased. Thoughtless prescribing does real harm.

A more productive approach is to assess the capacity for growth. What does a person actually want from the encounter and what type of relationship is being sought? What would be the nature of the therapeutic alliance? In what way would the patient like to grow and what are the barriers to growth? How can the patient move towards the best that he or she can be? I want to know what the patient's conscious intention is and try to understand what the *unconscious* intention may be. The next step might be to make some of the unconscious intention a little more conscious. The step after that might be to re-examine the perspective and to see if another mental set can be arrived at that might be a little more conducive to longer-term development.

Delusional Mood

Delusional mood is psychiatric term used to describe a state of perplexity in which the subject has a powerful sense that something very unusual, highly significant and pregnant with meaning is developing around them. I suggest that delusional mood is another form of archetypal crisis, which has an entirely different flavour to the dark night described above. It is the foundation layer from which serious psychiatric disorder can result and is traditionally associated with paranoia and schizophrenic states.[100] In delusional mood, dealings with everyday reality become suffused with meaning in a way that is so intense, so profoundly threatening, that the very existence of the self feels threatened. The quality of the mood is dark and sinister; there is a sense that something enormous and irresistible is about to happen and this mood is projected onto the external world.

In such a raw and sensitive state, threats to survival may be exaggerated, so that a glance from a stranger in a street may be interpreted as a threat. This heightens anxiety so that the person increases vigilance to further signs of danger, which are then more likely to be plucked from an increasingly hostile environment. The more arousing the environment; the greater the risk. An airport or crowded train station are among the higher-risk scenarios where the high levels of noise and activity are likely to fuel the developing delusional state. The person may then behave in an unusual way, which in turn may elicit certain responses from the environment and so a vicious circle propagates itself. A person in this condition becomes increasingly aroused but with impaired ability to discriminate between internal and external reality. This can be extremely dangerous. The degree of agitation and terror may cause impulsive and dangerous behaviour. Persecutory anxiety becomes reinforced by misperceptions of external stimuli and may become organized into paranoid delusions. Auditory hallucinations may develop with derogatory or commanding content. This is the stuff of the psychiatric emergency room and, once the situation has developed to this point, the person is usually unable to understand the difficulties in terms of an internal process and becomes a patient who progresses through the pathways of disease, hospital treatment and a career as a user of mental health services.

The tragedy of this scenario is that the setting is often profoundly unhelpful. The worst-case scenario is the exposure to the threat of aggression that often occurs in the police station or the acute psychiatric ward. This may be the only option to ensure safety for someone at high risk, but it further entrenches the persecutory anxiety and prolongs the illness. An unsupportive setting tends to hardwire the crystallization of the archetypal crisis into illness. The best scenario is treatment at home in a safe and caring environment with skilled professionals making a judgment as to whether an appropriate dose of minimally toxic medication would take some of the intensity away while allowing a slow process of encouraging the psychological mindset so that further psychological treatment and integration can occur. Modern psychiatry in the UK is now often able to do this. Home treatment teams may visit patients at home as an alternative to hospital treatment so that hospital admission is only used when there are issues of safety that cannot be properly attended to in the home setting. The treatment setting is much improved so people are less likely to be harmed by adverse settings but integration is often minimal and important opportunities for growth are overlooked.

Delusional mood is an archetypal crisis with a biological component, being strongly associated with schizophrenia. Dark nights occur in the more biological forms of depression and in psycho-social crisis. In the chapters that follow we will explore some other forms of archetypal crisis. How can we distinguish between the different types of crisis and what is the role of diagnosis? Is there a way in which the powerful archetypal energies, the forced encounter with the shadow can be better engaged with? Above all, how can we minimize the danger and maximise the opportunity?

CHAPTER 10

Breaking Down or Breaking Through

The fundamental mistake was supposing that the healing process was the disease, rather than the process whereby the disease is healed. The disease, if any, was the state previous to the 'psychosis'. The so-called 'psychosis' was an attempt towards spontaneous healing, it was a movement towards health, not a movement towards disease . . . it could be called mystical, a re-owning and discovery of parts of myself.

—Dick Price[101]

Archetypal Crisis or Mental Illness

Upstairs in the Crisis Service at the Royal London, the task is to understand the nature of our patients' important psychological issues and decide how we could best assist in promoting some resolution to free them, to some extent, from the restricting psychological structures that were causing them pain and restricting their progression through life. Although patients came to us in states of great distress, our model was tailored to much more than just the curing of the dis ease. We saw the crisis as an opportunity to resolve the underlying wounds, usually concerning trauma and loss, to promote a more healthy state for the future. We worked to benefit not only the patients themselves, but perhaps also their children and families, their friends and workmates. We thought that we were making it a little less likely that the issues of our patients, often involving multi-generational trauma, would be transmitted to the next generation. We thought this was good medicine. We rarely found diagnostic labels useful and I stopped people's unnecessary medication more often than I started necessary medication. We were always alert to the possibility of a serious depression, perhaps an underlying bipolar disorder or developing psychosis. The mantra was that missing a serious psychiatric disorder and not organising proper treatment for it would be a very serious error. But the vast majority of our patients needed and responded to the psychological treatment that we provided for them so that the crisis ran its course to some lasting benefit.

People often came to the Crisis Service after a numinous moment, a dark night involving suicidal thought, but, by the time they came to us, the archetypal nature of the crisis was dwindling and the therapeutic work generally addressed their psycho-social issues. Downstairs in the emergency room, our patients were more likely to suffer an unfolding archetypal crisis—often associated with a psychiatric illness such as schizophrenia or bipolar disorder. Psychiatry uses medication to achieve symptom reduction in such circumstances and often this is a helpful and appropriate approach. However, psychiatry tends to be blind to those archetypal crises that do not fit the pattern of those illnesses that are familiar to us and does not consider that these less-common conditions may sometimes represent an opportunity for growth.

Jung's crisis gives us a useful model for the understanding of an archetypal crisis that did not conform to psychiatric classification systems. Jung considered his crisis to be a hazardous but an inherently natural and growth-orientated process that needed to run its course; indeed interrupting or aborting the process would have been harmful. The eventual outcome for Jung was excellent (although it came at the price of immense suffering) and medical treatment would have been inappropriate. Jung's type of crisis is rare and mental-illness scenarios are much more common. How then should we distinguish carefully and reliably between, on the one hand, an archetypal crisis, which may be an opportunity for growth and, on the other hand, an archetypal crisis that is related to mental illness? How does this distinction influence the treatment that would be given to people seeking help with these conditions? Is this even a useful distinction to make, could mental illness be better understood as a failure to negotiate an archetypal crisis?

The Importance of Good Diagnosis

We need to begin with a brief discussion as to why diagnosis as a concept is important, especially as labels are so often seen as unhelpful and stigmatising. The medical model of illness involves a patient coming to a doctor in distress. A patient is someone seeking help and a solution to their dis-ease. The doctor has the honour of providing that help and the term *patient* recognises the sanctity of the relationship between the doctor and the person who entrusts the doctor with his or her concerns. In the medical model, the doctor first of all makes a thorough assessment of the patient with the aim of naming the condition or reaching a diagnosis. The nature of a fault needs to be identified so that the correct remedy can be applied. Thus the primary purpose of diagnosis is to inform and drive the treatment plan. Often the diagnosis is not clear and a number of possibilities are held in mind. This is called the differential diagnosis.

Sometimes, after investigating the condition and patient further, the range of possible diagnoses is narrowed down and a final diagnosis is made. Sometimes it is more complicated in that it may be difficult to reach a final diagnosis or there may be interplay between different disease processes. Proper use of the medical model is to always work in the patients best interests, working as an advisor to the patient and using the best available information to provide the correct treatment. The advantages of any treatment need to outweigh any disadvantages. If, as often happens, the first treatment is not effective, another treatment is tried. Decisions about treatment are based on evidence from research as well as other factors that are less easy to define such as experience, intuition or knowledge of patient and family.

Diagnostic classifications are developed to achieve a common understanding of what a condition actually is. With hypertension and diabetes, there are biomarkers, such as blood pressure and blood sugar, which are the crucial factors in making the diagnosis. With psychological states, it is more complicated as we do not have reliable biomarkers that can be measured to make a diagnosis. There are no blood tests or diagnostic imaging procedures, such as MRI scanning, that can make a reliable diagnosis of psychiatric disorders. The standard classification systems DSM and ICD use a syndromal classification, agreeing on clusters of symptoms that typically comprise a condition.[102] This is only useful if it leads to improved management, treatment and outcomes.

When I started training as a psychiatrist in the mid 1980s, there was much confusion about the diagnosis of schizophrenia. Most psychiatrists would agree that someone who had developed a severe, chronically deluded and hallucinated state without prominent mood abnormality and who had difficulties managing independent adult living, suffered from schizophrenia. But how about the milder versions where people had some unusual symptoms or brief psychotic states? Were they milder forms of schizophrenia or something more benign, like growing pains? Some clinicians thought that schizophrenia was a psychological condition and there were various theories as to how this might arise. Others thought that schizophrenia was more like a neurological illness with abnormalities in the brain being the primary cause of the symptoms and disability. There was also a school of thought that schizophrenia was merely a social construct to marginalise and punish people who did not conform to social norms.

My first trainer was a psychiatrist who hardly ever made a diagnosis of schizophrenia and my second trainer tended to make a diagnosis of schizophrenia in anyone with unusual symptoms. With my first trainer, there were people who did not receive the treatment that would have probably been helpful and, in the second case, sometimes people were inappropriately treated with medication that often had unpleasant side effects and impeded their forward progress. It is important to make a diagnosis even if the diagnosis is that there is nothing seriously the matter with the patient. Good classification systems and training help to standardise the boundaries and definitions of disease and dis-ease that helps doctors, patients and families to make the best decisions about treatment based on best available evidence. This is good medicine.

Fundamentalism

Fundamentalism is where a partial explanation is used as a total explanation; a partial cause is taken as a whole cause. Fundamentalism is a major problem in the understanding of human behaviour; especially in it's more unusual states. We all tend towards the perspective gained through the particular lens of our experience, training and culture. Medical models and classification systems are tools that can be used wisely or unwisely. An unfortunate use of the medical model sometimes happens with a medical reductionist perspective where anything that we don't understand or which is outside of our expectations is pathologized and treated medically.

DSM5 and ICD10, the numbers representing the version of the classification systems as they have developed over time, are consensus systems developed by committees. As the classification systems develop, some so-called 'conditions' fall out of the diagnostic criteria and are no longer considered to be a 'disease'. It now seems ludicrous, for example, that homosexuality was considered a psychiatric disorder until 1973. But it is much more common for new conditions to be added than deleted and the latest edition, DSM5 launched in 2013, has been criticised for its secrecy, the undue influence of the pharmaceutical industry and its description of new diagnostic categories that seem insufficiently supported by research. DSM is hugely influential. Its categories guide research and treatment for millions of patients in America and elsewhere. Crucially, it also acts as a driver for the psychiatry industry. If a disorder is included in the DSM, insurers are more likely to pay for it to be assessed and treated, and pharmaceutical companies will try to get their products licensed to treat it. There is concern that this will lead to the over-diagnosis and inappropriate medicalization of the range of human experience, which will ultimately benefits psychiatrists and drug companies rather than the individuals concerned.

Medical or biological fundamentalism occurs when someone is inappropriately put in a medical diagnostic box and treated with medication where no medication is required. This is a frequent occurrence. The medicalization of human misery leads to the mass prescription of antidepressants for mild depressed states that do not respond well to medication. The usual consequence is not only side effects, such as weight gain, but also a tendency for that person to abdicate a sense of responsibility for growth and taking the necessary action to move out of the adverse situation. If a person is judged by a doctor to be unwell and if that person is allocated a sick role and medication from the doctor, then this often holds that person in a dependent and regressed position. Why should they make the effort to address their growing pains, their maturational challenges if the doctor says they are ill? So the medical intervention often serves to entrench stasis and impede growth. Psychiatry at its worst involves the use of DSM as a sacred tract, with people being fitted into a diagnostic system without due consideration of the complexities of the individual. The goal of the DSM fundamentalist is to reduce all that is considered 'not normal' to a diagnostic label, which in turn leads to a treatment protocol and often the prescription of a medication. This is bad medicine.

Each branch of psychiatry and psychology tends to over emphasise its importance. Biological psychiatry, with the financial might of the pharmaceutical industry behind it, tends to believe that medication is the way forward and that the future is chemical. The various schools of psychoanalytic psychotherapy would be optimistic that psychotherapy of appropriate frequency and duration would enable the working through of most intrapsychic and interpersonal issues. The sociologist would point out the adverse effects of environment and deprivation, and would look to politicians to make the necessary socio-economic adjustments. Clearly, there is merit in all these approaches and a good clinician will be familiar with a bio-psycho-social model in trying to understand and help patients.

There is also a risk of archetypal fundamentalism, of inflating the importance of the archetypal perspective. There is a school of thought that there is no such thing as mental illness, that everything is inherently a 'spiritual emergency', that support and attention of the right intensity and duration is the only measure required in every case and that medication damages or impedes this natural process. I applaud the wish to provide intensive support, but sometimes this is not enough and denies the reality of serious psychiatric disorder. This approach runs a very serious risk of being blind to those people who really do have a serious and severe mental illness that would probably respond well to the medical model. Sometimes such people are put at risk by ideology.

Of course, what is required a careful and balanced assessment using a variety of different perspectives. Skilled clinicians are usually good at working with the bio-psycho-social perspective, using drug treatments when necessary and avoiding them when they are not, developing an understanding of the psycho-social issues and recommending a psychological treatment or social intervention. What is usually missing from the model is an understanding of the archetypal dimension of human experience, the potential healing power of numinous states and the potential for difficulties to arise in states of heightened archetypal penetrance. A bio-psycho-socio-archetypal (BPSA) model would enable a better understanding of some aspects of function of the psyche that are not well explained by accepted theories and a recognition that some states currently seen as pathological can be used for growth.

Kundalini

Kundalini states provide a good example of an archetypal crisis that can lead to a more mature psycho spiritual state, but if misunderstood or mismanaged can be harmful. Kundalini is not recognised by classification systems such as DSM and does not conform to our favoured Western models of mind, body and disease processes. Kundalini, originally described in advanced yoga practice, is considered to be related to a non-physical energy or life force known as *Prana* or *Shakti*, often visualised symbolically as lying coiled at the base of the spine, like a serpent. A Kundalini awakening involves a perception of this energy rising through the spinal area in a forceful and highly charged manner accompanied by various physical, emotional and perceptual manifestations. If this happens in the prescribed manner with good preparation and integration it is said to be a profound and enlightening experience, a purifying and balancing process. But if it occurs spontaneously or without careful preparation and integration, it leads to a Kundalini crisis.

Ideally, Kundalini awakening should develop slowly as part of advanced spiritual practice, allowing a gradual adjustment to the lowering of ego defences and the opening to the deeper layers of mind. Classical descriptions from the Yogic scriptures describe the full process of Kundalini awakening as taking at least 3 years in the most advanced initiates. Experiences with similar characteristics in the West can be much shorter, but more problematic. The American psychiatrist and ophthalmologist Lee Sannella distinguishes a 'physio–kundalini' syndrome, which has the characteristics and sensations of the archetypal inrush, without the complete integrated process of a full Kundalini awakening.[103]

We have no way of properly understanding what occurs in these states, but a useful model envisages the activating energy coming into contact with the bio-psycho-social organism of our mind and body and creating turbulence as it encounters blocks or resistances in us. Sannella describes it in metaphorical terms:

> Just as an intense flow of water through a thick rubber pipe will cause the hose to whip around violently, while the same flow through a fire hose would hardly be noticed, so also does the flow of Kundalini through obstructed 'channels' within the body or mind cause motions of those areas until the obstructions have been washed out and the channels 'widened'. The terms channel, widen, blocks, must be taken metaphorically. They may not refer to actual structures, dimensions and processes, but be only useful analogies for understanding this model of Kundalini. The actual process is undoubtedly much more subtle and complex.[104]

Ram Dass likens the inrush of energy to an overdose of electricity: 'If you were a toaster, it would be like sticking your plug into 220 volts rather than 110 volts'. He goes on to describe his first experience of Kundalini:

> I thought I had damaged myself because it was so violent. As it started up my spine, it felt like a thousand snakes. As the Kundalini reached my second chakra I ejaculated automatically and it continued to rise. I remember being really frightened.[105]

Thus, we could conceptualise a Kundalini state as an archetypal crisis—usually developing out of intense spiritual practice, although it may occur spontaneously—whereas delusional mood is an archetypal crisis associated with psychiatric disorder. There is probably a spectrum of mixed states. Studying such states is likely to be helpful in distinguishing those crises where supporting the unfolding process is the best treatment from the crises where the symptoms need some suppression in order to make progress. This is a difficult area with little research evidence to guide us, although Sannella has made a detailed study of Kundalini crises, arising in a number of cultures and contexts, and provides some guidelines for distinguishing between Kundalini crisis and psychosis.[106]

According to Sannella the characteristics of Kundalini crisis include:[107]

- Sensations of heat, vibrations or fluttering moving through the body, involuntary jerks, tremors, shaking, itching or tingling
- Energy rushes or feelings of electricity circulating the body
- Intense heat (sweating) or cold

- Spontaneous pranayama, asanas, mudras and bandhas[108]
- Visions or sounds at times associated with a particular chakra
- Diminished or conversely extreme sexual desire sometimes leading to a state of constant or whole-body orgasm
- Emotional upheavals or surfacing of unwanted and repressed feelings or thoughts with certain repressed emotions becoming dominant in the conscious mind for short or long periods of time
- Other perceptual disturbances such as bright lights and pains in the head
- Unusual breathing patterns
- Any auditory hallucinations are simple such as chirping or whistling sounds but rarely intrusive voices
- If voices are heard, they are perceived as coming from within and not mistaken for outer realities
- People experiencing these states are less likely to act out or become hostile compared to people with acute psychosis
- People having Kundalini experiences are more likely to be psychologically minded and interested in their inner process

A Kundalini crisis is a period of exquisite vulnerability for the person undergoing it. Sannella reports that an adverse reaction, a schizophrenic-like condition, can result if the individual receives negative feedback either from society or from internal resistances.[109] But—and this is the most important point—the process is essentially benign and growth orientated. If the process and the individual are supported through the crisis, people report improvements in interpersonal relationships, an enhanced sense of wellbeing and a subtle but profound psychospiritual transformation.

The American Buddhist writer and teacher, Jack Kornfield describes a Kundalini-type reaction to excessive meditation at a three-month retreat.[110] It involved an overzealous young man who wanted a maximum intensity experience and sought this by meditating non-stop for 24 hours without moving. He sat through the pain that inevitably developed in his body and abruptly experienced an altered state of consciousness.

> When he got up after 24 hours, he was filled with explosive energy. He strode into the middle of the dining hall filled with one hundred silent retreatants and began to yell and practice his karate manoeuvres at triple speed. The whole room was bursting with his energy and in the silence he could feel the fear that arose in the people around him, who were very sensitive after 2 months of silence. He said 'when I look at you, I see behind you a whole trail of bodies showing your past lives'. He could not sit still or focus for a moment. Instead he was very fearful and agitated, moving in a wild and manic state, as if he had temporarily gone crazy.

Now if something like this were to happen in a public place, it is quite possible that such a person would be brought to hospital for an emergency psychiatric assessment—possibly by the Police. One can imagine a very difficult situation developing, perhaps even involving handcuffs and medication. In such a sensitive condition any perception of aggressive or unsympathetic treatment could dramatically worsen the outcome.

Experienced spiritual retreat centres are familiar with these unusual situations and have developed strategies to deal with them. This was a 'manic' high energy state which was clearly triggered by an overdose of meditation. The person concerned was overwhelmed by his highly activated psyche and couldn't integrate his experiences. Kornfield goes on to describe how they stopped him meditating and tried to harness his physical energy. They had him running, digging the garden and taking hot baths. They fed him high doses of meat, to help ground him, while every one else on the retreat was eating vegetarian food. Most importantly, they had one person with him at all times. After three days he could sleep again and was able to resume meditating slowly and carefully.

Bipolar Disorder

Medical students often joke that psychiatry only has two proper illnesses and often we cannot make up our minds which of these illnesses any particular patient is suffering from. There is a grain of truth in this. Sometimes with a person suffering their first ever psychotic illness, it is difficult to know whether their condition is bipolar disorder with psychotic features or whether it is schizophrenia with excitement and agitation. It is a useful distinction to make as the course of the two conditions and treatments are different. The diagnosis usually becomes clear in time as the person has further bouts of illness that conform more to a recognized pattern. So someone with bipolar disorder would have symptoms predominantly affecting mood—either depressed or manic—while a person with schizophrenia would often have typical hallucinatory voices, disorders of thinking and delusions without major abnormalities of mood. Schizophrenia is primarily a neurodevelopmental disorder, although environmental factors influence the onset and the course. Typically, there are the so-called negative symptoms of schizophrenia with apathy and a progressive inability to cope with the demands of the everyday world, whereas people with bipolar disorder make a more complete recovery between episodes.

The point I am making here is that often we don't know exactly how any condition will progress, and the same applies to states that seem to be more like Kundalini or spiritual emergencies. If someone has a crisis involving some unusual behavior and perceptions, we may wish for this to be a spiritual emergence requiring understanding and support, with a positive outcome within a few days, but often this does not occur. For example, with Jack Kornfield's retreatant, it is just possible that this may have been the first manifestation of a bipolar illness that was triggered by the intense stress of the retreat, although it is likely that the model of spiritual emergency or archetypal crisis is more appropriate. He seemed to settle after a few days and the precipitant was a very intense spiritual practice. Someone with a manic state of this severity due to bipolar disorder would be highly unlikely to settle so quickly; it would take weeks or even months. But we do not know this with certainty.

Bipolar disorder is a relapsing condition. 50% of people who have recovered from a serious bipolar illness will have a recurrence within one year. If someone who has a manic-type state in a spiritual context (like Kornfield's retreatant) and it does not recur in the next five years or so then we could say that it is unlikely to be bipolar disorder. Why is this important? Because bipolar disorder is a deeply distressing and disabling condition, which can usually be well managed with expert help and medication. It is painful to see a young person recovering from a bipolar illness, doing the hard work of re-establishing his or her life, returning to work or education and then abruptly stopping the medication and suffering a devastating relapse. So psychiatrists are cautious; we try to avoid relapses if at all possible and encourage people to stay on their medication if we think that it will help them.

No one wants to take medication if it is unnecessary. There are significant physical side-effects and they can certainly cause an impediment to progress and growth. It is not good enough to simply assume that any excited state is diagnostic of bipolar disorder requiring lifelong medication. Improved discrimination and diagnostic acumen are required. So how does one distinguish those manic states, which may be due to the archetypal crisis of spiritual emergence, from the manic states that are due to bipolar disorder? If a condition is recurrent, if there is an excited state of longer duration or where there is a family history of bipolar disorder, it is more likely to be bipolar disorder. But sometimes, we simply do not know.

Sean Blackwell gives a vivid account of a manic state in his book *Am I Bipolar or Just Waking Up?* Sean attended a workshop, The Forum, at a time of great crisis in his life, which triggered an excited, manic-type state. Eventually, Sean thought that he was dead and waited to get to heaven:

> But the path to heaven was much more difficult than I'd imagined. I'd done everything possible to get there. I'd stripped naked, tried to push myself through a concrete floor, knocked on all the ballroom doors, even tried to turn the lights out in a hotel! That's when the cops grabbed me.[111]

Sean had an unpleasant but brief hospital admission and seems to have largely recovered with a day or two. He felt strongly that the illness paradigm was not helpful for him, more that he was undergoing a profound spiritual process that needed to be explored and developed. He immersed himself in literature such *The Autobiography of a Yogi* and *The Tibetan Book of Living and Dying* and found a psychospiritual practice in holotropic breathwork where he could gently rediscover and integrate his experiences. Ten years later, there had been no further episodes and Sean was convinced that his apparent illness had been an important part of his awakening, a true spiritual emergence. Sean's story shows how an abrupt onset manic state triggered by intense psychospiritual practice, with rapid resolution accompanied by a highly motivated psychological mindset, does not necessarily develop into bipolar disorder and can be better understood as an archetypal crisis in the context of spiritual emergence.

The American psychologist David Lukoff is a co-author of the 'religious or spiritual problem' diagnostic category that made its appearance in the fourth version of DSM in 1994. He has personal experience, describing his own crisis as follows:

> My interest in spirituality and mental health dates back to 1971, when I spent 2 months in a spiritual crisis—convinced that I was a reincarnation of Buddha and Christ with a messianic mission to save the world. In my clinical practice as a psychologist and my work with the Spiritual Emergence Network for the past 25 years, I have often found myself face-to-face with individuals with the same beliefs. By giving me a rare opportunity to go through the complete cycle and phenomenology of a naturally resolving psychotic episode, my spiritual emergency was a valuable clinical experience as well as a spiritual awakening![112]

Spiritual Emergency

Spiritual emergency was a term coined by the psychiatrist Stanislav Grof and his wife Christina to describe the variety of unusual mental states that can arise as crises of personal transformation. The term *spiritual emergency* is a play on words suggesting both a serious crisis (an 'emergency') but also the inherent opportunity for *emergence* to a higher level of psychological organization with an enhanced sense of spirituality. There are three crucial points that the Grofs emphasize:[113]

- These visionary states have played a crucial part in our social and religious heritage. Indeed, preindustrial cultures placed high value on such non-ordinary states of consciousness.

- Such states are perfectly natural. They have a natural tendency towards positive resolution and should be supported rather than suppressed with medication.
- They should not be confused with diseases that have a biological cause and which require medical treatment, but modern psychiatry, psychology and medicine has little understanding or indeed interest in these non-ordinary states.

Spiritual emergencies are a subset of archetypal crisis. If a person has a mindset, such as Sean Blackwell's, that understands the crisis in spiritual terms then the concept of spiritual emergency is likely to be enormously helpful. However, in my experience it is only a small minority of people in archetypal crisis that have such a mindset. Moreover, as the Grofs point out, there is a real danger of spiritual fundamentalism by seeking to understand all abnormal mental states as spiritual opportunities and not providing appropriate treatment for an organic problem.[114] A balanced approach is required.

Mixed States—Marion's Story

Sometimes both archetypal crisis and bipolar disorder co-exist causing a mixed state.

The defining moment of Marion's life happened when she was twenty-four and she accompanied her boyfriend to a retreat at Esalen for an experience of holotropic breathwork. She later described it as like a near-death experience in that she thought that she had died. She went through a tunnel and into the light where she felt connected with incredible bliss and unity. This was in the days before these states involving tunnels and light had become common knowledge; Marion had not heard accounts of such experiences before.

Marion was brought up in New York. She was clever—excelling at school, high-minded and always interested in religious and spiritual matters in a way that was not particularly encouraged by her family. She was of the generation that was involved in the protest movement against the war in Vietnam. Her experience at Esalen changed the direction of her life from a budding career in finance towards spiritual pursuits. She couldn't see any point in going to any more retreats or doing any more holotropic breathwork as she felt that she had been given the experience that she needed to redefine her life. She had found her path. She found a spiritual community in Britain where she stayed for some years. The community later ran into problems but by then Marion had come to a point where she needed new challenges and wanted to participate in the world in a different way. She returned to the USA and developed a career in the hotel industry with the man who became her husband and they started a family. She meditated every day and her spiritual life seemed to sit comfortably alongside her material life. So far, so good.

She was in her early fifties and the hotel business was going through a difficult period. Besides, it didn't seem to interest her so much anymore. Her marriage was fine on the surface but she and her husband didn't talk very much and they had stopped making love. She wasn't depressed, but life seemed a little grey and uninspired. She went on a retreat. This was not just a standard meditation retreat but one that involved fasting, long periods of sustained meditation and some intense group sessions. One evening, at the closing meditation, she felt a deep sense of connection to the cosmos and she re-experienced the same numinous feelings of bliss and unity that she had had all those years ago at Esalen. Although the experience was transient, its impact remained. The rest of the retreat passed uneventfully. She meditated, she ate and she slept normally—but she knew that something in herself had fundamentally shifted.

She went home and told her husband that she wanted to sell the business. The children were grown up by now and she felt she had fulfilled her obligations to the family. She wanted to go back to Britain and reconnect with her spiritual life. Her mother was English, she felt connected to the place and she felt that her future lay there. She told her husband about her numinous experience at the retreat and her husband was most concerned. He did not like what he was hearing and he most certainly did not want to move to the UK. He took Marion to a psychiatrist and explained that she had been behaving strangely, had some odd ideas about cosmic oneness and bliss, and that she wanted to sell the business. The psychiatrist made a diagnosis of bipolar disorder and medication was started.

Forward a few years: Marion comes to see me in London. The lady that walked into my consulting room was a most impressive and mature human being who radiated calm, humility and wisdom nicely mixed with humor. The story that emerged indicated to me that both her retreat experiences, separated by some 30 years, had all the hallmarks of a spiritual epiphany, a numinous experience of the beautiful kind, without any of the hallmarks of psychiatric disorder. I didn't think that these experiences could be reduced to bipolar disorder at all. But, to complicate matters, within a year or so of the retreat Marion had suffered a difficult bout of depression lasting a few weeks followed by a period when she experienced accelerated thought, and increased energy and well being. She was talking faster than normal, she had reduced need for sleep and she found himself getting into arguments, which was most unusual for her. This lasted for a

few weeks and then settled without causing any major problems. It had
happened on two occasions since. Marion had been keeping a mood chart,
which showed precisely these times when she had developed hypomanic
states.

These states seemed entirely consistent with a mild form of bipolar
disorder. I reviewed her story again very carefully. It was clear that she
had not shown any signs of bipolar disorder before her fifties, but she did
have two relatives with bipolar disorder and one aunt had suffered from it
badly. She certainly had a family history indicating a probable genetic
predisposition.

I acquired Marion's notes from her previous psychiatrists (there had
been a few by now) and I met her new partner who thought she was absolutely normal, if rather over-medicated. Putting it all together, it seemed to
me that she had her two numinous experiences or archetypal crises that had
shaped her life in a profound way and which were not caused by any psychiatric disorder. Then, in her mid fifties, she had developed mild bipolar
disorder, which was now in remission. The current issue was her strong
feeling that her ongoing journey through life was being impaired by medication and she wondered if she could stop it. It seemed an easy decision to
tell her that she could indeed stop this medication. Of course, there was a
risk of a relapse of bipolar disorder one day in the future, but I felt confident that any recurrence would probably be mild, that we could work well
together if there were any further problems and that she had the ideal mindset to manage and integrate any unusual experiences.

The relationship between bipolar disorder and numinous experience is
complex. Certainly, religious epiphanies frequently occur as part of a
manic illness, but, in practice, they are rarely integrated and do not often
lead to positive change. Someone who was developing a bipolar-type
manic upswing might attend a workshop or retreat which would then accelerate the condition, but most people who have epiphanies at retreats do not
go on to develop recurrent mood disorders. My suspicion is that the genetic
inheritance predisposing to mood disorders may also predispose to a raising of archetypal penetrance. So it may be that people with more than the
average amount of genetic predisposition to psychiatric disorders are more
likely to have archetypal crises, including spiritual epiphanies. Once again,
madness and mysticism may both arise from an increased sensitivity to the
archetypal.

CHAPTER 11

The Journey to the Self

We shall not cease from exploration

And the end of all our exploring

Will be to arrive where we started

And know the place for the first time.

—T. S. Eliot, 'Little Gidding'.

The Grail Within

Like all good legends, the tale of King Arthur and his knights is loaded with symbolism.[115] Arthur is the boy of destiny who develops his ego structures wisely and becomes a great king at Camelot. Merlin is the wise elder, the mutative presence, the shape-shifter who can change things through a deeper knowledge of the mysteries of existence. We have the wonderfully phallic sword Excalibur, emerging from the womb of the lake presented by its supernatural Lady. There are beautiful women and gallant men. Arthurian knights are rumbustious; it is a manly world with much cleaving of heads from bodies, but there is a prevailing mood of chivalry that promotes decency and ethical behavior. Arthur models how to be a wise leader, a first among equals around the Round Table. There are many remarkable adventures; the Court flourishes and becomes the envy of the world.

Once again, the Court symbolizes the persona and in Camelot we see the shaping of an idyllic structure, a symbol of a balanced and functional ego. But inevitably, there are challenges. There is a mid-life crisis at Camelot as the knights become disturbed by an esoteric vision and start abandoning the Court to seek the mysterious Holy Grail. There is an encounter with the shadow as dark forces gather. There is depression as the land becomes barren through a 'dolorous stroke', a complex wound of body and soul. The perfect queen, Guinevere commits adultery with the best knight, Sir Lancelot. There is a final battle where Arthur meets his shadow figure, Sir Mordred. Both meet their end but there is the promise of rebirth as Arthur is borne away by the Lady of the Lake and waits in mythic Avalon.[116]

The Grail legend is probably a fusion of Celtic mythology and Christianity. For the Celts, the Cauldron was a mutative ceremonial vessel while, according to Christian lore, Joseph of Arimathea caught the blood of Jesus in a chalice and transported it to England for safe keeping. The Grail vision provokes an archetypal crisis for Arthur and the assembled knights at Camelot. It has a tantalizing captivating quality; once it has been glimpsed, the yearning to find it again trumps other considerations and many knights immediately embark on a quest to find it. It turns out to be a dangerous quest; half of the knights either do not return or meet ruin.

Arthur's knights are used to getting what they want. This is a world where might is right, but the Grail, this numinous life-giving object, cannot be won by these means; entirely different qualities are required. It transpires that it can only be won by virtue, not strength. Lancelot comes close but cannot grasp hold of it because he is an adulterer. According to one legend, Sir Galahad, the most perfect gentle knight, eventually gained access to the Grail. His life became complete and together with the Grail he ascended to Heaven. According to another version, the Grail is won by Perceval, a boy of simplicity, an uncorrupted child of nature who is not at all attracted to material considerations. The Grail is entirely non-physical so it cannot be grasped by flesh and blood. It is a symbol of our transcendent core and the Grail legend is the story of our interior journey, the passage to the Self.

Atman or Self

The psyche in its deepest reaches, participates in a form of existence beyond space and time, and thus partakes of what is inadequately and symbolically described as eternity.[117]

Carl Jung

The first documented pioneers of the interior world were the Hindu sages of the Upanishads. They found that by progressively deeper meditation, by turning towards their interior and analysing the data presented by the mind, that they could penetrate below their perceptions to a bedrock beyond time and space where any sense of a separate ego entirely disappeared. This bedrock lay below a layer of ceaseless flux of matter dissolving and coming together in different forms, which we now know is analogous to the perspective of quantum physics. It was something changeless, an infinite indivisible reality quite different to the transient data of our common experience.

The Brahmins called the bedrock Brahma, the divine Ground of existence distinguishing it from the illusory, deceptive world of our senses, which they termed Maya. Brahma is everywhere and everything; it is continuous with the spark within us, which the Hindus called Atman.[118] Atman pervades us utterly, as Krishna tells the hero of the Bhagavad Gita: 'I am the Self in the heart of every creature, Arjuna, and the beginning, middle and end of their existence'.[119]

The Self is Jung's God term, comparable to Plato's form of the Good and to the Hindu Atman. The term *Self* can be confusing as it is entirely different to the personal self (or ego) or the part of our ego that we chose to show to the world (our persona). The Self is at the apex of the pyramid of archetypes; indeed, it is beyond archetype, for it is the primal unity from which archetypes flow. For Jung, the Self and the archetypes provided a top-down organising function in the psyche while the ego awakens in a world that is already structured by the archetypes. The anima and animus are mid-zone archetypes and Jungians generally consider that monotheistic religions derive from the Self archetype, while polytheistic religions originate from the anima / animus structures. The Self, like every archetype, is unknowable but we can taste an archetypal image of the Self in many ways. An opening to Self may provide a peak experience, a memorable moment of cosmic union, but more commonly it will be a modest experience, a quiet moment, the still small voice. The Self comes to us as symbols in many ways. It never leaves us.

For the materialist, for whom all mental phenomena derive from physical matter, the postulated presence of Atman or the Self is a more sophisticated version of the tooth fairy or Father Christmas. It is a vestige of an out-dated and primitive worldview. There is no objective evidence for the existence of the Self for it has no mass, no chemical structure, it is not part of the electromagnetic spectrum and it cannot be located using brain imaging techniques. The empirical evidence for the Self is gained by introspection; it may take some years but the contemplative path is available to anyone. However, evidence gained by an individual will not necessarily persuade anyone else and, besides, it fails the crucial test of science by not being falsifiable.[120]

A psychoanalytic interpretation of the Self concept would include two major themes: Firstly, our narcissistic need to defend the psyche against fear of extinction and death; and secondly our projection of the nourishing, protecting all-powerful breast with its power to soothe and restore harmony onto a different canvas. Is Atman merely a projection of an idyllic version of our earliest infantile relationship?

The Self can seem an abstract and mystical construct. Does it really exist or is it a primitive fantasy? Is it a useful concept? How does it help us in our lives? This is one those great questions that promises creativity or division. It certainly divides the Jungians from the Freudians, the personal psychologists from those of a transpersonal persuasion, and the mystics from the materialists. From an archetypal perspective, the concept of the Self is absolutely central. Indeed, finding a closer relationship with the Self could be considered to the whole point of the journey through life. But— and this is a very big but—the Self can only be accessed if, like the knights of the Round Table putting away their swords and seeking virtue, we abandon the aggressively self- assertive ego. Any victory for Self inevitably feels like a defeat for ego, as Jung observed. How then, can we in the modern world find a way of putting enough ego function aside to create a space where there can be a reunion with Self? This leads us to the theme of ego death and rebirth—a process described by Joseph Campbell as the hero's journey.[121]

Joseph Campbell and the Hero's Journey

Joseph Campbell (1904-1987) is widely acknowledged to be the world's greatest expert on mythology. He was influenced by Krishnamurti as a young man, then by Jung. In his maturity, he became an influential mentor to the burgeoning transpersonal psychology movement that emerged in the 1960s, shaping the views of people such as Stanislav Grof, the psychiatrist who became the leading authority on the therapeutic use of non-ordinary states of consciousness. Campbell described how myths from cultures throughout the world and throughout time tell essentially the same story. This is the story of spiritual awakening and an encounter with the great mystery that brings us away from the path of the ego towards the Self. It is the story of individuation, of moving towards a position of greater wholeness.

Campbell called this archetypal story the 'monomyth', or the hero's journey, as it is more popularly known. The hero is someone who hears a call and follows it. Usually the person is reasonably well adjusted but has a yearning for something different from the everyday realities of life. This call can take many forms but typically has a numinous flavour, ranging in intensity from subtle to strident. Like the first sighting of the Holy Grail, it is mutative, it can't be ignored and it is either acted on or actively squashed. Acting on the call means upsetting the status quo and precipitating a set of changes or a crisis. The structures of a life such as family, income or mortgage often have to be addressed before the journey begins.

The hero's journey is always a struggle, which is why heroic qualities are required. There is a confrontation bringing a death of the old self and a birth of a new structure—the ego-infused-with-Self—as the hero returns enriched and reborn. Along the way, the hero gets help through this journey of transformation, often in mysterious ways. There may be synchronicities indicating the presence of grace and a deeper sense of destiny. He may receive gifts of power. Thus armed, the hero goes to the threshold of another world, a gate or an entrance that is guarded by a guardian or demons (including the hero's demons). A confrontation takes place between the hero and the guardian, which is somehow resolved and integrated so that the hero can continue through the threshold with the transformed guardian by his side.

The hero finds himself in an extraordinary place, the 'Mysterium', the enchanted forest, and experiences a different sort of reality. Feeling strengthened by the encounter with the guardian, he meets his supreme ordeal, the great battle. This is the point where there may be a difficult numinous experience, a moment of madness, an encounter with the shadow. In facing his greatest challenge, the hero finds the treasure or his Holy Grail. This is a gift of life or rebirth and with it the hero leaves the Mysterium behind. He returns home, the awareness and insights of his voyage remain with him, and he takes his place in the world, enriched and reborn.

Jack's Magical Beans

There is a tide in the affairs of men, which taken at the flood, leads on to fortune. Omitted, all the voyage of their life is bound in shallows and in miseries. On such a full sea are we now afloat, And we must take the current when it serves, Or lose our ventures.[122]

William Shakespeare

Once upon a time, there was a poor widow who had a son called Jack. Their only possessions were her house and her cow, Milky White. All they had to live on was the cow's milk, which they sold at the market. But Milky White's milk dried up and they didn't know what to do. This was a crisis. The widow was desperate, depressed and pessimistic while Jack, being a cheerful lad, felt sure that something would turn up. They decided to sell the cow, so Jack took the cow to market. He hadn't gone far when he met a funny little old man who said 'hello Jack'. Jack wondered how he knew his name, as he didn't remember having seen him before. So they started talking and one thing led to another and Jack found himself swapping the cow for a handful of beans. It seemed like a good idea at the time. There was something rather special about the old man, his twinkle, his promise that the beans were magical and that it would be an excellent exchange. Jack was completely dazzled by him and went home with a spring in his step, feeling that he was indeed a clever and fortunate fellow.

Of course, his mother didn't see it that way at all. She called him an idiot for being tricked by an old scoundrel into parting with their only possession of any value. She knew that this would mean destitution. She was furious, worried and very disappointed in Jack. She swore at him and threw the stupid beans right out of the window. But the beans were indeed magical; they sprouted overnight and an enormous structure had grown, which extended as far as the eye could see, right up into the heavens. Jack, being a bold lad, went scurrying up. He was probably desperate to get away from his mother. It was like climbing a ladder, not hard at all. He went right up into the sky and eventually reached another land. He stepped off and there was a road that led directly to a house, a very big house indeed.

Jack is in a different world now, but he doesn't seem at all bothered as he steps merrily down the road to the house, where he finds a very tall woman, a giantess. She is friendly and feeds him, which is very welcome because he is very hungry. This woman, who is larger than life, warns him that he is in great danger because her man, the ogre, will be coming home soon and there is nothing that he likes more than boys on toast for his breakfast. Sure enough, the ground starts shaking, the ogre is returning. Jack is in mortal danger and hides in the oven. But the ogre senses his presence:

> Fee-fi-fo-fum,
> I smell the blood of an Englishman,
> Be he alive, or be he dead,
> I'll grind his bones to make my bread

But the giantess throws him off the scent and protects Jack, saying it must be the lingering aroma of yesterday's Englishman. The ogre eats three calves for breakfast instead and goes to sleep. Jack hears him snoring, seizes his moment to escape and takes something of value with him. There are different versions of what happens next, but the essential ingredient is the goose that lays the golden eggs. Some versions have a magic harp that plays the most beautiful music. Some versions have Jack making three trips, some have just the one trip. The giant wakes up and chases Jack, who has to run for his life holding his booty. No doubt this is the most terrifying moment of his life. He races down the beanstalk, takes an axe and brings the edifice crashing down so that the ogre falls to his death. His mother is overjoyed that he has not only survived but that their problems are suddenly resolved. They have wealth, in the form of golden eggs, and they will live happily ever after.

This is a deeply condensed story rich in meaning on a number of different levels. It is worth unpicking the main themes in some detail. They can be summarised as follows:

- The crisis
- The incomplete family
- The fool
- The trickster
- Turning away from material things
- Dark night of the soul
- Something sprouts
- Journey to the upper world
- Sense of mortal danger
- Help from an unexpected source
- Overcoming something big and terrifying
- Taking home the golden goose
- Permanent enrichment by something of great value that comes from within

Milky White

There are different layers to the crisis. The bottom layer is one of basic biological survival. Jack and his mother are hungry. They are destitute and the source of their meagre and precarious living has dried up. There is something very symbolic in the cow and her milk. The name Milky White has connotations of the breast, not only as a source of nourishment but also as a sexual characteristic. This points to Jack's development crisis as an adolescent trying to navigate his way from the needs of childhood to the needs of an adult man. An adolescent boy living with his single mother is always going to have some difficulties negotiating the complicated feelings around his awakening sexuality, maintaining a loving relationship with his mother while keeping her out of his masturbation fantasies.

There is a psychoanalytic interpretation of Jack and the beanstalk by Bruno Bettelheim in his interpretation of fairy tales—*The Uses of Enchantment*.[123] Bettelheim understands Jack's journey as a progression from the Freudian oral to phallic phase of development. Jack swaps the cow, representing maternal milk, for seeds which sprout in the night. This is a phallic structure on which he climbs hand over hand and, from a Freudian perspective, this seems a clear reference to masturbation. Indeed, his mother is very impressed by the structure associated with seeds that grows in the night, just outside the door. In Bettelheim's analysis, Jack engages in an oedipal struggle with the ogre and wins over the favour of the ogre's wife. Thus, his own internal oedipal struggles related to his mother are transposed to another arena and another parental couple. By putting his axe to the ogre, Jack decisively gains maturity by freeing himself of the view of the father as a destructive ogre and moves on from his belief in the magical power of the phallus being magically able to bring him all the things that he needs in life. A story with archetypal significance and a high intensity of meaning will always be interpretable on a number of different levels and Bettelheim's perspective is valid in relation to the development of a functional ego. But the story means so much more than this.

The Fool

Jack was a common name for the hero in medieval fairy tales and holds the meaning of a joker—a Jack the lad. He is like the fool in the tarot deck, an immortal wanderer, a rebellious upsetter of the established order. The tarot fool is a deeply archetypal figure representing the hero at the outset of the journey. The fool urges us on through places where the thinking rational mind would hold us back. This is someone who is destined to take the high and difficult road, the road with all its challenges, its potential for disaster and the possibility of mutative transformation. Like Shakespeare's Puck in *A Midsummer Night's Dream*, he can wander between the worlds, the world of ordinary reality and the world of non-ordinary reality. Like Puck, he may sometimes mix up these different levels of reality and cause confusion to himself and others. This is his prime function—to bring us insights from the deeper psyche. Jack is potentially a Promethean figure who brings us the gift of fire from the gods.

Jack stands for not being entirely logical, not being driven solely by the left brain but blessed with a touch of genius. In his case, his genius is the ability to be in tune with the deeper Self and to trust in Grace. Jack will do his best to get on in the material world and he is not unwilling to play the bio-psycho-social game. He will do his best to make progress in everyday reality, and he will try to escape from poverty and look after his family. He has an understanding of what his duties and obligations are but he is open to the magical and the divine. He may be seen as foolish, but he has energy and courage. As the story unfolds, we also see that Jack is completely amoral. He travels light and he takes what he needs. He's a thief.

We all need an inner Jack. But Jack has a dark side and we should not be seduced by him. The Pied Piper of Hamelin represents a Jack-like figure who robbed a community of its vitality and life by enticing away the children. The Pied Piper was a dazzling character who played intoxicating music and wore a multitude of colours. This is an archetypal image, which may have its roots in a historical event, such as the plague or the children's crusade. It also applies to the period of the 1960s when many parents would have felt that their children were lost to an intoxicating mixture of magical colours, music and a mental state that their parents could not understand.[124] Peter Pan lived in a place of magical fantasy, Never Never Land. He stayed with his gang, the lost boys, and he declined the development challenge, he failed to grow up at all. Indeed, the inspiration for the Peter Pan figure was the author's brother who died in a skating accident at the age of 13 when thin ice gave way and he disappeared into the lake beneath him.

So the fool is a very vulnerable figure. As is always the case in a crisis, there is potential for a good or bad outcome. It could go either way; this is the stage in the process where the next intervention is crucial. Whatever happens in this critical period will have a disproportionate effect. The fool, and what the fool represents in ourselves, is in a highly suggestible state and unusually sensitive to influence.

Then Jack meets the trickster, as we all do at some stage in our life, who gives us a clear choice between stasis and growth. Why did Jack make an apparently irrational decision with his family's most valuable asset? Did Jack recognise something in the trickster figure, perhaps a certain cast of eye that indicated a knowledge of deeper realities? What did he hear in the old man's voice? In accepting the transaction, Jack makes a decisive turn away from Main Street. He has accepted the call. There are a number of factors that may affect whether we opt for the slow-growth, low-risk route or the perilous hero's journey. There is always risk involved; there is a dynamic tension between staying too safe to grow and being so open to change that there are no roots to support growth. We may need a catalyst such as the trickster, or we may have a genetic predisposition for numinous experience or we may be at a time of crisis in our life. Why indeed would we upset a settled life if there were no crisis of some kind to upset the status quo?

There is a story attributed to the Tibetan Buddhist teacher Chogyam Trungpa Rimpoche that illustrates the importance of understanding the potential perils of the journey to the Self. This is not a path for the half-hearted and there should be a process of informed consent. In other words, people embarking on it need to develop an appropriate mindset, even if they find themselves thrust onto the path without consciously intending it. They need to know that there are significant side effects and that they need to have staying power and determination. Trungpa was giving a talk to a large assembly and he asked for a show of hands of those who were new to meditation or spiritual practice. A large number of people raised their hands. 'My suggestion is that you go home' he said:

We will give you your money back and you can go home now and not get started in this difficult process. It is a lot more difficult than you think. Once you start it is very difficult to stop. So my suggestion is that you do not begin. Best not to start at all. But if you do—it is best to finish.[125]

CHAPTER 12

Icarus and Narcissus

Your task is not to seek for love, but merely to seek and find all the barriers within yourself that you have built against it.

—Rumi

The great myths are simple stories with deeper layers of meaning that speak to the great themes that course through our human lives. The myths of Icarus and Narcissus show us some of the ways in which people may be damaged by the journey out of Plato's cave into the dazzling light of the sun. The hero's journey has its side effects and its casualties.

In classical Greece, Icarus was the foolish youth who flew too high. He rose so close to the sun that the wax holding his wings together was melted by the heat, so he fell. The fall of Icarus is a fragment of a much larger story, but it symbolises the sudden tragic end, the hubris of the moth that is dazzled and burned by the brightness of the light. Icarus did not fall a little way and learn from his mistake. This was not a false step on the heroic journey. Icarus was killed stone dead. There was no growth for Icarus.

Icarus was the son of the enormously talented Daedalus, the magician and advisor to kings. Daedalus was the wise man of his age. It was Daedalus who made the wings out of feathers and wax to escape imprisonment in a tower. It was Daedalus who had helped the mythic hero Theseus slay the Minotaur, the shadowy monstrous devourer of golden youth, who was kept hidden in the labyrinth. Icarus was presumably earmarked to be the heir, the hero apparent. Daedalus had told him not to fly too close to the sun but Icarus just could not resist.

The sun that burned his wings symbolises the lure of the Self archetype that holds such numinous intensity that it can overwhelm and achieve primacy over all over considerations. These high-intensity images of the Self may have a gravitational pull that is so strong, so compelling, that the wise voice of counsel is neither heard nor heeded. The wings, symbolising the ego structures that carry us, are melted by the power, the heat, the intensity of the sun so that there is no structure left to sustain our flight and we crash.

Psychiatric disorders, with their exposure to numinous experience, not infrequently provide Icarus-type experiences. These can happen literally or metaphorically. The problem for Icarus was that he did not have the equipment, the maturity of personality, to manage his exposure to the image of the archetypal Self. Some psychiatric disorders not only make it more likely that a person may experience a numinous Self image, but, because of the nature of the illness, they also make the experience of the Self particularly difficult to manage and integrate.

Simon and the Madonna

Simon had a severe form of bipolar disorder. There was no doubt about the diagnosis for he was now in his thirties and had a number of classical manic episodes since the age of 18. He had a typical relapse signature with increasing elation, reduced need for sleep and increasingly bizarre behaviour usually culminating in an act of aggression or disinhibition in a public place leading to hospitalisation. In between his illnesses, he functioned well, living with his very supportive family and working on his Ph.D. thesis. He came from a family that was mildly religious and he described himself as 'relaxed Jewish'.

Every time Simon became ill, he became very religious. Indeed, his family had learned to recognise that Simon becoming more religious was a sign of developing illness. They did not associate being religious with mental illness in general terms but it certainly seemed to work that way with Simon. Often the family were able to summon psychiatric help for Simon before matters got out of hand. When Simon was well, he fully agreed that a developing preoccupation with religion was an early sign of illness and that he would get some help. But when he started to relapse, his religious sense became so profound and so intense for him that it trumped any other consideration. When it started, all he really wanted to do was to go deeper into it. He wanted the experience to become more intense and more sacred; the last thing that he wanted was help. In psychiatric terminology, Simon lost insight very early.

Now insight is one of those controversial terms. It could be defined as whether or not a patient is in agreement with the psychiatrist's interpretation of their condition. If you don't agree with your psychiatrist, then the psychiatrist might say that you lack insight and need more treatment. Often, as patients become more experienced, they become more adept at recognising the early warning signs of their condition and distinguishing these from the vicissitudes and mood states of everyday life. Often they can manage the symptoms themselves or seek the appropriate help, but sometimes the developing mental state is so powerful and so intense that it dominates consciousness to the extent that previous perspectives are lost. This is what invariably happened to Simon.

When I met Simon for the first time, he had literally fallen like Icarus from a high place and he was seriously injured. He was still unconscious on the neurosurgical unit, his face was swollen from his facial fractures and he had undergone an evacuation of a blood clot from his brain. The early indications were that he would be fortunate to avoid some permanent brain damage. But he would survive. He was safe and he was being well looked after. He had fallen or jumped from the top storey of his house. His family told the trauma team that he had been showing some early signs of relapse of his bipolar disorder, so I was called to assess him. Inevitably, it was some days before he was able to tell me what had happened leading up to his fall. In the meantime, I had started him on the medication that always seemed to work for him when he was manic. By the time he was able to speak to me, his mood state was almost back to normal. He understood what had happened to him but his memory was hazy and he could not remember anything that had happened on the day of his injury.

His most important memory began some days before his fall. He remembered a rising delicious spiritual feeling that gained great intensity. It was such a gorgeous experience, he said. He became increasingly aware of a close connection to transcendent figures such as Krishna and the Virgin Mary. He felt their presence. It wasn't that he saw them or heard them, he actually felt them and it was the most beautiful thing. He remembers developing a notion that he had to sacrifice himself in order to placate or develop his relationship with these figures. He wanted to do this more than anything else, even if it would cost him his life. The Madonna became the dominant figure. He could not describe to me how beautiful she was. He wanted to be with her.

Luke Meets His Mother Again

Luke was 17 when his mother died. She had a late diagnosis of cancer and went from being a normal healthy mother to a dead mother within a few months. Luke's father was a man of few words. He didn't really know how to deal with his own grief let alone the grief of his son. They didn't talk much. They visited her grave together a couple of times and then the matter was quietly dropped. There was no flowing of tears, no healing grieving process. Luke was supposed to get on with it, like a good young

Englishman. Luke was very clever. He threw himself into his studies and got a place at a good university. In his first term he took LSD for the first time. He remembers going to a very beautiful place in his mind where all was beautiful and perfect, it was like a heavenly garden. He remembers an extraordinary spiritual feeling. He understood for the first time that all the stuff of the scriptures and religion was essentially true. He understood that the universe was composed of love. He had a meeting with the spirit of his mother who was serene and happy. His mother stayed with him for a while in the garden and all was well.

Hours passed and Luke stayed in a blissful state where there was no pain. He felt that this was the most important experience of his life. The LSD wore off but Luke never entirely returned to how he was. University seemed meaningless and he couldn't see much point in it anymore. The effort and demands of everyday life had lost its appeal. All Luke really wanted to do was see his mother again in the beautiful garden. He took LSD again and he tried increasing the dose. He tried other drugs too—but nothing seemed to work. He wasn't able to get back to the garden. Meanwhile, university was going badly and he was beginning to alienate people with his behaviour. He started hearing voices. At first the voices were soft and he hoped they might be a manifestation of his mother but gradually they became more unpleasant, derogatory and threatening. One thing led to another and he found himself in a psychiatric unit.

Judging from the hospital records that were sent to me, his psychiatrist clearly hoped that this was a drug-induced psychosis and that Luke would return to his normal self with some good care, a safe environment and abstinence from substances. But this didn't happen. Some low dose medication was started, but the antipsychotics didn't seem to be very effective either. Very gradually, over a period of a few months, Luke seemed to settle, the voices were diminishing and had become less unpleasant. Luke started to have some leave at home with his father. On one such visit, he walked out of the hospital to the nearest train station and jumped from the railway bridge on to the track below.

Simon and Luke both had intoxicating encounters with a female figure of great allure, a numinous mother figure, which fuelled their developing illness. Both had a yearning for an empathic female figure and Luke had a degree of grief for his mother that was very raw and deeply painful for him. Simon and Luke both eventually walked out of hospital and returned to their regular psychiatric teams for on-going care. Both of them were of unusually high intelligence and both had damaged their brains to some extent, which would make it their forward progress significantly harder for them. The body has its shock absorbers, the crumple zones that give some protection to the vital organs, the spinal cord and brain when a person falls in a feet first position. Brain and spinal cord injuries are surprisingly uncommon in people who survive these falls. But Simon and Luke were unlucky in many ways.

I do not know if anything could have been done to prevent these events. I thought that their treatment was generally of a high standard before their respective falls. A psychotherapist had been working gently and progressively with Luke in his unit before he jumped and Simon had been closely supervised by his family and his psychiatric team, but ultimately they were both unable to resist the allure of their numinous encounters. The pull of the sacred was too strong and overcame their rational selves. We agreed that it would be very difficult to help them to stay safe in the future. They both admitted to a yearning to have those beautiful feelings again. They both needed treatment to keep their conditions under control and, of course, there was a real tension between their wish to remain 'well', which would involve taking anti-psychotic medication and their wish to stop the medication and seek another taste of the numinous.

Max the Seeker

Max was indeed a man who fell to earth. He had walked off a balcony three stories above the ground. The phone call from the trauma surgeon indicated that he seemed confused and was talking about sauce. When I spoke to him on the Intensive Care unit, he told me that he had indeed wanted to merge with the Source. He still did. He indicated to me an aching, a longing to be joined with the divine. Max was in a very serious condition. He had sustained the typical multiple fractures that you get when your body hits the ground feet first including a complicated fracture to his pelvis. His nervous system was not damaged. The surgeons had fixed his broken femurs but he would be on bed rest while his pelvis mended and he was going to be with us at the Royal London Hospital for about 2 months.

Max's story emerged slowly. I saw him a number of times and his mother filled in some gaps. He had been a sensitive child. His parents had split up when he was young and for some years it had just been Max and his mother. Max admired his father, but contact with him was limited and petered out. His mother told me that life had been difficult and she had not been in a good place herself. When Max was reaching puberty, his mother had remarried. Soon afterwards she had a baby girl. Max had really minded. He didn't get on with his stepfather and he didn't like his baby sister. He wasn't shy of showing his feelings of anger and resentment and he gave his mother a hard time. He had never been very sociable at school, but he seemed to withdraw into himself further. He had some friends, but didn't seem to be close to anyone. After leaving school with good grades, he carried on living at home. He studied psychology and spent as much time as he could with his mother. He got along more amicably with his stepfather and his little sister by now but his mother was always his primary relationship.

One day Max decided to see a guru who was passing through his hometown. The guru was famous and came from India. It was a large meeting but the guru spoke individually to each person there. Max described a certain look in his eyes and a feeling of peace and wonderment when the guru spoke a few words to him. It was not so much the words, it was more his tone and the look in his eye. It seemed to convey a transcendent sense of love and compassion. The guru touched him and something like an electric shock went through him. Max felt that his world had changed in that moment. He told me that he felt that the particles of his being had been fundamentally rearranged. He left the meeting and suddenly the rest of the world and indeed his life seemed dull and nondescript. He decided that there was nothing of the conventional world that interested him. He determined to take the 'spiritual path'.

Max threw himself into his task. He sought gurus and workshops, epiphanies and retreats all over the world. He wanted quick results. He was not interested in meditating for years or joining an ashram. He didn't want to study with one particular organisation. No, he wanted peak experiences and he wanted them quickly. Max seemed unable to find a benign father figure and I gained the impression that he had a talent for finding the disturbed, the extreme and the abusive gurus and teachers. He told me of at least one guru who sexually abused him. It seemed that he spent a great deal of his mother's money. His developing career in psychology petered out.

Sometimes Max felt he was getting somewhere. There had been a few times when he had had a glimpse of 'the light' as he put it. There had been a retreat in the desert in Arizona with fasting, sweat lodges and chanting where he had a sense of ecstatic reunion with God or cosmic oneness. When the retreat had ended, he had felt bereft and had tried to drown himself in a bucket of water. He wanted to dissolve his ego, he wanted to be 'with the divine' and thought that ending his life was the most sure way of achieving this. He spent a few days in a psychiatric unit afterwards but was discharged without treatment.

His money had run out eventually and he came back to live with his mother. He was in his thirties now and he had not worked for a while. He had no real friends and had never had a long-term relationship. His stepfather and sister had moved out and for a while he had his mother to himself but now his mother was developing a close friendship with another man. Max told me that he didn't want to die, exactly. He certainly wasn't depressed, but he wanted to go to Heaven. He just walked off the balcony to be with the light.

Narcissism and Psychic Retreats

Narcissus was a good-looking boy and he knew it.[126] The beautiful nymph Echo fell in love with his beauty and pursued him. She declared her feelings for him but he rejected her. Narcissus was so vain that he did not want to have a relationship with anybody at all. Enter Nemesis the goddess of revenge and retribution. Nemesis lured Narcissus to a forest glen where there was a pool of water, clear and still, just like a mirror. Narcissus looked upon the image on the water and fell hopelessly in love with it. He had projected his self-love onto another object and related to it as though it was someone else—but it was not. He is transfixed and cannot move. This is a fatal injury for him and he dies. In some versions of the myth, he turns to stone; in others he kills himself because he cannot have the object of his desire.

Narcissism is the term used to denote people who are fixated with themselves. This usually flows from a profound unmet need or emotional deprivation during the formative years. Narcissistic people develop narcissistic object relationships. They cannot form mutually nourishing relationships because they can only relate to projections of themselves that they attribute to others; the role of any relationship is to reflect their glory. Narcissism is a place of no growth. A degree of self-centred behaviour is entirely healthy, especially as we develop our egos and as we learn to derive self-regard from the environment and become assertive and confident. But if the preoccupation with self is central and the pursuit of power or self-gratification is detrimental causing suffering to the person or to other people, it is termed a *narcissistic personality disorder*.

Numinous experiences are just experiences. They are important experiences in that they can cause an awakening, a change of life's direction, but they should not be an end in themselves. The consensus of spiritual traditions is that spiritual growth only gains its momentum and traction through sustained practice and by embedding it in everyday life.[127] There are many different types of spiritual path that may emphasize different goals, but usually the aim is to provide a liberation, an emancipation from self-centeredness while maintaining rich and compassionate interpersonal relationships and enjoying the full range of human emotions. Spiritual growth is not intended to make one immune to difficult feelings, such as loss although it can provide a peace beyond the fluctuating emotions we experience. The problem for Max was that his addiction to the pursuit of the numinous was acting as a self- reflecting mirror for his narcissism. His field of relationships and his emotional range were diminishing. He seemed unable to do any mourning; he was in a place of developmental stasis that held him in a dependent, despondent and deeply dysfunctional position.

The term *psychic retreat* was developed by the psychoanalyst John Steiner to describe the ways in which we can find refuge in comforting mental sanctuaries to provide us with some relief from anxiety.[128] While we all have our psychic retreats to some extent, a prolonged immersion in a psychic retreat profoundly inhibits engagement in everyday life and therefore limits the way in which we can gain developmental traction from our environment. Steiner's work with patients in psychoanalysis suggested that these narcissistic defences arose as a result of not having the benefit of formative relationships that show a real understanding and empathy. For Max, his constant search for another numinous experience functioned as a psychic retreat to support his narcissistic avoidance of any engagement with the world outside of his own experience. His numinous experience and sudden attachment to that first guru, the yearned for father figure, gave him an excuse to avoid developing relationships or a career. He had persuaded himself that these were of no import. He was able to comfort himself with the memory of his numinous experience, which also protected him from anxiety about living and dying. How could he be anxious if he knew deep down that life was just a prelude to be joined in eternal bliss with the divine, he asked.

Max had no idea of how to develop a broader perspective directed towards engagement with the everyday world, concern for others and the long slow journey of a normal human life. Max's mother had encouraged him in the past to join a mainstream spiritual community such as a Buddhist group. Max had tried this but found it too slow and boring, and he didn't like the community aspects. He didn't really want to do anything. He wasn't depressed; it was more that he had lost the backbone, the essential skeleton of personality required to make any progress towards a more independent, multifaceted lifestyle. Indeed, it was very difficult to see a way forward for Max. I thought that he would benefit most from long-term treatment in a unit working with people with personality disorders. This unit offered outpatient treatment for two years with individual and group psychotherapy with a view to eventually getting a job and living as an independent adult. I suggested to Max that he had done enough transpersonal workshops, perhaps he had even become addicted to them — it was time to develop other parts of his psyche. But Max really didn't like this idea very much, insisting that he was on a spiritual path. By the end of his hospital stay, after much discussion, he was willing to go the unit for assessment. I heard later from his mother that he had discharged himself.

Psychic retreats and narcissistic personality structures are easily organised around brief glimpses of the Self archetype. There is a mutual attraction between narcissistic gurus and people looking to organise their own narcissism around perverse forms of the Self archetype. The people who flew the planes into the World Trade Centre believing that they would rest in the gardens of Paradise while the unbelievers would perish were products of this type of system. Religious cults typically have a prophet preaching a vision of light in close relationship with eternal damnation (loss of the light) unless the collective psychic structure of the cult is defended by a rigid adherence to doctrine and rules. Typically, this leads to an egotistical and exploitative leadership pattern in which no opposition is tolerated and people in these movements either become subservient or get expelled.

There are some indications that exploitation of people is more common in transpersonally orientated psychological groups, perhaps because the normal boundaries don't seem to apply and there are ideologies that can be found to support boundary transgressions.[129] Theoretical models and super-vision are often lacking in such groups and may be entirely absent.

Residues of the Infantile

One of the most difficult aspects of good psychiatry is the mixing of dif-ferent theoretical models to better understand and assist the patient. If someone, like Max, makes a determined attempt to commit suicide, the first step is to attempt a diagnostic formulation, which then informs the choice of treatment. A formulation is a diagnostic paragraph rather than just a diagnostic label. A formulation seeks to provide a more comprehen-sive explanation of the condition. So if a person has a psychotic illness, a medical model will usually take pole position, although the psychological factors and social situation will be taken into account. For someone like Max, where psychological factors are primary, there is a range of models and theories as to the nature of the basic lesion in the development of his psyche.

I thought that the most useful model to help us understand Max's personality development was the 'core complex theory'. This describes the situation where a person regresses to a much more primitive level of functioning deriving from the primary relationship of the infant at the breast.[130] One component of this relationship is a profound yearning for an idyllic state of closeness or blissful union with mother.[131] However, this urge to merge is accompanied by anxiety about annihilation if the merging is successful. This sort of conflict is characterised in adult life by a deep ambivalence in relationships that can be played out in various ways often involving aggression or a perverse use of sexuality. Relationships with other people are tightly controlled in an attempt to navigate the need for unity and the need for separation.

Only the most disturbed people fail to resolve the core complex. Max was unusual in that this infantile residue seemed to be projected onto a larger screen and reinforced by the amplified archetypal energies of his retreats and workshops. In his spiritual seeking he found exactly the type of relationship that he had been unconsciously seeking, with the combination of blissful states interspersed with rejection, abuse and isolation. The workshops and retreats had infused these infantile dynamics with a genuine archetypal power, but the numinous experiences had totally failed to resolve his deep-seated personality problems. It seemed likely that some of the perverse gurus with whom he had worked probably had similar personality characteristics. Indeed, if Max had been more psychologically robust he might well have become a charismatic and controlling cult leader himself. This illustrates how primitive psychological states can find an archetypal expression and how the combination of archetypal energy and personality disorder can be dangerous.

Ego Inflation

I found God quite early in my psychiatric career. He was on a long-stay ward of one of our old asylums. In fact, I had noticed him walking around the grounds. He seemed a peaceful man who did indeed have long flowing grey hair and a beard. He was originally a Polish refugee from the German invasion of his country in 1940. His file was thin although he had been in the hospital for 30 years or so. I was to see him for his annual review. He was not on any medication. Some years ago he had been deluded and occasionally aggressive but those days were long gone. The nurses said that he was a delightful man but completely disorganised. If he had any money he liked to give it away. His preference was to be naked but he got dressed when the nurses asked him to. He liked to be called God and didn't respond to his own name which was Josep. He spoke quite good English and was delighted to see me. After exchanging pleasantries, I tried to get some information about him and his life before the asylum, but he was unforthcoming. That was before he became God, he told me. I asked him what he does and he told me that he was busy with his flock, the human race and the universe. He had some help from his angels, he told me, gesturing towards the nurses. Looking through his records, it seemed that his story was entirely consistent with diagnosis of chronic schizophrenia. But his residual delusion was a pleasant one and he did indeed seem to have a certain quality of benign transcendence about him.

Ego inflation is the term used when an experience of the numinous Self is conflated with the personal self. As Roberto Assagioli, the pioneer of psychosynthesis, explains; the distinction between the personal self and archetypal Self is the key to understanding mental states of self-exaltation and self-glorification.[132] There arises a confusion of levels between the personal and the archetypal. Such confusion is not uncommon among people who become dazzled by truths too great or energies too powerful for their mental capacities to grasp and their personality to assimilate.[133]

Numinous experiences typically promote a degree of ego degradation. Usually, this carries a degree of difficulty and occasionally it is overwhelming. Ideally, this leads to a period of reorganisation that leads to a more harmonious way of being in the world with ego structures being illuminated and recalibrated by the Self. This process does not happen for the narcissist; instead, the person will develop a narcissistic relationship with an idea of the Self, using an unintegrated numinous experience to develop an inflated sense of importance and self-esteem. Power will be directed not to serve other people in a growth-oriented way, but to submerge other people, while promoting the maintenance of the inflated ego structure.

CHAPTER 13

Into the Darkness

The unconscious is not just evil by nature, it is also the source of the highest good: not only dark but also light, not only bestial, semi-human, and demonic but superhuman, spiritual, and, in the classical sense of the word, 'divine.'

—C. G. Jung.

The Shadow

Our passage towards a more complete version of ourselves inevitably leads us to the dark stranger that is within us all. Jung called this the shadow. The shadow is our dark side. It is a nebulous concept that has intrigued man since our earliest days with a persistent refrain of returning to explore aspects of ourselves that are destructive, hidden and mysterious.

The shadow side of our personality is complex and nuanced; it is the unseen reflection of the 'persona', which is the mask we use to present ourselves to the world. We all have a shadow; it is an inevitable part of being human and possessing ego structures; it is the part of our psyche that is around the corner and hidden from our sight. If light symbolises the visible aspect of consciousness, the shadow represents the part of ourselves that we do not choose to show to ourselves or anyone else. It is that part of the personality that has been repressed for the sake of the ego ideal. The shadow is not limited to unpleasant aspects of the repressed psyche, it may have great potential for creativity, for example, containing the repressed childlike playful side of the mature adult, or the feminine part of the masculine male and vice versa. It may even include the potential for love and altruism for people who have denied these aspects of their personalities. But generally, because it represents the qualities deemed unacceptable to us, the shadow is experienced as murky, lacking in morals, shameful and self- centred.

As our ego begins to take shape in infancy, our capacity for destructiveness is thought to flow from the primitive feelings of greed and envy that develop in the primary mother infant relationship.[134] The shadow, however, is more than the Freudian unconscious.[135] The shadow includes the parts of id, ego and super ego of which we are unaware but adds an archetypal component and it is impossible to discuss archetypal shadow without a brief mention of evil.[136] The monotheistic religions since Zoroastrianism, have been constructed around battles between archetypal good and evil, which could be understood as representing the tension between archetypal Self and archetypal shadow. If the Self stands for compassion, empathy and nurture, then the shadow stands for those parts of our individual and collective persona that has yet to be illuminated by those qualities. To make matters more complicated, the Self is at once light and dark, as much destructive as creative. So shadow is an integral part of Self and somehow destructive qualities need to be owned and integrated for the Self to be more fully realised.

The shadow is always by our side requiring active suppression to keep it from our sight, and this acts as a drain on our psychological and energetic resources. If we can shine the light of conscious awareness into those dark places, if the shadow can be integrated and incorporated into a larger and more nuanced version of ourselves, we are immeasurably richer. Energy that was drained by defence mechanisms to protect the ego from the shadow can then be diverted to more creative use. Perhaps the ego might even readjust its goals towards a life direction that was previously buried in the shadow. For most of us, the meeting with the shadow is a tremendously difficult and potentially dangerous process. We can volunteer to meet it, usually through a commitment to a certain path, such as psychotherapy, or it can be an involuntary encounter. Psychotherapy involves a gradual uncovering and guided exploration of the personal shadow where there is an engagement with the animal energies of the id, the negative emotions of the ego structures, the repressed pain, the envy and the negative transference.

In any process of growth, whether psychotherapy, meditation or any other psychospiritual practice, there is a tendency to drop out when the process begins to bite, the pain becomes more intense and some of the repellent aspects of personality are brought into focus. Without assistance, this is the rock upon which we can founder —our sustaining structures, our relationships, our bodies and our sanity may be seriously threatened. But we have to go there—the encounter with the shadow is the stuff of any serious process of psycho spiritual growth; it is the first firm step on the path to individuation. Growth without meeting the shadow is precarious growth, a move away from integration, based on denial and characterised by a cheerful optimism, a 'happy clappy' perspective and a vulnerability to unexpected expressions of the disowned psyche.

The outcome of the engagement with the shadow is determined largely by the nature of the underlying biological and psychological framework, the mindset, the degree of support in the setting, and the nature of the integration process. In psychotherapy, the patient is help-seeking and reflective. The work gathers momentum once the therapeutic alliance is established and a secure attachment is formed so that the therapist and patient can explore together the darker recesses of the psyche where the light of consciousness has failed to penetrate.

Moments of intense numinosity are rare and many of us will go through life without such an experience. Most of us will have lesser experiences of a dark numinosity and a few of us may have the more sublime experiences of positive numinosity, but it is unlikely that we will be overwhelmed by them. We can perhaps trigger a taste of a dark numinosity by watching a horror film and we can probably induce numinous experience by using certain psychotropic drugs or using various techniques to access non-ordinary states of consciousness. But the most dramatic and potentially dangerous numinous states are those encountered in illness, particularly some mental illnesses and unusual mental states.

It is my intention here to describe the highly problematic encounters with the shadow that occur when the mindset is unprepared, the setting unfavourable and the integrative process is totally lacking. Milder forms of the encounter with the shadow may involve some low-mood, guilt, aggression or acting out but an encounter of archetypal intensity has a different quality altogether. Numinous shadow has an extraordinary quality of dreadfulness, hopelessness and evil. The ego is overwhelmed and often seeks to extinguish itself and the human body attached to it. There is a high risk of suicide. I have also found the integration process after the crisis of archetypal shadow to be extraordinarily difficult. As with Adam in chapter 1, I simply could not find a way of helping him to make sense of his dreadful experience – he shrank from it. As Marie-Louise von Franz puts it:

> The emotional nature of one's inferior personality traits makes insight into one's personal shadow difficult, but when shadow projections arise from the archetypal psyche, insights come with almost insuperable difficulties.[137]

The crisis associated with the shadow encounter is seen in a number of guises. The vignettes that follow include the shadow's expression in physical illness, trauma and abuse, schizophrenia, the 'bad trip' and depression.

Gary on the Neurology Ward

'I had to come and see Gary urgently', said the nurse in charge on the neurology unit. 'He had turned very nasty', she explained. 'He used to be such a nice man but now he's attacking people and saying horrible things to his family'. More than one nurse had been hurt and his wife and daughters were very distressed. I learned that Gary had lung cancer and did not have long to live. He was in hospital because of complications of his cancer affecting his brain. He had a condition called para neoplastic syndrome that was making him confused and affecting his coordination and balance.[138] His personality had suddenly changed in a most distressing manner.

He had taken to hitting people. He couldn't generate a lot of power because of his weakened state, but he would attack without any warning. The nurses realised that he tried to lull them into a false sense of security so they would come very close to attend to him and then he would strike them. His family were distraught as Gary was saying horrible things to them that made them very upset. Indeed, the things that he was saying seemed to be calculated to cause the worst possible trauma to them. I cannot repeat the things that he was saying, but the sexual content was high. He told his wife in the most graphic terms about the times that he had had intercourse with his children and with his grandchildren.

His family were absolutely clear that none of this had any basis in reality. Gary was a straightforward and decent man who never seemed to have put a foot wrong in his life. If anything, he was a little too normal, said his wife, but everyone liked him; he was a kind man. No one could understand why he was saying these things. His wife said that it was as though he had been taken over by evil. The obvious answer was that Gary had a brain condition related to his cancer that had caused this change. But somehow the physical changes in his brain had caused him to express a part of his personality that seemed completely alien to him.

This was an unusual clinical scenario. The changes in Gary's brain that had led to this expression of the shadow side of his personality were also making it impossible for him to process or integrate it. He was confused and his cognitive function was failing. I could not have a meaningful conversation with Gary and my task was to work with the nurses and family to minimise the risk of harm, both physical and psychological, and to provide the nurses with an explanatory model so they could take care of him without being provoked by his unpleasant behaviour. I had a meeting with the family, which began with their very painful expressions of anger and distress. They told me that they were beginning to lose sight of the Gary that he had been to them and they did not want to remember him as he had now become. As the meeting progressed, their anger softened as they described to me the Gary that they knew and loved. It seemed that Gary materialised again for us in the room as they spoke—a highly controlled man of duty and responsibility, a kind man who never raised his voice or showed aggression. As they restored their connection to a more complete version of Gary, they were able to understand his current condition as just an artefact of terminal illness, an expression of 'badness' that was utterly alien to how he had lived his life. As we spoke, the tears of frustration evolved into a gentle and deeply moving expression of love and commitment to him. They were beginning their process of mourning.

Collective Shadow—The Heart of Darkness.

The concept of the shadow includes a cultural or collective level. Expressions of the shadow by groups usually have an amplifying effect so that behaviour that would normally be taboo becomes acceptable and sanctioned by the social group. This can lead to a situation where the most primitive and murderous fantasies can be acted out. These flames are fanned by the archetypal wind to create those situations that we can barely imagine—the heart of darkness, the place of rape and pillage, and the holocaust. This is the place of evil in us, where there is no compassion, no love, no virtue and no hope, the place where the light of the Self seems extinguished.

A chilling account of an expression of the communal shadow came from Joseph, a Congolese priest who was being treated for tuberculosis on a medical ward at the Royal London Hospital. I was asked to see him as he was screaming in the middle of the night. He was frightening the other patients, and the nurses said that he seemed terrified. Joseph told me that he was having nightmares. He had suffered them for years and he told me that they concerned some very bad things that he had seen in his country. I saw Joseph on a number of occasions. He didn't want to talk about his experiences and I certainly wasn't going to traumatise him by asking him to do so before he was ready.

He seemed to find some reassurance in my explanation of post-traumatic stress disorder. I told him that it wasn't his fault that he was having these experiences, that he wasn't going mad but people who had seen terrible things often had terrible nightmares. We discussed some possible treatment options and he decided to try some medication to see if it would diminish the nightmares and help him sleep. It did indeed help a little. The last time I saw him, before he was discharged home, he told me in a few sentences the horror of what he had seen. The rebel army had suddenly occupied his village one day. The soldiers had gone wild. It was like a party for them; they were drinking and smoking weed. They cut and they hacked with their machetes, they penetrated with their penises and their bayonets. They were dancing, laughing and whooping. They took pictures on their phones of people being raped and killed. He recognised some of the soldiers who had been his pupils. They had been good kids, he told me.

Joseph told me that he could not stay in the Congo after that. He thought his country had been broken beyond repair. He had lost hope in the human race and his faith was sorely tested. But since arriving in London, he had been learning about the Truth and Reconciliation Committee in South Africa that was set up in an attempt to heal the wounds of apartheid. He liked what he learned and he hoped to be part of a similar process one day in the Congo. Whenever he seriously considered returning to the Congo, his nightmares became worse, but we discussed how treatment could help his symptoms and perhaps make it possible for him to go home one day. He was under no illusions about the difficulty, but he knew that the horrors had to be acknowledged and faced before his people could start to heal their wounds. He wanted to go back and find these boys. He wanted to talk to them and try to forgive them. Joseph could not understand why the rest of the world, its media and its governments, seemed to ignore the horrors in his country. 'They do not want to know' he said; 'they do not want to look at it and if they don't look, then the killing continues. Why won't they help us, we are all the same people?'.

The Congo was chosen as the setting for Joseph Conrad for his book *The Heart of Darkness* to explore the depths of depravity that a white man can access if he has the power and is hidden from his peers. There are many layers to this theme. The Congo represents the fullness of Mother Earth, with its majestic jungle, the arterial river and its inexhaustible resources. If the natural bounty of the Congo represents the fullness of the breast in the mother infant dyad, then the plundering of resources in collusion with corrupt and abusive governments represents a savage attack on the breast. Of course, this is a theme that plays out in many places and many different ways across the world but the Congo is unusual as it remains hidden. We are able to avert our gaze and the shadow is rampant.

Perhaps the task of Plato's ideal philosopher ruler, the true statesman, is to help us to own and integrate our part of the collective shadow. In the same way that the menacing horrors in our dreams at night offer the opportunity to work with a shadow part of our psyche, it may be that the horrors in the world; the destructiveness, the poverty, fundamentalism, greed and exploitation may perform a similar task on a collective level. We need to engage with the ways in which we contribute to the darkness in the world. It does not belong to 'them'; it belongs to Us. It is part of our collective developmental journey.

Sexually Abused Children

When I did my six months of child psychiatry training in the mid 1980s, the fact that children were being sexually abused in huge numbers still lay deep in the shadow. Not many children or adults volunteered information about abuse and it wasn't something that health professionals usually enquired about. If a child had disclosed sexual abuse, he or she would probably not have been believed. My trainer in child psychiatry was one of the pioneers shouting from the rooftops to say that sexual abuse of children is real; if children say that they are being sexually abused then they almost certainly are. This is not the product of a childish oedipal fantasy, as Freud suggested.

A few years later, when I started work in east London with its high proportion of Bangladeshi families, I was told that Asian children do not get sexually abused because the family structures are stronger and children are more closely supervised. There is some truth in that statement—but I soon found out that Asian kids do get abused too. We know now that sexual abuse is ubiquitous. Over the last generation, we have been reminded again and again that countless children have been subjected to unwanted and illegal sexual experiences at the hands of adults who usually had a position of responsibility to them. In every place where children live, men (and it is almost always men) were doing unspeakable things for their own gratification.[139] No one really knew about it other than the people involved. It was in our collective shadow.

Of course, it is no longer buried within the collective shadow. Years of revelations about abuse, especially recent high-profile cases, have taught us more about our responsibility, our social task, to protect children. It is now in our collective consciousness and we are more knowledgeable about this dark part of our collective psyche. The clinical task is to treat the consequences of the trauma to the children who are now adults and whose lives are often shaped by abuse. In the crisis service it sometimes seemed as though we spent much of our professional lives trying to heal some of the damage that was caused. Often our clinical meetings featured case after case of suicidal adults whose problems flowed primarily from their sexual abuse as children.

I learned to expect that the muscle-bound, masculine man walking aggressively into my consulting room would crumble when I asked if anything bad had happened to him as a child. The small, frightened child inside him wished he had been able to defend himself against the person who shamed and hurt him all those years ago. He was too weak to defend himself then and he will make sure that he is never physically vulnerable again. I try to ask my question in such a way that invites but does not pressurize, but usually such men are grateful to be asked. This, after all, is why they have come to see me.

Perhaps a drunken uncle touched them inappropriately when they were little. Often, it was much worse than that. The result was a deep humiliation, blazing anger and frequently some sexual anxiety. These emotions and repercussions from the abusive sexual encounter played out in many different ways affecting their engagement with the stuff of life— their friends, their partners, their children and their workmates. Usually they had not told anyone—no one at all—until they came to the Crisis Service. Once the damage is recognized, the healing work can begin. It begins with the attentive hearing of their story, supporting them through their tears and rage, and reflecting with them on their passage through life. Part of their being is being brought gently in from the shadow land, where it has been for very many years, to a place that is more whole.

The Problem of Evil

If the integration of the shadow is fundamental to psychological growth, how can we work with the difficult, unappetizing, repulsive, sometimes just plain evil side of ourselves and other people? How can we bring the shadow usefully into the light? Why indeed is it there at all?

I have lived much of my life as a psychiatrist in the shadow lands, where people have often been seriously damaged by the encounter with it. There are places of great pain where people have been injured by the actions of others. There are days when my clinical encounters with psychic pain seem almost entirely due to male aggression, often fuelled by alcohol or drugs. There are stories that I heard of men who went from their workplace to the pub and came home drunk to terrorize their families—stories of the fathers who raped their daughters and beat their sons. There are the sexually abused children who grow into adults who put their own children in positions where they too will be abused. There are the shadows cast by the institutions—the Church, the orphanages, the boarding schools. There are the shadows that we create ourselves everyday with our thoughtlessness.

Many people do not want to look at their shadow and have no interest in change. The shadow has gained the upper hand and they are powerless to stop its effects. I have had many meetings in the emergency department with someone who may be claiming to be suicidal and whose problems are self-inflicted with drink and drugs and antisocial behavior. They may have little control over the animal forces of the id. They may say that they want some help but without making any changes themselves and with no inclination to do anything that might be difficult. As I see a man dying of alcoholic liver disease who wants to discharge himself from hospital to get a bottle of vodka, it seems that the prospect of any growth is remote. These people seem destined to waste the opportunity that a human life offers them, while creating a lot of collateral damage to other people. As a team we ask ourselves how can we help, how can we make any difference. We know that often we cannot—but we try. It is always our task to offer a focused compassion, the prospect of help, the opportunity to make meaningful change, to show that life can be different, that there are choices, that they can perhaps find a better version of themselves.

For me these encounters are a participatory experience from which I learn something valuable about humanity, my colleagues and indeed myself. It is a challenge to apply focussed compassion, but we are after all connected as human beings. If circumstances were different, I could be in their position as the vagrant whose original trauma had been dissolved in alcohol and they could be in my position as the person trying to point to a different route. We are each expressing different parts of the whole range of human experience. Ultimately, we are all human with the same range of limitations, frailties, vulnerability and capacity to harm.

The task in psychiatry is often to help people who have suffered a more immediate and unexpected encounter with the shadow. Frequently, this is expressed by suicidal thoughts and acts. The fruitful integration with shadow is an inevitable component of the process of symbolic ego death followed by a rebirth of an ego structure more connected with Self. The problem is that when the more archetypal or numinous layers of shadow are encountered, this ego death is often accompanied by a compelling urge to die, any sense of a psychological journey tends to be lost and there is a risk of a very real death of the physical body.

If we consider that archetypal evil is the shadow of the light half of the Self, then it is an integral component of our totality but an unimaginable intensification of our dark side.[140] As Jung expressed it: 'It is quite within the bounds of possibility for a man to recognize the relative evil of his nature, but it is a rare and shattering experience for him to gaze into the face of absolute evil'.[141]

Hearing Voices

The hallucinatory voices of psychotic states such as acute schizophrenia have a special quality. For years I was puzzled as to why it was that patients found it so hard to tell me what their voices were saying. I really wanted to know and they really didn't want to tell me. Often I knew them well and they trusted me enough to tell me about other difficult parts of their lives, but they were still too ashamed to tell me about the voices. It seemed that the voices had a special way of honing in on something that was particularly unacceptable for them and was excruciatingly embarrassing. Often there was a sexual content, so my male patients, for example, would often be called a nonce by the voices, which is prison slang for a paedophile. Calling someone a nonce in London is one of the worst insults imaginable.

The voices in acute psychotic conditions are often derogatory. They may form a running commentary that has a sneering quality or they may point out a person's inadequacies, telling them they are useless and worthless. They may give commands, which may be very compelling, dangerous and difficult to ignore. We know that hearing voices is not always pathological and that many people hear voices that may be benign, helpful or sometimes inspiring. Socrates famously heard a voice that gave him helpful advice about what he should not do, although it never told him what he should do. For Socrates this was a form of divine guidance.[142] Hearing voices seems to be part of the normal human range of experience, but in psychiatry we often see people who are deeply tormented by their voices in a way that feels entirely destructive.

One of my more frightening patients was Dennis who had relapsing schizophrenia and a liking for crack cocaine. I tried to look after Dennis for some years and after a while I found I could assess his mental state, to some extent, just by the look on his face. When he was well he had a certain charm, a ready smile and no voices. At other times he looked over-stimulated, menacing and very dangerous. When Dennis heard voices he thought they were totally real. He thought that people such as pedestrians or people on a building site were calling him names, bad names and he wanted to kill them. Sometimes he carried a knife. My task was to keep some sort of connection with Dennis and bring him into hospital when he became unwell, before someone got hurt. It was high-intensity work. When Dennis was well he sometimes appreciated my efforts, but when he was unwell he didn't. Most community psychiatrists have been chased around the block by their patients at some stage and I was certainly chased by Dennis. If the crack cocaine he smoked hadn't damaged his lungs, he may even have caught me.

Hallucinatory voices seem entirely real. In psychiatry emergencies, we often see a person being distracted and looking around trying to find the source of the voices. People may describe the neighbours shouting out at them or people hurling insults from the street. They truly believe that this is the case but their relatives assure us that their complaints have no basis in external reality. We don't entirely understand the mechanisms in the brain that cause these misperceptions, but the content of the voices are representations of the patient's psyche. They are internally generated but experienced as external. These voices are profoundly alien to the person's idea of who they are and it seems reasonable to suggest that the voices are expressions of disowned aspects of their personas.

If voices emanate from the shadow and if the integration of the shadow is helpful, then surely we need to listen to the voices with the person who is experiencing them to try to help them to understand and come to terms with them. From this perspective the voices are not enemies but a potential source of insight into solvable emotional problems. The problem is that the voices are crude and concrete, so that thinking symbolically and divining the meaning behind the voice is very difficult, especially in a highly aroused and distressed state.[143] It is not surprising that so few people are able to make progress on their own in these circumstances; the right kind of assistance is needed. There is a developing 'hearing voices' movement where people meet in organised groups to share their experiences, support each other and try to make sense of the voices. Traditionally, psychiatry has been poor at this and quick to use medication as the primary solution.[144] Of course, sometimes with a very disturbed and inaccessible patient, medication needs to be the primary treatment but often the premature or heavy use of medication runs the risk of dulling any processing and integrative function and makes it less likely that any useful psychological progress can be achieved.

The small Scandinavian country of Finland has led the world in the integrative approach, developing an Open Dialogue programme where people with voices and other psychotic symptoms are engaged in talking treatments aimed at finding some potential meaning in their experiences. Medication is sometimes used but as a support for the psychotherapy rather than as the primary treatment. The results from this approach are very promising showing lower hospitalization rates, less recurrence and much less disability when compared with the usual treatment of psychosis. For example, in a five-year follow-up 83% of patients had returned to their jobs or studies or were job seeking, thus not receiving government disability.[145] Indeed, schizophrenia in Finland seems to be disappearing as a chronic disabling condition.[146]

The secret of this success seems to be an early and a continuing process of talking and exploration creating an open dialogue with families and social networks. The task of the staff is not primarily to function as experts providing solutions to the crisis, but instead to generate reflective processes.[147] The key is to keep talking about the experience, to find a language to describe it, to bring it in from the cold, to bring the shadow into consciousness.

There is a certain power in working with groups and families. The Jungian analyst and writer Murray Stein observes that the shadow may be available to some extent through introspection, but the ego's defenses are usually so effective that little can penetrate them and the shadow is difficult to bring into conscious awareness. Asking close friends or family is a particularly useful method of gathering information about the ego's shadow operations.[148] So it is not surprising that this process of working with families, an average of 25 meetings in the Open Dialogue model to set up patterns of inquiry and communication, is so effective. This would often have more power and enable a continuing process, compared to a person attending an individual psychotherapy session where the intensity of the experience can easily dissipate and be lost.

A variation on this theme is *avatar therapy*, which is being researched in London by Professor Julian Leff's team. People with troublesome and persistent voices create a computer-based avatar by choosing a voice and a face that they believe best represents the primary person talking to them through the voices. The therapist, in another room, says characteristically unpleasant things through the avatar on the screen, whose lips are synchronized to the speech to make it as real as possible. The patient knows that the avatar cannot hurt them and develops confidence in interacting with their persecutor in a more confident and assertive way. Early results show that for some people who had suffered voices for many years, the treatment was successful in stopping the voices, sometimes the voices persisted but were less malevolent so that the person felt less helpless and the quality of life was improved.[149] In some other cases, the person was unable to complete the course—as the voices told them not to.

When I contrast this approach to my experience of some psychiatric units, it is deeply uncomfortable. At its worst, a psychiatric ward is a frightening place with nurses retreating into the fortress that is the locked office, emerging to dispense medication, patients being steered into the weekly ward round and being questioned in an atmosphere that is often experienced at intimidating. Patients may find themselves in an environment that re-enacts the dysfunctional and disturbing early environment that contributed to their problems in the first place. Often, there is a culture in the psychiatric team that discourages any reflective process in favor of decision making.

I know that, with hindsight, there are some patients with whom I was perhaps too early with medication. Perhaps I should have tried harder to talk, to get through their reluctance, to build some bridges of words and understanding. On the other hand there may have been some people who I was too slow to medicate, so that they suffered perhaps for longer than was necessary – it is a difficult balance to get right. I think that part of the difficulty is that in order to help people to work with their own shadow, we are inevitably put in touch with aspects of our own shadow. This is deeply uncomfortable and often we recoil from it. It is not a conscious process but we make a choice not to engage with that territory. Working in a team with a specific mandate to do this difficult work has a considerable advantage. The team develops a culture that can reflect and can explore. The team members learn to support each other, as well as their patients, in facing the shadow together.

The Bad Trip

Psychedelic drugs such as LSD appear to act as amplifiers of the archetypal layer of the psyche. The Jungian scholar, Scott Hill, describes his own difficult psychedelic experiences, which illustrate a confrontation with the personal and archetypal levels of the shadow:

> After having taken LSD on the evening before moving out of a rented house, I came across a number of things I needed to pack or dispose of. Feeling hopelessly overwhelmed with the tasks before me, and recalling the kind old couple from whom we were renting the house, I was suddenly overcome with guilt at the thought that I would be leaving the house in a mess. As I stood looking down at a pile of old newspapers, I had, despite the lack of any previous religious inclination, a vision of standing below a panel of heavenly judges. It was the Last Judgment. Hanging my head in shame, I felt crushed by irredeemable guilt. Not only did I feel guilty for my personal transgressions, I felt profoundly ashamed for being a human in an absolutely sinful world. Life in this world was, I knew then, nothing but folly. Standing on a beach later that night, I had the terrifying feeling that I was being pulled into the ocean to my death—and to God—and I desperately fought my way back into this world, which I knew was Hell. . . . My friend and I later drove to a secluded cliff, and in windswept darkness, we threw our unwanted things into the surf below. As my long overcoat flapped violently in the wind, and as I raised a box over my head and flung it into the darkness—I was evil incarnate. A few months later, during my next LSD trip, I attempted to honor God's command that I kill myself to free my soul from Hell.[150]

Hill did not take his life but was left fascinated by the extraordinary power of his experiences. A mild feeling of guilt had escalated into an identification with archetypal evil. He understood that the psychedelic substance in itself was not dangerous; what was dangerous was the setting in which he took it and the material that it uncovered in his psyche. 'The trouble was that I, and who knows how many other uninformed, immature or foolhardy psychedelic cowboys, just didn't do it right'.[151] His journey to explore and process his shadow encounter took four decades and culminated in the publication of his book, *Confrontation with the Unconscious*, in 2013 We will meet him again in chapter 21.

The Golden Boy

Ian was brought into hospital after jumping under a train on the London Underground. He had chosen a station notorious for its long platform and fast approach. He stationed himself right at the end of the platform where the train would be going fastest but he landed in the pit, the wheels missed him, and the train passed overhead. He'd broken a bone and suffered concussion but he was expected to make a full recovery. He was very lucky but Ian did not consider himself as lucky at all. He still wanted to die.

Ian was not exactly pleased to see me but, being a well-mannered young man, he responded to my introducing myself and we were able to begin a conversation about what had brought him to hospital. I particularly wanted to know what had been in his mind when he tried to end his life and how he felt about still being alive. He told me slowly and with hesitation that he was in a place of great pain. He profoundly regretted letting down his family, his girlfriend and his friends, but he felt that his life had come to an end and he did not want to be alive any more. He told me that he was sorry and he recognised that people wanted to help him but it was hopeless. He would have to find a more effective way of killing himself next time. It was very clear that Ian was at great risk, so we had a nurse sitting with him to keep him safe and I saw Ian every day that he was in hospital. I met his father, his girlfriend and his best friend. I tried to put together a picture of Ian's personality, the way in which his life had unfolded and how his path had led him to where he found himself.

A severe depressive illness has some typical characteristics. Someone who is ill with this more physiological type of depression suffers a constant unremitting low mood and has lost the capacity to enjoy pleasurable activities. They develop the 'biological' symptoms of early waking, usually around 3 or 4 am, together with loss of appetite and libido and an impairment of concentration. They often describe a feeling of mental and physical sluggishness that is worse in the morning. These biological symptoms are accompanied by 'cognitive' symptoms of depression such as feelings of guilt, worthlessness and hopelessness, which will range along a spectrum of severity. In the more severe cases, there will inevitably be some thoughts of death, of life no longer being worth living, and some ideas about how to end their life. Often, there is genuine suicidal risk.

Ian was unusual in that he did not seem to have this constellation of symptoms. He seemed to be sleeping quite well, he still enjoyed the company of friends and his girlfriend and his libido was fine. There were no problems with his concentration and he was doing well in his high-powered job at a reputable city law firm. It was hard to find evidence of any problems at all in Ian's history. His family seemed to be unusually nice, well balanced and healthy. He grew up with secure attachment patterns, there were no difficulties or separations in his early life and he was a much-loved child. He enjoyed his schooling and had many friends—in fact everybody loved him. He was at the top of his class and he excelled at sport. He seemed to effortlessly achieve everything that he set his sights on. He went to Oxford University to study law and he had a long-term girlfriend who adored him. There had been no major life events, no bereavements, no difficult family issues and no separations.

His difficulties seemed to have started a month or so previously. An issue had developed at work where he felt that he was being asked to meet standards of moral integrity that were less than what he was used to. His boss had told him to take a certain position that was technically legal, but which Ian felt had an element of dishonesty. He did as his boss requested, but felt very uncomfortable. He started to brood about it. It was as though a door had opened beneath him and all his certainties and moral structures seemed to fall away. For the first time in his life, it felt as if he did not really know who he was. He started to drink in the evenings, not socially but on his own. He picked some arguments with his girlfriend and this troubled him. He could see that he was being unfair to her. He felt that he was failing not only himself but all those who loved him. If they could see what sort of person he was turning into, they would be deeply pained.

The revenge fantasy is one of the most common triggers for a suicidal act. Often this is conscious and has the overt aim of punishing parents, lover or employer—'look how you have made me suffer, look how you have failed to protect me', may be the underlying message. Sometimes, to put this in psychoanalytic terms, it is deeply unconscious reproach to the mother or maternal object for allowing them to be hurt in the cruel world rather than stay in the idyllic state of infancy or childhood. A son or daughter who takes their own life deprives their parents of their most precious possession, but perhaps this a just punishment for the child's ejection from the Garden of Eden. We often understand aggression, with this desire to hurt and punish, as a fundamental feature of the suicidal mindset. Ian and his family all told me that he didn't 'do aggression'. Any form of expression of aggression was totally alien to his nature.

I was beginning to wonder if Ian was the golden youth with no awareness of shadow. The brighter the light—and his was bright indeed—the more obscure the shadow and the more shattering it can be when it suddenly appears. Ian had no previous experience that he could remember of managing feelings of shame and inadequacy. He just didn't know how to, as it was outside of his experience. Any negative or difficult emotions had been firmly repressed so that when they finally became available to conscious awareness, the residue of the accumulated shadow from the past was particularly powerful.

The more I talked to Ian, the more this model of understanding him made sense to both of us. His feelings of utter hopelessness were receding and he was beginning to think that there might be a fruitful way forward. I met with him and his family to discuss his safety and supervision so that he could continue his treatment at home. With this framework in place, he came immediately to an experienced therapist in the crisis service and, when his 12 weeks of treatment had passed, I saw him for a while longer until a suitable longer-term therapist could be found. Ian was learning to explore and tolerate his feelings of shame and inadequacy. We learned that there was an important family dimension as his maternal grandfather had a public humiliation when his mother was a child, which had affected his mother very deeply and created a powerful family ethos of righteousness. His grandfather's shadow was being processed too.

Nigredo States

The process of growth according to the Sufi tradition involves a cleansing of the lens of perception so that we can relate to the world in a more authentic manner. This process involves learning to see and to hear in different ways and an encounter with the ways in which we may be blind or deaf, figuratively speaking. Typically, this involves a sacrifice in the outer, material world, so that we may gain in the inner world. Usually this leads to a loss of redundant ego structures so that a more mature personality can evolve. This is a process that is alien and painful for us; it is a death of the old so that the new can emerge. Jung likened this process of psycho-spiritual transformation to alchemy, where the 'base metal' of shadow is transformed by complicated procedures into the gold of the Self.[152] The mythical descent into the underworld of the shadow is termed the *nigredo*, the darkness which is 'blacker than black'. This is the bleak inhospitable place of raw, primitive and dreadful power. This is the dark night of the soul, the hellish place, the place of putrefaction.

The nigredo is the place where a person is most enmired and stuck but this state of dissolution is a prerequisite for the redemptive process that follows—there is a light in the darkness, for those fortunate enough to find it. The catalyst may be a manifestation of the animus / anima archetype, perhaps the emergence of a wise figure, a higher guiding principle that leads us out of the darkness. This light, the *albedo*, is the inrush of illumination, the rebirth after the near death. It may even have the detached quality of a mountaintop epiphany, but we can't stay on the mountain top; we need to descend safely again. The totality of the experience, the cy :le of *nigredo* to *albedo*, has to be incorporated into actual life. It has o be brought together as the union of opposites, which is termed the *rubedo* or reddening. This is where the shadow projections are realized and transmuted into gold as they are brought back into consciousness. The insights are incorporated into our everyday lives as the new ego-Self structure of the individuating person gives us a sounder platform for a life well lived.

The *nigredo* state can be subtle; it may manifest as mid-life crisis, grumbling low mood or a nagging dissatisfaction. But some *nigredo* states are so intense, so overwhelming, that progress through the alchemical process becomes arrested. This may be because the setting is poor and the mindset unprepared or the experiences may simply be too intense and frightening to be integrated. For some people the *nigredo* appears to erupt out of nowhere in a particularly powerful and dangerous form. The intensity of archetypal energy is not a fire that purifies but becomes a fire that consumes. The destructive urge is not directed towards a symbolic ego death but towards a very real physical death.

Jumpers, Stabbers and Hangers

There are few places where the high risk of such states is more apparent than in the Liaison Psychiatry team at the Royal London Hospital. Every day there are people brought in as emergencies who have been overwhelmed by extraordinary states of emotional intensity. They may come to the Emergency Room themselves seeking help, they may be brought in by a concerned police officer or they may come in on a stretcher after a serious injury sustained as a direct result of their numinous experience. The Royal London is a hospital specialising in trauma and serves as the base for the helicopter ambulance serving greater London, so people who were seriously injured after suicide attempts were more likely to be brought to us than to other hospitals.

To give a flavour of the drama and tragedy of such people, I will describe a simple research project that I undertook with some colleagues, Peter Martin and Chloe Beale, studying 200 consecutive people that were referred to us at the Royal London as psychiatric emergencies by the trauma team. Of these 200 hundred people, over 100 had jumped from a high place, over 60 had stabbed or cut themselves, 20 had thrown themselves under moving vehicles such as trains, and 10 had tried to hang themselves. Hospitals are fond of abbreviations that incorporate the black humour that serves as a psychological defence to help us to deal with the awfulness of the suffering, and we termed them jumpers, stabbers and hangers.

When a person jumps from a height, if they drop feet first, the skeleton acts as a crumple zone. Typically, the bones that are broken are the long bones of the body such as the femur and tibia and perhaps the heel bone, the pelvis and some vertebrae. It is a testament to the design of the body that the vital structures are well protected and spinal cord injuries are not common, although they do occur. People who jump from heights, if they survive, will usually walk away from hospital although it may take some months before they get to that stage and they are unlikely to recover their previous level of fitness. People who jump under trains are more likely to lose limbs and, indeed, one third of our patients who went under trains suffered a traumatic amputation. The people in this study who cut themselves had not merely lacerated their wrists, but caused serious and life-threatening wounds with knives penetrating their abdomens, chests or necks. This being Britain, where guns are strictly controlled, gunshot wounds were rare.

All of these people could have died. Some of them came very close to death and would not have survived if it had not been for the rapid transport to hospital and the expertise of the trauma team. They had all done dreadful things to themselves because of the intensity of their emotional experience. Many of our patients were known to be vulnerable; about 45% had harmed themselves before, about 60% had seen a psychiatrist at some point in their lives and one third of our sample had been seen by their psychiatric service in the week before they harmed themselves. Some of our patients continued to be in a state of great emotional distress; about 20% were still suicidal when we saw them and required intensive supervision, support and treatment.

So it is no surprise that the majority of our trauma patients were suffering from a psychiatric disorder of some kind. What was more surprising was that many of them did not. Sixty of our two hundred trauma patients, about 30% of the sample, had a normal mental state by the time we saw them for assessment. They were not clinically depressed, they regretted their actions, and whatever had troubled them enough to make them suicidal had passed. For half of these patients, we could understand easily enough what had happened to them: either they were in a state of intoxication or there had been a very clear trigger, such the ending of a relationship. But for 15% of our patients, about thirty people in total of our sample, we had little understanding of why they had tried to harm themselves—and nor had they.

The usual story was that something difficult had happened to turn a normal day into a difficult day. Perhaps there had been a presentation at work that had not gone well, triggering thoughts of humiliation, of letting down the family, of being a failure. Such scenarios are commonplace. But in our patients, this had led to a darkening of their mood that was so powerful and all consuming that any balancing perspective was lost. Often, they were able to tell me that their world suddenly changed, becoming highly charged, sinister and menacing. To my ears, this sounded reminiscent of delusional mood, but instead of becoming deluded or paranoid they became depressed and desolate. Suddenly, there was no hope, all was lost and their entire world had become bad and horrible – a wasteland. Indeed, it was so dreadful that they just could not bear it any more. It is difficult for us to imagine the strength and depth of a feeling that would cause someone to jump from a high place or under a train, but this is what they did. When they tried to describe to me their state of mind before the suicidal act, they would run out of words. As their disturbance gathered momentum and power, their experience fell increasingly outside the normal human range, it was beyond description. Some would liken it to a 'bad trip'.

By the time they are able to talk to me in their hospital bed a day or so later, the moment of horror has passed. They generally deeply regret their actions, and their friends and family tell me that it is completely out of character. My usual approach at this stage would be to work towards a shared understanding of the stresses that triggered the crisis and how this might resonate with any previous areas of difficulty. How can the person learn from this, how can best use be made of this second chance of life, and where is the potential for growth? This is the approach that the Crisis team used to excellent effect with suicidal people. But the Crisis service patients had not experienced the same level of archetypal intensity and had not harmed themselves so dramatically. The striking difference about the hospitalised trauma patients was that they just could not work in this way. They could not reflect and typically they could not even begin to integrate their experience. They wanted to just button it all up and go home. At first we thought that this was due to the physical effects of the trauma and the pain-killing medication. But, no, the same observation held true when I saw some of them in my clinic weeks and months afterwards. I wasn't sure if these people had suffered such an indigestible archetypal crisis because they could not emotionally process and reflect on issues before their suicide attempt — or if there was something about such an archetypal crisis that so seared the psyche that reflection and integration became more difficult subsequently. It seemed that the experience had been so indescribably dreadful that thinking about it was almost impossible. Conventional methods of psychological treatment and support simply did not seem helpful in processing and integrating the extraordinary power of archetypal shadow. Their passage through the *nigredo,* if that is what it was, had been catastrophic and an *albedo* seemed a forlorn prospect.

CHAPTER 14

The Numinous Feminine

I think the biggest disease the world suffers from in this day and age is the disease of people feeling unloved. I know that I can give love for a minute, for half an hour, for a day, for a month, but I can give. I am very happy to do that, I want to do that.

—Diana, Princess of Wales

Death of a Princess

Piccadilly was transformed for those first few days of September 1997. A mood had developed that had a distinct sacred quality. It was a special place of soft steps and hushed tones; people were careful with each other; it was a place of great gentleness. I had never experienced a London quite like this before. Diana, the Princess of Wales, had been killed with two others in a car crash in Paris a couple of days previously and something extraordinary was happening. Piccadilly had metamorphosed into a garden of flowers and poetry. All over the country, over the world, people were feeling full of emotion. There was an outpouring of grief but also of something else that I struggled to understand. I had some sympathy for Diana. I thought she was a complex woman in a difficult situation but I had no particular feeling or interest in her beyond that. Why then was I myself so affected? Why did the whole country seem to be in tears as the funeral cortege passed through London and up the motorway to her ancestral burial grounds?

Diana's state funeral was viewed across the world and there is some evidence of a measurable ripple effect through the noosphere, the sphere of human thought, as a sizeable proportion of the world's population briefly developed a more coherent meaning-filled state of mind.[153] The emotional currents were transcending the usual boundaries in a way that seemed to defy rational explanation. There were clearly some people who felt they had a personal connection with her through the media, even though they didn't know her personally. There was a level in which we were expressing unresolved grief for the losses that we had suffered in our personal lives, maybe the losses that we would face ourselves in the future. There was clearly a powerful collective grief process that had gathered momentum.

Even taking these factors into account, I thought it was more complicated than this and that there was another layer underneath the grief. Diana, for all her faults and complexities, was known as the Princess of Hearts. She did seem to have a gift for a real and deep compassion. She was the one who went to the dark places on our planet; the war zones and the hospital wards where she held the maimed, the deprived and the suffering. She seemed to have a wonderful presence that lit people up, that gave them something that was good and sustaining. The sense of the sacred, which was so apparent when Piccadilly morphed from bustling London's West End into a memorial garden, points clearly to the presence of an archetype. Her passing, and the numinous mood that followed, seemed to hold something of the archetypal Feminine. We were not so much mourning Diana the person as we were being touched by the image that she represented for us of a higher form of a feminine principle.

The archetypal Feminine has many forms and names— witness the variety of the goddesses in the world's traditions. Although the Feminine has a darker version, the archetype captured by Diana's death seemed to resonate with the receptive, the fertile, the nourishing and the compassionate. The Feminine is, above all, the vehicle for life. There are a number of different types of archetypal crisis associated with the Feminine and we will begin by looking at anorexia nervosa, which might be understood as the denial of the feminine.

Anorexia Nervosa

Melody had a severe form of anorexia nervosa. She was in her late thirties and she had been anorectic for as long as she could remember. She had been brought into hospital in a state of physical collapse. Blood tests showed that her sodium and potassium levels were deranged and her blood pressure was dangerously low. She was in a life-threatening situation due to risk of heart failure. She allowed the physicians to insert a nasogastric tube to give her fluids and salts but she declined anything with calories either by mouth or by tube and she would not allow herself to be weighed. She told the physicians that she was under the care of the local eating-disorders unit, which was true. She said that she did not need to be weighed and that she was eating food brought in by friends, which was not true.

She did not have any friends that visited and she was not eating anything at all. Melody had been in hospital for 10 days or so by the time she was referred to me. A bizarre and dangerous situation had developed where she had seduced the medical team into allowing her to stay in hospital, taking fluids through a tube but slowly dying of starvation. Her face looked relatively normal and well hydrated and she hid her body with baggy clothes. She was very plausible.

I watched her walk slowly along the ward corridor. She was wearing a pristine white gown and a seraphic half smile. She looked very serene and had a certain ethereal radiance. She was quite friendly when I introduced myself. We established that she lived with her parents and has always done so. She has a part-time office job and her colleagues had initiated the admission to hospital after she had collapsed at work. She had never had a sexual relationship. We established slowly that she had a regular pattern of admission to the eating disorders unit where she would be fed up to her 'target weight', the weight that is deemed to be normal for someone of her height and age and compatible with health. As soon as she is discharged, she starts dieting again. Weight loss is usually slow to begin with but she told me that she always gets better at it. The times when she feels best about herself are when she is eating almost nothing and her weight is dangerously low. She doesn't want to die, she said, but she doesn't really care either way. Why is this the best time I wondered to her? 'Oh, that is a difficult one', she said, and, indeed, she seemed lost for words for a moment. 'It's a time when life gets very simple, and focussed and clear; it's a very special time'. She smiled sweetly.

Anorexia is a fascinating and frustrating condition. Adolescent anorectics undergoing a full treatment programme will usually make a recovery, but often people with this condition do not get completely better and it becomes a chronic illness. As a general rule, one fifth recover completely, three fifths have a long-term condition that fluctuates to a greater or lesser degree, and about one fifth have a chronic severe form of the illness, as in the case of Melody.[154] The mortality rate, from alcoholism, suicide and the physical complications of chronic starvation, is high. Conventional treatment focuses on achieving and maintaining weight gain to target weight, together with psychological treatment, both as an individual and as a family to address the underlying psychological issues.

The bio-psycho-social factors associated with anorexia are numerous and well documented. Some of them are fairly obvious, some less so. We generally understand anorexia as a developmental crisis concerning the transition from childhood to womanhood. Anorexia puts the biological clock into reverse, stopping the menstrual cycle and shutting down the sex hormones together with the turbulent and confusing feelings that go with them. There is an unconscious fantasy of reversing the fall from paradise that occurs as childhood gives way to the pressures of adolescence and a much more complex and threatening world. As the pressure on the family increases, there is often a profound split between the parents about how to deal with the situation, while the anorectic feels an increasing sense of persecution and injustice.

The obsessional focus on food and weight loss forms a 'psychic retreat'. This means that the focus on one preoccupation allows other potential concerns to be blocked out. But the cost of this psychic retreat is high — there is a stunting of psychological growth, as the normal developmental tasks of life are not engaged with. Usually, the anorectic becomes the focus of the family's attention. This can seem to provide a useful function within the family, binding the family together and serving as a perverse method of getting emotional nourishment for the anorectic. But the suffering and unhappiness continues as family life enters a wintry zone of no growth and stasis. According to the psychoanalyst Marilyn Lawrence:

> Whenever one meets a patient in the grip of anorexia nervosa, one knows that some sort of catastrophe has taken place. Without knowing how or why, it seems that psychically the patient has given up on the idea of relationships and crucially the possibility of development. It is as though unconsciously some sort of decision has been made. All sense of relatedness to an object is lost.[155]

The Shadow of the Feminine

The biological factors in anorexia are powerful and complicated. The effect of starvation itself has a paradoxical effect. Rather than stimulating appetite and life force, in the anorectic the pull towards starvation and death intensifies. The psychological and family issues are often deep-seated and obvious. But is there something more? Is there another component in addition to the usual bio-psycho-social formulation? What is the nature of the archetypal territory that these women (for they usually are women) find themselves in? Is there a perverse transcendence, a subtle numinous quality that is delicate and unusually difficult to pin down? If so, then this would be in the domain of a darkening of the feminine principle and the encounter with death.

From an archetypal perspective, anorexia could be understood as a denial of the feminine. It represents a failure of transformation into womanhood and a profound horror of appetite, passion, sexuality, fertility, love of life and abundance. Goddess figures such as Aphrodite, Ishtar and

Lakshmi represent qualities of radiance, pleasure, sensuality and vitality. They hold the qualities of harmony, easy equilibrium and beautiful flowing movement. The archetype of Venus in its highest octave is love, but a particular feminine version of love. Anorexia abhors these qualities. Indeed, the qualities associated with the Aphrodite or Venus archetype would be completely foreign to the anorectic. But anorexia is more than the shadow of Aphrodite. Anorexia also represents something altogether darker, the seductive flirtation with death and an immersion in the underworld, the land of the shades. The myth of Persephone gives us some of this flavour.

The name Persephone means 'the one who loves the darkness'. But she did not start out like this. She had an idyllic childhood, in the company of her playmates and protected by her mother, the goddess Demeter, from the stresses of the outside world. Her childhood name, Kore, means eternally young girl—the archetypal maiden. Then, adult sexuality reared its head in a most traumatic way as she was raped by Hades, the god of the underworld (the Roman Pluto). In fact, her father Zeus had promised her to his brother Hades but omitted to tell Kore's mother, Demeter. Persephone is taken from her earthly paradise with all its colour and vibrancy to a dark, soulless place and into an overwhelming and intense relationship with the Lord of Death. We can imagine the awfulness of this transition. The journey into the land of death is a one-way journey; there is no return ticket and no prospect of returning home. Her mother sinks into despair and, as the goddess of fertility and harvest, Demeter is no longer able to fertilise and breathe life into the earth. Spring does not arrive, the crops fail, humans start to starve and everything is in danger of extinction. A permanent winter descends. This is comparable to an archetypal form of anorexia, a permanent sterile winter of the body, mind and soul. It is a destructive frozen wasteland where nothing grows for the anorectic or her family.

The myth eventually progresses to a satisfactory conclusion. The gods fear that mankind will be extinguished and that there will be no one left to worship them. They intervene with Hades and a compromise is reached. Persephone is allowed to return from the underworld, but only for eight months of every year. She has eaten the seeds of the pomegranate, which symbolically bind her to staying with Hades as Queen of the Underworld for four months of every year. This is the time when the earth becomes sterile and non-productive. This is winter. But Persephone retains a special gift as a result of this arrangement. She becomes comfortable in two worlds. She can master the everyday world with its sunlight and laughter, it's beauty and social mores, but she also remains mistress of the underworld. She knows how to navigate in the darkness. Having progressed through her encounter with the shadow, Persephone becomes a goddess of fertility, worshipped alongside her mother as the bringer of the flowering and abundance of spring. She is the bringer of the life force after the barren death of winter. The mysteries of Eleusis in Ancient Greece gave a further layer to the Persephone story as a profound symbol of death and rebirth, of symbolic ego death and renewal as well as preparation for the death of the physical body. We will pay Eleusis a visit in chapter 21.

The Persephone myth gives an insight into the tenacious and seductive relationship with death that can be so difficult to treat in severe anorexia. Sometimes the pull towards death is so profound and irresistible that society has a dilemma whether or not to intervene. Instead of Zeus and the Gods, we may require the highest law in the land to pull the anorexic back from Hades. To give an example, a Court of Protection in London made a ruling that a woman with severe anorexia, who wanted to be allowed to die, should be force fed in her 'best interests'. The judge had decided that she did not have the capacity to make decisions for herself. When the case was brought to court, her death was imminent. She was refusing to eat and was taking only a small amount of water. The judge ruled that 'She does not seek death, but above all she does not want to eat or to be fed. She sees her life as pointless and wants to be allowed to make her own choices, realising that refusal to eat must lead to her death'. He said that it was a very difficult decision for him to make because it required 'a balance to be struck between the weight objectively to be given to life on one hand and to personal independence on the other'. Giving his reasons, the judge said that although she was 'gravely unwell, she is not incurable . . . it would not be right to turn down the final chance of helping this very vulnerable young woman'. Every effort was to be made to bring this young woman back from the underworld.[156]

Anorexia and Sainthood

There is a long tradition of fasting and mortification of the flesh to achieve transcendence. Usually the goal is to move beyond the chattering mind with its everyday concerns towards a higher transcendent reality. Sometimes in fasting states there is an imperative to conquer greed and gluttony in all its forms, sometimes there is a clear wish to use starvation to achieve numinous experience. The *Samkkhya* philosophy of ancient India sought a truth that lay beyond ordinary human experience, but, rather than look for salvation in external gods, they looked within.[157] They wanted liberation from the clinging, constricting, over- talkative ego. They sought to transcend the *dukka*, which stands for the highly unsatisfactory pleasures and pitfalls of the everyday world and all it's suffering and illusions. The problem was that *dukka* is not easily transcended. How does one go beyond the chattering mind? How can a person prise free the attachment of the ego to its environment?

The explorers of the inner world of the Hindu tradition developed a strict moral code requiring disciplined self denial and abstinence from intoxicants and sex. They developed physical techniques such as yoga to help with this task. Yoga was very different in those early days to the contemporary version widely practised in the West with its emphasis on physical fitness and stress management. In those days, it was a sustained campaign requiring the utmost discipline. Examples of this practice would include physical postures, working with the breath and various ascetic practices including fasting.[158] Sometimes people became competitive about their asceticism and fasting, and people occasionally died. The problem with ascetic practices is that, although they can be a useful tool to practise discipline, they are not a direct route to enlightenment. This is certainly what the Buddha found after he had fasted to the point where he was close to death. Having practised the abasements that were common among ascetics in those times, including eating and drinking his own urine and faeces, self-mutilation and starvation, he found that the chattering mind was not stopped at all. What worked for Buddha was a deeper understanding of the causes of suffering, compassion practice, loving kindness and an opening of the heart.[159]

In the West there has also been a well-documented association between spiritual seeking and ascetic practices such as self starvation.[160] In the middle ages a number of women, some of whom became saints, starved themselves in the pursuit of purity and religious purpose. Many of these ascetics did not have the modern condition that we call anorexia nervosa but there was a degree of overlap and some of them did show anorectic ways of thinking. Saint Catherine of Sienna who died aged 33 in fourteenth century Italy had a traumatic family background by any standards. She was born around the time of the Black Death. She and her twin sister were her parents' 23rd and 24th children. Her twin sister died, as had half of her siblings. Around puberty, her elder sister died in childbirth and her youngest sister (child number 25) also died. Her parents wanted her to marry her sister's widower but Catherine went on a fast. She went through a period of profound withdrawal, rejecting her family and her family's food. Her biographer records that after a command from Jesus she changed her lifestyle to become a carer for the poor and the ill and became more active in public life. She achieved prominence, eventually corresponding with the pope and seeking reform of the clergy.[161]

Meanwhile the Church had become concerned about the use of extreme fasting as an indicator of spirituality and as a criterion for sainthood. Indeed, Catherine of Siena was told by Church authorities to pray that she would be able to eat again, but she was unable to give up fasting. Over the years, Catherine had eaten less and less, claiming that she found no nourishment in earthly food. Instead, she received the Holy Communion virtually on a daily basis. The severity of her fasting appeared unhealthy in the eyes of the clergy and her own sisterhood, and her confessor, Blessed Raymond, ordered her again to eat properly. But Catherine claimed that she was unable to comply, describing her inability to eat as an illness. She would disgorge what she swallowed, and suffered severe stomach pains, which she bore with patience as another penance.

In medieval times, this type of extreme fasting was called *anorexia mirabilis* and was often combined with other ascetic practices including flagellation and self mutilation. Typically, practitioners would refuse food except for the holy Eucharist, perhaps lice from vagrants and the scabs and pus from the pestilent. The piety associated with *anorexia mirabilis* would impress the congregation with the primacy of spirit over bodily needs and show that the delicious banquet of God was sufficient to maintain body and soul. This was a specifically female achievement. These women claimed a degree of spiritual grace from their fasting and the possession of special powers such as visions, healing powers and miracles.

Over the years, I have treated a number of people who have developed psychotic states that were triggered by fasting in a religious context. Invariably, they were women and usually they belonged to an evangelical Christian church. I have learned to expect such cases at Easter, although the phenomenon is not just limited to that time. Typically, there is a state of increasing religious fervour with chanting and praying. A mental state develops that is dominated by an ecstatic feeling of a close relationship to God. Sometimes people in such states do extraordinarily dangerous things. One woman jumped out of a window because she knew that God would save her and stop her coming to harm. She had fasted and chanted for three days and thought that the fall from the window would be the final stage in union with God. I have found that these women gradually recover to their normal mental states within a few days, they do not usually develop a serious psychiatric disorder and they do not need longer-term treatment. It seems to me that their condition is best understood as an archetypal crisis related to fasting and intense religious practice; a spiritual emergency.

Ana Cool

Modern anorexia nervosa has something in common with the *anorexia mirabilis* of the religious orders. Anorexia nervosa includes ritualistic behaviours, physical exercise and discipline, self-denial and sometimes obedience to a higher power. There is even a modern archetype of anorexia represented by Ana. Ana is the subject of the 'pro Ana' websites, which typically endorse anorexia as a desirable state providing a strong sense of community and common identity for anorectics with mutual support, 'thinspiration' areas and the communication of techniques to facilitate weight loss. Pro Ana sites have a certain spiritual flavour often depicting the thin emaciated individuals as angels who are pure and full of light.[162] Many pro Ana tips and words of advice use spiritual and religious terminology such as bodily purity, guilt and salvation. Patients with anorexia also talk of Ana, the disease personified, as someone to be followed and obeyed. Anorexic communities often defend their disease as a way of life, a way of following their deity Ana, which other people do not understand. This description of anorexia is almost like the creation of a new religion. Religious symbolism is also obvious in the Ana Commandments, giving directions such as:

- Thou shall not eat without feeling guilty
- Thou shall not eat fattening food without punishing oneself afterwards
- Thou shall count calories and restrict intake accordingly.

There is an Ana creed, which is interesting because it gives a flavour not only of self loathing and self punishment. but also a taste of a yearning for transcendence. For example:

- I believe that I am the most vile, worthless and useless person ever to have existed on this planet, and that I am totally unworthy of anyone's time and attention.
- I believe in control, the only force mighty enough to bring order in the chaos that is my world.
- I believe in perfection and strive to attain it.
- I believe in salvation through starvation.

Sometimes mild forms of anorexia may confer some advantage and be sustainable. Consider the supermodels, the skinny icons of chic. Some may be clinically anorexic and others may flirt with it. They presumably have appetites but seem able to control them. They are the mistresses of their destiny while transmitting a sense of ennui. Life may be pointless and we will play it on our own terms, they seem to say. We will make the rules. They transcend, they captivate. Above all, they are cool. People want to be like them.

Sophie was 19 when I first met her and she weighed under seventy pounds.[2] I remember going into her room at the hospital to introduce myself and to begin the long journey of getting to know her and winning her trust. In my countertransference, I felt huge, clumsy, gross and afraid of breaking something. She seemed to be in an unreachable zone, serene and calm. She was not unfriendly but definitely icy. She was distressed about being in hospital. A part of her accepted that her lack of eating had got out of control and that she had become too weak to function at college. This part of her recognised that her life had become narrow and restricted and that she was losing her friends. But she could not bear the thought of giving up her anorexia.

Sophie became my long-term psychotherapy patient. I saw her every week for a couple of years and became deeply immersed in her struggle. It took some time before she could speak freely to me about her relationship with anorexia. She told me once of a peak moment when she was walking around the Covent Garden area of London. She was very thin, she was losing weight and felt in control, but had not yet become weak. She knew that other girls were looking at her and were envious of her thin shape. She felt fantastic. She felt as though she was separate from the human race and all of their problems and pettiness. She felt as though she was in a special place. She struggled to describe the quality of this feeling. It seemed to have a sacred and indefinable quality. 'I felt like a goddess', she said.

The problem with this sort of numinous experience is that it becomes very addictive. It is like the first drunk or the first transcendent drug experience. You have touched the heights and want to touch them again. There are other factors of a bio-psycho-social nature that predispose towards a turning away from the difficult engagement with everyday reality, but the developing archetypal flavour acts as an accelerant; it pours petrol on the flames. As the condition progresses, the numinous feeling becomes more elusive but the memory of transcendence remains and drives the addiction.

If we accept that there may be a hidden archetypal component to anorexia, then we should explore the implications of this for treatment programmes. If there is an element of perverse numinosity, a searching for the sacred, then there could be potential for a spiritual emergence as part of a psychospiritual maturation process. There is no reason why a therapeutic effort aimed at the archetypal layer of psyche should not sit comfortably alongside treatments aimed at the bio-psycho-social elements aimed at the

---

[2] Thirty kilos.

restoration and maintenance of weight and the treatment of the underlying issues in personal and family psychotherapy.

What would such a treatment programme look like? We can make some tentative suggestions. People with anorexia are difficult to engage with so it should be gradual, non-threatening, gently engaging and carefully nuanced. Yoga could be a good place to start. The physical benefits of gentle exercise would be obvious to fragile and starved bodies with depleted bone density and atrophied muscles. The typical anorectic would also welcome the opportunity to burn some calories. Yoga would provide the opportunity to introduce some simple breathing exercises or some meditation techniques and this could pave the way for the introduction of more complex methods. Mindfulness practise or loving kindness meditation could soften the harsh and punitive cognitions that afflict these patients who find it so very hard to be kind and gentle with themselves. Such treatments could be a useful adjunct to conventional treatment.[163]

Internet forums are raising the suggestion that psychotherapy augmented by the drug MDMA, colloquially known as ecstasy, could be useful in the treatment of anorexia, particularly by decreasing the degree of self-loathing and hatred of the body. There is a growing interest in the possible use of MDMA as an aid to psychotherapy in some psychiatric disorders (such as PTSD), although there is no research evidence yet to support its use for treatment of anorexia. MDMA is not yet licensed as a treatment, but I will discuss in chapter 21 how it holds the characteristics of the Aphrodite archetype, which is exactly the quality that is denied in anorexia.

The Anima

The archetypal principles of anima and animus are notoriously difficult concepts to understand.[164] The anima is said to hold inner feminine qualities for the male psyche while the animus represents the inner masculine version of the female psyche. But this is an over simplification, the gender issues of anima are less important than her bridging role which ultimately brings ego into a closer relationship with Self. An integration of the anima or animus is considered by Jungians to be an advanced stage on the path to individuation, taking the psyche to a deeper, more functional level.[165] Anima has an 'otherness' quality, she seems to belong partly to our individual ego, but partly to something else altogether.

The archetypal nature of anima and animus is best portrayed in the gods and goddesses of old, and the myths and legends about them. For the Gnostics, the feminine principle was represented by Sophia and it was the task of ego, of consciousness, to find a way of liberating this feminine part of the Divine from captivity, so that she could take her rightful place in nature and in the material world. In polytheistic religions, it would be unimaginable to have gods without their goddesses, as the qualities that they hold are entirely different. The goddess that I tend to associate most with the anima archetype is Athena. Athena is the Greek goddess of civilisation, justice and courage. It seems appropriate that Athens, the home of Socrates, Plato and Aristotle was named in her honour. Athena holds very different qualities to Aphrodite. She is a virgin who represents progress and growth, supporting learning, science and the arts. Athena is the guiding principle of the heroic journey. She befriends hero figures in Greek mythology, often giving them gifts or magical assistance. However anima may take a very different shape to the perfection of Athena. When we first encounter the anima principle, it is often much more primitive, sometimes frightening. Anima figures can take us unawares, surprise us with their intensity and the assistance that they give us can come in an unexpected form.

The most frightening dream that I ever had occurred in my childhood. It involved an image that seared my mind; it shook me to my core and I tried not to think about it for years afterwards. The image was a simple one: it was a female face that held a look of concentrated venom. She didn't move and she didn't say anything; she simply stared. She was just plain evil and she did not like me. Years later, I tried to understand this image in psychodynamic terms and I'm sure that there were elements of my relationship with my mother that came into the equation. But this was, above all, an archetypal image and it held a very dark numinosity. Although it certainly did not seem helpful at the time, this terrifying dream shaped me powerfully in some indefinable way and seemed to act as a conduit bringing material from shadow towards a more illuminated position. This dream drew me towards an interest in the psyche and has played a role in my passage through life that led to this book forming in my mind. I understand this image now as a manifestation of the dark feminine principle, a primitive encounter with a version of anima that is gnarled, jagged and dreadful. It comes from the shadow, it is the archetypal feminine that has been alienated and rejected so that the first meeting with it is likely to be difficult.

These primitive forms of the feminine can be paralysing rather than helpful. In Greek mythology, the archetypal hero Perseus encounters Medusa, the dreadful female gorgon with a hideous face and snakes in place of hair. Medusa is a terrifying presence that is totally opposed to growth, anyone who gazes upon her is turned to stone. However Perseus is befriended by Athena who gives him a highly polished shield. He uses this shield as a mirror so he can see the reflection of Medusa well enough to lop off her head without making eye contact. Thus the guiding principle represented by Athena enables the hero to take an entirely new perspective. The hero becomes able to see the situation in a different way so that the paralysing influence of shadow is overcome.[166] Perseus continues on his heroic journey using the power of his mutative encounter with shadow (Medusa's head) to marry the beautiful Andromeda and eventually having a star named after him – representing the successful realisation of Self.

CHAPTER 15

Ego Death and the Midlife Crisis

Much has been written about the near death experience. Yet every psychiatrist is confronted daily with people not living but surviving. I have observed that the fear of dying is directly proportional to the sense of not having lived. The psyche knows that there is a real danger of missing the boat.

—Andrew Powell

The Challenge of Midlife

What is it about the living dead, the zombies and vampires, that have so caught our collective imagination? These dreadful, unfeeling creatures are incapable of compassion, being driven only by base appetites that compel and consume them. Zombies are the slow-witted, relentless and damaged beings who swarm like locusts and destroy those of us who have flowing blood and warm hearts. Vampires are more conscious consumers of vitality to give their archaic frames some form of life force, when they should be dead and decayed. It seems that they fascinate us because they show us something about ourselves. They are a representation of our shadow, the unconscious aspect of our individual and collective psyche that is entirely self centred and dominated by appetite. They point to the part of us that is mindless, complacent, consuming and entirely anti-growth.

The most extreme form of zombie-like behaviour that I see is the addict. Not the addict who is stabilised on support, therapy or medication; not the addict who has built some stability into their lives; but the addict for whom every waking moment is dominated by craving and who will do anything to satisfy that thirst. For addicts of this kind, all their behaviour is organised around that primary appetite. Addiction takes many forms; perhaps we all have this innate tendency, to some extent, related to our animal appetites, the demands of our ego and its addiction to the things that gratify it, the things that we think we need and the things to which we become attached. Perhaps the midlife transition is the journey of taming the inner zombie, of becoming less asleep to who we really are.

The idea that I will explore here is that the midlife crisis is essentially a crisis of meaning. The term 'midlife crisis' is potentially misleading as the process I am describing can occur at any age from adolescence to old age. However the midlife crisis is most likely to occur in middle age when a person has successfully navigated many of life's hurdles, managed the basic issues of adult independence and achieved security. But somehow these things are not enough. There is a lingering feeling of dissatisfaction, of dis-ease. As Joseph Campbell once said, 'you may have got to the top of the ladder, but perhaps the ladder is leaning against the wrong wall'. Surely there is more than this. But what else is there?

The midlife crisis classically occurs in association with a threat to the ego. Death is the ultimate threat and, by definition, the midlife period brings the realisation that we are closer to the exit than the entrance. We are on the downward slope to our extinction. The ego structures that have served their purpose well over the first part of life become less useful and need to be re-arranged. Sometimes this process flows smoothly, but the ego is nothing if not tough and resilient, and often it resists this process strongly. The midlife crisis then develops as a battle between the ego that was and the ego that needs to be brought into being. It is a battle of ego death and rebirth. There is often a trigger that brings matters to a head. The trigger is a challenge to the established ego regime. It may be an important relationship change involving partner, family life or employment or there may be a change of role such as retirement or children leaving home. It may involve illness or an encounter with death. It may be a numinous experience or an archetypal experience of some kind.

I don't think many are spared one of the many manifestations of the midlife crisis. For many of us, it is a nagging grumbling presence with mild dis-ease. For some of us, it may be more severe, although it is rarely as dramatic as the type of psycho-social crises that we worked with in the crisis intervention service where people became suicidal after a difficult life event. On the various retreats and workshops that I have done over the last ten years, many of my fellow participants had certainly undergone some form of midlife crisis, and it was this crisis that led them eventually to some form of spiritual practice and thence to the retreats that we shared. A few of them have had encounters with psychiatry, which often left them feeling misunderstood and frustrated. Many of them seemed to instinctively gravitate towards a community that seemed to hold some integrity and a promise of a deeper way of understanding and relating. Such a community may be simply an organisation that provides occasional seminars, a forum for some discussion and the proximity of like-minded people. It may be a more formal structure such as a church, a Buddhist centre or a training programme. It may be a yoga class or a meditation practice. The function of such a community is to provide a safe, encouraging and nourishing setting, a compass to show which way is North, if North symbolises the Self. It is much harder to navigate this territory alone and sometimes people get very lost.

The philosopher Michael Washburn has developed a useful model that describes this process.[167] For Washburn, there is an underlying layer of undifferentiated archetypal energy that he calls the Dynamic Ground. This is primal life force, the source of energy and creativity, the bedrock of consciousness. In this model, the ego is a personal construct that emerges from the Ground and, as the ego takes shape, we increasingly identify with it so that we repress the Ground, which becomes the deep unconscious. Washburn describes how the over-identification with ego eventually becomes counterproductive, as we become disconnected from the nutritive energy of the Ground. We lose vitality and our mood tends to become depressed. For Washburn, the midlife crisis holds the difficult but essential task of loosening the grip of ego and reconnecting to the dynamic potentials of the Ground so that psychospiritual growth can continue.

The problem is that the ego is a crucial part of who we think we are, the very basis of our identity—so it is not surprising that the death throes of our ego structures can be associated with such a profound sense of meaninglessness and alienation. This is a low archetypal penetrance state bringing a bleak flatness of spirit; an anhedonia where pleasure is lost. This is the long dark tunnel of life with no light at the end of it. We may redouble attempts to find some pleasure in the things that have served us before. We may buy the red sports car, go partying or have an affair. But these attempts to support the foundering ego by rekindling the relics of our youthful ideals don't work for us any longer and the consequences of such behaviour may deepen the crisis.

For Washburn and others, the midlife crisis is part of a developmental process that allows the redundant ego structures to properly perish as a prelude to a regeneration or rebirth. This is a complicated process. We will take a look at two examples. The first is a classical spiritual emergency and the second is a psychiatric emergency.

Stefan and the Sami

Stefan was an engineer. He lived in Chicago and held a senior position as an engineer in a large company. His crisis began in his forties when he had everything that he aspired to. His marriage was sound and fulfilling and he had a good relationship with his daughter. 'It was all going so well', he told me, but despite his success he felt increasingly unhappy. He wasn't depressed in any clinical sense; he functioned well at work and at home and no one would have guessed that anything was the matter with him. But it was all beginning to seem so meaningless. He looked back on his achievements and could take no pleasure in them. Okay, so he had built some good bridges. But if he hadn't built them, then someone else would have done. What had he ever done that really meant something?

The state of the world depressed him and reinforced his ennui. He pondered that everyone was out to enrich themselves at the expense of other people and the planet. He stopped watching news programmes and he gradually dropped his social contacts. He simply couldn't see the point in it. People were just talking about their achievements, their holidays and their houses. He went through a phase of excess, of eating and drinking too much, but he disgusted himself even more and was able to stop it. He found himself thinking about death more and more. On one hand, he felt that he would welcome a terminal illness; on the other hand, he found himself becoming more anxious about his health and had a number of consultations with his doctor. Antidepressants were discussed, but he didn't think pills were the answer and he didn't think his doctor thought so either.

He felt increasingly desperate. He really didn't know what to do with himself. He could see himself just turning into a morose old man, like his father had done before him. He had always been able to find solace in nature, but it felt as though this was deserting him too. The mountains had lost their magic—they were, after all, just big rocks. The trees seemed gloomy and the great expanses of the lake, which had always delighted him, just looked cold and grey. It felt as though the juices of life had dried up.

In midlife crisis, the turning point often arrives from a completely unexpected direction. On impulse Stefan accompanied a friend to an evening lecture about the practices of the Sami, the indigenous people of northern Scandinavia. One of the presenters was an old Sami shaman who made a profound impression on him. He held a stillness, vitality and power that seemed utterly authentic. It spoke to something deep and half forgotten inside him and, to his surprise, a little while later Stefan found himself at his first shamanic workshop. He felt something stirring in his depths, something in his soul seemed to be coming alive. He began a serious study of shamanic journeying and found that this helped him to find a path through his inner turmoil to reconnect him in an important way to nature. So far, so good. He had found a path with which he felt some resonance and people who he felt had some important knowledge. He went on another more intense retreat, which involved a vision quest in the Arizona desert and he had one of those wonderful moments, while sitting on a mountain, of peace, clarity and bliss. He felt cured of all his neuroses and empowered for whatever the future held.

So why did everything start going wrong again when he returned to Chicago? He felt full of power and a newfound confidence. He wanted to tell people how the way in which they were living their lives was wrong. He could see their mistakes so clearly and wanted to put them right. He antagonised his colleagues and his adult daughter told him one day that she couldn't talk to him any more as he was too irritable and rigid in his views. Stefan began to see that his experience had made him arrogant and dogmatic. He wondered if he had suffered some sort of breakdown.

The Italian psychiatrist Roberto Assagioli has something very interesting to say about the complications of peak experiences such as Stefan's mountain top epiphany. The influx of energy from the Self, he says, will cause the sharp edges and less agreeable traits of the personality to recede into the background and we see a new and lovable individual. Sometimes the integrative energy of the Self and the maturity of the ego is sufficient to allow a permanent transformation. However, sometimes, as the energy of the Self recedes, the personality traits reassert themselves with renewed force. All the rocks and rubbish of our ego and personality, which had been covered by the high tide of energy, emerge again.[168] Of course, the advantage can be that this shadow aspect is now available to be worked upon, if it is recognised for what it is.

Stefan describes a dawning realisation that he had not treated people with respect and compassion. He had not been skilful in the use of his new insights. He realised that he had some interpersonal and family-of-origin issues that needed attention if he was to make further progress, and he sought some help from a psychotherapist. He continued his shamanic practice and found inspiration in it. When I met him at a meditation retreat a few years later, he told me that he had been surprised at the direction that his midlife crisis had taken him, but he felt grateful and refreshed by the process. The crisis was over, his relationships were flourishing and he had found a path to continue his growth.[169]

The Archetypes of the Chakra System

For those of us who are trained in the Western scientific and medical tradition, chakras may be associated with 'New-Age' ideas of dubious validity but I am introducing the chakra system here from an archetypal perspective, organized around states of meaning and significance. The traditional understanding of the chakra system shows seven distinct nodal points along the midline of body from sacrum to brow but this is symbolic and there is no evidence that these nodes have a physical existence. According to the Ayurvedic model, each chakra resonates with and captures different octaves of energy or 'prana' from the universal energy field. The word *chakra* is translated from Sanskrit as a vertex or wheel, which gives a flavor of the dynamic and energetic nature of the concept. There are three aspects of this theoretical model that I would like to consider:

- All of the levels are necessary—in a condition of health all the chakras are said to be open and balanced with no obstruction to the free flow of energy. But when the flow of energy is blocked, our human organism can become unbalanced and potentially unwell.

- Midlife crisis is best understood as an imbalance; with overweening lower levels, particularly the third level, and an under development of the archetype of compassion associated with the fourth level. This in turn suppresses sources of potential inspiration from the higher levels.

- The higher levels give a model for numinous experience with its potential benefits and side effects. Indeed, the American psychiatrist John Nelson has developed a comprehensive theory showing how difficulties relating to the archetypal energies of the chakra system combine with our biological and psychological systems to produce various psychiatric disorders.[170]

The British psychiatrist Andrew Powell, who founded the Spirituality and Psychiatry group of the Royal College of Psychiatrists, shows us how chakras can also be understood as archetypal principles representing the developmental journey of the ego.[171] For Powell, the lower chakras relate to the development of the personality while the higher chakras point beyond the personal psyche towards the transpersonal. The first three chakras relate to the development of the area of psyche described by Freud, while Jung is more concerned with the journey onward from the third chakra. The level of the fourth chakra is the transitional zone where the ego starts to recede in importance and there is a decisive shift away from egocentricity and increased capacity for compassion and altruism. There may (or may not) follow a progressive opening to the archetypal layers before the final seventh chakra, which is said to be the primal place of unity that is beyond archetypes and indeed beyond words.[172]

The first level or root chakra symbolizes the basic and instinctive drive to survive. This is the life force of the human animal that concerns security, survival and response to danger. It concerns the maintenance of the body, appetite, feeding, hunting and its modern-day equivalents. The way in which this survival drive is expressed ranges from the suckling and crying of the newborn to the disparate ways in which adults seek to satisfy their various appetites. This is the level that binds and grounds consciousness from the pre-personal, pre-ego undifferentiated state into the demands of physical reality.

The second level or the genital chakra is concerned with the development of emotional range, the perpetuation of the species, sexual energy and generativity. The expression of this energy will be highly variable according to stage of life and the modifying effect of other physical and psychological factors.

The third level or solar plexus chakra is concerned with power, will, hierarchy and issues of social organization in individuals and groups. It is the most worldly level and its concerns are domination and submission, manipulation and the erection of structure. This is the level where the ego is at its most dominant, being organized around role, status and station in life.

The middle level or heart chakra is the crucial transitional point between the personal and transpersonal, where further development depends less on intellectual or rational knowledge of a scientific kind and more on a certain form of emotional development, 'Gnosis Kardias', the knowledge of the heart. This turning point occurs as survival, procreation and status no longer dominate the agenda and different values are sought. This may involve the paradigm clash of the midlife crisis or it can take the form of a gradual progressive softening of the rigid structures of the ego. Ideally, the demands of the ego begin to give way to higher emotional functions with the affective tones of altruism, love, compassion, grief and joy. This tends to bring about a new relationship with the world based on a dis-identification with 'me' (egocentric) towards identification with 'us' (ethnocentric), an identification with 'all of us' (worldcentric) and perhaps ultimately to identification with 'the All' (kosmocentric).[173]

The last three chakras are the levels involving transpersonal experience, beyond the individual ego and which move progressively to domains of mind that are not governed by our conventional sense of space and time. The fifth level or throat chakra is a state of increased archetypal penetrance that can be problematic; it is associated with mysticism and madness depending on how the archetypal material is construed by the human being concerned. This is said to be the level of consciousness associated with creative genius. A composer may talk of a mysterious process where the music is gleaned from the ether or an author may describe a plot or a character arriving fully formed in the mind. Art tends to describe this level better than words and visionary artists make their interpretations of it available for us. Aldous Huxley described a process where light seems to spill out from the interior world to the exterior world.[174] This is a kind of visionary experience that people have with their eyes open and which consists of a positive transfiguration of the external world so that it seems overwhelmingly beautiful and alive and shining.

Glimpses of this fifth-chakra level occur not infrequently in everyday life in quieter contemplative moments. There may be mild transcendent experiences in nature or with music or more intense and pressing numinous moments whether sublime or frightening. I suggest that the major developmental transitions of life such as adolescence, midlife and end of life have a tendency to raise archetypal penetrance so that such glimpses become more frequent and intense during these periods. The glimpses may occur at any time of life, they may be fleeting, but if the intensity is high and if the experience is supported and integrated, the impact may be profound. These can be valuable moments for the midlife navigator of crisis, potentially perilous but pregnant with potential. Jung's 'creative illness', with his visions and non-physical guides, probably emanated from this level.

The sixth or brow chakra is said to take us further into the realm of the transpersonal, where space-time is transcended and consciousness is no longer experienced as arising from the self. This is a level where all things seem connected. The opening to this level can be perilous for the uninitiated but is pregnant with potential. People who are familiar with this level, such as very experienced mediators, may have enhanced capacity for psi or 'siddhis'.[175] Nelson compares people at this level to the sighted person in the land of blind, clearly a perilous position.[176] The blind people with no knowledge of vision would tend to see the sighted people as abnormal and threatening to their worldview. Perhaps they would be kept in secluded areas and measures would be taken to deprive them of their sight, suggests Nelson—alluding to the potential for psychiatry to misunderstand these states. We can perhaps see parallels with Plato's philosophers returning to the cave after their ascent and being persecuted by the people of the shadow world. While the 6th level is the summit of the achievement of the individual organism, it is not surprising that people with experience of this area of mind tend to be discrete.

If the 5th level looks back to the previous four levels, the 6th level looks forward to the ultimate dissolution of the 7th. The seventh level is the non-dual, the state of bliss or Samadhi described by the few mystics and contemplatives who have direct experience of this level. Here there is no duality, no observer and observed. There are no boundaries and no thoughts. There is just unity. This is a truly transpersonal state where the individual ego has been entirely transcended.

It is not uncommon for people whose primary area of function is firmly rooted in the egoic levels to have fleeting experiences of transpersonal levels, which can act as important signposts, holding the germ of transformation by dislodging the identification of consciousness with the ego and the worldview that is based on it. These experiences of the numinous may strongly suggest a sense of direction for future travel or they can cause an archetypal crisis. I do not want to over-simplify a complex process, but the chakra perspective highlights the midlife crisis as a fundamental imbalance, with hypertrophied ego structures collapsing under their own weight. An identification with the archetypal forces of the 4th chakra, with compassion and altruistic love to the forefront, may resolve this dilemma for the ego but this is not without risk. The territory of the heart chakra brings with it an increased potential for opening to further transpersonal experiences, which in turn have the potential to be helpful or to cause confusion thus deepening the crisis. A failure to make this progression may have devastating consequences.

Heart Opening

Many of the patients that I saw on the trauma unit at the Royal London had done terrible things to themselves. I met Terry after he had plunged a knife into his chest in a crowded London supermarket. The police used an electroshock instrument to immobilise him before he damaged himself further, or indeed anyone else. In hospital he was resuscitated and the trauma surgeons repaired his wound. He had lacerated the left ventricle of his heart. As his story unfolded, it seemed to me that his developing ego death was very nearly accompanied by physical death.

When I met him he was terrified that someone was going to harm him. Indeed, he knew that 'they' would probably kill him slowly and horribly. He didn't know who they were, but he knew they were out there and waiting for him. He told me that he tried to end his own life in a quick and painless way before these people could get to him. His first day in hospital was stormy. He felt in great danger and tried to escape from the intensive care unit, pulling out his tubes and drains as he did so. Our primary task at that stage was to take care of his physical health and ensure his survival. There was no question of allowing him to leave the hospital. He had a nurse sitting with him and I gave him a sedative antipsychotic to lessen the intensity of his distress and terror. It was a few days before he could tell me his story.

Terry told me that he had been feeling stressed for a year or so. He was in his late forties, and working harder than ever. His marriage was in trouble and there never seemed to be enough money. He wasn't sleeping very well and his alcohol consumption was increasing. He came from a large family, he followed his football team, he loved his children and he walked his dogs. He was a steady sort of fellow who enjoyed life and was not prone to depression. He had never seen a psychiatrist before and it never occurred to him that he would. He had started to feel depressed and irritable; he and his wife seemed to have less and less to say to each other, and his libido was waning. He missed her. One day at a family party, he saw his wife and his brother exchange a smile and he described a sudden moment of realisation that they were having an affair. We later established that his wife and his brother were not romantically involved in any way, shape or form, and Terry accepted this, but at the time of this party, Terry was totally persuaded that they were in a conspiracy together from which he was excluded.

From this point onwards, Terry's world was suffused with an entirely different meaning state of mounting suspicion and fear. His level of vigilance increased. Everything began to seem loaded with a hidden meaning. It was very intense and his sense of being on the edge of something huge, overwhelming and sinister became more and more powerful. He couldn't sleep and lay awake at night trying to figure it out. At this stage, the 'feeling' dominated his every moment; he was utterly preoccupied, but he couldn't name it and he didn't have a theory about it, except the memory of his suspicion about his wife.

He confronted his wife under the influence of alcohol. He frightened her and she asked him to leave the family home. He went to live with his father but he missed his children dreadfully and it seemed as though the bottom had fallen out of his life. He just didn't know what to do with himself. Then he noticed the policemen watching him. Whenever he was in the streets, there seemed to be a policeman in the vicinity and it seemed as though they were signalling to each other about him. The signals varied but usually involved a gesture of hand, or a movement of eye. Then he noticed that people in plain clothes were using the same gestures. They seemed to be young Asian women. Terry felt that wherever he went, the young Asian women were keeping him under surveillance.

Terry had no idea what was happening to him and couldn't really describe afterwards how he felt. He tried to find words: 'it felt big' he said, 'bigger than anything'. He couldn't sleep, and he couldn't think of any ways to escape the net that he felt was closing in around him. He knew that he was powerless to resist. He knew that the end when it came would involve unimaginable pain. He took a handful of tablets to try to end his life, but his father found him and he was brought to hospital. While awaiting the psychiatrist, he thought he was in danger from assassins, so he fled. He went to a shopping mall thinking at first that he might be safer in a crowded place, but he could see people around him, Asian women, gesturing with hands and eyes. He knew they were coming for him. It was time to die.

Terry's paranoia resolved surprisingly quickly in hospital. After a couple of days of antipsychotic medication, the fear had left him and he felt restored to something resembling his normal self. He found it very difficult to find the words to describe his experiences. He told me that it was like being in a horror film, that there was no escape, he felt that he had been singled out to be destroyed like a nut in a big crushing machine. Now that he was clearly and decisively in an entirely different archetypal landscape, the task changed to the integration of his experience to help him emerge from his crisis to maximum benefit. Indeed, he felt he'd been given a second chance. He felt that much of his problems were associated with alcohol and resolved to become abstinent. His wife came to visit him in hospital and it seemed that they were finding ways to communicate again. His wife was making no promises but it looked as though he would be returning to the family home once he'd finished his convalescence. Terry just wanted to be with his family again.

Terry was most unusual with the severity and drama of his presentation and the speed and completeness of his recovery. As days passed, his memories of his state of terror became blurred and he found it harder and harder to bring them into his consciousness. Apart from a few moments that retained a stark clarity, it faded like a vivid dream. Psychiatry would label Terry as having developed a brief psychotic illness and would consider that bio-psycho-social factors had been involved in its causation. His illness would probably not have developed if he hadn't been drinking so much alcohol. Perhaps he also had a genetic predisposition to psychotic disorder, although there didn't seem to be anyone else in his extended family who had suffered similar experiences. He'd been developing the signs and symptoms of chronic and increasing stress for some time, although he hadn't developed a depressive illness. A psychoanalyst would suggest that anxiety had led to an expression of the infantile psyche with a projection of psychotic anxiety onto the external world. Perhaps the incident with his wife represented the triggering of an unresolved Oedipus complex, with a sense of life changing and catastrophic betrayal by his wife resonating with buried feelings about his mother.

These models are all helpful and relevant but perhaps there is another layer. I wondered if Terry's experience was an unusual and malignant form of midlife crisis with all the features of an archetypal experience. His 'feeling' was ineffable and it dominated his every moment with an unbearable intensity. There was a strong sense of being involved in something bigger than himself but with a profoundly negative and dangerous nature. How can we understand this using archetypal imagery? He had experienced a death-rebirth process but in an external and life-threatening way. He had no way of using a reflective process to make sense of his experiences. His images of being killed horribly, torn to pieces could be understood as a concrete version of the tensions surrounding ego death and the resistance put up by the ego structures whose survival is threatened.[177]

His crisis had been fuelled by his perception of a personal rejection from his wife, which became paranoid and acquired a delusional component. He felt that the Asian ladies were conspiring to torture him—a clear pointer to the darker aspect of the feminine principle being expressed in a delusional manner. There are many goddess figures that capture some of the power of the encounter with death. The Hindu goddess Kali is associated with death and destruction, a dreadful power, but Kali is also the penetrator of Maya, the world of illusion. So Kali represents a mutative process; she will brings you to your demons but she can also be the demon slayer. She is fierce and destructive but has a nourishing maternal side. Kali is an embodiment of the dark feminine. The Jungian analyst Monika Wikman speaks of the encounter with the suppressed feminine, the rejecting feminine and how it is inevitably difficult and jagged at first, but it softens as it is integrated into our consciousness.[178] Terry's experience contains a number of clues as to the presence of a rejected feminine and, indeed, he seemed to recognise this, recognising that he needed to become softer, gentler and more co-operative.

I have seen a number of people who, like Terry, have performed a perverse and concrete form of heart opening by stabbing themselves in the heart. Although they are different and do not all conform to a pattern, I have observed a pattern none the less. They are almost always men in midlife crisis who are experiencing a profound alienation from their loved ones and from themselves. They develop a sense of self-loathing that translates into behaviour that puts further distance between them and their support systems. They often drink too much alcohol and develop acute psychotic symptoms that are implicated in their suicide attempt. This illustrates an extreme version of ego death: a profound loss of their emotional bearings accompanied by feelings of worthlessness and hopelessness. As the intensity of this state of meaning increases, it completely overwhelms the capacity of the conscious mind for integration and the process of ego death becomes translated into an irresistible urge towards extinction.

These men, when I see them after their suicide attempts, often settle quite quickly and the extraordinary intensity of their state of mind fades within a few days. Their course is very different to those with acute schizophrenia or a severe mood disorder where recovery would take weeks or months. It is unusual for me in clinical practice to see such dramatic changes in people and I have learned to recognise this as a hallmark of the structural change in the deep psyche that can occur in archetypal crisis. It is as though this extraordinarily close and vivid encounter with death has caused a fundamental shift in ego structures so that the symbolic ego death has indeed occurred. There has been a transition and these people are usually very clear that they are no longer suicidal. Usually, there is a sense of gratitude that they have survived and they can cautiously sense a new lease of life. So the task for myself and my colleagues is to work with them to make some sense of what they have been through and how they are changed by it. We can begin the work of integration to shape with them a new way of being in the world.

Egolescence

For many of us, the turning away from the flickering shadows of our cultural trance is not an intentional process. We do not stride confidently through Plato's cave towards the exit; we hesitate, we slouch and we stumble. In mid life crisis there is likely to be a powerful undertow of low mood. It is a state of unstable archetypal penetrance, where the pervasive greyness of the LAP state may be interspersed by periods of higher archetypal penetrance. These higher penetrance states hold the potential for various forms of numinous experience that may accelerate the mutative process. In mid life crisis, the ego has to begin to fail significantly to stop the repression of Self. So the process needs to be supported in two crucial ways, firstly to allow the ego to fail in a safe and supported way and secondly to allow an emergence, an uncovering of Self. A developed mid life crisis, as we saw with Stefan, has elements of both. While ego is foundering, the Self may be beckoning – if we can only become aware it. It follows that any practice that amplifies the beckoning Self by increasing archetypal penetrance, may be very helpful, but correct mindset, setting and integration are absolutely crucial for this endeavour.

The midlife crisis may seem to arise out of nowhere or it may be triggered by external events. A life event that frequently causes a developmental crisis in adult life is the birth of a baby and becoming a parent. I do not mean to suggest that parenthood is the only way or the best way to undergo this process, merely that it is the most common and the tensions between satisfying our own ego and the service to others are often particularly stark. For some this may be a smooth and progressive maturation, for others it may be a profoundly uncomfortable assault on our ego structures as our lives are abruptly restructured to serve the demands of another small and demanding being. Many other people will go through a similar process in service of community, of friends or partners. The key ingredient is often developing the practice of selflessness, altruism and kindness in some form, and I suggest that an encounter with this force of compassion is often the tipping point, the crucial fulcrum in this process of ego regeneration.

We have seen how the midlife process fundamentally changes the ego. The familiar ego structures are found wanting and new ego structures, new ways of being in the world, are tried on for size. Sometimes this is a straightforward process, following the examples set by role models or by a community. Sometimes, as with Stefan, it is a more precarious process that can amplify and perpetuate the midlife crisis before a more stable equilibrium is found. Ego death and rebirth are like the weeding of a garden. The constricting and growth depleting parts of ego, like the weeds, have a powerful tendency to grow back. Sometimes it is the same type of weed that reappears and sometimes they are different weeds. The point that I want to make is that the weeding process needs repeating.

Egolescence is a useful term to capture that period of precarious uncertainty between two phases of ego. As we move uncertainly from dying ego to ego reborn, there is great potential for mistakes as we veer off the established pathway with its familiar stability towards the less certain path of the new ego structure. The natural tendency is towards a more organised state, but once again much depends on mindset, setting and integration

We are all familiar with the manner in which people navigate their adolescence in very different ways. Adolescence is different to the biological process of puberty although the two processes are inextricably entwined. One person can go through puberty progressing seamlessly from childhood to adult responsibilities—it can seem like business as usual although the perspective becomes more permeated by hormones and their imperatives. For another person, the onset of puberty can lead to an adolescence that is much harder, darker and destabilising, full of tension and uncomfortable nuance. Egolescence is the adolescence of the midlife crisis. However, the drive in egolescence is in the opposite direction, the adolescent moves towards establishing strong and viable ego structures, while egolescence is towards diminishing some redundant aspects of ego, in favour of an enhanced relationship with the Self.

There is a danger in pushing the analogy too far because the maturity is very different at 40 compared to 14, at 50 compared to 15, although some of the processes are similar. Indeed for some people the midlife crisis may occur shortly after adolescence, egolescence does not only occur in middle age. Adolescence is associated with a sexual epiphany with the first orgasm. The orgasm is a moment beyond ego but the ego wants more orgasms and tends to organise behaviour to that end. The midlife crisis may be associated with an archetypal epiphany which can be likened to an orgasm of a spiritual nature; it is a crossing of a threshold. While adolescence is fuelled by hormones, egolescence is a quickening to the Ground. One cannot go back to the pre-epiphany state, although some people may try. Epiphanies are by their very nature antagonistic to ego structures.

The spiritual awakening, as opposed to the sexual awakening, affects fundamentally how you see the world, your place in it and your interpersonal relationships. Both are periods of intellectual and moral awakening with a compelling shift in perspective and relational attitudes towards the world and its people. In egolescence there is inevitably a revisiting of some of the unresolved themes of adolescence. Both phases are typically suffused with a heightened archetypal imagery and a numinosity that may be vague but pregnant with potential. Both phases are prone to introspection and narcissism. Both represent a shift from the concrete. Both can lead to a cynical alienation from norms, parental ideals and society. Both can predispose to naïve idealism, looking to abstract principles and ideals as offering solutions to ethical difficulties.

Transformation in 'O'

How does one start to emerge from midlife crisis? How does the failing dispirited ego respond constructively to the whispers from the deep? Sometimes the charge of archetypal energy and spiritual insight can be followed by a disappointment, an alienation and abandonment, as the connection to the numinous is lost. For those of us who have been through the process, it can indeed be a long dark night of the soul that seems interminable and never-ending. The reassurances that this is a natural healthy process, that the dark night will be followed by bright dawn, sound naïve and fantastic. Yes, it makes sense to practice kindness, to do yoga or meditation, to listen to beautiful music and to spend time in nature. But sometimes this just doesn't seem to work. What, then, is there but to wait and hope that there may be something inchoate, something emergent, and something gestating?

As a decorated tank commander at the close of the First World War, the British psychoanalyst Wilfred Bion (1897–1979) knew something about life and death. After the war, he transferred his attention to the world within and became a highly respected psychoanalyst of the Kleinian school, also noted for his experiments in group analysis. In his 'late' phase, he became a psychoanalytic heretic, to the point where he felt the need to escape from his psychoanalytic peer group who 'hedged' him in.[179] He left London for the freshness of California so that he could develop his ideas further.

Bion had learned that psychic change occurred in psychoanalysis in the rational thinking mind, attached to brain and body with sensory input, object relationships and biological imperatives. His point of departure with psychoanalysis was his discovery of an entirely different sphere of mind, which he called the 'O' zone. He considered this to be an undifferentiated germ cell layer of mind with much greater transformative power than rational mind. Bion considered that people such as Leonardo and Shakespeare were nourished by and derived their inspiration from the O zone.

Bion attempted to convert the analytic couch into a setting more conducive to transformation in O. He recommended a turning away from rational thought, which he considered restrictive, to be replaced by a receptive reverie where there is 'no memory, no desire, no coherence, no understanding'. This is heresy for psychoanalysts but is easier to understand for people conversant with the various schools of meditation and non-ordinary states of consciousness.

Bion's O zone may sound familiar. His description of a living subterranean flow of power and mystery has a resonance with Bohm's implicate order, Washburn's Dynamic Ground and Jung's collective unconscious. Bion was influenced by Kant and Plato's theory of forms or archetypes and even found evidence of a pre-natal and hallucinatory zone linked to the O zone, which resonates with Grof's model of the psyche with perinatal and transpersonal layers.

Bion, who liked mathematical constructs, thought that there was movement in the O zone from infinity to the finite and the key point in this process is the birth of the finite, the thought, from the infinite zone.[180] This could be likened to the quantum process where wave (infinite zone) becomes particle (finite zone). This is a valuable point that Bion emphasises – that the key is the point of emergence from O, the birth of the idea. Try to articulate the emerging thought, the whisper, too early and words become a form of constriction, a strangling at birth. But once something has emerged from O, it has to be prized and engaged with.

Bion's task was difficult indeed, applying a transpersonal concept, the O zone, to a psychoanalytic setting that is not conducive to it. Experience from work in states of non-ordinary consciousness, where emergence from the O zone is commonplace, show us that fundamental determinants of outcome are not only the set and setting, but the very careful integration of the material that emerges, so that it is incorporated as much as possible into ego function. The integration occurs using a variety of means, and non-verbal methods are particularly helpful in capturing the symbolism of the deep unconscious. The most obvious example of this is Jung's *Red Book* with his use of artwork to capture the profundity of his experience.

How does this apply to our dilemma of the dark night? For Bion, it is indeed a gestation. Something will emerge when the time is right if the process is supported and held in the right way. Often non-verbal processes such as art, music, film are most helpful in providing some sail cloth to capture the transformative wind and lend it some shape and direction. The reborn state of mind needs carful holding and nurturing to be integrated in the body of consciousness using every means available.[181] The points of emergence in egolescence are births of crucial importance. If we have techniques to access the O zone, as we shall see later, then we have an advantage.

CHAPTER 16

Pain and the Perinatal

Emotional and physical pain can reach such extraordinary intensity . . . that he or she can feel that they have transcended the boundaries of individual suffering and is experiencing the pain of entire groups of individuals, all of humanity or even all of life. . . . Confrontation with pain at this depth tends to be intimately interwoven with phenomena related to the birth process.

—Stanislav Grof

Police Officer Sandy and the Moment of Impact

Sandy was aiming for a career in the covert surveillance section of the London Metropolitan Police. She was in her late twenties and had been a police officer for six years. She loved the training and her service as a uniformed officer on the tough streets of Hackney. She thrived on the adrenaline and she thought nothing of confronting large and violent men. She loved making arrests or 'nicking villains' as she put it. Now she was in a plain-clothes role in a special rapid response unit responsible for emergency situations developing in the nation's capital. She loved the camaraderie of the police and would have worked every day if she could. She had a boyfriend, Jim, who was in the firearms unit and had similar feelings about the job.[182] She said that the only person she could have a relationship with was another policeman; no one else would tolerate her. Of course, Sandy was super fit. She did exercise every day; she ran, she swam and she cycled. If she and Jim were ever able to take a holiday at the same time, they would try to do a triathlon together. Sandy was living the dream. This was the life she had always wanted to lead.

The accident happened in winter. It was raining and although it was only six o'clock in the evening, it was already dark. She was partnered with Mark and this was the third response call of their shift. The 'blues and twos' were on, the flashing blue light and the two-tone siren. She thought that Mark was driving a little faster than he needed to but she was busy navigating and listening to the communications. She was just doing her job. She was aware that Mark was turning right through a red light. He was going fast. They said later that he took the bend at 60 mph. The back wheels lost grip and she was aware of the car slipping and sliding. She looked up and saw that they were skidding into a big red London bus that was coming towards them. The bus hit them on her side of the car and it was like being punched by a giant fist. The police car bounced off and spun around in the road. She could see a lorry coming at them and trying to stop. She shut her eyes but the car ricocheted off the lorry and turned over a couple of times before coming to a halt on its roof. It started to fill up with smoke.

Sandy told me that there were three separate times when she knew she was either going to be killed or seriously injured. In fact, she needn't have worried about the smoke because it was only the chalk from the air-bags that had been deployed. But she didn't know that and she thought that the car was about to explode. She tried to get back into police officer mode, exit the vehicle and take charge of the situation. But she couldn't move her legs. She thought that she had been paralysed and the idea came into her mind that her life was effectively over. She would never be able to run again. She wouldn't be able to make arrests again. She would be in a wheelchair.

Mark had a minor injury and returned to work within a couple of weeks. Sandy was not paralysed but her feet had been trapped in the foot well of the car and she had suffered a complex crush injury. She needed to be cut out of the car. She spent a few days in hospital and was discharged home with both feet in plaster. She would not be putting any weight on her feet for at least three months. So Sandy found herself alone at home. She was in pain and she couldn't move very much at all. Jim took care of her as best he could, but he was always at work or out running and she felt very envious of him. She suffered great pain from her legs and great pain from her mind. She was unaccustomed to inactivity; she had so much time to fill and she just did not know how to fill it.

The worst problem was the nightmares. Every night she would have a dream that the accident was happening again. The dreams were incredibly vivid and took her to the place that she feared most, that place where she was about to die: once when they hit the bus, twice when they ricocheted into the lorry and the third time when she thought that the car would explode with her trapped inside it. She would awake screaming and it would take some time before she realised that it was a dream. She would be drenched in sweat with her heart pumping and her breath gasping. She would be in such a state of arousal that she would be unable to return to sleep for a couple of hours. She couldn't get up because it was too much effort with her legs in plaster. So she just lay there and felt desperate.

Sandy treated her recovery like the training for a triathlon. She broke it into sections and set herself targets. One plaster was removed and then the other. She started putting some weight on her feet and walking with a frame. She did her physiotherapy assiduously. She was desperate to get back to work. She was in some pain from her feet but the surgeon said that they were healing and she assumed the pain would gradually get better. She and Jim weren't getting along so well. She had lost her libido. She hurt all the time and just did not feel very sexy. Besides, he had moved into the spare bedroom to sleep as she kept waking him up with her nightmares.

Six months after the accident, Sandy went back to work. She knew that she wasn't really fit but she could walk and she did not want to go on to half pay. She thought that a return to duty would help her. She had been so bored just sitting at home. She went into work and one the first people that she saw was Mark. This triggered a panic attack—she felt dizzy, short of breath and nauseous. Her heart was thumping so loud that she thought everyone would hear it. She wondered if she was having a heart attack. She went to the ladies and sat for a while gathering herself. That night she had one of the worst nightmares she had ever had and was sleepless for the rest of the night. She was very tired. The next day she went out in a patrol car. She had a different driver; she knew that she would not have been able to get in the car with Mark again. This driver was older and more cautious. But when the first emergency of the day came in and the car deployed its siren and lights, she had another panic attack. Every fibre of her being was urging her to get out of the car but she stayed put and tried to concentrate on her task. She didn't tell anyone about her panic attacks. She was a police officer. She would tough it out. Surely it would get better.

But it didn't get better. Every working day she had panic attacks. She had dreams about the accident that woke her from sleep in a state of terror. She lay awake most of the night dreading sleep and dreading work. She forced herself to get to work. She forced herself to get in the patrol car. She didn't speak to any of her friends anymore and Jim was moving out. She was determined not to tell anyone about her psychological symptoms as she didn't want people to think she was 'mental'. And her feet were getting worse and worse.

Pain in the Brain

In fact, it was Sandy's feet that eventually led her to my door. She had not been able to carry on with her job as her feet were too painful and she had not been able to pass the fitness tests. She couldn't do any of the things that she wanted to, she was miserable, lonely and single and she had still not told anyone about her panic attacks. Sandy told me that her life was a living hell. She felt that everything was against her. Her feet were excruciatingly painful and the pain was getting worse. Now that she wasn't going to work anymore, the nightmares had mostly stopped although she had to avoid watching police dramas on TV, because hearing a siren would bring on a panic attack. She was not getting paid and she was struggling to keep up with the payments on her house. She had applied for medical retirement from the police, which would at least give her a modicum of income. But the doctors could not understand why she could not work; they had put her feet through X-rays and MRI scans but could not find anything demonstrably wrong with them. They seemed to think that the pain might even be in her mind.

Now I had seen the various reports from the orthopaedic surgeons and the pain physicians before I saw Sandy. There was a consensus that there was no physical pathology to account for her complaint of pain and disability. They could not understand why she seemed to be so disabled. It seemed that she had developed a chronic pain syndrome, a condition where the pain is entirely real but related more to the central nervous system rather than damage in the body. I had seen some people with a symptom profile similar to Sandy before and it didn't take long to clarify that she had post-traumatic stress disorder or PTSD as it is usually called. PTSD only occurs after an event that threatens death or serious injury. Most of the police officers that I have seen with PTSD, and I have seen many, develop it after a sudden and unexpected event for which they are totally unprepared. It as though the adrenaline surge that results from the shock never goes away, leaving them in a permanent fight-or-flight mode.

Most people have heard of the nightmares and flashbacks that typify PTSD, but the less obvious symptoms are often the ones that cause the most damage—the constant feeling of hyper-vigilance and exaggerated startle response, the irritability, some loss of the ability to have loving feelings, the loss of enjoyment, the tension and the absence of libido. For people with PTSD, their relationship with the world around them has fundamentally changed; the world is no longer a benign place but a place of incipient threat and danger; it feels as though there is no possibility of a good future. Severe PTSD has a profoundly archetypal quality; it is a place of dread; it has a numinous quality of oppression.

Sandy had been in a state of insoluble tension. There was a part of her that desperately wanted to return to work, to re-engage with normal life and her career trajectory. But there was another part of her that dreaded the anxiety triggered by work and the panic attacks caused by the emergency calls. There was no obvious answer. The solution that resolved this dilemma was the deteriorating condition of her legs. It was her anxiety that caused her brain to perceive pain, not the pain receptors in her body. The pain was not in her mind, it was entirely real but it was a pain that seemed to be generated by the brain rather than her feet. Indeed, it seemed that the problem causing her perception of pain was more psychiatric than physical. Sandy had developed a somatoform pain disorder.[183]

There is much that could be said about Sandy and her battle back to herself. The first time I saw her I was deeply impressed by the pervasive quality of her pain. Indeed, she told me herself that she no longer knew where the emotional pain stopped and the physical pain began. She was feeling compressed and attacked from all sides. The police authorities were being difficult, she had no means of income and it looked as though she would lose her house. The litigation process was also proving stressful and she was most distressed that some the doctors seemed to be saying that there was nothing physically the matter with her. Was she going mad, she wondered? Life had boiled down to a hopeless battle against impossible odds. The forces against her just seemed too great. The quality of her dreams had changed too. Although she still had some dreams about the accident, she also had dreams of being trapped, of being caught in a crushing machine, even her legs felt as though she was in a vice. There was no way out; pain had become her world. She admitted that if it were not for the distress that it would cause her mother, she would take her own life.

Sandy's case is complex and encompasses the bio-psycho-socio-archetypal spectrum of experience. Sandy had suffered because of her strength of character. She had pushed herself to work despite a serious condition, her PTSD. She had not had the trauma-focussed psychotherapy that is usually effective in treating PTSD. We know that there are cases where the anxiety, depression and emotional distress affect the way in which the central nervous system perceives pain, providing an amplifying effect. As her condition progressed, her physical pain was offering her an exit from a situation at work that had become intolerable for her. She was not taking sick leave for psychological reasons but for physical reasons. At least her colleagues wouldn't be able to say she was mental. There was a strategy to treat Sandy. It would take some time, but I knew that her innate fighting spirit and resilience would be a huge asset to her once she was engaged in a treatment plan. Sandy's case sheds some light on the archetypal quality found in depression and constriction. But there is a further layer of psyche that we also need to explore that often provides a link between the personal story of our personality development and the archetypal domain.

Enter Stanislav Grof

When I was undergoing my group analytic training, I became very inter-ested in the deeper, invisible layers of depression. How do they form and take shape, why do they affect some of us more than others and how can they be relieved? One of Freud's most important papers, *Mourning and Melancholia*, focussed on the crucial importance of the healthy flow of grief so that guilt and anger do not become directed inwardly.[184] I was impressed by the ideas of the psychoanalyst Melanie Klein who had deduced from her work with children that the basic templates for depression arose in the very early relationships between the mother and the infant. But it seemed to me that there was another deeper layer of depression that did not easily fit into the conventional models. Some years later, I came across the Czech psychiatrist Stanislav Grof and his work on the perinatal layer of psycho-logical experience. This seemed to be the missing piece of the puzzle. The perinatal layer of psyche is the mental life relating to the birth process and it appears to provide a particularly close link with the archetypal.

Grof, in my opinion, is of similar stature to Jung. He has developed some of Jung's ideas and made two highly original contributions. Firstly, he has pioneered the mapping of the perinatal area of psychological and archetypal experience. Secondly, with his wife Christina, he has developed holotropic breathwork as a safe and reliable method of accessing and inte-grating material from the deep psyche. Grof outlined his perinatal theories in his first book, *Realms of the Human Unconscious,* in 1975. The subtitle of the book was 'observations in LSD research'. Grof's clinical research program had found that LSD seemed to catapult people into the archetypal domain, which opened up this area of psyche for inspection, often for the first time. Grof's original training was in Freudian psychoanalysis but he found that some of the phenomena encountered in his patients simply could not be explained in Freudian terms.[185]

The LSD research that Grof was referring to occurred in the era when such research was entirely legal and respectable, attracting enormous aca-demic and clinical interest. But by the time his book was published, LSD research had been closed down and the drug had been demonised. Indeed, I had come across Grof's work a few times in the 1980s and 1990s and dismissed his theories out of hand when I came across the word LSD. As a clinical psychiatrist being exposed on a daily basis to people whose lives have been devastated by drugs, I instinctively took the position that any-thing concerned with psychedelic drugs was of no interest to me. I know now that I was mistaken to take such a dismissive attitude, but this has helped me to understand why Grof's pioneering work has been so neglected in some countries.

Grof reports that in the non-ordinary state of consciousness induced by LSD, people often experienced moving beyond the level of memories from childhood and infancy, encountering emotions and physical sensations of extreme intensity that held a strange mixture of themes of birth and death. These included images, emotions and physical experiences that seemed related to the birth process itself. Grof introduces the perinatal layer as follows:

> The basic characteristics of perinatal experience and their central focus are the problems of biological birth, physical pain and agony, aging, disease and decrepitude, dying and death. Inevitably the shattering encounter with these critical aspects of human existence and the deep realisation of the frailty and impermanence of man as a biological creature is accompanied by an agonising existential crisis.[186]

The Perinatal Layer of Psyche

I had a recurrent dream through my childhood. I would not say that it was a nightmare but it tended to wake me in a state of alarm. I would tell my parents that I couldn't describe it, but it was like being swallowed by an ocean. The dream involved a titanic rhythmic pulsing; feeling powerless, engulfed and overwhelmed by something that was enormous and irresistible. I had this dream for the last time when I was in my twenties and it dawned on me finally that the dream was a re-enactment of my birth.[189]

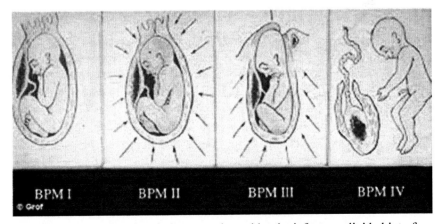

Figure 2. The perinatal period as experienced by the infant are divided into four stages.[187] Grof terms them basic perinatal matrices abbreviated to BPM.[188]

Let us imagine the birth process from the perspective of the baby rather than that of the mother. To begin with there is the serenity of the womb, but this leads to the cataclysmic shock of the onset of labour, the struggle through the birth canal and the exhausted relief of delivery. These four distinct meaning states comprise Grof's perinatal matrices.

The first perinatal matrix (BPM 1) is the resting state that lasts until the onset of the contractions of labour. The baby develops peacefully in the amniotic sac with her entire needs being met by the encompassing and nourishing mother. Occasionally this resting state becomes poisonous, perhaps due to medication, toxins or lack of oxygen.

The second perinatal matrix (BPM 2) is the physical onset of labour where the uterus contracts against a closed cervix. There is no available exit so this state involves an experience of constriction, entrapment and fear; the baby faces death.

The third perinatal matrix (BPM 3) represents the physical process of movement out of constricted uterus through the opening cervix followed by the 'life or death struggle' through the birth canal. There is, after all, some light at the end of tunnel.

The fourth perinatal matrix (BPM 4) is the birth, the emergence into the light, the first intake of breath and the recovery phase for mother and baby. The ordeal is over and they can meet each other for the first time in the outside world.

In the archetypal states that correspond to the perinatal journey, the first perinatal matrix involving good-womb experiences would equate to oceanic feelings of bliss and cosmic unity. A toxic womb state would equate to feeling in a bad place; poisoned or paranoid. The second perinatal matrix would involve profound hopelessness, despair and the encounter with death. This is the territory of the 'bad trip' after the paradise of the first matrix is lost. The third perinatal matrix is the archetypal hero's journey, the call to arms, the tumultuous and perilous struggle. The fourth perinatal matrix holds themes of triumph, fortuitous escape from danger, revolution, decompression and expansion of space, radiant light and colour. This is Jack returning home with the golden goose and perhaps even living happily ever after.

Grof reports that the perinatal matrices and their archetypal manifestations are most vividly encountered in states of non-ordinary consciousness but they also occur in routine clinical situations and are insufficiently understood by contemporary psychiatry. I believe that Grof is correct and, while he may sometimes overstate his case, his research gives us valuable insights into a layer of archetypal experience that is otherwise difficult to define.

Psychological states corresponding to the second matrix are particularly difficult to treat due to the sheer hopelessness of the situation. There is an archetypal amplification of catastrophe; it feels as though titanic forces are ranged against you. There really is no exit and no point in trying to find one. There may be a prevailing mood of cynicism and meaninglessness. We might identify with Macbeth, in one of Shakespeare's bleaker passages:

> Out, out, brief candle!
> Life's but a walking shadow, a poor player,
> That struts and frets his hour upon the stage,
> And then is heard no more.
> It is a tale
> Told by an idiot, full of sound and fury,
> Signifying nothing.

The severe depressive illness captures the archetype of the second perinatal matrix. As a new trainee in psychiatry, one of my first patients was a woman with psychotic depression. She thought she was in hell and was being eaten by rats. She was screaming that she was being crushed and there was no escape. She was scouring herself with her fingernails and she was refusing food. She was the most distressed human being that I had ever seen at that point in my life. She was also the first person to whom I administered ECT and witnessed the miracle of her complete recovery over the next 2 or 3 weeks.[190]

More commonly, I believe that second matrix states often occur, in more subtle forms, in the existential crises of midlife. Such people may be functioning perfectly well but will be aware of a weight and a compression that is hard to define. It may feel like an uncomfortable swaddling, an oppression by forces that are too big to be resisted. There is a feeling of misery and desperation, of cynicism, as though the world is corrupted and superficial. This is a deep crisis of meaning and there is indeed no obvious escape. The natural trajectory of second matrix states in labour is towards a sudden unexpected opportunity as the archetypal cervix opens. But in the psychological territory of ego-death and rebirth, a successful rebirth is not a forgone conclusion, and the ego-death experience may seem impossibly difficult. Many people either get very stuck, as in the case of Sandy, or find partial solutions or partial recoveries that seem to ease the pressure but do not allow a satisfactory rebirth and merely perpetuate the problem.

The problem is that conventional psychiatry and psychotherapy often do not have an understanding or methods that are helpful for these states of second matrix compression. The Freudian or Kleinian areas of the psyche do not seem relevant or helpful and certainly biological treatments such as medication are not effective unless someone is suffering from a more severe depressive illness. Kindness and care will support the process, but how is one to find the mutative exit from the compressed and suffocating space? How do you access and work with that archetypal level of psyche so that second matrix 'stuckness' can flow into a natural ego-death and rebirth?

Sandy Remoulded

In Sandy's case, we can see how her relationship with the outside world became profoundly changed by the accident. There is a parallel with the onset of the labour and the beginning of the second perinatal matrix when the mother and the baby move from the idyll of the womb to a situation where each is causing the other pain. The change is irrevocable and there is no going back. Each contraction is a hammer blow to the status quo. Each constriction—by pain, by employers, by finances, by litigation, by social relationships—drives her deeper into the no-exit despair. She was in that place of unbearable, untreatable pain.[191]

In fact, Sandy did well—she did find her exit in the end. My task was to organise treatment for her and to advise the police medical team about her future and her capacity for work. It seemed clear that she would never return to response-car driving. Even if the treatment of her PTSD was successful, there would be too high a risk of a relapse if there were any more accidents or near misses in a response car. But it would be premature to recommend medical retirement before treatment had even been started. So Sandy saw a cognitive psychotherapist to work on her anxiety and she saw a physiotherapist to plan a sensible rehabilitation programme. We worked with the pain physician to wean her off her oxycontin and she went to a pain management course where she was given information about non-pharmacological methods of pain management. Sandy started yoga, which appealed to her as a way of building up her body in a balanced way after a couple of years of inactivity. Being Sandy, once she was given a task that she felt was safe and appropriate, she approached it as she had approached her training. She found that the physical exercises and asanas in yoga calmed her mind and took away some of her worry. She found that as she became less anxious—the pain was less intrusive. Her yoga instructor introduced her to a meditation teacher who worked with her on mindfulness-based pain reduction.

The last time I saw Sandy she was back at work on light duties. She was starting to run again. Her feet still hurt but, as she put it, the pain did not control her any more, it simply didn't bother as much. She told me that she had learned in the yoga and the mindfulness practice that there was a part of her that was entirely separate from the pain. She was finding that life was opening up new vistas. She was clear that she did not want to go back to her past self that she now thought was obsessive and rigid. She was developing as a softer, more nuanced person. She had a new partner, who was a woman and they planned to have a baby.

Sandy was emerging from her crisis as an entirely different human being. There had been the crash, followed by the brutal end to her ego's aspirations. She faced the loss of all that was dear to her—her life, her fitness, her partner and her career. She lived in the grip of the archetypal forces associated with PTSD and her physical pain. Somehow, she had negotiated a passage from the place of compression. She knew that she had a long way to go, but now she had the tools to travel.

The Tumultuous Struggle to Be Born

As labour progresses, the cervix is forced open and the baby begins its passage through the birth canal. The uterus contracts compressing the baby's body while the head pushes against the muscle of the cervix. The baby and the mother work together at this stage to end the suffering that they are inflicting on each other. As the uterine walls contract, the blood flow through the umbilical artery is diminished adding a feeling of suffocation and insufficiency to the struggle. We can assume that the levels of stress hormones such as adrenaline are high. This is the third perinatal matrix, which forms the prototype for the life-and-death struggle.

On an archetypal level, Grof associates this matrix with the Pluto archetype symbolizing extraordinary and unimaginable power; the cycle of life and death, destruction and renovation. Pluto is represented by Shiva, the terrifying destroyer of Hindu mythology, who also creates new life. Pluto stands for the underworld with its dark, demonic, shadowy, sometimes perverse quality. For Liz Greene, Pluto is an image of the dark maternal roots of the psyche, which is forever pulling us out of life and back into the womb of the Mother, either for renewal or death.[192] Above all Pluto stands for the epic process of transformation. There is nothing subtle about this process; it has an overwhelming force; an inevitability. Nothing can stand in its way.

We see this theme played out in titanic struggles through history. Grof describes how Lenin's life resonated with the third matrix as the revolutionary who reacted to a vision of compression, which he associated with the Russian autocracy and international capitalism. Lenin's life was defined by the struggle against oppression and the epic life-and-death struggle to birth a brave new world.[193] Some people live their lives in a third-matrix manner choosing to perpetually struggle through a metaphorical birth canal, fighting oppression and seeking a distant dream of paradise. For many of us, this is the rat race; the people packed together on the mass transit systems and offices struggling to emerge from compression towards a better future. We mostly know that paradise is unobtainable, but that misses the point: the struggle holds the meaning of life. Some of these people are entrepreneurs, politicians or freedom fighters. Some of them are more shadowy underworld figures. They live their lives with an adrenaline-fuelled intensity. Nothing suits them better than the activating forces of compression driving through a tight passage. There has to be a promise of a brave new world ahead of them but if they found it they would probably pass it by and embark on a tumultuous life or death struggle to find another one.

Catherine lived her life driven by this Plutonic third matrix archetype. She was at her most fulfilled in emergency rooms and war zones. I met her when we were both junior doctors working in the accident and emergency department in a busy city hospital. She liked to do the resuscitations and cardiac arrests, while I was happiest with the minor surgery, the suturing, the setting of broken wrists and dislocated shoulder joints. So we fitted well together in the workplace. I moved on to psychiatry and she became a specialist in intensive care. But before long she was in the Lebanon, working in a refugee camp, then I heard she was in Afghanistan as an army medic. Then she was back in London, she'd become a mother and was planning to go trekking in South America with her baby. She moved on to New York and worked as a hospital doctor for a while, but this was not stimulating enough. She had ideas and she started an IT company building medical software. There was a real prospect of material success over the longer term although she was deeply in debt and her twenty employees depended on her for their monthly pay. Bankruptcy and financial death loomed unless she could get at least one big contract. Catherine was jetting around the world, bidding for contracts, trying to manage her business out of constriction, through the hazards of the birth canal into a viable future. If her company becomes successful, I have little doubt she will leave it behind to find another challenge. For Catherine, the third matrix defines her passage through life and there is no sign of this changing.

The COEX

As any mental experience becomes more intense, the archetypal flavors tend to become more pronounced and pull towards it other fragments of our mental life with a similar resonance of meaning. These may be emotionally charged memories from our life experiences, our childhood or perhaps even our perinatal experience. Thus a complicated mental structure emerges which has a number of different components all with a similar meaning tone. The point I want to emphasize is that meaning is the organizing factor. It can be likened to the same musical note with different octaves. The note represents the meaning state such as constriction, excitement or peace and the octave represents the level upon which the meaning state is experienced, whether biographical memory, perinatal or archetypal.

Returning to Sandy, there were reasons why she was so driven in the way that she lived her life and she could understand how this related to her experiences of stasis and constriction when she was a child. She told me about some of these. The most obvious was her experience of being the only girl with three brothers in a household where the girl was expected to do the household chores while the boys did their sporting activities. She hated this, telling herself that one day she would be out in the world enjoying the exciting activities and would never be constrained doing housework again. No doubt there were deeper layers of her biographical psyche, further back in her childhood and infancy that held a similar meaning tone. From a perinatal perspective, her post-accident state resonated with the compressed and stuck second matrix and this meaning state eventually developed an overwhelming archetypal intensity for her, finally manifesting as her chronic pain syndrome.

Grof found, in his work with non-ordinary states of consciousness that people in these states tend to move easily between the different octaves of a particular meaning state. An emotional state that seems primarily related to a childhood experience may, in these high archetypal penetrance states, then mutate to a perinatal theme with the same emotional resonance and then to an archetypal experience with a mythic or dreamlike quality. He termed this mental complex a 'system of condensed experience' or COEX for short. Grof explains that the disparate memories or feelings belonging to a particular COEX system are associated with a strong emotional charge of the same quality. Each COEX system has a basic theme that permeates all its layers and provides a common denominator. Different people will have a different number and flavour of COEX systems and each COEX system will have a characteristic relationship to psychological defenses. Some COEX systems may have a particular weight due to the accumulation of experiences associated with a meaning state, particularly if associated with trauma. Usually experiences from later in life lie in the more accessible superficial layers of the COEX systems but the core of the COEX derives from earlier childhood and birth.[194]

Grof's concept of the COEX helps us to understand the relationship between the different layers of psyche. Intense mental states cannot be understood according to just one level or model of psyche; rather, there is a sliding scale between the different levels with the same meaning tone. Thus, people with a psychodynamic structure predisposing to certain feeling states will be more likely to experience those feeling states with numinous intensity in high penetrance archetypal states. Turning this around, it seems likely that high archetypal penetrance states may offer an opportunity to access and resolve some of the hidden psychodynamic areas that may be problematic for us. We will examine this further in chapters 21 and 22.

In chapter 1 we met Adam, who severely injured himself during a terrifying archetypal crisis, and Martin, who had a positive numinous experience of beauty and unity. Neither had a psychiatric disorder beforehand and the experiences developed very quickly for both of them. Adam was in a slightly agitated state beforehand, with some concerns about work, while Martin was on quiet country walk on a gorgeous summer's day. It seems likely that there were some psychodynamic determinants of both of their different mental states, although we do not know what these dynamics were. It may well be the case that the psychoanalysts are correct in postulating a relationship between these dramatic mental states and the very early vicissitudes of personality development with the primary object. Perhaps Adam had a predisposition to persecutory or annihilatory anxiety while Martin, on the other hand, was inherently well adjusted and secure in his attachment patterns. On another level, according to Grofian perinatal theory, Adam's experience related to the second and third matrix while Martin's was a blissful expression of the first matrix. Both of their states of mind rapidly escalated to the higher reaches of archetypal experience with very different results.

I do not know why Adam and Martin both progressed from relatively mild moods to their separate archetypal crises. They both occurred in nature, which seemed to have an archetypal accelerant quality. The COEX model helps us to clarify the passage from mood state to archetypal crisis although we do not understand entirely why this occurs spontaneously for some people. The COEX system provides a model of psyche where meaning states are primary. We can envisage, perhaps, psychodynamic influences pushing from below and archetypes pulling from above, all being played out on the biological playing field in our material world.

CHAPTER 17

Matters of Heart

It is rather embarrassing to have given one's entire life to pondering the human predicament and to find that in the end one has little more to say than

'Try to be a little kinder'

—Aldous Huxley[195]

The Second World War for the British was very different from the First World War. We were spared the mass slaughter of the previous generation in the trenches and we did not suffer the European horrors of invasion or the holocaust. The Soviet armies and the Russian winter broke the back of the Wehrmacht while the dynamism and might of the American industrial and military machine finally cleared the path to Berlin. For the British, it felt like a truly heroic journey, fighting a just war against the evil empire. The process mirrored an archetypal or perinatal journey with a time of great peril and compression followed by an epic death-defying struggle and a victorious emergence.

My two grandfathers fought in the World War 1 and my father fought in World War 2. Generations of the male members of my family had been reared in those English boarding schools that provided the training to equip them as officers of Empire. We were reared in Spartan academies, educated on the classics and subjected to harsh conditions and brutal discipline. We were a martial people, trained to endure, to strive and to dominate. Masculine qualities were encouraged and reached their best expressions in team sports. We were reared to be tough and our emotional development suffered. Kindness, emotional nourishment, caring, emotional articulacy and vulnerability were discouraged. This way of being in the world began to change after World War 2 as Britain and Europe sought a softer, perhaps a more feminine, nurturing aspect. Britain was exhausted when the guns stopped firing. The wartime government of Winston Churchill was voted out of office and a reforming Labour government came into power. The task was to make the land fit for returning heroes, to build a compassionate and fair country with equal opportunities for all, irrespective of the old class system. There was a new spirit in the air.

Lady NHS

The National Health Service was the fruit of that epoch. The NHS was born on the 5th July 1948 when the Minister for Health, Aneurin Bevan, stated: 'We now have the moral leadership of the world'. A grandiose statement perhaps, but the NHS was the first publicly funded comprehensive healthcare system that was totally free of charge to all that had need of it. The same treatment was provided to everyone irrespective of birth, wealth or status. No one would suffer unnecessarily because they could not afford medical fees. Everyone was to have the best available healthcare.

I was a medical student when the NHS was in her mid thirties. She was still very attractive to us, although we all knew that she had her flaws. We knew that a few senior doctors neglected their NHS work for lucrative private work in Harley Street in London's West End. We all knew that when we qualified as doctors, we would be working in excess of 100 hours per week. We came from across the range of the political spectrum: a few of us were socialists but most of us were not. Irrespective of our politics and background, we all loved the NHS—we believed in it and we wanted it to work.

The press often refers to the NHS as the 'sacred cow' of British politics. Governments try to reform her as she ages; they put her on a diet and give her supplements; they try to make her fitter and leaner and they give her management consultants. But the NHS is like the Royal family. It seems to represent something that has almost holy status for many of the population. It is sacrosanct. Killing it would be unthinkable, we are told.

So the NHS has a quality of an archetypal image. Archetypal forces meshed with the ashes of war and the social reforming zeal of the time to create something in the image of the great mother of infinite compassion. This is the sacred mother who takes you in and holds you, irrespective of your condition, heedless perhaps of your sins. From an archetypal perspective, this is the feminine principle, the Great Mother Goddess with her succour, patience and heart. She loves us and we love her.

The lure of archetype can seduce us into neglecting the small print, the practicalities that make any system function properly. Sure enough, there were always the resource constraints, the underfunding, the inherent inefficiencies and mismanagement. The lady groaned and moaned but we knew that her great beating heart was marching in step with ours. We always understood, even when we were tired and bruised in body and soul, that we were engaged in a proud endeavor, an idea that was greater than ourselves. We mostly didn't count the hours and we stayed late if our patients needed us. Although we didn't articulate it very often, we felt inspired to be part of the NHS and we imbibed the spirit of compassion from her. To a small but significant degree we were able to participate in the archetypal current that had led to the NHS in the first place. Flawed perhaps, but we knew it was morally right. It seems to me that there was a mutually reinforcing system where we captured some archetypal wind in our individual sails, which led to a perpetuation of the compassionate ethos of the great mother archetype. And so the great ship sailed on.

For the system to work, for the lady to work her magic, the system needs replenishing by the archetype that inspired it. The compassion at the very heart of it needs nurturing and nourishing. Many of us believe that if good staff are supported in their clinical work, in reasonable conditions and with enough resources to do their jobs, that the battle is mostly won. The vast majority of staff in the NHS are inherently compassionate. They have the necessary human qualities and a sense of vocation. The enemies of compassion are burnout and bureaucracy.

Fatigue traditionally has been the curse of the junior doctor. When I qualified in the 1980s I was working a 'one in two'. This meant that as well as the normal working hours from Monday to Friday; there was the requirement to be on duty alternate nights and weekends. This averages out at one-hundred-and-twelve hours a week. Some of this time is spent asleep so it wasn't quite as much as it sounds. For my internal medicine internship, the hours were less, a 'one in three', but the nights were busier and the weekends on call involved working from Friday morning until Monday afternoon with perhaps a few hours sleep during that entire period. We all found that simple tasks like the insertion of a cannula in a vein would be easy enough on the Friday but by Sunday evening we would be so tired that our motor coordination started to fail and simple tasks became difficult. We all knew that this was an initiation ritual that we all had to pass through in order to become proper doctors. We accepted it, but the price was high and compassion tended to be the casualty.

Some ten years later, when I was the new Consultant Psychiatrist at the Royal London Hospital, a young intern, Alistair, approached me with a view to setting up a support group for his fellow interns, a 'houseman's group'. I thought this was an excellent idea, primarily to provide support but also to encourage a degree of psychological thinking about their clinical work. I was interested in the work of Isobel Menzies Lyth, who had explored the psychological denial occurring in hospital staff when exposed to the powerful and primitive currents of suffering, decay and death, and how they form defensive organizations to protect themselves against anxiety.[196] It seemed obvious to me that bringing these anxieties into a more conscious focus could be helpful in addressing the clinical task.

Alistair had a great deal of energy and his enthusiasm communicated to his colleagues so the newly qualified doctors found time in their busy diaries and attended the lunchtime weekly group. The houseman's group started in the autumn with interns who were in the first month or two of their working lives. They were bright eyed, fresh and enthusiastic. They generally considered it an honor to be woken at night to perform a useful duty on the ward when they were on call. The first group meetings were filled with excited chatter about the practical demands and duties of their jobs. As time passed, we were able to talk about the deeper layers of their experience and explore the power and intensity of being with people who were suffering and often terminally ill. This seemed to be the work that we needed to do together, not to be overcome by emotion, but not to deny the emotion either. Our challenge was to stay with the suffering people, to look them in their eyes, to help them professionally and with humanity—to face it with them and not look away.

The original group of interns moved on to another post after six months. A new cohort of interns came to the Royal London who had mostly done their first six months in other hospitals and the Wednesday lunchtime group continued to meet. As the year progressed, the tone of the group changed dramatically. The young doctors in their second post had become angry, depressed and burnt out. They were so very tired. They felt that their training and skills were not being used properly. They felt abused by their hours, the conditions and sometimes their bosses. They spoke of their need for time away from hospital work to rediscover how to be a young person again. As they became increasingly brutalized, it was clear that there had been a profound loss of compassion towards their patients. I was shocked by some of the things that they said in that group although I was reminded that I had gone through exactly the same process myself some years before.

I remember as a medical intern myself learning a lesson that served me well and still causes me shame when I recall it. It was one of my first days on a neurology ward. I had just qualified, I had a long list of tasks to do, such as take bloods for tests, organise investigations, do lumbar punctures and clerk in the new patients. I did not want to fail in these tasks and I most certainly did not want to be chastised by my seniors. The man in the side room had suffered a brain stem stroke; he had a 'locked in syndrome' and couldn't move anything below his eyebrows. He was unable to speak. Because of the wasting of his muscles it took a few attempts before I managed to cannulate a vein and draw some blood out of his arm when I noticed a tear rolling down his cheek. I suddenly realised the enormity of what I had done. I was in such a hurry that I hadn't introduced myself, or spoken to him or explained what I was doing. I had treated him like an object, in an inhumane way. It was one of those moments of looking at myself in the mirror and being appalled by what I saw. I resolved that whatever I did in the future, whatever pressures I was under, that I would always remember to treat people with respect as fellow human beings and not forget my compassion, or indeed my manners.

Raymond's Last Rampage

Raymond was a large man, with a loud voice and a tendency to drama. When he was upset, his presence was amplified and you always knew when he was in your vicinity. So when he came into the emergency room, dishevelled and threatening suicide, he was referred to the psychiatric liaison team in double-quick time. It was past midnight, it had been a busy evening and the staff were stretched. He was drunk, he was threatening and he was suicidal. He said that he needed help, that he was depressed and that he was definitely 'going to do it this time'. He said that he would jump in the river or under a train.

His medical records told us that he was in his early forties. He had a history of alcohol dependence with some signs of liver failure and possibly some early signs of alcoholic dementia. But he had not presented with depression before and there was no record of him being suicidal. There are some people who make a habit of coming to hospital threatening suicide when drunk. They know that they get to stay in the department overnight for assessment and they generally leave in a better mood in the morning. Raymond did not seem to fall into this category.

There followed the sequence of events that often happen with people like Raymond as their disorderly internal world becomes re-enacted in the relationships that develop in the external world. This is not a conscious process, but typically life has been one long list of setbacks, rejections and failures of caregiving. These psychological structures becomes hardwired as 'internal object relationships' and they become very adept at triggering further rejection. Sure enough, the emergency room staff wanted him out of the department. From their perspective he was a drunken nuisance interfering with their proper duties of managing trauma cases and medical emergencies. Raymond picked up the atmosphere that he was not a welcome guest and became louder. In fact, he became a lot louder. He started walking around the department looking for trouble. He poked his head into some cubicles where other patients were waiting for treatment. He was rude to the psychiatric nurse who came to assess him, but he said that he was hearing voices, that he wanted to kill himself and he expected some help.

The assessment of Raymond continued. It was clear that he needed proper psychiatric assessment and supervision and could not be unceremoniously discharged. He was not in alcohol withdrawal and did not have delirium tremens although he did appear to have alcoholic hallucinosis.[197] His complaint of hallucinatory voices seemed genuine and he needed to be transferred from the emergency room to the psychiatric unit. The psychiatric unit was reluctant to take him based on long experience of admitting people like Raymond in the middle of the night, with the entire unit being disturbed by his arrival, other patients losing sleep and temper, the nurses being harassed and the admitted patient walking out cheerfully after breakfast the next day leaving a bruised ward behind.

There was a further problem as he did not have an address and it was not clear that he was entitled to a bed in our local psychiatric hospital, which served a strict geographical area. The duty nurse at the psychiatric unit did not want to get into trouble the next day for allowing him into hospital if he did not fit the criteria. There were a number of phone calls made to try to find a bed for him in neighbouring psychiatric units. The hospital serving his most recent address would not accept him. Raymond was still walking around the emergency room making a nuisance of himself and the security guard had to be called. Raymond took offence and was becoming more aggressive. The senior psychiatrist on call and the senior manager to the mental health service were phoned at 4 am by the exasperated doctor in charge of the emergency room. 'Get this man out of my department' were the words that were used.

So Raymond is having a drunken tantrum. He is claiming to be hearing voices telling him to commit suicide. The night-duty psychiatry team have no way of knowing if he is telling the truth or if he is trying to manipulate a hospital admission to avoid a social difficulty. The local alcoholics and vagrants know that hearing voices commanding suicide are their ticket to a hospital admission for a few days respite. But, as so little is known about Raymond, he has to be taken very seriously. He has disrupted the working of the emergency room, upset patients, threatened staff, caused acrimony between the teams and exposed the fault lines in our services. The senior staff who have been woken up for consultation have the usual adrenaline rush that happens when the phone goes in the middle of the night and will struggle to get back to sleep. I know because it was me who was called that night. The feeling is that Raymond has ruined the next day before it has started.

Time passes, arrangements are made and eventually Raymond is waiting for transport to take him to the psychiatric ward. Just as I am about to get back to sleep, I am phoned to say that Raymond had sobered up a little, decided he was thirsty and reported that he was no longer suicidal. He said the voices had stopped, threatened the security guard with his walking stick and walked out. The staff informed the police feeling that he had not been fully assessed and may still be at risk.

The next morning, I am sitting with the team in the small and window-less room in the emergency room that is allocated to the psychiatry service. We are having the morning meeting. We go through the caseload and dis-cuss each patient to clarify what needs to be done and who will do it. It's going to be a busy day; there is a lot to do and no time to waste. There is a loud knock on the door. We recognise the familiar knock that indicates that the person knocking has an urgent problem that they want to hand over to us as quickly as they can. Sure enough, a police officer is standing outside who tells me that they have returned Raymond to our care.

I look around the room at my colleagues hoping to be persuaded that someone else in the team might assess him, but they know that it has to be me and so do I. A patient who is high risk, complicated and has caused political problems between the various services has to be seen by the senior psychiatrist. I know that the interview and the aftermath will probably take at least two hours and I have a number of other patients to see and tasks to complete. I realise once again that I do not feel very kindly disposed to Raymond. This is a warning sign for me to spend a moment or two, reflect-ing and balancing myself, taking note of my state of mind to better under-stand the patient and not react in an inappropriate manner. We constantly remind ourselves as a team that people's expressions of distress are often lacking in fragrance and we must be very careful and meticulous in our countertransference, our emotional response to them. Many of our patients who have been abused tend to unconsciously set up situations that invite abusive responses. People like Raymond are vulnerable to being treated badly as a result. Indeed, the countertransference is an enormously valu-able clinical tool. Raymond was eliciting the classic 'fuck off then' emo-tional response that requires very careful consideration and sensitive management.

At this stage of my life, I had become very interested in the concept of the higher Self. I wondered if it had an ontological reality or was it a philo-sophical bauble. I thought that I would probably never know the answer, but even if it were just a psychological construct, it might be a very useful one and I would see if I could take advantage of it. So, as an exercise, I had taken to acknowledging my hypothetical higher Self as a private mental ritual before challenging encounters. I found it a helpful way of grounding myself in the course of a busy day, when the bullets are flying and tempers are frazzling. I knew that my colleagues would have considered me eccentric if I had told anyone about my mental preparation routines, but I found it usefully humbling to acknowledge that my Self, Raymond's Self and indeed everybody else's Self are theoretically the same. It helped me to remain compassionate. So I try to hold these thoughts in mind as I go to the cubicle where Raymond was being guarded by the police.

When I walk into the cubicle, it is immediately clear that the situation has moved on. Raymond is not drunk, although not entirely sober, and his mood has changed. He is convivial but reflective. He is patiently waiting to see me and seems on excellent terms with the two police officers who have brought him. It seems clear that the presence of the police officers is no longer necessary. I check this out with Raymond and the police before thanking the officers for bringing him back and letting them go.

The story that emerges is of a man who has lost everything. Always a heavy social drinker, he submerged himself in alcoholism after his wife died 12 years previously. He told me a little about his childhood. His father was a terrifying figure who worked as a builder, came home drunk and spoke with his fists. His mother was a tired and frightened woman who took to alcohol herself. Raymond tried to be different from his father. He worked as a crane driver on construction projects. He was good at his work and proud of his family. His wife was everything to him and when she died of cancer, the bottom fell out of his world. He was furious about the injustice of her death; he railed against the fates and his anger came to colour his important relationships. He became estranged from his children and friends. He lost his job, his income and his home. He had lived on the street for a while and he drifted from hostel to hostel. He had been badly beaten on more than one occasion.

The one constant presence in his life over the last few years was his landlord Derek who had rented him a small room. Derek was an ex-alcoholic who had now been sober for over 20 years. He told me that Derek had been very patient with him and seemed to have some faith in a better version of Raymond. It was Derek who eventually persuaded Raymond to seek treatment and, in due course, he had been accepted for an alcohol rehabilitation unit. A vacancy on the unit had come up and he was about to embark on alcohol withdrawal followed by abstinence and the rehabilitation program. The entire programme would take six months. This was his last big binge, his farewell to alcohol. He had been drinking constantly for a few days and now he had spent all his money. Raymond had been in a reflective state as he approached his change of life. He had been thinking of all the harm that he had done to other people, he was feeling ashamed, and, in his weakened state, was doubting whether he could give up alcohol or whether he was even worthy of the treatment place. The hallucinatory voices that arose as a consequence of high blood-alcohol levels and his vulnerable brain tissue were deeply disturbing for him. He heard his father telling him loudly that he was useless and should kill himself.

Raymond looked me in the eye and said 'You know Doc, I think my problem is basically spiritual'. Now I thought that was a very interesting and unusual thing to say. If this were a spiritual problem, then it has caused absolute havoc for a number of people over the last 12 hours and it was not obvious that issues to do with spirituality had brought him to the emergency room. It seemed to me that he had brought us his distress flavoured by his narcissistic personality with the self-centred nature of his demands being fuelled by alcohol, his grief and anger, his declining health and his knowledge that he is slowly dying. He was testing his faintly beating hope that the competent, loving parent figure, that he never had, would come and look after him properly at last, contain his tantrums and make everything okay.

So I asked him what he meant by spiritual? Raymond said that he knew that he had issues with his family and that the alcohol helped him to numb his grief. But he thought that when he first started drinking, it was because he felt so alone and that no one cared. The alcohol made him feel warm, he enjoyed the sense of fellowship from carousing and the world seemed a better place. Indeed, sometimes when he'd been drinking, he felt genuinely good, he could see the goodness in other people and in himself. He could see the love and kindness in the world and sometimes, he told me, he thought he could even believe in God. He so much wanted more of this better version of the world that he associated it entirely with alcohol and redoubled his attempts to find it. Then, as the structures supporting his life dissolved into the alcohol, he lost his contact with God and that was so distressing for him that he drank to forget that too.

What changed for him was Derek. He just couldn't understand why someone like Derek would want to help him. Derek had received nothing back from him except problems. He knew that Derek would have been much better renting his room out to someone else. But Derek had not done that. Derek had no ulterior motive; he just wanted to be of help. Raymond told me that he slowly became aware again that perhaps there was some goodness in the world, something that was genuine and undeniable. 'Solid gold goodness', said Raymond, 'even when I haven't deserved it'.

So I made some phone calls and I established that Raymond was telling the truth. He had a few more days before his rehab place was available. I spoke to Derek who agreed to come to see me with Raymond in the next few days. Apart from the usual ambivalence about stopping drinking, there was something about Raymond that troubled me. I thought that he was someone who had the potential to benefit from treatment, but if he sabotaged the treatment, as many people do, I thought there was a high risk that he would kill himself. My phone call to Derek confirmed that he had the same view.

So Derek and Raymond duly came up to the third floor of the Royal London Hospital to see me in the Crisis Intervention Service. The receptionist told me that two big tough looking men with tattoos were asking for Dr Read. I reassured her that I was expecting them and they followed me to my office. Raymond had recovered from his big night out. I had prescribed him some medication calculated to keep the withdrawals at bay if he didn't drink and not to dangerously sedate him if he did. The home treatment team had visited him to make sure he was safe and to administer the medication.

Raymond was just about holding himself together. He wanted to believe that life could become sweet, but the prospect was almost too frightening for him. We talked about the rules and boundaries that he would have to respect in the months ahead, how there would be zero tolerance of aggressive behaviour or drinking. Raymond was unusual in that he understood this and had a realistic idea of the hard, gritty discipline required for rehabilitation and the maintenance of abstinence. We talked about facing his pain without alcohol and being supported in his grief and anger. We discussed his internal saboteur, how he would test the boundaries and invite rejection. He had a good understanding of that too.

The most difficult issue for him was the allowance of hope. Better, he said, to have no hope than to dare to hope and have it taken away from you. We knew what he meant. Raymond was really asking himself and us and the people who would be working with him in rehab if there could really be such a thing as goodness. Could there be some Grace left over for him? He sometimes dared to hope that there was. Derek had taught him that. Then we talked about kindness, about Derek's kindness and how he had learned to bring kindness into his life. We talked about the lack of kindness in Raymond's life and how the trigger for feeling suicidal was often a realisation that he had been unkind to people that he loved. And we talked about the big question: could he address the difficult task of being kind enough to himself?

He told me that when he left the emergency room that day, he was planning to kill himself. He felt tortured by the voice of his father and felt full of all the hate, cruelty and despair that he remembered him by. He went home to say goodbye to Derek and just as Derek opened the door, the police arrived. Derek smiled and looked pleased to see him. The policeman looked solid, genuine and friendly and said 'hello mate, we've come to take you back to hospital so they can take care of you'. Raymond said that in his weakened, hung-over, turbulent state, there was a sudden extraordinary revelation that these were good people after all and he was going to trust them. He did not need to listen to his father any more. Goodness was real. It existed.

Unkindness

It was a two-bedded unit on the neurology ward. I had arrived to see a patient, but he was still emerging from sedation so I was standing by the door reading his file and waiting to see if he would become alert enough to talk to me. I suddenly became aware of a flurry of activity as a young man with a patrician bearing and a small entourage strode down the corridor. He swept into the room and addressed the other patient who was sitting up in bed. He didn't introduce himself.

'The scans are clear', announced the confident young man. 'You do not have a neurosurgical problem. So it's all OK. You can go'.

The patient looked bemused. 'But I can't walk', he said.

'Oh well, never mind about that, the scans are clear. So you can go now.'

'But I can't walk', repeated the patient.

'Well you don't have a neurosurgical problem', said the young man; 'so you will have to go'.

'But what am I supposed to do because my legs don't work', said the patient. I could see that the nurses were beginning to look uncomfortable.

'Well, you don't have a neurosurgical problem and you can't stay here', said the surgeon. And that decided the matter.

The entourage swept out of the room and I could hear the discussion in the corridor. 'Where does this fellow live', said the young surgeon. It turned out he lived in a provincial town, just outside of London. 'So how do we get him out of here', said the surgeon. The nurses suggested that he needed further assessment to find the cause of his apparent paralysis. 'Well, can't we put him in a taxi and get him dropped off at his local hospital?', said the surgeon. The entourage was getting uncomfortable: 'we don't things like that here', said the nurse in charge. The young surgeon swept off.

The patient was eventually properly assessed and treated. I spoke with the nurse in charge and established that he had been extensively investigated with scans and tests and there was no physical or organic cause to his apparent paralysis. It seemed that he had a 'medically unexplained symptom', probably a conversion disorder. This is a psychiatric condition where the underlying problem is an unbearable anxiety that becomes 'converted' to a physical symptom. These conditions are usually very treatable once the correct diagnosis is made and they can be directed to psychiatry rather than surgery. Indeed, one of my colleagues who specialises in this clinical scenario was able to see him later in the day and appropriate treatment was organised.

One of the strengths of surgeons is a certain narrowness and determination of focus. I knew that the neurosurgical unit had an allocation of twelve beds in the hospital. This patient had become a 'bed blocker', someone whose presence in hospital meant that the next person could not be brought in from the waiting list for a scheduled operation. So the bed blocker had to go. Surgeons like to perform surgery. Junior surgeons are eager to get operating experience and it is also part of their job to facilitate discharge of patients to maintain turnover. I remember on my first day as a surgical intern, I was told by my boss that my job was to check people in, book them for surgery and then get them out of hospital as quickly as possible afterwards.

The term *patient* indicates a special contract between a person who is suffering and who seeks a skilled and compassionate response to their distress. A patient is not a customer, nor a client. The surgeon's suggestion that the patient be carted off in a taxi and dumped at another hospital was outrageous and could have got him into serious trouble. But he seemed quite oblivious to his dereliction of duty. The narrowness of his focus had blinded him to his responsibilities as a doctor towards a human being in his care. This casual violence of thoughtless unkindness is acted out many times every day in clinical settings.

The NHS that I entered was under-managed. When I left the NHS, in 2013, it was over-managed. A new managerial fundamentalism had taken over. There were targets that had to be met and a raft of administrative tasks of varying relevance that made less time available for clinical work. Many of us could see the parallels with the overweening bureaucracies of the old communist regimes of Eastern Europe with regimes of managers becoming more numerous and authoritarian as they struggled to enforce increasingly unrealistic and politically motivated targets. The atmosphere became more and more persecutory as people had to be bullied by managers to achieve the targets at the expense of useful clinical work. Inevitably, bullies are recruited to do the bullying. The system is maintained as the new breed of managers become dependent on the higher salary, their status and the pension enhancement. Their clinical skills may atrophy and they become alienated from the clinical workforce. The divide between the managers and the clinical staff widens and the respect given to clinical skill decreases. Human values can become secondary to the spreadsheets and the targets. As the original revolutionary values of the NHS become hijacked, the words of the great Russian author Vasily Grossman may come to mind:

> The hide was being flayed off the still living body of the Revolution so that a new age could slip into it; as for the red, bloody meat, the steaming innards, they were thrown on the scrapheap. The new age needed only the hide of the Revolution—and this was being flayed off people who were still alive. Those who then slipped into it spoke the language of the Revolution and mimicked its gestures, but their lungs, livers and eyes were utterly different.[198]

I was called to see a woman with a severe form of lupus, an autoimmune disease that can affect any part of the body. The ward doctor told me that she was suicidal and was threatening the nurses. I had seen Melanie before on one of her previous hospital stays. She had a complex and emotionally unstable personality with a history of intense and turbulent relationships with just about anyone that she met. Her mood swings were amplified by the high-dose steroids that she needed to keep her lupus under control. She was in a lot of pain and often felt that life was not worth living. In fact, I knew that suicide was against her very strong religious beliefs, but she was clearly very upset.

Melanie had severe arthritis as part of her condition and she'd been brought to hospital in the middle of the night with swollen painful joints. She was admitted to the medical assessment unit and prescribed the high-dose steroids that she required. It was hoped that her condition would settle so that she could go home within a day or two. But her condition did not settle; in fact, it got worse. It would take more than a few days for her to recover sufficiently to go home. To complicate matters, there was a new target that the assessment unit had to achieve: no patient was to be on the unit for more than three days. Within 72 hours of admission a patient either had to be discharged home or moved to another ward. The night manager noticed that Melanie was going to breach this target if she were still on the ward at three in the morning. So at 2 am, she was woken up, put in a wheelchair, taken outside the building on a bitterly cold night and transferred to another ward. She was very upset.

This would be an appalling way to treat any human being let alone someone who is unwell. To compound matters, Melanie had been brought up by a mother who had bipolar disorder and alcohol issues. Melanie's childhood had been blighted by her mother's unpredictable moods. Sometimes when Melanie most needed her mother to be sane and supportive, her mother was mad and unsupportive and this went some way towards explaining why Melanie had such difficulties with her personality and relationships. Her treatment by the hospital had sent her back to a very difficult psychological place where she was once again the vulnerable and abused child. We talked this through and she settled down a little. 'I thought my mum was mad', said Melanie. 'But the hospital makes her look like the Virgin f...... Mary. What sort of system allows them to treat people like that?'

Intelligent Kindness

Many years ago I had a colleague who didn't believe in kindness; he didn't see the point in it. He thought that kindness was a sentiment that could muddle the complex decision making processes that doctors have to make. 'Where is the evidence that being nice to people is clinically effective?' he would say. He thought that being harsh to his staff was a way of maintaining standards, but people were frightened of him. As a result, patients often didn't come to their appointments and he didn't get the best out of his team. Most of us know on a very deep level that kindness is absolutely fundamental to every human relationship and is the bedrock upon which every human and professional interaction must rest. We do not need scientific evidence to tell us this.

I have completed two long and challenging psychotherapy trainings. The first was psychoanalytic in nature and the second was transpersonal / archetypal. Both involved the learning and understanding of theory, much exploration of hitherto hidden parts of psyche, a range of emotional experience, some good times and some less good times. But the most important and lasting result of both, I believe, was to help me to be more conscious, humane and kinder in my relationships. To put it another way, I became progressively less blind to the ways in which I was unkind.

But the term *kindness* is one of these words that can cause people to recoil. It can seem too fuzzy or idealistic, perhaps disconnected with the real world. There are types of kindness that serve a psychological purpose but which can be harmful rather than helpful. Every parent, every doctor, everyone who has responsible relationships knows that kindness sometimes has to be tough, even fierce. Dr Paramandhu Groves in his book *Practical Buddhism* distinguishes between the false kindnesses and true kindness.[199] There are the facades of looking kind while being weak, manipulative or overly controlling. There is 'stupid kindness' where a generalised wash of goodwill is actually thoughtless and insensitive and does not respond to the requirements of the situation. There is laziness and sentimental attachment masquerading as kindness. No wonder the word can make us uneasy.

Intelligent Kindness is the title of the book written by John Ballatt and Penelope Campling. It has been widely praised; Dr Claire Gerada, while president of the Royal College of General Practitioners in the UK, said in 2013 that it was the one book that every doctor should read.[200] The authors define kindness as '*a binding, creative and problem solving force that inspires and focuses imagination and goodwill*'.[201] They take a psycho-social perspective on kinship and its expression in a compassionate relationship between the doctor and the patient, and suggest an investment in understanding what helps and what hinders kindness as well as the roots and causes of unkindness. They analyse how the modern industrialisation of medicine has pursued efficiency at the expense of relationship and how the basic core function of healthcare—the caring part of it—has been neglected, creating a 'pull towards perversion'. At worst, this leads to disasters, where compassion ceases to exist and patients become units to be abused in the pursuit of financial, managerial or political targets.

We now know, as a result of a public enquiry, that in the Mid-Staffordshire NHS Foundation Trust in Britain, between 2005 and 2009 some 400 to 1200 people attending the emergency department apparently lost their lives due to cost cutting, target driven behaviour and poor management, caused by an inappropriate focus on financial and business imperatives.[202] Ballatt and Campling conclude with a plea to apply our collective intelligence and solidarity to the process of reform of the culture and the systems so that intelligent kindness can become central to the healing relationship.[203]

The Saturn Archetype

Much of this is so obvious that we may wonder how we can possibly become parted from our basic principles of compassion in such a way. How can the complicated process of the management of financial and political risk in our healthcare systems have such a confounding effect on our altruism? We can understand some of the collective psycho-social stresses, we can study the dynamics of organizations and the structures of power, but is there also an archetypal element at work, which is dazzling, dominating and befuddling?

The archetypal principle traditionally represented by Saturn underpins our need for structure and endurance. For students of archetypal psychology, Saturn (or the *Senex*) brings form to the formless. We could liken the role of the Saturn principle to the manifestation of the particle from the wave form of the quantum world. Saturn also holds those qualities required for the slow building of the ego from undifferentiated psyche, forming the ego structures that we need to navigate this world. But Saturn is difficult. The darker side of Saturn is the tendency to bind, restrict and tyrannize.

He (for Saturn is a patriarchal archetype) does not have a sense of humor, but is grave and serious. He is associated with the march of time and the inevitability of decay and death. Saturn stands for thrift, caution and fear, resistance to change and the rigidity of age. Saturn represents the drudgery of life, the rigor, and the sheer effort that life entails, but also the rewards of hard work and organization and the steadfast qualities of loyalty and constancy.

We would not bother to grow without the impetus of some pain and discomfort. It is Saturn that provides a stiffening of sinews, a vulcanization of ego to provide hardening and strength. Liz Greene describes the Saturn archetype as a psychological process by which an individual may utilize the experiences of pain, restriction and discipline as a means for greater consciousness and fulfillment.[204] We need Saturn in our passage towards a more whole and complete version of ourselves. But Saturn is not a cheerful companion and is difficult to integrate in the correct proportions. When Saturn dominates the archetypal soup in which we swim, it gives a particular perspective that dominates the worldview. This harder version of Saturn is the place of impossible constriction, of no hope, no escape. This is the place of the Grofian second perinatal matrix, the prison camp, the frozen waste where nothing can grow or flourish.

For the archetypal cosmologist Renn Butler, a well-integrated Saturn confers in people feelings of responsibility, humility and patience. They will live comfortably within nature's material boundaries while recognizing that consciousness is without boundaries. Saturn's negative form can manifest as religious and scientific fundamentalism, a slavish identification with one's job and social role, or narrowed horizons. In contrast, people who have not integrated Saturn's imperatives, the 'reality principle', will have trouble accepting any kind of discipline or structure. They may lack strength and focus.[205]

The unfolding story of the NHS casts some light on the tension between the archetypal forces of compassion and the archetypal forces represented by Saturn. They both need each other in order to flourish and function effectively, but a healthy balance is difficult to achieve. The same archetypal tensions are played out within us all on an individual level as we grow through our lives. A well-integrated Saturn is one of the hardest developmental tasks, requiring typical Saturnine qualities of hard work and application to tread the path between an unfocussed mushiness and the inner Stalin.

The Saturn archetype does not allow us any short cuts or easy answers. Growing up, like healthcare, is hard work. Dealing with people like

Raymond is difficult, and there really does need to be a judicious mixture of compassion and boundaries. The love does indeed sometimes need to be tough. Similarly, the organizational issues raised by Ballatt and Campling in *Intelligent Kindness* will not simply go away but will need to be addressed methodically, skillfully and painfully over time. It will be hard but necessary work.

Saturn is a subtle archetype because it is so integral to our development. The archetypal crisis driven by Saturn does not have a rapid onset numinous quality; rather, it is a cumulative process, a gradual immersion that is difficult to navigate partly because we are so unconscious of its presence. It is shadowy in that there is great potential for the manifestation of its shadow. In individuals it often emerges in the midlife crisis with a state of entrapment that feels hopelessly inescapable. It can present as a depression, but this is not a depression that is likely to respond to medication or traditional psychological methods. In organizations, a Saturnine crisis brings rigidity, conflict, fear and redundancy. It is the antithesis of creativity.

The Saturn archetype needs to be carefully brought into conscious awareness so that we can understand it's meaning and purpose rather than be oppressed by meaninglessness and purposelessness. Some awareness of how the archetypal current with this flavor moves through us, both as individuals and in institutions, could be a useful tool in our struggle to achieve a functional and compassionate balance. The other way to address the tension between compassion and rigidity is to engage in practices that encourage the flow and expression of compassion – and that is the primary task of the next section.

SECTION THREE

Working with the Numinous

. . . .but it is good to have died and been trodden out

trodden to nought in sour, dead earth

quite to nought

absolutely to nothing

nothing, nothing

nothing.

For when it is quite, quite nothing, then it is everything.

When I am trodden quite out, quite, quite out

every vestige gone, then I am here risen,

and setting my foot on another world . . .

myself, the same as before, yet unaccountably new

—D.H.Lawrence.

'New Heaven and Earth'

experiences (OBEs) and research involving recovered memories.[210] Much of this work remains neglected and relatively unknown. For example, the work of the late Canadian psychiatrist Ian Stevenson, continued by Dr Jim Tucker over a 40-year period, studies cases of children who talk to their families about a life that has been lived before.[211] Stevenson was the chairman of the Department of Psychiatry at the University of Virginia with a wide range of academic publications and an interest in psychosomatic medicine. In the 1950s he became aware of accounts from around the world of young children who reported memories of previous lives. Stevenson studied 44 of these reports; he found that that a clear pattern emerged in the cases and concluded that this was a real phenomenon worthy of further study. He travelled to India and Sri Lanka to find new cases to investigate and this developed into his life's work based in the Division of Personality Studies at the University of Virginia.

Stevenson found that when children give narratives of other lives, the child starts talking about their memories shortly after speech develops. The memories subsequently fade to be followed by normal development. There are over 2500 cases on record in Stevenson's unit. The primary characteristics of these children are as follows:

- The memories appear between the age of two and four
- The memories fade between the age of five and eight
- The child behaves like an adult when discussing the memories; for example, giving detail about the opposite sex that no two-year-old would usually know.
- The child claims the new body feels strange
- Vivid events of the other life are remembered
- A large percentage of the cases remember a violent death
- There may be a phobia of objects connected with previous death
- When children visit their previous home they can point out changes, which are corroborated by current inhabitants
- The child has skills not taught or learned
- Children may have desires for alcohol or tobacco that are alien to their culture but consistent with their previous personality
- Some have large birthmarks or deformities in the same place as a previous life injury
- There may be memories of an interlife period or selection of parents

Stevenson had a reputation as a highly methodical, cautious and painstaking man who accumulated a wealth of data that simply cannot be ignored.[212] Other researchers such as Keil in Australia, Pasricha in India, Mills in the USA and Haraldsson in Iceland have reached similar conclusions that some children report events from other lives.[213] This is the type of research that cannot be proved by brain imaging or the measurement of biomarkers. It is a softer science reliant on careful painstaking investigation and the integrity of the researchers involved. It seems a little old fashioned in these days of technology and multi-center research, and this probably contributes to the lack of attention that this research has received. The implications, however, are paradigm changing for the materialist model of mind favored in the West—although many cultures, particularly in Asia, would take such matters for granted.

The most impressive cases are those where there is independent corroboration from people outside of the family that the child's memories of the other life are factually correct. To give a recent example, James Leininger, an American boy born in 1998, had disturbing dreams from the age of 2 that he was a pilot flying from a boat called Natoma, whose plane was shot down by the Japanese. As a small child, before he was potty trained, he showed intimate knowledge of World War II and the aircraft of that era. He spoke of a friend who was called Jack Larsen. His father was intrigued by his son's story and investigated further, despite his religious beliefs that were opposed to the concept of reincarnation. He found that there was an aircraft carrier called the Natoma Bay that supported the invasion of Iwo Jima in World War II. A plane flown by a pilot called Jack Huston was shot down over Iwo Jima. Through the Natoma Bay reunion meetings, he found pilots who witnessed Huston's death and who corroborated the same vivid detail that little James Leininger was describing about the circumstances of his death.[214] Little James eventually met Jack Larsen, who his father had tracked down, and he had a phone conversation with James Huston's elderly sister Annie who was able to corroborate his memories of their early family life. It seemed clear that little James had access to James Huston's memories.[215]

There is always debate about the credibility of such stories, and it would be a mistake to place too much reliance on one individual account. However, there are many other similar cases that suggest a transfer of conscious experience from one life through death to another life. This does not prove that the child involved has lived that previous life but it does provide some evidence that individual consciousness is not extinguished with neuronal death. Although reincarnation is often offered as an explanation, this is not the only possibility; it may be that the memory is more like a download; that the child is participating in the memory of a life that has been lived before. It is possible that some of these experiences may turn out to have other explanations, including fraud, but a weight of evidence is accumulating that cannot be easily dismissed. For the open-minded and curious, it would be hard to escape the conclusion that, while we do not know whether some aspects of consciousness survive death, it is certainly a possibility worthy of serious consideration.

The Ascent of the Dragonfly

The poet Percy Bysshe Shelly penned the line: 'He is not dead, he does not sleep, he has awakened from the dream of life', after the premature death of John Keats.[216] Is this sentiment only a sugarcoated pill that we swallow to help us through the pain of bereavement or could it also contain a kernel of truth? Is there a part of our life cycle that is hidden from us? We cannot know the answer, but we can be open to the question.

There are some simple stories that illustrate the change from a familiar state of 'being' to a state of 'becoming' that is completely unimaginable in the original state. Examples are the condition of the baby in utero who has yet to be born into the world or the fish that is miraculously transported from the sea to explore the unfamiliar territory of land. If anyone had told the baby in the womb or the fish in the sea that there were these other worlds, they would not have believed it. These stories point to the possibility of a transformation of our state of being after the conclusion of our physical life here on planet Earth, implying that our natural life cycle could hold more complexity than many of us imagine. Here is the fable of the dragonfly, which illustrates this point.

The insects lived simply and comfortably among the weeds and lilies in the muddy pond. Not much happened to disturb them. Every now and again one of the insects would go missing. He or she would climb up the stem of a weed and would never be seen again. One day, one little insect felt an urge to climb up that stem. It was a powerful urge and he couldn't resist it. He was quite sure that he would not leave forever. He would come back and tell his friends what he had found at the top.

When he reached the top and climbed out of the water onto the surface of the lily pad, he was very tired,. The sun felt warm and he decided to take a rest. He fell asleep and, as he slept, his body changed. When he woke up, he found to his surprise that he found that he had grown broad wings, a long blue tail and a slender body designed for flying. He had turned into a dragonfly.

He tried out his wings and they worked. This was amazing. As he flew, he saw the beauty of a whole new world with colours and textures and many wonderful things that he had never known existed. This was so much more interesting than the pond. Then he remembered his friends and family back in the muddy water. He wanted to go back to tell them what he had seen and explain to them that he was now more alive than he had ever been before. His life had been fulfilled rather than ended. But he found that his new body would not go down into the water. He could not get back to tell his friends the good news; it just was not possible. Then he realised they would join him when the time was right for them to do so and they would understand what he now understood. He opened his wings and joyfully flew off to explore.

Archetypes of Near Death

The classic near-death experience or NDE has become part of our collective culture. We have all heard the stories of the cardiac arrest followed by the separation of consciousness from the body, the flowing through a tunnel towards the light, encounters with a welcoming committee of dead relatives, and perhaps a divine presence. NDEs occur in about 10–12% of people who have suffered cardiac arrests although the recall and the quality of the experience is variable. In 1–2% of cases, there may be difficult 'hellish' experiences, but usually the experience is one of deeply positive numinosity colored by an intense feeling of love. Typically, the survivors enjoy a loss of fear of death and an enhanced enjoyment of being alive. It is easier for NDE survivors to give a narrative of their experience but much harder for them to describe the extraordinary emotional intensity, the peace, happiness and the sense of coming home.[217]

Many people who have had a numinous NDE experience struggle to accommodate the disappointment of the return to everyday life, often in a vulnerable body and there is a risk of a depressive reaction. This was the case for Jung after a heart attack in his late sixties. He described an ascent where he found himself looking down on Earth from space, followed by a sloughing off of all the relics of his earthly existence so that only his essential self remained. He found himself in a structure that reminded him of a Buddhist Temple in Sri Lanka and he describes how the answers to all his deepest questions were revealed to him.[218] He felt able to frame his life in a context of what had gone before and where his life was flowing, but then he received a message that he had no right to leave the Earth and must return. For some time afterwards he was depressed and angry at his return to life. His days were difficult but at night he would wake from sleep in an entirely different mood with the most exquisite numinous experiences that he likened to the 'sweet smell of the Holy Ghost'. Once he had recovered fully, Jung describes feeling more objective about his experience and felt able to develop his ideas more creatively. The numinosity of his NDE seemed to provide an important function in providing the fuel for the final stage of his life where he was extraordinarily productive, writing many of his principal works during this period.[219]

There is uncertainty as to what the NDEs actually represent: Do they offer a glimpse into an afterlife or are they an artifact of fading brain? We cannot know for sure although people who have experienced NDEs are in no doubt that they have accessed a realm that is entirely real. Certainly, the survivors of the NDE have been nearly dead rather than finally dead; they have not passed that final barrier as they have returned to life. From a medical perspective, we know that the blood supply to the brain stops immediately after a cardiac arrest and we know that the EEG measuring brain activity becomes electrically inactive, showing no brain activity within 10 to 20 seconds. This indicates that when people report images of medical teams attending to their cardiac arrest, they are reporting these sensory perceptions despite an inert brain. This is theoretically impossible according to the materialist paradigm and points to an entirely different type of consciousness in operation, which is not dependent on brain tissue. The counter argument is that there may be aspects of brain activity that may linger in the deeper structures of brain after cardiac arrest, which may not be detectable. Whatever we may believe may happen after we take our last breath and our heart stops beating, there is no doubt that NDEs occur and that they are among the most powerful archetypal experiences available to humankind.

Post-traumatic stress disorder, commonly abbreviated to PTSD, is the polar opposite of an NDE. It is an extraordinarily intense encounter with death that has a dread-filled quality and causes a major impediment to growth. The trauma that causes PTSD is always of sufficient magnitude to cause a perception of threat to life, even if the person emerges from it physically unscathed. It is an overwhelming and terrifying experience that is outside of the normal range of human experience. We do not fully understand the biological mechanisms that underlie PTSD but it is often likened it to an overreaction of the adrenaline system, so that the fight-or-flight response remains highly activated even after the actual threat has disappeared. The cardinal symptoms of PTSD are the nightmares and flashbacks that re-enact the trauma and cause a reliving of the emotions involved with same quality of terror and powerlessness.

It is difficult for people to find words to describe the fear with which they wake from these nightmares, drenched in sweat, heart pounding and too stimulated to get back to sleep again. This version of the encounter with death is jagged, shocking and disturbing to the core; it is like a blast zone where important psychological structures and integrative mechanisms are demolished. Milder cases of PTSD make a full recovery without long-term consequences, but many of the people that I see with PTSD are towards the more severe end of the spectrum. Their symptoms involve an enduring and intense meaning-state of terror and imminent catastrophe, which utterly dominates their conscious experience. Some of my PTSD patients have come very close indeed to death but not a single one of them has undergone an NDE. Because of my interest in this area, I always enquire in some detail as to what happened after the moment of trauma, but no one with PTSD has ever reported to me an out-of-body experience, a passage towards the light or any transcendent experience. It seems that PTSD flows from an encounter with death that is indigestible and totally toxic.

The trauma unit at the Royal London had many such patients, some with unusually severe forms of PTSD, who were very difficult to help. Simon was working on a construction site when he was crushed by a truck. He was standing by the side of a building when truck reversed towards him. He moved to get out of the way but stumbled and fell. He was unable to take evasive action. The beeping noise of the reversing mechanism continued as the truck slowly reversed over his legs. He knew without a shadow of doubt that he was going to die and there was nothing he could about it. He was shouting and screaming but the truck driver didn't hear him. He could smell the diesel fumes and the noise of the engine was getting louder in his ears. The front wheels of the truck were coming towards his head as he lay trapped on the ground. He knew that he had seconds to live.

The truck stopped just short of his head. His screams were heard before he lost consciousness and he was brought to the Royal London Hospital by the helicopter ambulance. His leg fractures were fixed but he needed three months bed rest in hospital to allow his badly broken pelvis to heal. I was asked to see him because of his nightmares that woke him screaming at night.

Simon was my patient for two years. His nightmares improved with treatment while he was in hospital. He needed some medication to help him to sleep and we began the slow and very gentle process of the talking treatment. My nursing colleague, Peter Martin, accompanied him on his first few short trips in a wheelchair outside the hospital building to become acclimatized to the sound of engines and trucks. We know from experience that people like Simon can appear to be making a good recovery from PTSD in hospital but that is because they are protected from certain reminders of their trauma and they may suffer a dramatic increase in symptoms when they leave hospital and hear the sound of traffic, which triggers flashbacks. After discharge, when he felt ready, we treated him with a trauma-focused psychotherapy to help him to process the PTSD. I saw him in the

Crisis Service for follow up. I also saw his wife and I arranged a further course of treatment with a psychologist specializing in eye-movement desensitization and reprocessing therapy (EMDR).

Despite the high-quality treatment over a long period, very sadly Simon did not do well. He remained in a state of terror. He could not leave his house easily as the sound of engines, particularly heavy diesel engines, caused flashbacks and panic attacks. If he heard the beeping sound of a vehicle reversing he suffered a vivid and highly distressing re-experiencing of the trauma. When these flashbacks occurred, he was transported right back under the truck knowing that he was going to die and feeling terrified and unprepared for his death. He dreaded going to sleep because of the nightmares that he knew would follow. He couldn't go back to work and lost his job. He existed in permanent state of vigilance that something disastrous would happen either to him or his family. His stress tolerance was impaired, he couldn't concentrate, his libido was non-existent and he was very irritable. His wife told me that the family felt that they walking on eggshells around him. He became excessively protective about his teenage children and relationships deteriorated. Eventually, Simon separated from his family and moved to a rural location where he would not be troubled by engine noise.

PTSD holds that intense archetypal quality of tremulous fear where the world is no longer benign but has become threatening and highly charged. It is a numinous experience of the darkest kind flowing from an un integrated experience of the dread-filled encounter with death. The mindset and setting of the encounter with death are crucial determinants of the development of PTSD. Death erupts out of nowhere, in an instant and in a manner that is profoundly shocking. The setting is traumatic and totally unsupportive and the mindset is unprepared and overwhelmed. Any meaningful integration of the experience is such circumstances is impossible. The dominant mindset perceives that the world is inherently threatening, the future is bleak and another dreadful event is imminent. There is nothing that promotes growth in PTSD; it is a psychological winter.

We have touched on the two extreme forms of the encounter with death and their very different archetypal characteristics. The third scenario is the sentence of death, the loss of innocence and the knowledge that the final journey towards death has begun. The diagnosis of terminal illness triggers a highly complex process. The challenge has many levels: the putting of one's affairs in order, the managing of relationships and the possibility of healing past traumas. Death can concentrate the mind wonderfully and some of the things that seemed so important suddenly seem trivial. The toys of ego fall away—there is an altogether different task to address.

Philippa's Story

Philippa was 33 when she was found to have an aggressive form of breast cancer. It had already spread to some lymph nodes. She had two young children, both girls. She knew that she would probably not see her daughters reach teenage years let alone adulthood, but she was determined to stay alive and be their mother for as long as she could. So she underwent treatment after treatment: surgery, high-dose chemotherapy and bone-marrow transplant, radiation and more chemotherapy. Her hair fell out, her body changed shape and there was much physical and emotional pain. She wanted to try every possible treatment that held the potential to slow the spread of cancer and its effect on her body. She explored complementary medicine, she consulted a psychotherapist, she did reiki, she ate organic food, she worked at positive thinking and she tried to meditate. Against the odds, she survived for another seven years, dying in the arms of her family when she was forty.

Philippa was someone with an appetite for life. As a teenager she rode a motorbike and she hitchhiked through Europe. She liked good food, good wine and lively company. She was an extrovert who was not much interested in the world of the interior or philosophical issues but, as her illness progressed, she became preoccupied by the big questions of life and death. Inevitably, she sought answers of a spiritual nature and eventually she found the nourishing home that she sought in the Anthroposophical Church.

Philippa was my sister. She was living in Argentina with her family when she became ill and we had stayed very close despite the geographical distance between us. I was doing my psychotherapy training at the time. Perhaps I over-identified with the psychoanalytic models that I was learning about and I tended to understand her new found religious orientation as a psychological defense system against the tragedy of her impending death. With my aversion to organized religion, I would even say that there was a barrier between us for a while. But as time progressed, I could see that, while her developing spirituality may have started as a defense, it had become much more than that. She was growing and finding a maturity, fulfillment and peace that came to fill her with a calm radiance that supported her and continued to nourish her family after she was gone. Her last days were extraordinarily happy and transfused with love and compassion.

The Crystal Bowl is the one of the fruits of her short life. She wrote it in the style of a children's story as it represents her legacy to her daughters, who were still young when she died and I am reproducing it here in her own words.[220] It is an allegorical story about the journey of Being, the gathering of the baubles of personality, the purpose of their accumulation and their eventual surrender to something altogether greater. It tells us about her higher guiding principle — we could call it an anima figure although Philippa called her an angel. Most of all, the Crystal Bowl tells us something about the complex relationship with the transcendent Self and of the search for meaning in suffering. This is what she has to say about the meaning of the mysterious passage through our human life towards our death.

The Crystal Bowl

Once upon a time, in a beautiful land of gentle, lush hills, a baby girl was born to joyous parents. As she was dearly loved and much cherished, she grew strongly from a chubby babe to a graceful child with soft locks of lustrous hair and eyes like the depths of a mountain pool. One night as she lay asleep in her chamber, her guardian angel visited her in a dream and spoke to her thus:

> Sweet child, arrived from the realm of the skies to live your life on earth, don't be afraid, for I am your angel and I shall ever stay near you, though you see me not. I shall accompany you along life's paths be they straight or twisting, be they narrow or generous, be they of shadow or bathed in light. I have a gift from the heavens to bestow upon you, which shall be carried in your soul for as long as you live. This gift may be seen only with your mind's eye and as time passes you will become ever more able to appreciate its unique beauty. The gift may be held in the hands of your soul, and with the passing of time, you will become ever more able to feel its unique strength.[221]

With these words the angel held out a bowl of the finest crystal towards the child, a bowl that seemed to be of every imaginable shape in the world and of all the colours that will ever be seen. With infinite tenderness, the angel placed the wondrous vessel in the soft receiving hands of the child.

'This bowl may always be found should you lose it, my dear', said the angel and added

> but it will not be found unless you seek it with love in your heart. Into it you may place a jewel, but only a jewel that no eye of flesh can see and no hand of flesh and blood may touch. For this crystal bowl is to hold the jewels of your soul, the fruits of your journeys along life's paths, the essence pure of all your joys and sufferings, of your affections and distastes, of your fulfilled wishes and your disappointed desires. The tears of your pain shall mingle with the sunlight of your happiness.

The girl stirred in her slumber and murmured, so low that it could have been a sigh. 'And what shall I do, dear friend, when the crystal bowl is full?'

The guardian from the skies smiled.

> It is good that the bowl shall be filled, as life on your earth must be as a rose, which bears thorns as it bears also its velvet blooms, and as a landscape with high peaks and low valleys. It takes courage to continue the journey of Being, to reach ever further into the unknown, ready to greet the dawn and bid the dusk farewell. On your journeys my sweeting, you will fill your crystal bowl to overflowing, and then you must take it in the hands of your heart and climb the staircase to the stars where the Lord Of All Worlds abides.

> Your trembling hands will hold up the crystal bowl to the Lord, and your heart will nigh be torn in two. With all your love and devotion will you wish to bestow your gift upon the Lord, and yet will you fear to give up the jewels of your experience in the crystal bowl made of all shapes and all colours.

Again the child stirred in her sleep, her small body was warm and an invisible glow radiated from her form. Her eyelashes fluttered and the clenched fists of her little hands unfurled as the fingers stretched and opened. But she did not wake.

The years passed by and the child grew and flourished and came to maturity. She was blessed with a living filled with much love and coloured by great adventures. Myriad paths stretched out before her from which she could choose her own way. She encountered the deepest shades of darkness and the thickest swirling fog as well as the threshold of the realm of light. Many were the times when she had to wrestle with misery and despair. But more numerous still were the times when she felt the warm breath of joy as she broke free of the Shadow and could live in peace and happiness.

When the day came when she was once again obliged to forsake the gentle green hills where she lived in peace and plenty, to journey out into the unknown once more, great dark gems and glittering jewels of all hues nearly filled her crystal bowl. The girl— grown woman—felt as though darkness was taking root in her very soul and she suffered greatly in her pain and in her fear.

Just as she was wondering if the light would ever return to brighten her days, a wise woman approached her on the path and introducing herself only briefly, begged to be permitted to recount a short tale. Her voice resounded with music as she spoke, and in the tones of the wise woman

were revealed the wishes of the guardian, who had made the gift, so long
ago, of the crystal bowl.

Take the gems of your soul
Soul—life turned to jewels
Jewels gladly given
Given in a bowl of crystal
Crystal pure for the master
Master Of The Worlds
Worlds beyond the staircase
Staircase to the stars
To the stars take the gems . . .

The girl—grown woman—who is named with all the names in the world,
took the crystal bowl of every shape in the world, glowing with all the
colours in the world, overflowing with a world full of jewels, and held it
firmly in those soft, supple hands which reach out from the heart. She shut
her eyes and saw the staircase to the stars rise in front of her. In the gleaming radiance that gathered about her, she began to ascend the steps.

The higher the girl—grown woman—named with all the names in the
world, climbed, the greater grew the radiance, a radiance so gentle that it
did not dazzle or burn. At the end of the staircase waited the Lord of The
Skies who is also Lord Of The Earth. He greeted her with love, and spoke
all her names with one long sound, and bade her to give Him her gift if she
so desired.

Kneeling before Him in wonder and devotion she lifted her hands with
the precious jewel filled bowl. Her hands trembled and she felt as though
her heart would be split in two, so dearly did she wish to give up her gift of
love and so greatly did she fear to part with the jewels of her experience
and the crystal bowl of all colours and shapes.

The might voice of the Lord Of All Realms resounded in the very
centre of her being

Let go of the crystal bowl
The crystal bowl be let free
Let free from a trusting soul
A trusting soul who has learnt
Learnt with love to let go . . .

The girl—grown woman—with all the names in the world, gathered all her
strength and thrust forth her fears. With a dawning light of understanding,
she opened her hands that cradled the crystal bowl. Taking on the form
of an arrowhead, the crystal bowl cut through the air, and sparks of all

imaginable hues illuminated its fall as it fell farther and lower. The tinkling tones of smashing crystal flocked expectantly, preparing to resound when the crystal bowl crashed to the ground.

But the tinkling tones waited in vain. It wasn't they who resounded through the skies, but the softly swelling chords of harmony, which are the companion of Peace.

The girl—grown woman—with all the names in the world, turned her sight from the radiant glow of the Lord Of All Realms to seek the cause of that exquisite sound. Far below over a landscape of pinnacles and precipices, she beheld the hands of the Lord Of All Realms, nurturing in their cupped form, her jewel filled crystal bowl.

CHAPTER 19

Mindfulness and the Empathic Observer

Life is an incredible curriculum in which we live richly and passionately as a way of awakening to the deepest truths of our being.

—Ram Dass

Without self knowledge, without understanding the working and functions of his machine, man cannot be free, he cannot govern himself and he will always remain a slave.

—G.I. Gurdjieff

Let us return briefly to Plato's cave with the people chained in position gazing at the shadows flickering on the back of the cave. This is their two-dimensional reality and they can conceive of no other. The chains that hold them in place prevent their direct experience of the multi-dimensioned primary reality outside the cave. Those chains symbolise those attachments that hold us back from growth. They represent the anxieties, the insecurities, the addictions, the greed, the rigidity and the unkindness to name just a few. The chains include the mind chatter, those purposeless repetitive patterns of thoughts that swirl around our outer consciousness, but these chains are metaphorical and they can be shed.[222]

Our natural state is orientated towards growth although there are many impediments that can get in the way. As our bodies are predetermined to mature, our psyche has an inbuilt drive to learn from experience and become more complex to a greater or lesser degree. From an archetypal viewpoint, there is assumed to be an inner intelligence that is orientated towards us becoming more whole, more complete, more fully human, deeper, richer and wiser.[223] There is a perspective that every moment of our lives holds perfection, a potential for us to learn and grow. Each moment has a poetry, if we can only appreciate it, capture it and be mindful of it. The various methods of mindfulness practice are techniques to help us become more conscious of each moment—more aware of being alive.

We mostly recognise our everyday experiences that hold a greater intensity of meaning as being life-enhancing. We find these moments in music and the arts, being in nature, taking pleasure in friends and family or intimacy with a partner. But there is growth and learning to be had in the darker moments too. Indeed, the harder the moment, the more potential there may be for growth—although this is an advanced practice. Ram Dass, for example, describes his recovery from a stroke, receiving his affliction and disability as a form of Grace providing developmental opportunities and learning that would not otherwise have been available: 'If you want to live a full life, you have to take the full curriculum'.[224]

The fruit of years of meditation practice is the ability to live mindfully in a way that most of us cannot imagine. But we do not have to be life long meditators to benefit; mindfulness practice is easy to learn and teach and has a number of useful clinical applications. The primary result is a movement towards dis-identification with pain and suffering and becoming an empathic observer of one's condition.

Meditation and the Chattering Mind

The first lesson that we learn in any meditation practice is that we have a chattering mind. If we start by counting our breaths, we may find that we lose count before we have reached more than five or six. Our mind has a mind of its own; it simply wanders off. But in taking up meditation we begin to examine our mind chatter so that we become more conscious of the paths that it takes and how we are led by our anxieties and our attachments. We gradually become familiar with a rich seam of subliminal experience and, over the course of time, we may become less identified with our restless ego and its superficial wanderings. The ego, in taking up meditation, embarks on a process of sowing the seeds of its downfall as the dominant force in the psyche.[225]

In a receptive meditation practice such as Vipassana, we are encouraged to become aware of our breathing.[226] When thoughts arise, we note them and then turn our attention calmly to the breathing again. We are encouraged to treat the thoughts like clouds in the sky. They pass—they are just thoughts. But these thoughts are remarkably persistent. As our practice progresses, we become more aware of the seething, turbulent, ever-changing currents of our inner experience. We find that our minds are not the finely honed tools that we imagined; we find that this conscious rational mind is but a small fraction of our mental life. There is layer upon layer of mental activity that becomes uncovered, much of it driven by desire and aversion, much of it very trivial. By paying attention, our minds gradually become quieter allowing us to catch the more subtle thoughts with all their diversity and richness. This effect is often compared to the setting of the sun (the ego) allowing the multitude of the stars to become visible in the night sky.

We find that much of our mind chatter is our ego whispering to us about the things that we think we want or that we don't want. These thoughts carry a strong charge for us and we are very attached to them. They pull towards us those things that will soothe and we push away those things that cause pain or angst. The problem is that these attachments, with their constant pushing and pulling, reduce the range and flexibility of the mind.

I suggest that it is these attachments and our cultural conditioning that make up much of those allegorical chains that confine us, looking at the flickering shadows at the back of Plato's cave. As the prolonged practice of meditation gradually softens and loosens the ego structures, we may be able to take some steps away from the back wall of the cave. We may be able to turn our attention away from the flickering two-dimensional shadows and we may become more aware of the sunlight filtering into the cave. We may learn to distinguish between chattering mind and whispering Self; we may even begin a tentative ascent into primary reality. This process is not without its challenges, and we may gain some bruises and abrasions on the way. There is likely to be some immersion in difficult parts of ourselves. Aspects of the shadow will arise and we need to accept and integrate them rather than recoil.

This is difficult work and serious meditation should always be done within a community where guidance is available from people who have travelled further along the same path. For a few people there may be powerful archetypal experiences. These may be exquisite and joyful or they may be powerful eruptions of a more unsettling kind, sometimes amounting to a spiritual emergency. Michael Washburn describes how long-term meditators tend to 'hit a wall', which is the final barrier between the ego and the archetypal domain. Once this wall is broached, it is likened to an oil strike and the numinous power of the Dynamic Ground (Washburn's term) becomes available.[227]

There is a consensus that going to a meditation retreat will accelerate progress. Indeed, it may be very difficult to progress beyond a certain stage unless the practice is deepened by the more intense discipline and distance from everyday life that a retreat offers. Retreats require a mindset orientated towards growth, a setting that is protective, supportive and nourishing, and conducive to integration. The usual characteristics of retreats include:

- Seclusion with separation from the demands of work and domestic life
- No regular contact with family or friends

- The food is usually vegetarian
- Separation from media, emails and internet (this may be partial)
- Rules governing the degree of communication, such as periods of silence
- Programmed activities, meditation or other practices
- Usually some programmed physical activity, i.e., walking meditation or moving to music
- Programmed teaching and instruction
- Induction and integration processes at the beginning and the end
- Clear guidelines for aftercare if required

Mindfulness Practice

Mindfulness is the practice of non-judgemental attention to the present moment. It seeks to isolate the essential components of meditation practice to make the practical benefits more easily available. If long-term meditation is likened to psychoanalysis, a complex practice requiring unusual levels of commitment, then mindfulness practice is more like CBT: short, easier to practice, goal orientated and demonstrably efficacious. Simple mindfulness practice serves to stabilise ego rather than transcend it. It is unlikely to lead to numinous experience or a profound psychospiritual transformation but it can be very helpful in navigating difficult territory, providing stability and thus promoting growth.

The founder of modern mindfulness practice, Jon Kabat-Zinn, defines mindfulness as paying attention in a particular way: on purpose, in the present moment and non judgementally.[228] Instructions for a simple mindfulness exercise follow:

- Find a comfortable posture sitting in a chair or on the floor in a quiet room.
- Sit straight without putting strain on the body. Let the eyes close.
- Bring your awareness to the body. Be aware of the sensations of contact wherever your body feels supported. Discover how this feels.
- Bring your attention to the breath. Become aware of the changing sensations of the abdomen and the chest as the breath moves in and out of the body.
- Simply breathe as normal and try to maintain awareness throughout each breath.
- Whenever the mind wanders, bring the awareness back to the breath and the movement of the abdomen. Do this over and over again. This is the practice and you are doing it well.
- Be patient. If you find yourself becoming impatient, remind yourself that it is just another thought. Bring your mind back to the breath.

- After a period time, usually fifteen minutes, bring your awareness gently back to your whole body, sitting in the room.
- Open you eyes and be ready for whatever happens next.

Kabat-Zinn's great contribution was to strip mindfulness of any religious or spiritual connotations to devise a standard eight-week programme called 'mindfulness based stress reduction' or MBSR. The programme includes some teaching or psycho-education about factors that trigger and maintain stress alongside training in mindfulness. A class is held each week where new techniques are introduced and the participant is required to practice mindfulness for 30 minutes each day.

There are many variations on the basic theme, all with their own acronyms.[229] Mindfulness based cognitive therapy (MBCT) was originally designed for people with recurrent depression. Dialectical behaviour therapy (DBT) is designed to reduce self harm. Acceptance and commitment therapy (ACT) has a greater emphasis on cognitive 'defusion', a deliberate dis-identification from thoughts and an identification with the transcendent Self. KBT is a training in the cultivation of kindness through meditation, with consideration of what kindness really is and what it is not.[230]

Mindfulness techniques work. There is an evidence base for its effectiveness for anxiety, stress reduction, depression and pain.[231] Mindfulness is at least as effective as antidepressants in preventing a relapse of recurrent depression. In the UK, the National Institute for Clinical Excellence (NICE) recommends MBCT for anyone who has had three or more depressive episodes. It seems likely that an increase in self-compassion may account for much of the therapeutic effect to counteract the painfully punitive negative thoughts that characterize depression. There may be some side effects that are more likely to become apparent in more intensive retreats including restlessness, anxiety, depression and guilt, but these are rarely problematic.[232]

These days mindfulness is becoming embedded in our culture. A quiet revolution is taking place as schools, multinational companies and government bodies are increasingly recognising the benefits. In healthcare, many of us believe that the true potential of mindfulness is nowhere near being realized and that applications of mindfulness would be a simple, cost-effective way of alleviating suffering associated with a variety of conditions. Perhaps part of the problem is that it is so simple. You do not need medical degrees, expensive training, costly technologies or plush settings to apply mindfulness. But you do need to be mindful and, for many of us, that is potentially challenging, perhaps bringing us into conflict with some of the ways in which we go about our lives. This is the true challenge of mindfulness, that we cannot avoid gaining some insight into the sharper edges of our ego function.

Mindfulness and meditation seem to exert their effects by modulating our bio-psycho-social settings. There is evidence of a reduction in the body's arousal systems, mediated by the nervous system and our stress-related hormones. Parameters such as blood pressure generally fall. Functional MRI scans of experienced meditators show that different brain pathways are activated as the meditators become more successful in regulating negative emotional responses.[233] There is some evidence of increased density in the hippocampus, which is associated with memory and attention while the amygdala, which is associated with anger and arousal levels, shows decreased grey-matter density. There can be little doubt that meditation affects the hardware of our brain and that this is reflected in some psycho-social changes in how we interact with our environment.

I suspect that mindfulness practice of any type may also have a balancing effect on archetypal penetrance in the early stages with an increase in archetypal penetrance in advanced practice. This is a complex process in which there can be an intensification of unresolved psychological issues, but the tendency is for these to settle and resolve if the process is supported and allowed to unfold. The ego chatter diminishes allowing a more focused ego function and an increased permeability to the archetypal domain, which gathers momentum with duration and intensity of practice. There can certainly be an encounter with the shadow but the advanced stages lead to an immersion in a peaceful joyous state that is beyond words.

As a psychiatrist working closely with surgeons and physicians, I see many people with a combination of physical pain and depression. I find that severe painful states have an archetypal quality; the pain is intense and dominant, looming over large in mental life and holding an awesome, dreadful quality. In these high archetypal penetrance states, we are one with the pain, we are one with the depression and the distress is overwhelming. Sometimes the medical efforts to relieve pain are counterproductive. Opiate analgesics cause dependence and torpor, and antidepressants tend to promote weight gain, which in turn amplifies the physical disability. Mindfulness practice seems to be effective by decreasing the archetypal quality of the pain, allowing a gradual dis-identification with the state of suffering.

In some states of very high archetypal penetrance, a person is unable to meditate as the mind is too aroused and disturbed, but an awareness of mindfulness techniques can sometimes allow a safer passage through the crisis by defusing the identification with the intensity of the moment. For people suffering from paranoia or disturbing voices, the standard mindfulness practice requires some adaptation to prevent people becoming lost in a struggle with their symptoms. Paul Chadwick, a clinical psychologist with long experience in the application of mindfulness with people suffering distressing psychosis, suggests that 10 minutes of mindfulness practice is sufficient with spoken guidance every 30 to 60 seconds to avoid long silences.[234]

Mindfulness in the Emergency Room

I have sometimes found mindfulness techniques useful when people in archetypal crisis are brought into the emergency room. Much depends on the severity of the condition. If people have a severe mood disorder, paranoia or fixed delusions, they remain strongly identified with their viewpoint and it is difficult for them to dis-identify with it. With less severe states, a gentle and grounding engagement can help the person to develop a position of becoming a more empathic observer of their distress. If this can be achieved, the degree of arousal diminishes, the setting feels less threatening, a therapeutic alliance develops and with it a mindset of working towards the management of the internal process.

Jim was a patient that I had looked after over the years at the Royal London and I tell his story here to illustrate how mindfulness can sometimes be helpful in emergency situations. Jim was a local character who hinted at a significant criminal background. He had a large and complicated family who had intense and highly charged relationships with each other. Jim had been seriously assaulted some years before and had developed agoraphobia, being too anxious to leave his home on his own. He had bought a puppy from a friend so that he could leave the house, with his dog for security without suffering panic attacks. Jim loved his puppy, but it grew into a large dog with sharp teeth and an excitable temperament. One evening Jim was arguing with his wife, they were shouting and objects were thrown. The dog caught the mood, joined in the affray and bit them both. Jim and his wife had to come to hospital to have their wounds sutured and the dog had to find another home. So Jim was largely housebound again. He found that the only thing that helped his anxiety was cannabis and he smoked a lot of it. It may have been the cannabis that triggered his first manic episode requiring in-patient treatment. After he was discharged from the psychiatric unit, he came to see me again in the Crisis Service. We agreed that he would try to reduce his cannabis use and that I would work with him towards regulating his affect, his anxiety and his tendency to over-react to environmental stress.

Jim surprised us both by taking to some simple mindfulness techniques and he duly went to the East London Buddhist Centre to attend a mindfulness course. He didn't complete the entire course but he attended some sessions. Some months later, Jim was brought into hospital again by his family. He had been staying up all night and he thought someone was watching his house. He was frightened and angry, and he had a selection of weapons ready for use in the kitchen in case he was attacked. His family said that his speech was not making sense—he was talking too fast and couldn't sit still. Jim was pleased to see me when I entered his cubicle in the emergency room, although he was suspicious of my intentions towards him. He recognized that he was in need of help and he was grateful to his family for bringing him to hospital but he was very frightened. He was in state of high arousal and he was weighing every perception to see if it held peril for him. The various sounds of the emergency room, the voices of the staff and patients, the sounds of doors being opened and closed, the trolley wheels on the corridor were all fuelling his mental state and triggering thoughts that he was in danger.

With patients in such exquisitely sensitive states, I always begin with an attempt to make the setting as safe as possible for them and clarify the purpose of the interview. I tell them that this is a hospital, a safe place, with good people who will try to protect and be of assistance to them. As we spoke, Jim settled a little and after some more discussion we agreed to use some simple mindfulness techniques. We began by focusing on regulating his breathing and he relaxed a little more. He spoke about his feelings and he was able to identify that, yes, it was indeed fear and paranoia he was experiencing. We watched his fear and paranoia together for a while and agreed together that it would pass. He felt a little safer and he gave me the knife he had concealed in his sock. Jim told me that he had found the body scan exercise at the Buddhist center was very helpful to him. He agreed to lie down on the mattress of the emergency room and I talked him through a simple body scan: take your attention to the feet and feel the sensations there, the toes, the feet, then become aware of the legs, the knees and so on gradually to the head. This seemed to help and as he became calmer, we talked some more and then we did another body scan. Jim said that doing the body scan in the fraught setting of the emergency room reminded him of the calm and peaceful setting of the Buddhist center and this seemed to settle him further. He took the medication that I offered him and eventually he went home with his family. The home treatment team visited him at home over the next few days and he completed his recovery.

Yoga and the House of Many Rooms

I confess to being one of those people who is in favour of meditation but who has failed to establish a stable meditation practice. I am not proud of my record as a failed meditator of some thirty or so years standing. I started when I was a medical student with transcendental meditation. I studied in a Tibetan monastery in India in my twenties and I have been to numerous meditation centres in London over the years. I knew that the practice of focusing attention, quieting the mind and creating some mental spaciousness was an important skill to cultivate, but, somehow, I could never get past the first base. I could meditate every day for weeks, but never months—I simply could not settle enough to maintain the routine. At first, I tended to blame the method—too slow, too uncomfortable, too much Buddhism, too little Buddhism— but, of course, it was my monkey mind and my lack of discipline. I had a nagging anxiety that meditation would reduce my 'edge', my healthy aggression, perhaps make me sedate and boring. I knew that my ego defences were probably getting the better of me and I was not impressed with my lack of application and progress. I enjoyed Zen with the alternation of sitting and walking meditation, which helped me towards the realisation that sitting meditation was not necessarily the only method. I accept now that I am a sporadic meditator. I go through periods when I can sit regularly and watch my breathing, and I sometimes use other practices to help me navigate my path through the shadows.

Many people take up yoga as a form of physical exercise, often unaware of its history as a serious spiritual practice. Indeed, I started yoga precisely to ease some backache and vary my exercise regime. My first few yoga sessions were memorable for the discomfort as my stiff back was bent into unaccustomed positions. I enjoyed working with the breath, the discipline and the way in which the mind chatter gradually calms as the session progressed. I certainly enjoyed the moment that the session ended, but mostly I remember the physical strain, the watching of the clock and wondering how much more of this I could take. It did not feel like a psycho-spiritual practice.

Very soon after starting yoga I noticed a dramatic and surprising change in my sleep rhythm. I had a number of dreams that hinted strongly at an opening, of discovering hidden spaces and riches. Typically, the dream would involve being a small place, a caravan or an apartment, before opening a door and discovering other rooms that lay behind containing rooms covered in gorgeous tapestries and beautiful objects. The dreams held a sense of the sacred and I would waken feeling calm, energised and inspired as though sleep had taken me to a profound and beautiful place.

This phase did not last very long, perhaps a month or two, but it was the strongest indication to me that yoga was so much more than easing stiff backs and gentle exercise. The dreams of the many rooms had a numinous quality and it was clear to me that something quite profound in my psyche was being activated. For reasons that were beyond my understanding, my painful and inept yoga practice was unleashing something of an archetypal nature.

The Darkness Retreat

If I had more time, perhaps I would have gone on a long meditation retreat. But this was not a practical prospect with the demands of work and family life, so I sought out intensified retreats hoping for an accelerated process in a short period of time. The darkness retreat promised the type of high-intensity experience that I was seeking. It was a five-day retreat that involved four days and three nights of wearing a thick blindfold to ensure total darkness.[235] For two of those days the participants were in silence too. The setting was excellent with a variety of group activities designed to intensify and deepen the inner experience. I had previous experience and great respect for Simon Buxton and Naomi Lewis who led the retreat and there were two sighted assistants who guided us when necessary.

This was a complex journey with many twists and turns and my extract below is just a fraction of the total experience. It illustrates how the retreat setting with its enhanced archetypal intensity can resonate with unresolved psychological issues to trigger a crisis. The crucial point with these archetypal crises occurring in favourable supportive settings is that they need to run their course towards completion. The central assumption here is that the crisis is an opportunity for healing and resolution; it is inherently growth orientated and problems generally only arise if the process is interrupted or left unresolved. People working with deep states of consciousness need to understand this and support the unfolding process. The more the experience can be brought into consciousness, understood, worked on and integrated, the greater the reward. Integration takes time and effort, as there is layer upon layer of meaning to be mined. An experience without the integration is an experience wasted.

The recommended method for navigating such archetypal crises is to use mindfulness techniques, watching, accepting and being an empathic observer. The intensity of the moment will often temporarily overwhelm coping strategies and we can find ourselves just holding on and waiting for it to pass. It always does pass, as this level of intensity cannot be sustained. The complete resolution of such a crisis can pave the way for a positive numinous experience, a feeling of extraordinary wellbeing. In fact, this was the moment that persuaded me that once the chattering mind could be quieted there was a bedrock underneath of calm, peace and indescribable joy.

'The first full day of darkness was going well. The induction process had been intense and had the effect of driving the 16 participants far away from our everyday lives and preoccupations into a mindset of inner exploration. The conversation at the meal breaks was slowing and quietening and the same was happening in my mind. My thoughts were slowing down in a way that had never ever happened before. In the rest periods between the meditations, I found myself sitting in an armchair for quite long periods of time with remarkably little mind chatter, feeling still and peaceful. It was most unaccustomed and very pleasant. We were told to expect some visions, as our optic pathways become accustomed to a different level of stimulation. My visions usually involved the sun rising on bright green fields, with huts and sheep. But as soon as I brought my conscious attention to it, it faded. It was a little tantalising; it felt like I was paddling at the edge of the ocean of infinity and there was a sense of a hidden universe just beyond my perception, something subtle and delicate. I was aware of entering a highly sensitive state and that the entire workshop with its poetry, precise use of highly charged words, music and drumming was working on my suggestibility.

In our blindfolded state we are becoming adept at feeling our way around the walls and doors, but in the crowded dining hall the sighted helpers guide us round the obstacles, put food in front of us and station themselves strategically in case of need. It feels like an entirely safe and loving environment. The vegetarian food is delicious and we find that eating with fingers works well when you cannot see. It is a much more sensuous experience, eating very slowly and mindfully. The flavours are exquisite and I feel as though my relationship with food is changing irrevocably. I had not appreciated that there was such variety and richness in taste.

My crisis started at the supper table. With hindsight I can see that the trigger was the physical discomfort of feeling hot and trapped and, in my supersensitive state, that my anxiety developed from this feeling of disease. But, of course, the nature of an archetype is that the intensity of it robs one of the power to think, to rationalise. I had been led into my allotted berth at the dining table and sat down. My neighbour was making some desultory conversation that I did not welcome. My growing feeling of entrapment triggered thoughts and feelings about my father in the later stages of his dementia, in his nursing home, being led to his table and being dependent on the able-bodied carers. Eventually he needed a transfer to hospital, where in his final weeks, he was sat in a circle together with other people with dementia. It was a very different kind of circle to the one that I was in but the similarities were chilling to me at the time.

I found myself going into a profoundly difficult and unpleasant space. I became preoccupied with the futility of life, with the inevitability of decay, aging and death. I wondered at the barren and pointless nature of it all. What on earth am I doing here with a blindfold over my eyes when I should be at home enjoying my family and being in nature in the spring? But I couldn't imagine spring because my mental state was winter. It is always hard to describe the overwhelming bleakness of these states when they descend. It was a tunnel with no light at the end of—a state of desolation where there is no meaning, no meaning at all.

I could feel the panic rising. The thought of two more days and nights of this filled me with fear and loathing. I had an impulse to tear the blindfold from my face, to drive away and leave all this behind. But I knew that I couldn't do this. I had made this appointment. I had a commitment to this practice and I couldn't turn back now. I had started a process that had to be followed to its conclusion and I had to find a way through. I knew I had to use my resources and use some skill to navigate this. I made an exit from the confines of the dining hall, I found myself a quiet space, sat down and focussed on my breathing. I was finding that some thoughts of everyday life were bubbling up. Simon had told us what to do when this happened and I tried to follow his advice to surrender to the darkness, to drop, drop, drop back into depths of mind, to engage with the flow of whatever emerges. I reminded myself that I was in a state of non-ordinary consciousness and that I needed to trust the trajectory of the process. I knew that bringing myself back to everyday thoughts would just make the agitation and entrapment worse. I remembered Simon's instructions to 'keep the foot on accelerator' — don't take it off. Have faith through the dark night.

It eased, but left me wary and anxious. The drum beat was summoning us to the evening session. It was time to dance, to breathe some life into our bodies after a day spent mostly sitting. We stood in our space in the darkness and moved to the music. I felt stiff, clenched and old. I couldn't move freely, which added to my sense of failure. I imagined all the others dancing with grace, energy and ease while my movements were stiff and ugly. So be it! I would rejoice in being stiff and ugly. I would be the stiff and ugly one. Gradually my body relaxed and I could feel my way into some rhythm and, as the music moved through me, the mood started to pass. The music stopped. Simon told us in his strong and melodious voice that we were about to enter the period of silence, that in a few minutes the bell would sound and we would seal our lips. For the rest of the evening and the whole of the next day, we would be silent. We would be silent until the time came that we did not need to be silent any more.

This triggers another bout of panic. I will be blind and silent. I feel trapped in a nameless dread. In silence we exit the room. I have to find a way to control the waves of panic. Its just anxiety, I think to myself. I've been triggered. I'm in a crisis. It will pass. I remind myself to use my resources: easy breathing, focus, concentrate, get back to a safe place. I feel my way along the wall, towards the two steps, turn left through the door, feel my way along the rack and identify my shoes. I feel my way along the wall to the door leading outside.

It's cold outside with a gusting wind and rain. I find the guide rope and follow it along, slowly by the cattle grid, the fence, the trees, through the puddle, five steps down, turn left another two steps, combination lock to the door of the cottage, remember where I put my shoes, open the door into the kitchen, doorway to lounge, identify the table, calculate the angle across the room, feel along the wall to the stairs, 13 steps, turn right to the bedroom. Home. I lie down on the bed with a feeling of relief. I made it. I settle down and find some peace again as I settle into the colours and shapes of my life in the darkness. As my mind settles, I slowly realise that, in my sensitive state, I have accessed a well of unresolved psychological trauma concerning my father's final illness. I had been so concerned with my busy life and the practicalities of taking care of him that I had not allowed myself to feel what I needed to feel as that proud and independent man became confined and dependent. I felt a surge of love and kinship for him.

In the morning the crisis has passed. I write my journal and hope the ink is running so I will be able to read it when I am sighted again. The shower and teeth routine is easy now in the darkness behind the blindfold. I hear my neighbours stirring, getting ready for the day ahead. It's raining quite hard outside as I feel my way along the rope towards the main house. I open the door and hear heavenly glorious music. The dining room seems filled with the rich and peaceful choral music. Hands up if you would like coffee, whispers Anthony. Nod if you would like honey, banana and yoghurt on your muesli, says Lisa.

After the best breakfast in the world, I feel my way into the soft armchair in the lounge. I find myself in a mental space that I have tasted but not dwelt in before. The potency of the meaning state is almost overwhelming and I shed one or two quiet and gentle tears at the beauty of it. It is a heavenly place; I never want this to end. Occasionally, I hear someone glide past, the sound of fingers feeling along a wall, stocking feet picking a way carefully down stairs. Nothing else. The sound of silence. My mind is a clear still lake. I have never felt such peace and joy. I did not know that life could feel so good.'

Living Mindfully

'Man is asleep', said Gurdjieff. 'He has no real consciousness or will. He is not free; to him, everything 'happens'. He can become conscious and find his true place as a human being in the creation, but this requires a profound transformation. Man lives in only a small part of himself'.[236]

Different techniques develop different parts of consciousness. Psychoanalysis, meditation and the exploration of non-ordinary states will all bring different perspectives, different advantages and potential side effects. We need to find our own paths and our own teachers. What was right for one person is unlikely to be exactly right for the next. So how indeed can we find our own path towards wakefulness? How can we train ourselves to become more conscious? The first step towards greater consciousness is to develop the intention; this simple step accelerates our innate tendency towards integration and growth. If we try to reduce any activities or habits that are unhelpful then we gather momentum. If we then engage in practices that are orientated towards development then we are likely to make real progress.

Living mindfully involves an appreciation of every moment and every aspect of life. There is a perspective that each moment of our conscious experience is pitch perfect, every vicissitude and every pain is but a birth pang in an evolving field of consciousness. From this perspective, our suffering is simply the gristle of life with potential to enhance our growth. The key to understanding mental suffering is that our suffering is not caused by the external world; it is a subjective sensation as to how we are triggered into a subjective feeling of suffering. Indeed, as I found in the darkness retreat, the nature of the triggers holds vital clues about the issues that we need to work on. If we have the mindset and can avoid blaming everything on the outside world, suffering allows us to look inside ourselves to examine the wound that is exposed. This gives the opportunity to heal, and the deeper the wound; the greater the opportunity to heal.

If our wounds are most easily exposed in high archetypal penetrance (HAP) states, we should explore how these moment of crisis and intensity can be harnessed for our benefit. Tav Sparks, the Director of the Grof Transpersonal Training program, has developed a method using films in retreats, which he calls movie yoga.[237] For Sparks, movies are the modern expression of mythic themes giving us the opportunity to heal ourselves. Movies are chosen for their intensified archetypal content and the HAP state induced by the retreat setting increases the participant's sensitivity to the archetypal resonance of the movie. We are told to watch the movie and pay attention to our reactions to it. Sparks emphasizes that it is not the film that is causing our feelings; rather, the feelings belong to us and are merely triggered by it. We are encouraged to look deep inside ourselves, embrace the feeling as much as we can and allow it to emerge into awareness. As it takes shape, we take the position of the empathic observer, we hold on to the intensity of the feeling and we allow ourselves to be as fully moved as we need to be. Something shifts in our psyche when we do this. It may feel like a healing, an opening, a tenderness or perhaps part of our shadow brought into consciousness.

The key to movie yoga or working with dreams is that every aspect of the movie or dream is seen as an expression of our psyche. We cannot pick and choose which aspect we wish to identify with. Our natural inclination is to side with the attractive characters but we are poorer if we do not examine the parts of us that turn away from growth. As Le Grice tells us, in Star Wars we are as much Darth Vader as Luke Skywalker and Princess Leia.[238] We are Gollum as well as Frodo, we are Voldemort as well as Harry Potter.

Most of us do not want to entirely devote our lives towards becoming more mindful but would be interested in a little progress along the way. We can certainly become more aware of our internal processes and we can learn to become an empathic observer. We can look at how emotions are triggered by our encounters with our environment. We can become kinder and look at the ways in which we are unkind. We can take a little time out of our busy schedules to feel the wind, hear the stillness and look attentively at what we see before us. By being more mindful, we can simply enjoy the unfolding variety and richness of our unfolding adventure in human consciousness.

CHAPTER 20

The Way of the Imagination

Awakening is possible only for those who seek it and want it, for those who are ready to struggle with themselves and work on themselves for a very long time and very persistently in order to attain it.

—G. I. Gurdjieff

With hindsight, it is obvious that my sister's death intensified and entrenched my own midlife crisis. I certainly wasn't clinically depressed. I was functioning well at the hospital and none of my colleagues would have noticed any difference in me. Indeed, the only activities that did hold meaning for me were clinical work and supporting my family. Otherwise there was a pervasive greyness, a lack of meaning, an ennui—and I always seemed mildly unwell with one viral illness after another.

It was very difficult for me to find a path that held any promise. I dabbled with psychoanalysis, but it didn't generate any traction and nothing arose in the sessions that I found particularly interesting. I found myself reaching again for Jung, admiring his balance and wisdom but straining to understand precisely the message that he was trying to communicate. It seemed to me that Jung was pointing in the general direction that I needed to travel, but the path itself was vague and ill defined.

In this new voyage of discovery, I found myself in the position, once again, of being a novice. When I was a trainee psychiatrist trying to unravel the mysteries of the ego, I had the model of psychoanalysis and my training organisation to guide me. But at this stage in my life, it did not seem at all clear to me how to address the nebulous questions that interested me. I attended lectures and talks about death and dying, spirituality and transpersonal psychology, but it dawned on me that theory could only take me so far.[239] I didn't learn group analysis by reading about it, I learned by engaging in it and, similarly, I needed to learn about the deeper layers of consciousness by actually experiencing them. I needed to get out of my comfort zone, divest myself of my dogmas and start exploring.

This chapter outlines some of these explorations and some of the tentative conclusions that I drew from them. We will begin by revisiting Jung's crisis before examining some more contemporary schools of depth psychology. I worked only with people and organisations that I respected for their intellect, rigour, integrity and especially their humanity and compassion. I knew there were blind alleyways and narcissistic traps, which I tried to identify and avoid. I certainly made a few mistakes. I often wondered if I were seeking solace in spirituality as a psychic retreat to avoid the reality of extinction and perhaps even the reality of meaninglessness. Maybe I was simply going through a convoluted grief reaction or giving rein to my schizotypal tendencies. Perhaps—but I believe these are only partial explanations and I have been slowly persuaded that the concepts of transpersonal psychology hold important truths for us.

I remain a novice in this field, but a more experienced novice than before. Although I certainly do not know the answers, I have found that asking the questions is a profound and fascinating process.

Beyond the Personal Psyche

During Jung's period of crisis, he describes how a figure that arose from his imagination went on to develop a life of it's own. This figure, Philemon, seemed to have a foot inside Jung and a foot outside of him altogether. As time passed, the extra-psychic, transpersonal aspect of Philemon seemed to gather weight and eventually Jung saw him as a separate guru type figure. In the 1930s he reports a conversation with an elderly Indian visitor, who described his own personal teacher or guru as Shankaracharya, a Hindu reformer who had died in the ninth century. This Indian visitor did not consider that it was unusual to have a dead teacher: 'Most teachers are alive but there are always some people who have a spirit for a teacher', he said. This account of learning from a deceased and non-physical teacher encouraged Jung to consider Philemon as a real and distinct presence.

One explanation for Jung's experience is that he was psychotic, that he was not only having auditory hallucinations but also projecting an aspect of himself onto an external object and holding this idea with delusional intensity.[240] But before we reach this conclusion we should consider other models of psyche that offer an alternative explanatory model, namely the *transpersonal*.

Transpersonal psychology is a multi-disciplinary field incorporating insights from anthropology, theology, mythology, thanatology (the study of death), parapsychology and other disciplines. It includes the empirical study of unusual mental states and psychological experiences that do not easily fit traditional psychiatric diagnostic categories

Transpersonal, meaning beyond the personal, is the modern term to describe the deeper layer of the individual and collective psyche that stretches beyond the personal ego.[241] Transpersonal psychology is inclusive, seeking to build on personal psychology to address a greater range of human function, including spiritual experience. Transpersonal psychology recognises archetypes and dimensions of mind that can exist independently of us, whereas personal psychology usually does not. Transpersonal psychotherapy aims to help us towards a new relationship with the transcendent Self. If a transpersonal experience occurs in a religious context then it is a religious experience, but many spiritual and transpersonal experiences occur outside of organised religion and represent a universal aspect of human consciousness. Although the prevailing scientific paradigm holds that our consciousness is contained within the bony confines of our skull, according to the archetypal perspective, we are all subjected to the transpersonal in varying degrees all the time, with our psyche generally keeping the intensity of this archetypal exposure within manageable limits.

The terms *archetypal* and *transpersonal* overlap but are not synonymous.[242] Archetypes are assumed to be part of an underlying order that transgresses boundaries and permeates both the personal and the transpersonal layers of mind. Transpersonal experiences do not necessarily have the heightened intensity of meaning typical of an archetypal experience. A person involved in psi research, for example, may be engaging in a transpersonal activity by engaging in telepathic communication with a subject in another room, but this is unlikely to be a numinous experience.

There are various methods of accessing the transpersonal, of amplifying the archetypal element of consciousness, of 'going online' to a deeper level of consciousness. Jung was able to use Philemon as a teacher, companion and guide by undergoing a descent into the depths of his unconscious mind, but, for Jung, this was a Herculean task involving personal crisis, impaired function and sustained effort. His was a high-risk endeavour and cannot be recommended. How then, can we have a taste of this experience in a digestible form without the dangers and side effects?

Stalingrad with Woolger

My first venture into the world of transpersonal practice was through the work of Roger Woolger. I had read his book *Other Lives, Other Selves* and found it to be a most impressive introduction to past-life regression research and the various theories around reincarnation. I saw him speak at a conference and was impressed by his wisdom, humility and gentle humour.[243] Here was a man that I wanted to work with. Woolger had trained as a Jungian analyst of the archetypal school in Zurich, this being very different to the British Jungians who seemed to me more in tune with traditional psychoanalysis and distanced from the archetypal tradition. He developed his ideas as 'deep memory process' or DMP, which combines active imagination, bodywork and psychodrama.

My motivation for undergoing a 'past-life regression', as it was called in those days, was twofold. Firstly, as a psychiatrist and psychotherapist I was naturally interested in any powerful psychological tools to access and work with material from the deep psyche. Secondly, I was interested in the great question of death and the possibility of a hidden part of the human life cycle. I was more than a little apprehensive that my worldview might be changed by my explorations, and I remember a sense of gathering myself before a momentous journey. It would perhaps have been easier to have cancelled my appointment and stayed with the apparent certainties of the accepted Western scientific paradigm. I suspect that this 'trembling on the threshold' experience is common, probably normal.

So I found myself lying down on a mat in a living room in Oxford. I felt rather foolish but I had come a long way for this experience and wanted it to be productive (positive mindset). After some relaxation exercises I was asked to imagine myself walking through a cave and emerging from the back of it. Who was I, what was I feeling in my body, what was I wearing, where was I going, what was I going to do, what was my mood and what was in my mind?

This was very challenging for me as I tried to answer some of these questions. I was a rather embarrassed man on a mat. This had little to do with the curriculum required to become a member of the Royal College of Psychiatrists. I was apparently supposed to use my imagination and a lot of my medical training had been geared towards making my imagination as unobtrusive as possible. This was one of those moments that became familiar with repetition when it felt as though I was making something up, possibly cheating in some way, as a narrative emerged from my lips. I had a thought that this was a foolish endeavour, that I wasn't going to be any good at this, but I went along with it to be polite. To my surprise, I found myself describing a time when I was living with my wife in a muddy hovel in medieval Europe. Our proudest possession was a pig. A couple of soldiers on horses appeared and took the pig. My wife protested so they killed her with their spears. I protested and they killed me too.

Roger asked me what happened next. I said I didn't mind very much that I was dead, but what surprised me was the sense of 'otherness' that followed it. I found myself in a very peaceful place where I immediately forgave the soldiers. The anger that I felt when they killed my pig and my wife had totally evaporated. The perspective that seemed to come to me was that this was just one life of many, that it was all part of an evolutionary progress and I even felt a sense of relief at not having to live in the mud hut with my pig any more.

While I was having these thoughts, there was a part of me that was remembering that I had read about similar experiences in Roger's book. I accepted that I was in a suggestible state of mind and I assumed that this story had emerged from my brain based on my memories of Roger's book, my desire to please him and to have a fulfilling and constructive day. But it didn't seem to be a particularly deep and meaningful experience so far.

Roger encouraged me to go to another place, another time, another self. Suddenly, I found myself at Stalingrad. This was altogether different. The whole quality of the experience was highly charged; it seemed vivid, intense, almost real. I was a young soldier in the German army. The story that came from me was that I came from a small town and I was in my late teens, maybe 20. I was a proud German. I thought Hitler was a good strong leader and I believed in the Fatherland. I completely supported the war to make our country great and strong and to put right some of the wrongs that had been done to us. I thought we should take our rightful place as the greatest country in the world. War was a great adventure and I loved it. I enjoyed the camaraderie of the army and our skills as soldiers and I thought that we were invincible.

Then we came to the quagmire that was Stalingrad, where Hitler and Stalin and their armies became involved in an arm wrestle to the death. For the first time, we were not easily winning; for the first time the Soviets were holding us. Their supply lines worked better than ours and I witnessed the gradual degradation of the army and the souring of our dream. The glorious adventure became a journey into a hell as we ran out of food, there was disease and we were so very cold. We began to understand that the impossible was actually happening—we were losing.

The few survivors of our army were taken prisoner and I was taken to a concentration camp in Siberia. My life shrank to the confines of the labour camp, the cold, the hunger and the guards who hated us. I never lost hope of eventually returning home. I dreamed of home, my small and lovely town in Germany with its decent people, beautiful girls and warm, lively pubs. I longed for home with every fibre of my being. I couldn't believe that I had left my hometown thinking that war was sport and that Hitler was a great leader. I developed a hatred for liars and politicians, especially Hitler and Stalin. I felt so dreadfully cheated and deprived of the life that should have been mine. I came to see the world as a cruel and desolate place. I felt so trapped in my ghastly cold prison that was barren of any humanity and decency. This was the worst place in the world for a young man; I just wanted to go home. It was all I wanted, to touch my home again. I wanted it with every pulse of my fading life. I was a young man and I took a long time to die. I never believed I would die and didn't accept that anything could be so unfair. I died full of hatred and pain.

This was a very profound experience for me. I was very moved when I returned to ordinary consciousness.

There was nothing in this experience that could not have come from my own psyche. I had always been interested in World War Two and the German campaign in Russia, and I had read Solzhenitsyn's *The Gulag Archipelago* about the Soviet labour camps in Siberia. It seemed like a dream, but the most remarkable dream that I had ever had with clear narrative and an extraordinary condensation and intensity of meaning. Some years after the event, I still remember it with clarity. The themes seemed to have an emotional resonance with my life at the time. I identified with Sisyphus eternally rolling his boulder up the hill, with the hard labour and feelings of confinement with my work at the hospital and young children at home. But the intensity of these feelings had been greatly amplified and I was far beyond my comfort zone.

I didn't feel as though I had actually been that German boy. I did not have that the moment of recognition that some people describe, of a genuine past life that I had lived. But was it a past life that perhaps I had downloaded through the collective unconscious? Talking it through with Roger afterwards, we explored the idea of being able to access a life that someone else has lived, which has a particular resonance of meaning with your own emotional experience. Roger took a transpersonal perspective, gently suggesting that, as well as moving something forward in my own psyche, perhaps I was helping a fragment of consciousness that had lodged with this young German too. Roger's view was that there may be a layer of the collective psyche which is bound in trauma, particularly with the mass slaughter and brutality of the twentieth century, so that in doing this work we are freeing something not only for ourselves, but something in the collective psyche as well. The most intense mental states that people experience are associated with trauma and violent death so perhaps these memories are most likely to linger in our collective mind field. If this is so then it is not surprising that so many 'past life' regressions seem to access experiences of violent death.

The more that I thought about it, the more questions came to me. It was hugely refreshing to find that I really had no clear understanding of what had happened in that session with Roger, except that it had an emotional power that I had not previously experienced. This demonstrated to me the power of the non-ordinary state of consciousness to work in the deeper levels of the psyche that may not be otherwise accessible. I had to explore this further.

Cispersonal Psyche

The prefix 'Cis' means 'on the near side of'. The ancient Roman world contained Cisalpine Gaul and Transalpine Gaul. Cisalpine Gaul was the part of northern Italy that was inhabited by the Celtic Gauls. Over the course of time, Cisalpine Gaul became incorporated into Italy. Transalpine Gaul was on the other side of the Alps, from the Roman perspective and in due course became part of France. The great barrier of the Alps separated these two parts of Gaul.

Using the ancient Roman world as a metaphor for the psyche, we can cast modern man as a Roman. Rome represents the personal psyche, our ego, our perception of our environment as mediated by our organs of perception, our cognitive apparatus and the prevailing ideas and paradigms. Most of us either stay entirely in Rome, or we leave Rome only for brief periods. The Romans were deeply suspicious of the Gauls and similarly most of us are naturally cautious about leaving our familiar psychological territory.

We can cast the abnormal experience of non-ordinary states of consciousness as the land of the Gauls. If we leave the safety of our Rome-like psyche, with its high walls and defences, we immediately become much more vulnerable. Safety issues are paramount, so we need to have a mindset of curiosity balanced by some caution and the setting needs to be secure and carefully judged. We need to be in good company, led by someone who knows the territory, who has a map and most important of all, knows how to return to Rome. The further away from Rome that we go, the more important this is. It would not be uncommon for Romans to make short journeys outside the walls of Rome, edging into Cisalpine Gaul to indulge curiosity, but to go further afield it would be necessary to have a purpose, a mindset, an intention.

In the way that Cisalpine Gaul was an outlying Roman province until it became incorporated into Rome in 41BCE, the cispersonal psyche is more personal than transpersonal. The cispersonal psyche is the part of the psyche that is opening to material from the deeper layers of the unconscious but this material is rooted predominantly in the personal or the psycho-social layer of psyche. It is not an obviously transpersonal experience although there may be elements of the transpersonal.

In order to go to the truly transpersonal territory, it is often necessary to pass through a significant barrier, the Alpine ranges of the psyche. Of course, crossing the Alps was perilous in the old days. Travellers were subjected to very difficult conditions with hostile climate and inhabitants. Some people got lost and some travellers perished on the journey. Similarly, travellers to the truly transpersonal territories have a process of an intensification of meaning as they cross the dividing range. This often involves a death-rebirth experience with a numinous encounter of the challenging kind where ego is expunged, before emerging on the other side of the divide into the sunlit pastures.

By using this Rome analogy, I am suggesting that most experiences with a transpersonal element are better conceptualised as cispersonal. Cispersonal psyche is a deeply interesting place, Gauls abound and one can have a Gallic experience without necessarily going across the Alps. I believed that my Stalingrad experience was cispersonal, originating primarily from my own psyche, although Woolger suggested that it was more of a transpersonal journey with a download of a life that had been lived by the young German.

The borders between cispersonal and transpersonal are fuzzy, forming a spectrum of consciousness. Sometimes it feels as though there is a decisive move up or down the spectrum. Thus with Adam and Martin from chapter One, I suggest that Martin had a pure form of transpersonal experience where he suddenly and entirely transcended his personal psyche. Adam, on the other hand, nearly perished in the metaphorical Alps with a cispersonal experience that was presumably heavily contaminated by shadow. Perhaps this is an artificial distinction—the value of the experience lies in the symbolic content after all—but the point that I am trying to make is that what seems to be transpersonal may in fact be more related to biographical material and what may be appear to be predominantly personal may be more transpersonal than we think. This will bring us to one of the most common and problematic of the spiritual emergencies: the confusion of levels. But first we will look at some more examples of the cispersonal and the transpersonal and the mysterious relationship between the intra-psychic and the external world.

Active Imagination

Active imagination is Jung's distinctive contribution to psychotherapy. It is essentially a meditation where images and a narrative are encouraged to take shape and to flow. It is a distillation of the techniques that he found helpful in navigating his own crisis. The aim of the exercise is to bring to life material from the unconscious and provide a way of interacting with whatever emerges from it. There are a number of different techniques, including writing, talking out loud or being silent and developing an internal narrative. In Jungian psychotherapy, figures from dreams can be actively engaged with. Using dreams in this way, the totality of the dream, with each and every character, is seen as an expression of the psyche. So unattractive or persecutory characters represent important parts of ourselves, which need to be owned.

Active imagination helps a person to give voice and substance to some of those shadowy figures that are uncomfortable companions for the ego, with the aim of integrating this material to form a more complete and functional personality. The ability to follow the imagination, maintain focus and retain the images grows with practice.

Here is an example of instructions for an active imagination practice:

- Prepare the set and setting. Confirm that you are ready and willing for an active imagination journey.
- Try to empty the mind of everyday concerns. Do a body scan or a breathing exercise to release tension.
- Make an intention to be open, present and responsible to whatever comes up.
- Try to be open in heart and mind to allowing and developing a dialogue with the imagination.
- Try to define an intention. What is the purpose of this journey?
- Try to bring an intention of deepening a relationship with a figure, landscape, energy or a situation from a dream or a mood state.
- Bring yourself as you are just now, not your persona or who you think you should be.
- If you feel flooded by images or thoughts, bring your attention back to your intention, select one image that has arisen and engage in dialogue with that image with the hope of the dialogue deepening.
- The dialogue happens through many channels of perception, image, word, feelings, impulses, sensations, energetic change and felt presence.
- Be present with whatever or whoever arises.
- Be mindful of what arises, do not jump to early conclusions, continue to dialogue.
- Take notice of any changes in perceptions.

If nothing is happening or you feel stuck here are some methods that may help:

- See yourself sitting in a cave of the heart, bringing your attention to heart and mind and see who or what appears in the dark cave with you. Interact with this and allow the story to unfold.

- See yourself walking to a forest; you find a crossroads where three paths offer themselves to you. Select the one that feels right for you. As you take the path, who do you encounter?
- See yourself anywhere else that feels right, the sea, by a tree or mountain and allow the active imagination to unfold.

The Pink Spider

In September 2011 the Jungian analyst Monika Wikman joined the week-long holotropic breathwork training retreat in Somerset, where I was assisting as a facilitator.[244] It was an intense week, with four sessions of holotropic breathwork interspersed with Monika speaking about Jung's *Red Book*, archetypes and the collective unconscious. As the week progressed, it seemed as though a field of consciousness was developing between us all. People seemed to have some dreams with links to other people's experiences that they hadn't known about and synchronicities were being discovered over the breakfast table.

On the last day, the breathwork sessions lay behind us, Monika was finishing her series of talks and we settled down for an active imagination session. This was a good time to do such an exercise; we expected that our gradual opening through the retreat, with its amplification by the group process, would give it a particular power. I had been looking forward to this exercise, but as I settled into the active imagination, I found that I just couldn't seem to engage in it. I seemed to be going through the motions. I realised that I was tired. I felt disinterested in the transpersonal and the deep psyche and I wasn't even sure that I believed in it any more. I rather wanted to go home and see my family.

But I went through the motions. This seemed like a daydream emerging entirely from my own personal consciousness. I imagined catching a ride on a dolphin. It was good to feel the strong muscular dolphin carrying me along through the water. We arrived at a place that reminded me of the Golden Temple in Amritsar where I met an Indian guru figure who told me that I knew what I needed to do and should get on with it. He seemed brusque and perhaps disappointed in me. I seemed to have a moment of contact with my sister who had died some ten years previously. This was a pleasant moment of connection with her and I mused as to how she would have loved this retreat. There was a less pleasant moment when I seemed to be in the company of a huge spider, like the malign Shelob in *The Lord of the Rings*. My association to the image was of cancer, which I suppose followed from my encounter with my sister. Then it turned into a tiny pink spider that went in through my navel and emerged from my right side. That seemed quite strange and I didn't know what to make of it, but it was a benign little creature that seemed friendly. I was left with the image of the pink spider.

The exercise came to an end and we were instructed to go into the gardens and woods to think about our experience. I found a secluded area under a tree, gathered my thoughts and wrote in my notebook. As is often the case in such exercises, I felt that the experience was understandable in terms of my own psyche. I had enjoyed floating along on my imagination for a while, but it did feel like a product of my imagination and I could understand my daydream in terms of aspects of my thoughts and life experiences. Nothing of the transpersonal there, I thought—I was just making it up. I noted the mood of mild cynicism and disillusionment that seemed to be descending upon me. I wondered, not for the first time, if the entire transpersonal paradigm was a fantasy. I was falling asleep.

Then I noticed the tiny pink spiders. There were three or four of them scampering around my hands. There was no mistake about it: they were real and not in my imagination. But they had exactly the same shape, form and motion as the one that I had experienced in the active imagination. I have since found out that these tiny spider mites are not uncommon in the summer but my encounter with them, just after seeing them in the active imagination, was a very meaningful coincidence. I suddenly felt very awake and I could hear my heart beating. An image that had seemed like a curious fantasy of my internal world was repeated immediately afterwards in the outside external world. Something that I had thought to be predominantly intra-psychic or cispersonal had come from a much more transpersonal place than I had realised.

My faith was restored. As Samuel Coleridge once said 'Imagination is the power to disimprison the soul of fact'. It seemed that I was not wasting my time exploring the transpersonal after all. The synchronicity of the pink spiders had given me exactly the message that I needed at that point in time, implying that the transpersonal is indeed real and the psyche is much more complex than we imagine. Again a synchronicity reaffirms that the internal world and the external world are fundamentally aligned.

Shamanic Journeying

Jung used the term 'autonomous psychic fragment' to describe the figures that he engaged with during his journeys of imagination and he reported that they can develop a life and energy of their own. When Jung's *Red*

Book was published posthumously in 2009, we learned that Jung was told by one of these psychic fragments (who Jung knew as Elijah):

> You may call us symbols for the same reason that you call your fellow man symbols, if you wish to, but we are just as real as your fellow men. You invalidate nothing and solve nothing by calling us symbols. We are certainly what you call real. Here we are and you have to accept us. The choice is yours.[245]

So Jung was told in no uncertain terms that Elijah and his fellow autonomous psychic fragments had an ontological reality and were what we might call *spirits*.

Encounters with spirits are also fundamental to shamanism. The core practice used by shamans is the shamanic journey. This is the practice of altering consciousness to make a journey out of the body in order to access different levels of reality and encounter personal helpers and teachers. For shamans, these teachers and helpers are real and have an autonomous existence in non-physical worlds. Shamans use the simple word spirit to describe a complex concept and I will use this term when discussing shamanic practice. The use of the word spirit triggers an aversive response for many of us. Many Jungians believe that shamanic journeying is simply a version of active imagination, and I suggest that it is not necessary to believe in spirits to engage in and derive some benefit from shamanic journeying, although more advanced practice of shamanism depends entirely on working with spirits.

Shamans are the traditional healers, the ones who could bring information from beyond the veil of ordinary experience. Over millennia their techniques presumably evolved and became refined so that they were more likely to be effective. They engaged with the power of the archetypal world and learned to put it to good use. Many shamans probably used other methods available to them to augment their work with spirits, methods that we would now describe as cold reading, suggestion, use of counter-transference and perhaps even trickery. No doubt they were adept at the use of ritual to enhance set and setting to produce powerful experiences and amplify the placebo effect.

Shamanic practice is distinguished by journeying to three worlds—the upper, middle and lower worlds—to engage with the entities and animals of those worlds. The anthropologist and father of modern shamanic practice, Michael Harner, found that the descriptions of the shaman's cosmology, the worlds where shamans go, are consistent between peoples of different cultures who have never had contact. The implication for him is that these worlds have an ontological reality and do not just exist inside the shamans' minds. In his extraordinary book *Cave and Cosmos,* which is the culmination of over 50 years of experience, Harner gives detailed descriptions of the upper world of the shaman together with the experiences of his students who have travelled there. For Harner, the helpers and teachers that one meets in journeys to the upper world are compassionate spirits who are unconditionally ready to respond to anyone seeking advice or a healing. Moreover, they avoid giving any advice that might cause suffering or pain if carried back to our physical world.[246] Whether one believes in autonomous spirits or not, the notion of such compassionate, benevolent entities is a helpful contribution to mindset and setting.

Shamanic journeying is one of the easiest, most practical methods of accessing the transpersonal domain of the psyche. A non-ordinary state of consciousness is induced by sound (a sonic driver), usually a regular monotonous drumbeat at 200 to 220 beats per minute.[247] A specific question is framed and an inner journey is made to seek an answer to that question. The answer will usually be highly symbolic, with layers of meaning. Once the method is learned, a shamanic journey can be made in 10 to 15 minutes followed by a rapid resumption of everyday consciousness.

The practice of journeying described here was taught to me by the shamanic practitioner Dr Zoe Bran and has the advantage of simplicity and the use of technology to aid integration.[248] Shamanic journeying always requires a specific intention or question. This intention is repeated three times before each journey. Thus, the mindset is clearly defined. To start the journey I select the fifteen-minute drumming track on my music player and put on my headphones. I lie down on a mat, shut my eyes and repeat my intention. I have my recording device in my hand. The drumming starts in my earphones. I start my journey and speak my experience out loud into the recorder. When the journey is finished, I write out a full transcript of my recording, word for word. Then I start trying to understand the symbolism of the entire journey in reference to my stated intention.

The memory of the journey fades rapidly, like a dream, although the key features may linger for longer. Some of the material can be traced from my autobiographical memory and personal preoccupations and some cannot. I am always surprised when I listen to the playback of the recording how much has happened and how much I have forgotten. I find that the more I study my experience, the more layers of meaning become more apparent to me. One fifteen-minute journey can give me material to consider for some days. Numinous experience of mild to moderate intensity is commonplace, once you become accustomed and practiced in the method.

In workshops and training programs for shamanic practitioners, journeyers will often work in pairs. I have found repeatedly that I have elicited information from my journeys that revealed something about my partner that he or she confirms to be accurate and that I could not have guessed or deduced. The same applies for my partner's journeying on my behalf. This has demonstrated to me, beyond any reasonable doubt, that there were genuine transpersonal elements—of whatever nature —in our journeys.

Monroe and Hemi-Sync

I'm not interested in the details of your inner journey but I'm giving you the tools to make your own journey and training you to use them safely.

—Robert Monroe

Robert Monroe has an appealing down-to-earth quality. He was a success-ful businessman in Virginia who started having spontaneous out-of-body experiences (OBEs) in the 1950s. At first he thought he was ill but medical examination found nothing the matter with him. His OBEs continued and eventually he learned to induce them at will. He came from a practical background and, unlike most of the other transpersonal pioneers, he was not interested in Eastern mysticism, meditation or psychedelic drugs. He was an American male with the habits of his era: he ate hamburgers, he smoked cigarettes and he drank alcohol.

Monroe's three books written over three decades give an account of his experiences with OBEs, the development of his explorations and the lessons he learnt from them.[249] His early OBEs equated to the middle world in the shamanic terminology in that he would simply look down at his body from above or he would explore the local area. His experiences became more complex with time and practice and he describes progressing to a series of upper worlds where he met a succession of non-physical life forms who became his teachers and helpers. Eventually he came to believe that these figures were aspects of himself in some way. Indeed, one of the fascinating aspects of Monroe's books is that one can trace the gradual unfolding of his psychological development to a much larger transpersonal self. Above all, this is a story of an individuation.

Monroe developed a research centre, the Monroe Institute, and a method for inducing similar states in other people. He called this method 'Hemi-Sync', short for hemispheric synchronisation. The technique uses sound, different tones in each ear (binaural stimulation), to induce a mild non-ordinary state of consciousness. Research shows that Hemi-Sync induces brain wave patterns on EEG similar to those found in experienced meditators—mostly theta with occasional slowed alpha.[250] Monroe devel-oped Hemi-Sync with his 'explorers'—people who had a particular apti-tude and interest in OBEs. The explorers were blind to each other in that they did not know what experiences the others were having. Monroe found that his explorers described similar and repeatable experiences, suggesting that the places to which they travelled may have an ontological reality that was independent of the individual explorer's mind. They found that different binaural frequencies in the headphones tended to induce different brain states that produced a range of different experiences that Monroe called 'focus' levels. These focus levels represent a progressive moving away from the physical body to a domain of mind which he thought was separate from our worldly existence and which he termed the 'M field'.

Again, the set and setting are the crucial determinants of the Hemi-Sync experience. The absence of sensory stimulation and the use of an isolation chamber seemed important for those early explorations. Monroe developed an 'affirmation', which is repeated silently at the start of every Hemi-Sync exercise to affirm the mindset. This affirmation seems to be a prerequisite for journeys to the upper world using this method. Monroe considered that it 'gave the brain permission' to open to an expanded consciousness. The affirmation is as follows:

> I am more than my physical body. Because I am more than physical matter, I deeply desire to experience, understand and use such greater energies and energy systems that may be beneficial and constructive to me and those close to me. Also I deeply desire the help and cooperation of those individuals whose wisdom and experiences is equal or greater than my own.

Monroe took care to emphasise that no belief systems are involved, just the willingness to be open to the possibility of being more than just a physical body. However, the focus levels are orientated towards an assumption of reincarnation and an exploration of the interlife zone, so the mindset and setting are inevitably orientated towards this belief system. Indeed, one attraction of Monroe's method for me was that it addresses the question of what happens after death and offers the possibility of an exploration of the afterlife. Does an afterlife exist, is it real and what does it look like? Monroe communicated a map of the after-death dimension of life based on his explorations of OBEs, which he considered to represent the hidden part of our natural life cycle. He describes an interlife zone as a multi-level, psycho-plastic environment created in accordance with the way in which people's consciousness was expressed and focused when they were alive.[251] It interested me that his description of this interlife zone had much in common with Swedenborg's eighteenth-century model and Fontana's twenty-first-century model.[252]

The week-long Gateway Course is an introduction to the work of Monroe and Hemi-Sync and allows subsequent entry to the more advanced courses at the Monroe institute in Virginia. I found the Gateway Course to be a well-judged and gradual immersion into non-ordinary consciousness. Much of the day was spent lying on a mat wearing radio headphones using binaural stimulation. There were six or seven Hemi-Sync exercises a day using active imagination and shamanic journeying techniques. There was the usual careful attention to the setting with an emphasis on 'opening up to the higher self'. Again the biggest difficulty was to move attention away from everyday concerns and to still the chattering mind. People with a regular meditation or spiritual practice seemed to find it easier. We became familiar and comfortable with the first four focus levels and two or three people had brief out-of-body experiences.

The Gateway course fulfilled my expectations by raising more questions than answers and stimulating my curiosity further. I found that for some weeks following the Gateway course I would awake from sleep with a positive mildly numinous feeling, which persisted through the day in a manner that was definitely life enhancing. Aldous Huxley called this state a positive transfiguration, where the world seems richer, the colours are brighter and there is an intensification of meaning. I have always found after returning from an intense retreat that the adjustment to the time pressures and natural aggression of working life takes a week or so, but the connection with a more compassionate perspective endures for much longer. The practical benefit was that I felt deeply and mysteriously refreshed and able to be of better service in my clinical work.

With hindsight, the Gateway course also did me a great service in dispelling any notions that there were easy answers. I realised that I had been half expecting to find solutions to those eternal questions about the meaning of life and death and the true nature of our life cycle. Those who may have some tentative answers, people such Jung, Grof, Harner and Monroe, have invested decades of rigorous practice and courageous exploration to this end. My situation reminded me of my first encounter with group analysis many years before, which helped me to understand the magnitude and extent of my ignorance. It became clear to me that if I were serious about satisfying my curiosity, I would need to have a similar level of discipline, choose my vehicle carefully and prepare for years of practice.

Some dilemmas were being framed for me. Firstly, it was apparent that further exploration of the transpersonal required a group of trusted fellow travellers in a healthy, growth-orientated organisation. But such communities usually come together through shared ideas and values that can come close to beliefs systems. How could I be a true fellow traveller while maintaining a healthy scepticism for the valued ideas and dogma that any community seems to accrue?

The second dilemma was that I did not want to fully immerse myself in the depths of the unconscious. I remained fascinated by the shadow lands of Plato's cave and did not want to leave it behind, although I wanted to explore beyond the flickering shadows of the effigies and perhaps even pay a visit to the land outside the cave. It was clear to me that my interest in the transpersonal was an adjunct to professional and personal life rather than a primary goal; I saw myself as a psychiatrist first and foremost, not a mystic, not a shaman and not a monk. I would pursue my interest in the deep psyche, but perhaps my natural territory was cispersonal rather than transpersonal.

Confusion of Levels

When I do a shamanic journey, I understand it as a cispersonal experience. I suspect my experience in the journey is mostly an expression of my own psyche using its higher integrative function and responding to cues, imagery and ideas from my experiential world. However, my experience strongly suggests that there are some genuine transpersonal elements. My teachers, on the other hand, consider that shamanic journeying is a transpersonal experience in that the spirit world is real and communicates with us. The majority view, held by people who are unfamiliar with the transpersonal paradigm or these psycho-spiritual methods, is that these experiences are not transpersonal at all but are entirely a result of the integrative function of the brain, finding half-thought ideas and half-remembered information. I suspect the truth lies somewhere in the middle.

The point that I want to emphasise is that work of this nature is exploratory and the mindset should reflect this. These journeys of the imagination are usually guided by the aim of personal growth, service to the community and the search for a higher, more integrated version of oneself. I do not discount that adepts such as Harner and Monroe may very well be describing areas that have an ontological reality, but I suggest that, for relative novices such as myself, it is helpful to navigate a course between undue belief or disbelief. One of the most common pitfalls of non-ordinary states of consciousness is the confusion of levels where the symbolism of the inner experience is lost and is projected onto the external world. In some people, this may take the form of a subtle, encapsulated conviction that is rarely revealed. In other people, the conviction may come to dominate the way in which the person interacts with his or her environment and resemble a psychiatric condition such as delusional disorder. A confusion of levels is essentially a failure of integration and this is most likely to happen when a person has a high-intensity archetypal crisis in a suboptimal setting.

Confusion of levels can also occur in people who are experienced in transpersonal work. I recall a colleague who I respected for his wisdom and balance, who revealed to me a belief concerning aliens that he had encountered in an out-of-body experience. He told me of his conviction that these aliens, who apparently required supplies of animal blood from their human allies, were manipulating politicians by transferring technology to them in exchange for cattle. He told me they were watching him to make sure that he did not communicate this information and that, if he told his story to the press, he would probably be 'disappeared'. It transpired that he had received these insights while doing his own unsupervised work using a particular method in which he had received some training. He had been going through some life changes; he was in a vulnerable state and he hadn't used the normal methods for integration as he considered himself very experienced. I tentatively tried to explore the symbolic content, but he was entirely convinced of the ontological reality of his experience. Indeed, he seemed to have lost some capacity to think in a symbolic manner.

For me, this illustrates the importance of treating experiences lightly, being mindful, empathically observing the mindscapes but not over-identifying with them. It is absolutely crucial to understand that the language of meaning is symbolism and not to be taken literally. Some experiences are bigger than others and some are indeed life changing. But there is a constant balancing act between not taking it too seriously and yet seriously enough. I believe that an important component of the mindset is to enjoy not knowing the answers, to enjoy exploring the mystery without expectation of understanding it. People often lose their way when the wave of uncertainty becomes the particle of knowingness. Something becomes set in stone and something of the essential fluidity of the psyche is lost. A healthy attitude to attachment is so often the key to navigating through life's tensions. The same applies to ideas. Too close an attachment to an idea is rarely healthy or helpful. An idea is usually just that, an idea, a thought form.

CHAPTER 21

Psychedelics: Gateway to the Numinous

Psychedelics are the mindcraft of the noosphere. Like spacecraft, mindcraft must be used with crews who are well trained, with ground staff of high ability, planning operations and monitoring progress. It is not just a matter of shooting rockets off into space and hoping for the best.

—Humphrey Osmond[253]

This chapter explores the use of psychoactive substances to access the higher reaches of the sphere of human thought—the noosphere.[254] Ancient and modern cultures have used such methods to amplify the archetypal content of our psyches so that it dominates our consciousness. Sometimes space and time may be transcended altogether giving a particularly pure form of numinous experience. These methods are safe if performed properly and carefully but, if undertaken recklessly, they can be hazardous. The principles of mindset, setting and integration are absolutely crucial to this endeavour.

The Eleusinian Mysteries

According to Plutarch, the Eleusinian mysteries involved 'wandering astray in the beginning, tiresome walking in circles, some frightening paths in darkness that lead nowhere. Then before the end, all the terrible things—panic and shivering, sweat and amazement. And then some wonderful light comes to meet you, pure regions and meadows are there to greet you, with sounds and dances, sacred words and holy views.'[255]

The ceremonial rituals of the Eleusinian mysteries were extraordinarily successful, influencing the classical cultures of Greece and Rome for nearly 2000 years. The ceremonies began around 1500 BCE and were performed annually until the site was sacked by Alaric the Goth in the late fourth century CE. Pythagoras, Plato, Aristotle, Aeschylus as well as the

Roman emperors Hadrian, Julian, Augustus and Marcus Aurelius attended the mysteries. It seems likely that anyone undergoing the ritual was powerfully influenced by it. The ancient Greeks and Romans were often casual about religion but they took the Eleusinian mysteries very seriously.

The rites of passage at Eleusis involved anticipation, preparation, drinking a psychedelic potion and participating in a secret underground ceremony. There were two versions, the lesser mysteries were performed annually and the greater mystery, for initiates, every five years. The rituals revolved around the myth of Persephone's voyage to the underworld, with a descent, a search and a rapturous ascent. This followed the pattern of the mythic voyage to the subterranean, the land of the dead, the place where the sun does not shine. People who participated in the Eleusinian mysteries are said to have had a transformative encounter with death—an ego death, emerging afterwards with loss of fear of death and greater sense of being alive.

The mysteries were shrouded in secrecy; discussion was forbidden and punishable by execution. Anyone considering undergoing the mysteries would have been aware that it was a formidable undertaking, perhaps the greatest endeavour that could be achieved in spiritual life at the time. It would be a big decision to make, one that presumably would have involved much thought and discussion and a resetting of the compass to orientate their journey of life to take them towards Eleusis. This amplification of the mindset was a major part of the preparation and would be enhanced as the date in the diary approached. There would be a developing anxiety, fear, excitement and anticipation. One can imagine that the journey towards the site near Athens would have had a powerful sense of pilgrimage with an intensification of the sense of leaving behind the everyday world. There would be a quickening of psyche, an increase perhaps, of archetypal penetrance.

The intensification continues as the initiates gather in Athens where they fast for days and there is a ritual immersion in the river or sea and the sacrifice of a piglet to Persephone. Karen Armstrong describes how the pilgrims travelled together along the 16 mile road to Eleusis, some would be weakened by fasting and they would be apprehensive. There is chanting and some further softening up of ego in the form of deliberately intimidating behaviour from the people who had been initiated the year before. They arrive in Eleusis as the sun is setting, there are flickering torches and they become more disorientated by being herded through the streets before entering the initiation chamber, called the Telesterion. It is pitch dark. They have left much of their everyday persona behind. They are ripe for a numinous experience.[256]

We do not really know what happens after that. There was no teaching and no doctrine. Above all, this was a personal encounter with the sacred. We know that they drank a potion, 'kykeon', which had psychedelic qualities, perhaps from a fungal parasite of barley, ergot, that contains the alkaloid LSA, a precursor to LSD. It is likely that the setting was manipulated towards a dark numinosity and an encounter with the archetypal shadow. Karen Armstrong refers to something unspeakable, such as the sacrifice of a child who is saved at the eleventh hour. There is a ritual followed by the numinous ecstasy and rebirth into the world as a reconstituted human being.

We do not know how the process was integrated. Carefully designed rituals have an innate integrative effect and we can assume that the group process continued to some extent after the conclusion of the ceremony. There was the opportunity for repetition and for someone approaching the greater mysteries, the anticipatory journey before they could participate again could be as long as five years.

The Eleusinian mysteries provide a model for the optimization of mindset and the provision of a setting conducive to a high-intensity archetypal experience. There is the very gradual immersion in the process, perhaps beginning some years before the event with an acceleration towards the ritual itself. The cardinal features of this include:

- The decision to undertake the sacred ritual.
- The anticipation and mental preparation.
- Travelling.
- Fasting.
- Ritual preparation, immersion and sacrifice.
- Amplification by group process.
- The model of the Persephone myth as the descent to the underworld.
- Psychedelic potion to induce the non-ordinary state of consciousness.
- The entry into the chamber.
- The darkness.
- Encounter with shadow, the dark numinosity.
- Symbolic death and rebirth.
- Secrecy preventing trivialization.

Psychedelic/Archaidelic

Professor David Nutt is a leading psychiatrist and neuro-pharmacologist who has served and led various committees and academic organizations in Britain and Europe. He was famously sacked by the British government for his upholding of scientific fact above political expediency regarding the classification system used to classify controlled drugs.[257] According to Nutt:

> Psychedelic drugs are arguably the most important drugs for neuroscience. They produce profound alterations in many key elements of brain function such as perception, mood, insight and sense of self. For these reasons they have been used by different human societies for millennia. Currently there is very limited use of them in science because of the intense regulations that control their production and use. These regulations are based on the false premise that psychedelics are extremely harmful drugs.[258]

The term *psychedelic*, meaning 'mind manifesting', came into use in the late 1950s.[259] An alternative name for psychedelics could be 'archaidelics', for I suggest that these drugs create their effect by increasing archetypal penetrance. With their use, the archetypal domain is made manifest. These drugs are unusual in that the quality of the effect varies according to the dosage. In higher doses, there can be transpersonal experiences and a transcendence of the ego with high-grade and life-changing numinous experiences. In lower doses, there is a more cispersonal effect that is useful in psycholytic psychotherapy where psychodynamic issues and conflicts are brought into a brighter focus with amplification of meaning and intensity. In doses that are too small to exert a noticeable effect (microdosing), it is suggested that there may be a cognitive and creativity enhancing effect.[260]

There is a growing recognition, supported by research, that it has been a great mistake to prematurely consign these agents to the therapeutic dustbin. Why are we encouraged to over-prescribe psychoactive substances of limited use and significant side effects while neglecting to examine these agents of possible transformative change? We know that psychedelics are physiologically well tolerated with a low incidence of physical side effects. If used properly with appropriate set and setting, they are remarkably safe. A 1960 study of 5000 people who had taken LSD more than 25,000 times between them in clinical and research conditions, found that only 5 of these people had suffered a psychotic reaction lasting more than 24 hours.[261] If used carelessly without proper set and setting, the consequence can be a disastrous archetypal crisis. We are familiar with the stories of the LSD trip where internal reality was confused with external reality resulting in injury or worse. These are powerful tools indeed and to be treated with great respect and caution.

Many people are not aware that there was a time when considered use of and research into psychedelic drugs was not only respectable, but offered real therapeutic potential. The psychoactive effects of Lysergic Acid Diethylamide, LSD, was accidentally discovered by the chemist Albert Hofmann working at Sandoz[3] laboratories in Switzerland in 1943. Hofmann famously gave himself a tiny amount of LSD, not realizing how potent it was. He wobbled home through the streets of Basel on his bicycle, thought he would die, became paranoid and called the doctor who could find nothing the matter with him. Hofmann was in a terrified despairing state before the horror softened and evolved to a feeling of good fortune and gratitude. He particularly enjoyed the extraordinary intensity of shifting colors and synesthetic plays of shapes. He found that each sound generated a vividly changing image with its own form and color. The next day he awoke clear headed and refreshed:

> Breakfast tasted delicious and gave me extraordinary pleasure. When I walked out into the garden, in which the sun now shone after a spring rain, everything glistened and sparkled to a new light. The world was as if newly created. All my sense vibrated in a condition of the highest sensitivity, which persisted for the entire day.[262]

Hofmann realized that he had accidentally developed an extraordinarily powerful drug. It remains the most powerful psychoactive drug by a considerable distance, but there was no obvious use for it. Sandoz distributed it to psychiatrists and scientists for research and clinical use in the hope and expectation that a useful role would be found. Then, of course, LSD became associated with 1960s counterculture and opposition to the war in Vietnam. Reckless use outside of a clinical or research setting caused adverse publicity and, in the politically fraught context of the time, the authorities made it illegal. Clinical and research into psychedelics ceased.

The first generation of psychedelic research between 1950 and the mid 1960s published over 1000 scientific papers involving 40,000 patients. Many pioneers gave their careers to this field, hoping that psychedelic drugs could be to psychiatry what the microscope is to biology or the telescope is to astronomy: an essential tool to explore the parts of the internal world that are usually inaccessible. This research is almost entirely forgotten by modern psychiatry; indeed, much of the design of these studies falls short of modern standards so that the findings have to be treated with caution. However, we should note the evidence that LSD psychotherapy improved the prognosis of recovering alcoholics. One of the most interesting findings of this research was that for abstinent alcoholics who were

---

[3]   Swiss pharmaceutical company

engaged in the recovery process, the treatment was particularly effective if the patient had a numinous or spiritual experience as a result of the psychedelic sessions. Thus, it is assumed that the numinous experience causes any therapeutic effect that results rather than the drug itself. Psychedelics may also be particularly useful for those people with anxiety about death associated with terminal illness. LSD research in the terminally ill found a reduced need for analgesics with improved mood and reduced fear of death in 60–70% of cases. Again, the treatment response seemed to be correlated with the extent to which the patients experienced a mystical or transcendent state.[263]

The sober use of psychedelics as a method of treatment or self development is a journey through the landscape of the interior. In properly supported psychedelic sessions, any contact with the everyday world or interpersonal communication is kept to a useful minimum. A gentle, contemplative, spiritually oriented setting with the intention of opening to higher levels of consciousness predisposes to positive numinous experiences. Usually the subject puts on a blindfold and listens to music. The music is usually archetypally evocative and is an important aid to the process. In other words, this is not pop music or music that relates to egoic experiences; it typically has a transcendent quality.[264] In any psychedelic session, there is at least one person 'sitting'. The sitter is in a position of care and responsibility, and should have familiarity with the psychedelic territory and some of the mental states that may arise. The key role of the sitter is to support a naturally unfolding process that is assumed to have its own innate healing trajectory. The sitter takes a passive role and will not interfere with a person's process except on matters of care and safety, but is available to offer support if required. The support may be verbal, emotional or physical.

A landmark study by Roland Griffiths and colleagues entrenched the second generation of psychedelic research showing that psilocybin often caused life-changing numinous experiences.[265] This was a double-blind study administering either psilocybin (psychedelic) or methylphenidate (stimulant) in a non-clinical and supportive setting to volunteers who had not previously taken psychedelics and who had a regular spiritual or religious activity. Thus, people were selected who were likely to have a spiritually orientated mindset. 22 out of the 36 subjects who had taken the psilocybin described a mystical experience as opposed to 4 after taking methylphenidate.[266] At the two-month follow-up, 67% of the subjects rated the psilocybin experience as either the single most meaningful or in the top five meaningful experiences of their lives (compared to 8% with methylphenidate). These subjects reported that psilocybin enhanced their attitudes about life in general, their mood and their relationships with others and this was confirmed by independent ratings from family and friends.

Ben Sessa, a British psychiatrist, gives a comprehensive account of the modern era of psychedelic research in *The Psychedelic Renaissance*. The most promising psychoactive agents in the modern era of research are MDMA and psilocybin. LSD is rarely used, partly due to the difficulties associated with its long duration of action but also perhaps because of the persistent effects of the bad publicity from the 1960s. Sessa comments 'those three little letters L.S.D are still enough to strike fear into people's hearts and make research very difficult indeed'.[267]

In 2014, Peter Gasser's team published the first clinical research involving therapeutic use of LSD for over 40 years.[268] Using a controlled, randomized and blinded study design in 12 patients with distressing anxiety after the diagnosis of terminal cancer, they found significant reductions in anxiety and the absence of significant side effects. End-of-life anxiety is notoriously difficult to treat but, as Gasser put it, 'with LSD assisted psychotherapy, the anxiety went down and stayed down'. The key phrase here is *LSD assisted psychotherapy*, where the therapy is an ongoing process and the setting is carefully managed. The numbers of the patients involved in this study are far too small to produce firm evidence—larger scale studies are required for this—but it does provide proof of concept.

Gasser's team provide an excellent model for the psychotherapeutic work required. The characteristics are as follows:

1. Ongoing psychotherapy over 2–3 months.
2. 2 preparatory psychotherapy / explanatory sessions.
3. 2 full day LSD sessions 2–3 weeks apart.
4. Moderate dose of LSD, i.e., 200 mcgs—to avoid fully dissolving normal ego structures.
5. Each LSD session accompanied by male / female therapist pair.
6. Participants were instructed to focus their awareness inwards, usually assisted by music.
7. Lengthy discussions between the participants and the co-therapists were discouraged during the acute effects of the LSD.
8. The therapeutic session ended after 8 hours followed by a brief review of the day's experiences.
9. Each LSD sessions was followed by 3 non-drug psychotherapy sessions over a few weeks.
10. Most of the participants stated a preference for more than two LSD sessions and a longer treatment period.

Venus in a Tablet

MDMA is not a classical psychedelic.[269] It does not cause the perceptual disturbances or the variety of archetypal experience that can occur with LSD and it does not cause the encounter with the shadow or an archetypal encounter with death. MDMA is known for its ecstatic, powerful positive feelings of love where the world becomes suffused with beauty and goodness, hence its street name of ecstasy. Sessa describes MDMA as having all the required qualities to enhance psychotherapy. The drug is short-acting, has no dependence potential and is not toxic at therapeutic doses. It enhances the therapeutic alliance by amplifying a feeling of trust and closeness with the therapist, which in turn enables the addressing of trauma that may otherwise be too difficult. MDMA reduces depression and induces relaxation while simultaneously raising arousal levels for the therapy session. Most importantly, it is remarkably consistent in its effects, almost always causing an intensely pleasurable feeling.[270]

MDMA was used in the late 1970s and early 1980s by a growing number of psychotherapists until it was banned by the Drug Enforcement Administration (DEA) in the USA. Largely due to the efforts of the Multidisciplinary Association for Psychedelic Studies (MAPS) led by Rick Doblin, MDMA has been pioneered as potential treatment for severe post-traumatic stress disorder. PTSD in its severe form is one of the most difficult psychiatric conditions to treat and has a high mortality rate. It is estimated that more combat veterans died from suicide, presumed to be associated with PTSD, than died in combat in the Vietnam War.

In my psychiatric practice, I have patients who have suffered from years of the characteristic nightmares and flashbacks of PTSD, but the most disabling part of the condition is their constant feeling of being on the edge of a terrifying catastrophe. Such people lead constricted lives, often unable to leave the house and their irritability damages their relationships. They derive no pleasure from activities they previously enjoyed, they have no libido and they have no hope. Talking treatments are usually effective in cases of mild-to-moderate severity, but in the most severe cases it can be counterproductive as talking about the trauma is too difficult, often triggering a panic attack. Standard psychiatric medication for PTSD is of limited use so the therapeutic options are very limited. We desperately need a more effective treatment for severe PTSD.

Michael Mithoefer is a doctor who specialised in emergency medicine before moving to psychiatry. He and his wife Annie both completed the Grof Transpersonal Training and co-facilitated holotropic breathwork sessions for some years in association with Michael's psychiatry practice. They used many of the same principles derived from holotropic breathwork in their development of their model of MDMA-assisted psychotherapy for people with severe PTSD. Thus, mindset and setting are of prime importance. Patients are administered the MDMA and encouraged to use a blindfold, while listening to music designed to aid the internal process. Michael and Annie sit with their patient and at some stage the patient will start to talk about the trauma that caused them to develop the condition. The positive, 'loved-up' feeling induced by the MDMA allows patients to develop a different relationship with the trauma so that it is less overwhelming. They can begin to talk about it with the therapists and re-encounter the emotions associated with it in a manner that was previously impossible.

The early results from these well-designed research studies are very promising, although the numbers of patients were small. Mithoefer's first paper in 2010 reported on 20 patients with severe treatment-resistant PTSD: 12 received placebo and 8 received MDMA. All patients had preparation and non-drug psychotherapy before and after the drug-assisted sessions. At follow up, 83% of the MDMA group and 25% of the placebo group had a reduction in symptoms so that they no longer qualified for a diagnosis of PTSD.[271]

Despite these positive results, we are some way away from being able to use MDMA psychotherapy clinically. The studies have to be replicated with large groups of patients (phase three trials) before the drug is licenced for clinical use. It may be that the most difficult part of the clinical treatment will be the training of the therapists to match the Mithoefers' expertise and empathy. This is delicate psychotherapy requiring immense skill and some personal experience of MDMA.

I suggest that MDMA assisted psychotherapy is a bio-psycho-social-archetypal (BPSA) treatment. The drug enables a high intensity archetypal experience that allows a rebalancing of the relationship with the dark numinosity of the PTSD. The terrifying trembling at the edge of the precipice is met with an inrush of warm positive loving feelings that are mutative. This enables a fundamental change in symptoms that is expressed at a psycho-social level with a restoration of relationships and function.

Sacred Medicine

Richard Tarnas tells a story of a transpersonal psychology conference, where he and the other organizers discussed how it was that they had first become drawn to the subject. As they went around the table, giving their answers, it became clear that most of them had started the same way:

they had taken LSD and this had triggered an awareness that conscious-ness was far more complicated than they had previously thought.[272] Typ-ically, the experience had a spiritual tone with a deeply felt and positive sense of the sacred. This type of experience is enormously surprising for those who have no previous spiritual interest or who have an antipathy to spirituality caused by previous encounters with organized religion. Stanislav Grof observes that people who experience these numinous moments often develop a conviction about the utmost relevance of the spiritual dimension in the universal scheme of things. Even scientists deeply attached to a materialist perspective, uncompromising atheists or antireligious crusaders, such as Marxist philosophers and politicians, suddenly become interested in the spiritual quest after they have such an experience.[273]

It is clear that psychedelics predispose to mystical experience and that such experiences can be growth enhancing by opening a gateway to the transpersonal and signposting a direction of travel. However, the doors of perception swing shut again when the experience ends and the degree of archetypal penetrance gradually returns towards baseline.[274] The philoso-pher and religious scholar John Huston Smith gives a flavor of this process. He describes a ten-year period of Zen meditation practice including a period in a monastery in Japan, but ultimately he found the results disap-pointing. He felt that not much had changed for him. Then he was given LSD for the first time on New Year's Day 1961 and 'after about an hour, I was into the experience that for the previous fifteen or twenty years I had been trying to get by other means'.[275]

There is a complex relationship between the use of psychedelics and meditation. Someone like Huston Smith, with a spiritual mindset honed by years of practice, would have been highly likely to have a high-grade mys-tical experience with a high-dose LSD session. For serious students of the numinous this is a prize worth having but psychedelics generally have diminishing returns and the emergent spirituality needs to be buttressed by regular psycho-spiritual practice, usually meditation. Huston Smith reports that after about half a dozen powerful LSD experiences, the utility seemed to decrease and the bad trips increased. Ram Dass emphasizes that psyche-delics cannot give a permanent spiritual immersion, but they can provide an initial experience and some faith that serves as a foundation for future spiritual practice.[276]

Like Albert Hofmann, Huston Smith thought he was going to die on his first trip as he moved ever closer to an experience of 'the Absolute'. He describes the intermingled awe, fear and fascination that are typical of the high-intensity archetypal experience. He had no doubt that this was an authentic religious experience. Religious scholars tended to dismiss the experiences derived from psychedelics as pseudo-religious and of little significance. However, Huston Smith performed an experiment by taking reports of mystical experiences by Saints over the ages and mixing them up with reports of LSD experiences. He found that people who were knowledgeable about such states were unable to distinguish between the two categories. The mystics and the psychedelic explorers seemed to be describing exactly the same territory.[277]

Therapy of Substance

In psychotherapy, as a general rule, the greater the depth, the more mutative the therapeutic process.[278] Thus the deeper the level of psyche at which emotional material is processed and worked through, the greater is the prospect of lasting resolution and change. Freud made use of this with his amplification of the transference neurosis, where fundamental disturbances in formative relationships become re-enacted in the relationship with the analyst. This transference neurosis then becomes available for examination in the psychoanalytic encounter. The analytic setting enhanced the process by the opacity of the analyst and laying the patient on a couch so that there was no visual contact with the analyst.

The judicious use of psychedelics may take this process deeper by increasing archetypal penetrance. Psycholytic therapy involves a low-to-medium dose of a psychedelic agent with the aim of making available the repressed material from the psyche, which would otherwise be difficult to access. Typically, this generates an archetypal spotlight that becomes unerringly directed towards the fault lines in the psyche, the states of mind with turbulence and resonance of meaning that need to be worked with. Psycholytic work is very different to a psychedelic session; the patient is still rooted mainly in ordinary reality, has a functioning ego and is able to interact with people. Psycholytic psychotherapy has an innate gentleness; it involves working with defenses in a way that is not overwhelming so that the encounter with the shadow is a meeting rather than a confrontation.

Only one psychotherapist in the modern era has made available an account of psycholytic psychotherapy. Friederike Meckel Fischer is a medical doctor who specialized in psychotherapy and trained with Grof. She joined a group in Switzerland that trained therapists in psycholytic psychotherapy, mostly with MDMA and LSD, during the period of 1988 to 1993 when Swiss law allowed such treatment. When such therapy became illegal again, Dr Fischer continued the treatment as she was convinced of its efficacy and did not want to deprive some of her patients of the potential benefits. In 2009, her work as a psycholytic psychotherapist was terminated when she was briefly arrested by the Swiss authorities for working with substances that were classified as illegal.

Dr Fischer treated nearly 100 people over the years with psychedelics. They represented those 4% of her patients who felt they were not making progress in conventional treatment. The first step towards the psycholytic therapy involved an individual session with Dr Fischer using MDMA to become familiar with the drug's properties, to recognise the peaks and troughs of the experience and to manage their emotional responses accordingly. When deemed to be ready, the patient would join the group session, which would take place once a month over the course of a weekend. The weekend session would have a clear timetable: the Friday would be for preparation, the Saturday for the psycholytic session and the Sunday for the integration. Her patients would generally stay in the group for an average of 25 sessions spread over the course of a few years.

Dr Fischer's book contains the definitive account of psycholytic therapy and the complexity of her work is difficult to convey adequately in a brief account.[279] In outline, the psycholytic session on the Saturday is composed of quiet time interspersed with periods of interaction with the group and therapist. There are periods of lying on a mat in silence with suitable music acting as an amplifier of mental contents. This is interspersed with talking therapies to engage with and process the issues that are brought to light. Dr Fischer pays great attention to the integration process. The first stage of integration is directly after the drug-assisted session on the Saturday. The Sunday morning is taken up by a group meeting to discuss the work of the previous day. The third stage of integration is the preparation of a written report of their experience that is duly sent to Dr Fischer during the next few weeks. An individual (non-drug) session is always available with Dr Fischer if required.

The participants were taught a simple mindfulness technique—to be the empathic observer of their thoughts and mental experiences. In the early stages of therapy, there tended to be a re-engagement with emotionally laden aspects of their biographical experience whereas later in therapy there tended to be experiences with a spiritual tone. Dr Fischer reports that there were no serious adverse effects from the drugs that were used. Clearly, only therapists with impeccable training, credentials and ethics could undertake this type of work—there is scope for all manner of problems if the therapy deviates from the highest standards. At time of writing, psycholytic psychotherapy is not available for clinical use, but Dr Fischer has done us a great service by developing a comprehensive, modern model of psycholytic psychotherapy that could act as a template for further development.[280]

Integration

Jung said that most of what we need lies in the shadow. The shadow is the repressed content of our unseen psychological interior while the archetypal expression of shadow amplifies the challenging flavors of destruction, guilt, evil and horror. It is probably inevitable that emotionally problematic material laden with our biographical issues comes to the surface in the high archetypal penetrance states that arise in psychedelic sessions – and that this uncovered shadow will hold an archetypal intensity. The difficulty is that we need to access and integrate this shadow material in order to become more whole but this is usually the most difficult part of the process. Many people will encounter the shadow in the course of a bad trip but, at best, they may not be able to make use of it and, at worst, they may be traumatized by it.

Classical LSD psychotherapy, such as performed by Grof and colleagues in the 1950s, was repeated with each patient until the problematic psychological issues were properly worked through and resolved. Of course, this takes time; usually involving a course of carefully supported psychedelic sessions extending over months. Grof developed methods of integration, which we will discuss more fully in the next chapter. Sometimes a single psychedelic session may seem a complete process, as occurred with Hofmann's classical experience. Frequently, though, this is not the case and in an unsupported psychedelic session the shadow may be powerfully expressed but remain un-integrated. The bad trip with unprocessed shadow can represent a trauma in its own right, resulting in persistent psychological difficulties or flashbacks.

Many people who have been through an unresolved shadow experience in the form of a bad trip find that, in order to fully resolve it, it is necessary to go, once again, to the archetypal layer of psyche, which involves accessing a non-ordinary state of consciousness. This is an important observation; more superficial forms of therapy simply will not sufficiently engage with this layer of trauma. In my experience, it is not uncommon for people to attend holotropic breathwork sessions precisely to work on unresolved issues from previous psychedelic experiences.

Archetypal experiences have a tendency to resist the passage of time. Scott Hill gives a vivid account of powerful and disturbing flashbacks occurring over 40 years after the original LSD experience that caused them (see chapter 13). The strongest flashback occurred at the Burning Man festival in Nevada, where he was serving as a volunteer in the psychedelic emergency response team. He was so disturbed by his reaction that he sought help, and a few days later he underwent an MDMA-assisted psychotherapy session that took him back to the original traumas. This time, in his high archetypal penetrance state, he was able to face the pain of his traumatic memories, talk it through with the therapists, work through the powerful archetypal material that was causing him such distress and take a big step towards resolution.[281] Hill felt that the extraordinary power of his flashback was triggered by the heat and dust of the desert, the festival's otherworldly atmosphere and the work he had done supporting two people in crisis that had stirred up his memories from his own past psychedelic experiences. This illustrates the important point that high archetypal penetrance environments may express unresolved traumas in the archetypal layer of our psyche. This is likely to be challenging—taking the form of a bad trip perhaps—but it represents an important opportunity to resolve the trauma if sufficiently supported.

A different issue is the lack of the encounter with the shadow. There is a prevailing atmosphere at some psychedelic conferences that has an almost evangelical fervor, being enthusiastic about the highs, the surges of creativity and the mystical insights. There is a mood of excitement that these powerful psychoactive substances are being brought in from the cold so that their therapeutic potential can be re-examined. But there is a risk of failing to adequately examine the side effects and the difficulties, and disowning the gritty, developmental challenge of the shadow work. It may be that there are some people, the cheerful extroverts, who simply don't have many shadow experiences, so that this aspect remains un-integrated, to the detriment of the journey towards wholeness.

High doses of psychedelics can be counterproductive as the ego structures dissolve and memories of the experience cannot be retained. There may only be vague memories of something that is very difficult to describe. It requires discipline to emerge from a psychedelic experience and write, draw and talk the experience into consciousness. Some people seem unable to do this and the result can be the ungrounded ramblings hinting at the numinous, the illusion of growth and a failure to unlock the benefits in a useful manner. Rather than actively applying the insights of the psychedelic experience to engage in life in an enhanced manner, they simply revisit the psychedelic experience. Rather than having ego function enriched, the ego can become eroded. Rather than become self actualized, a person's function can be diminished. Sometimes there is a perception of development or spiritual growth but if the lessons are insufficiently incorporated into consciousness, the sails of psyche are not properly filled by the archetypal wind and the opportunity for growth is lost. At worst un-integrated experiences can be distressing, dangerous and damaging.[282]

Ayahuasca Retreat

Some years ago, in the days when ayahuasca ceremonies were of uncertain legal status and openly advertised in the UK, I attended an ayahuasca retreat.[283] Ayahuasca is a brew prepared by shamans from plants in the Amazonian rain forest. The mixture contains at least one plant containing DMT (a tryptamine giving all the classic features of the psychedelic experience) and one plant containing a mono amine oxidase inhibitor (MAOI) required to convert the DMT to a psychoactive form when ingested orally. It is never used recreationally but taken as part of a religious ceremony led by the shaman and accompanied by music and songs (*icaros*) designed to amplify and aid the inner journey. Ayahuasca was highlighted for its powerful properties by the community of people interested in the therapeutic uses of psychedelics and there has been some research indicating some benefit in the treatment of addictions, particularly in indigenous peoples with a poor response to conventional methods of treatment.[284]

I had not taken psychedelics for many years. As a student I experimented with LSD and psilocybin. It seemed to me to have similarities to mountain walking, being variously challenging, exhilarating and frightening. I didn't have any life-changing or spiritual experiences on psychedelics, but I was glad I had tried them and felt they gave me some useful insights into the complexity of the psyche. I certainly wasn't tempted to try them again and, like most psychiatrists, I developed a strong dislike for the drug culture, based on the harm that street drugs caused my patients. But the prospect of a legal ayahuasca ceremony with an authentic shaman with appropriate setting seemed like a unique opportunity. Ayahuasca has the reputation of being the most demanding but valuable of psychoactive substances, the 'queen of psychedelics', so this was a retreat that I clearly needed to do. The convener had written a book on the subject, having spent years working with Peruvians shamans, and he was accompanied by three kind and skilled assistants.

We had ayahuasca ceremonies on three consecutive nights. The dose was increased each night, the first night using a mild introductory dose and the third session using a strong dose. The setting could not be faulted: it was a large secluded country house and there was no contact with the outside world. The mindset of all the participants was sober and orientated towards a mindful exploration of the deep interior. The ritual before and during the drinking of the ayahuasca each night was powerful and reinforced for us that this was a serious undertaking. One at a time we walked through the hall to where the shaman stood at the altar, we drank the foultasting liquid and lay on our mats on the floor. The lights were low. The shaman played the traditional *icaros*, the haunting music of the Amazonian ceremonies, and it felt as though we were descending into the Telesterion of the rain forest.

Each journey that I made was pleasurable with vivid visual imagery, which seemed to be 'of the jungle', involving green serpents and foliage, filled with vitality. Each night left me with a strong sense of the power of the natural world. The ayahuasca sessions occurred in the evening and by the time the drug effect had worn off, it was approaching midnight. The ceremony was ritually concluded and I went to bed. On the first two nights I slept beautifully and awoke refreshed, but I could not remember very much about the ayahuasca session of the previous night. I had not taken the necessary steps to talk through, write or draw my experience into consciousness. The memories were lost and would not come back. I resolved to be more careful with my integration on the third and final night

Our final session involved the higher dose. Once again it was vivid and enjoyable, and I remember having emotions and insights that I wanted to retain in my memory. When the ceremony ended, it took longer for the perceptual disturbances to settle and through the night I felt unpleasantly stimulated as though I had taken strong coffee or a stimulant. The other participants were similarly affected. Sleep did not come, my thoughts were agitated and would not settle or take shape, and I could not do the writing that I had planned. One of the participants thought she was dying in the middle of the night, but we could not find any of the staff and those of us who tried to support her were still affected by the drug. Afterwards, she felt that it had been a profound and helpful experience for her — but any retreat needs staff available to support these unexpected crises and it was clearly a serious failure of setting.

The next day I could not remember anything that seemed of value from the ayahuasca session and I went home feeling tired and scratchy. At work the next week I was uncharacteristically irritable and found myself in a committee meeting caught up in an unnecessary argument that I would normally have avoided. It seemed to me that while the workshop had been of interest, there had a been a total failure of integration and ultimately it was of no value. This was an important lesson for me. I believe that psychedelics, if used wisely, have a valuable therapeutic potential as an archetypal amplifier, but the setting and integration really do have to be done properly and to a very high standard. This is not optional.

It also confirmed for me that I would prefer to continue my explorations of inner space without taking any drugs.

CHAPTER 22

Breathing

I lived for over 10 years at the Esalen Institute where I was director of programs, and in the course of those years virtually every conceivable form of therapy and personal transformation, great or small came through Esalen. In terms of therapeutic effectiveness, Grof's (holotropic breathwork) was by far the most powerful; there was no comparison.

—Richard Tarnas[285]

This book is about growth, the barriers to growth, the side effects of growth and some methods to enhance growth. Our lives are perfectly designed as vehicles for growth, if we wish to use them in this way. A life well lived has all the material required for this task, with our animal bodies, our relationships, our developmental stages and our natural environment. If life is an adventure in consciousness, then the difficulties in life are the developmental gristle and much of our growth can be derived from negotiating these obstacles. If we need assistance, there are a range of psychological methods that can untangle the damage caused by trauma in the formative years and there are methods for the management of problematic cognitions such as anxiety.

But for those of us who wish to take it further - how do we progress to the next stage? How can we get to the very deepest parts of the psyche, where the opportunities for learning, growth and change are perhaps the greatest? How can we access those parts of ourselves that are in the most pain, which are so deep, so intrinsic to us and thus so very difficult to help? How indeed can we reliably and safely, without taking any drugs or substances, access a high archetypal penetrance (HAP) state to aid our developmental trajectory? If we are able to achieve this, how can the insights and energy be harnessed so that growth is coherent and progressive and not wasted?

The archetypal psyche has both light and dark characteristics so it is inevitable that serious work will involve an encounter with the shadow. We may remember from the first chapter, Rudolph Otto's description of how incomplete or partial forms of numinous experience can have a nightmarish, primitive quality with an abrupt and capricious character, but that this crude stage with its ominous tone has the potential to be transcended as the numen reveals itself, the process unfolds and eventually becomes integrated by the more rational elements of consciousness. So any therapeutic method involving HAP states has to be completely committed to supporting any problematic manifestation of the numinous towards its natural conclusion.

My intention in this final chapter is to explore the history and variety of powerful dissociative states that predispose to transcendence. I will outline the practice of holotropic breathwork and discuss the possible mechanisms of therapeutic action as well as potential pitfalls. We will conclude by reflecting on the purpose of such practice. What is it exactly that we gain?

Esalen and the Transpersonal Movement

There are certain periods in history when the people transfixed by the flickering shadows in Plato's cave become restless and are moved to examine the shadows and the effigies in greater numbers. One such time was the 1960s with the social and political currents of the time amplified by the widespread use of archetypal amplifiers, particularly LSD. There were some casualties, and there was social and political turbulence followed by a strong reaction from the establishment—much as Plato predicted in his allegory of the cave. But there were some people who showed the tenacity and discipline of Plato's true philosopher and there were some important staging posts that assisted these journeys. One such place was Esalen.

The Esalen Institute was founded in 1962 with the primary aim of developing human potential. Situated on the Californian coast at Big Sur, the institute developed a flavour influenced by the transformative experiences of its two founders, Dick Price and Michael Murphy. Price had been hospitalised for a 'psychotic episode' that he came to understand as a necessary move towards health – a transformation rather than an illness. Murphy was a medical student who wandered into the wrong classroom one day and found himself listening to a lecture on comparative religion. This caught his attention to the point where he started a meditation practice and eventually had a life-changing moment while meditating on the shores of a lake. Murphy switched from medicine to psychology but continued his fascination with Eastern thought, living and studying for a while in Sri Aurobindo's ashram in India. Price and Murphy were both influenced by

Aldous Huxley and the intertwined themes of spiritual emergence and its vicissitudes, non-ordinary states of consciousness and Eastern religion continued as the culture at Esalen matured and deepened. There was a strong feeling that the favoured paradigms of Western psychiatry and psychology had an overly narrow focus, judging other cultures solely through the lens of the modern Western culture (ethnocentric) and disregarding any insights from non-ordinary states of consciousness (cognicentric).[286]

A procession of radical thinkers enriched the development of the community at Esalen, notably Stanislav Grof who became scholar in residence in 1973 staying for twelve years to develop his treatment methods with his wife Christina.[287] Richard Tarnas lodged with the Grofs for a period, forming a cross-fertilisation of ideas in the area of archetypal cosmology, which examines the relationship between the physical structures in the cosmos and the archetypal forces affecting human experience. The institute was just one of a number of creative epicentres of the human potential movement, but Esalen punched above its weight and has had a disproportionate influence on the development of the transpersonal movement.

One of the fruits of Esalen was the development of holotropic breathwork as a non-drug method of accessing and integrating archetypal domains of consciousness.[288] It was developed by Stanislav and Christina Grof to continue their work, once clinical and research work with psychedelics became illegal and Sandoz had stopped supplying LSD for therapeutic and academic purposes. Their method produces a similar amplification of archetype, with heightened intensity of meaning, to that which occurs in psychedelic sessions. The term *holotropic* is derived from Greek and means moving towards wholeness, it has a similar meaning to the Jungian term individuation and indicates a continuing process. I will describe holotropic breathwork in some detail as it sets the standard for current practice with regard to the induction of a powerful non-ordinary state of consciousness with appropriate set, setting and integration.

The Holotropic Breathwork Retreat[289]

Holotropic breathwork (HBW) is not for everyone. It is noisy, intense, labour-intensive and cumbersome. It is done either as a day-long or weekend workshop or as a six-day retreat where the breathwork is combined with either meditation or teaching. The retreat setting provides for a deeper longer immersion in a high archetypal penetrance state, which, according to Stanislav Grof, provides the richest and most integrative experience.[290] As with the Eleusinian mysteries, the preparation of the mindset starts some time before the retreat itself. The crucial first step is the statement of the intention by booking the retreat, then as it approaches, there is an intensification of mental activity with excitement and possibly a little anxiety. Instructions arrive from the convenor regarding the practical issues and supporting the mindset, such as advice to pay attention to our dreams and our unfolding mental processes.

The day arrives. There is a journey to be undertaken away from everyday life, perhaps there is even a sense of pilgrimage. The opening group session brings a further intensification, where the participants and the staff sit in a circle. All the participants introduce themselves in turn, saying a little about why we have come or how we are feeling. Already we are moving further away from our everyday selves, we are preparing to enter a symbolic Telesterion, the dimly lit initiatory chamber of the Eleusinian mysteries. Interpersonal chatter quietens as people become more focussed on their internal processes and the work ahead.

During each retreat of this nature, there are four breathwork sessions. The group is divided into pairs for the purpose of the breathwork; each person 'breathes' twice and 'sits' twice for his partner. Breathing involves lying on a mat with a blindfold. There is a further increase in intensity as the breathwork session approaches with a sharpening of the mindset, a gathering of purpose for the task, perhaps some agitation. There is an acceptance that the session may be positive and joyous or it may sometimes be more challenging and involve an encounter with the shadow. The induction process comprises a relaxation exercise and instruction to surrender completely to the experience, to pay attention to whatever comes up in the mind and body, and to trust the inner healing intelligence that the experience will be exactly what is required. The role of the sitter in holotropic breathwork is crucial and complex, giving focussed and unwavering attention to the breather throughout. The presence of the sitter allows the breather to relinquish any need to monitor their environment to ensure safety, so that the everyday world can be fully disengaged. It is as though the left brain can be temporarily switched off allowing the right brain to flourish.

The process generally lasts between two and three hours. The nonordinary state of consciousness is induced by hyperventilation, breathing a little deeper and more rapidly than normal as the music set begins. Hyperventilation causes some complex physiological changes with decreased carbon dioxide in the lungs and a corresponding rise in pH as the blood becomes more alkaline. Grof compares this state to being in high mountains, suggesting that the decreased oxygen and carbon dioxide causes some inhibition of the brain's cerebral cortex and intensifies activity in the older parts of the brain. This has the overall effect of making unconscious processes more available.[291]

The music is played at nightclub volume, and has a typical pattern and flow designed to be archetypally evocative and conducive to a positive experience. This is music redolent of meaning, with a mythic quality that speaks to the great themes of humanity. While the music is chosen for its high quality and intensity, it should not be well known and any lyrics should be a foreign language to avoid undue influence on the breather through its verbal content. The voice should seem just like another musical instrument. The music set has five distinct phases and the music is chosen accordingly. Grof describes the first half of the music set as follows:

> The session typically begins with activating music that is dynamic, flowing, and emotionally uplifting and reassuring. As the session continues, the music gradually increases in intensity and moves to powerful rhythmic pieces, preferably drawn from ritual and spiritual traditions of various native cultures. Although many of these performances can be aesthetically pleasing, the main purpose of the human groups that developed them is not entertainment, but induction of holotropic experiences. An example here could be the dance of the whirling dervishes accompanied by beautiful music and chants. It is not designed to be admired but to take people to the experience of God.[292]

The second half of the set is characterized by a reduction in beat and the introduction of 'breakthrough' music chosen for its intensity and sacred quality. It is designed to favour a positive numinous experience. This is flowed by 'heart' music with an emotional and loving quality. The final 20 minutes or so of music has a meditative mood with qualities of calm, peace and coming home.

There is a wide range of possible experiences such as:

- Dream-like states or emotionally charged visual imagery
- Profound feelings of joy or serenity
- Meditative states
- Intuitive insights or clarification of troublesome issues in participants' lives
- Re-experiencing and releasing physical or emotional trauma
- An experience of the birth process
- Encounters with mythic or archetypal themes
- Past-life or inter-life experiences
- Spiritual or religious awakenings
- An experience of energy felt emotionally or physically.

Some participants report transpersonal experiences, which may include a convincing sense of being other than oneself, whether another person, animal or plant. It is not necessary to have such experiences to benefit from holotropic breathwork; indeed, they may be a distraction, but they make a great impression on participants when they occur, providing evidence for them that the map of the human psyche is wider and more complex than previously imagined.[293] There may be experiences beyond space-time and consensus reality such as visions and experiences of archetypal beings or communication with non-physical entities. Occasionally, there may experiences (such as that described by Martin in chapter one) with an identification of cosmic unity or non-dual consciousness.[294] Jack Kornfield, who has worked with the Grofs for many years, explains:

> To witness a large group practicing holotropic breathwork is to see a remarkable range of experiences, reliving any stage of their own history or entering the realms of archetypes, of animals, of birth and death. Being present at a group breathwork session is like entering Dante's Divine Comedy with Paradiso, Purgatorio and Inferno all on display as breathers go through the profound process of breathing, healing and awakening.[295]

There is a degree of voluntary control over the depth of the psychological experience. It is possible to have a mild experience by limiting the hyperventilation and many people feel their way into the process at a pace that they feel comfortable with. Some people use some active imagination to kick-start the journey. A degree of engagement is necessary to intensify the experience. If a particular feeling or bodily sensation is developing, the advice is to 'make it bigger' to allow it to reach its natural conclusion.[296]

When the session comes to a natural end, and the breather has returned to everyday consciousness, the integration begins. If the breather is not returned to a normal state of consciousness, he or she continues until the process is completed, sometimes requiring assistance from the facilitators. Often, a breather will feel a conflation of emotion and bodily feeling, perhaps a tension or pain in a particular body area. Typically, this bodily sensation has a profound emotional charge, often associated with a trauma of some kind. The usual guidance is to breathe into this feeling, to intensify it so that it may run its natural course towards resolution. If the process is difficult or feels stuck, there are bodywork techniques that help towards intensification and release of the associated emotion. The bodywork typically involves providing some resistance for the breather to push against and is never an active process.[297] One of the revelations for me about holotropic breathwork was the way in which careful bodywork in these highly charged HAP states could be so powerfully transformative, releasing those inaccessible reservoirs of pain and trauma that people hold inside themselves.

The entire retreat is geared towards integration while treating each person and their experiences with exemplary care, compassion and respect. The integration has a number of phases. It begins with the breather recounting the detail of the experience with their sitter. This provides a narrative and some imprinting into memory. The role of the sitter as a witness with a mirroring, containing and supportive function has echoes of the mother-infant relationship, gradually reverting to a normal adult relationship as the integration progresses. The next phase is drawing a mandala, considered by Jung to be a symbol of wholeness. In practice, this is a sheet of white paper with the outline of a circle, the breather is encouraged to draw whatever comes to mind to capture some of the ineffable quality of the experience. Some of us, who struggle with drawing, still find it illuminating to see what emerges onto the paper, but use writing as the primary medium.

The breather is encouraged to stay with the experience, to think about it, mull it over, perhaps do some more writing or drawing later in the day. When the roles are switched so that the breather sits for their partner, archetypal penetrance is slightly raised again for the sitter during the session, which provides further impetus to the integrative effort. There is a group sharing in the evening where all the breathers will discuss briefly the core of their experience. An important aspect of this group work is that people are in a very sensitive state and need to be protected from any perception of aggression, which could impair the open and reflective state of mind that is optimal for integration. So any interpersonal interaction such as interpretation or 'therapizing' is strongly discouraged.

The last day of the retreat is set aside to complete the integrative process with group work so that people can place their experiences in a context before leaving and returning to their lives. It is imperative that each and every participant has completely returned to an everyday state of consciousness. The facilitators would be monitoring everyone throughout and would provide additional support if required. Of course, the integration continues afterwards, and participants are encouraged to pay attention to their unfolding inner processes. Often people report finding a new depth of meaning or an unfolding insight some time afterwards, perhaps in a dream, by looking at their mandala or simply through a subtly changed way of being in the world.

An Inner Healing Intelligence

When I completed my training in group analysis, I knew that it was a powerful and effective method and I felt as though I had achieved a good understanding of the psychodynamic mechanisms by which the process worked and achieved its therapeutic goals. When I completed my training in holotropic breathwork, I knew it was a powerful and effective method. I could see the benefit of the group retreat and how infantile and perhaps perinatal areas of pain, trauma and need in the psyche were being healed and nourished. There were certainly aspects of the process that were familiar to me and that could be understood in psychoanalytic terms. But there was another component altogether that remained mysterious to me.

The single most important concept in holotropic breathwork, and indeed in all high archetypal penetrance states, is that the process is entirely natural, integrative and orientated towards our growth. The assumption is that there is an inner intelligence with a benign trajectory, and that this trajectory becomes more powerful in the non-ordinary state of consciousness. The implication is that any material that arises in the psyche in such a non-ordinary state will be precisely what is required for the person's move towards wholeness. It is the role of the facilitator to simply support this natural unfolding process. This is the article of faith that Grof has derived after thousands of sessions of clinical work with psychedelics and holotropic breathwork. To some extent, this is the norm for any psychotherapeutic process where the patient makes available the part of psyche that needs attention; the model is trusted and a therapeutic alliance is achieved. In traditional psychotherapy, it is generally understood that the path may prove challenging as the problematic issues are engaged with, but that this is the route to an improved quality of life. It is a bigger leap of faith when working with the archetypal psyche as the intensity of the experience and the challenge can be so much greater.

What then can be expected after an experience of holotropic breathwork? Generally, people come to holotropic breathwork because they want to go deep inside their psyche. Sometimes this may because they wish to work on parts of themselves that may be hidden, causing distress or controlling their lives in a way that does not feel comfortable. Others attend seeking personal or spiritual development. Participants in workshops and retreats generally report a feeling of spiritual nourishment with enhanced vitality and a degree of transcendence of unwanted patterns of thought and behavior. Many will find relief for a range of emotional and physical problems and reach a more integrated level of functioning. The clinical research base is very limited but indicates some efficacy with the maintenance of abstinence from substance or alcohol addiction. The psychiatrist James Eyerman has used a modified version of the method in psychiatric patients and found it to be a safe, well tolerated and without adverse effects.[298]

Of course, psychological relief will result from many psychotherapeutic modalities, but the unusual feature of holotropic breathwork is its tendency to point beyond the concerns of ego. Many people who persevere at the practice will have a powerful numinous experience, which is often life changing. It takes a special skill to articulate the quality of this type of state; these are the words of the nineteenth century Poet Laureate, Alfred Lord Tennyson:

> A kind of waking trance that I have frequently had, from boyhood, when I have been all alone. This has generally come upon me through repeating my own name two or three times to myself silently, till all at once, as it were out of the intensity of the consciousness of individuality, the individuality itself seemed to dissolve and fade away into boundless being. This is not a confused state, but the clearest of the clearest, the surest of surest, the weirdest of weirdest, utterly beyond words, where death was an almost laughable impossibility, the loss of personality (if so it were) seeming no extinction but the only true life.[299]

The Eleusinian mysteries had the role of reducing fear of death and enhancing life and the same often holds true for holotropic breathwork. People draw their own conclusions about the nature of life and death, but the perspective that often develops in holotropic states is the notion that our life on Earth is part of a larger more complex cycle. This tends to be associated with a move towards a sustained spiritual practice of some kind or non-sectarian spiritual interests. Grof reports the development of a greater sense of planetary citizenship with warmer human relationships as well as a desire to live a more simple and satisfying life in harmony with nature and ecological values.[300]

Prolonged practice of holotropic breathwork is often combined with the Grof Transpersonal training course.[301] This involves at least 20 experiences of breathing spread over the course of a few years, supported by teaching in transpersonal theory and training in integrative methods. Typically, there may be an initial spiritual opening or numinous experience that supports the harder work of trauma resolution, integration of shadow and the experiences of ego death leading to the emergence of a reformed ego structure. At best, this is a milder, safer version of Jung's epic confrontation with the unconscious—a carefully judged ascent from and return to Plato's cave. Using Maslow's terminology, the peak experiences are just stepping stones on the way – the ultimate aim is to produce a self-actualized individual with the qualities of self sufficiency, low anxiety, being humorous and humble, loved and loving, and above all living a fulfilling and harmonious life.

My own four-year passage through the Grof Transpersonal Training gave me the experience that I was looking for; a controlled introduction to the parts of psyche that Jung had discovered and that I did not encounter in my psychodynamic training. I came to holotropic breathwork in something of a mid-life crisis associated with bereavement and loss. My first session gave me a paradigm changing 'proof-of-concept' experience that spiritual epiphany was real and powerful and that I had been wrong to discount it as a psychological defense mechanism.

The quality of any training is demonstrated by the quality of the people it produces. I found the facilitators led by Grof and Tav Sparks to be of the highest standard and I remain impressed by the commitment, compassion and integrity of the people involved.[302] The failures of setting and integration that I described in the ayahuasca retreat simply do not happen in the holotropic breathwork retreats that I have experienced.[303] The absence of dogma or pressure to conform to Grof's theories was important to me—the focus was entirely to allow people to find their own way towards a more complete and comfortable version of themselves. As my training progressed, I encountered archetypes, deeper parts of pain and unfolding shadow that added new dimensions to my understanding of psyche. That first positive numinous experience gave me the impetus and motivation to manage the more challenging experiences and with repeated exposure, the archetypal world became increasingly real and palpable.

In time, I found that my breathwork sessions continued to give me personal insights, but they increasingly seemed like immersions in a warm, loving, invigorating energy. I found myself cured of my symptoms of professional burn out and physical malaise, and I was able to engage in my clinical work with renewed compassion and energy. I think I did some of my best work during this period. Sitting for breathers helped me to sit more effectively in different ways with patients and with the dying. Witnessing some of my fellow breathers working on, processing and eventually resolving their psychological traumas, which I believe would have been resistant to other treatment methods, profoundly impressed me. Breathwork does indeed appear to operate in parts of the psyche that other psychotherapies do not approach.

I do not want to over-idealize the training; like any other method, it assists, it helps the flow but does not by any means conclude the journey. There were some side effects and, some years after I concluded my training, I am still working on the integration.[304]

Hysteria and Dissociative States

It appears that holotropic breathwork involves the induction of a dissociative state in a highly supportive and conducive setting, which allows an unusually high degree of archetypal penetrance. This implies an engagement with a heightened energy holding an intensification of meaning and the full range of numinous experience. This energy does not have a physical substrate that we are aware of and could be defined as spirit, Ground, *prana*, implicate order or any term of similar resonance that we feel comfortable with. The point that I want to make is that if the mechanism lies beyond our current understanding, it does not mean that it does not exist.

This heightened energy inevitably highlights our problematic areas, the places in our minds and bodies where we hold pain and tension and the places where we have barriers to growth. If we allow ourselves to open to this energy, we have the opportunity for resolution and healing, and perhaps we move to a higher octave of our function. In order to access this energy, we need to disengage for a while from everyday reality in a setting designed to allow a safe, sustained immersion in the high archetypal penetrance state. The act of detaching from everyday consciousness is termed dissociation. Dissociative states are usually associated with pathology such as conversion disorders in medicine and psychiatry, but there is a great range of dissociative states, some of which are highly complex and predispose to positive outcomes rather than dysfunction.[305]

Anton Mesmer was the first to use dissociative states in a secular manner to promote the flow of energy for healing. He is well known for his development of 'animal magnetism' in eighteenth century Europe and he used his flamboyant personality to amplify the hypnotic effect he exerted on his subjects. It seems clear with hindsight that his patients developed a powerful transference to him and this 'rapport' was an important component of his cures. Liz Greene gives a hilarious account of him at the height of his powers in Paris when he was visited by two members of the French Society of Medicine:

> In the center of room stood a 'bacquet', a big tub full of magnetized water bristling with metal rods. Dozens of women stood with a hand on one of the rods, some of them fainting, some of them convulsing, some shrieking and crying and some staring blankly in a state of trance. Some were being carried off by assistants to the padded crisis rooms. All the while, music poured out from a small chamber orchestra; and over this Neptunian bacchanalia presided Mesmer, dressed in a cloak of gold lace and purple silk suit, occasionally joining the musicians on his glass harmonica. All this was rather too much for the gentleman of the society. What was worse, the patients were getting better.[306]

Mesmer had found a way of not only inducing dissociative states but also using the setting to amplify the results. His method was obviously powerful but the forces that he was working with remained mysterious. Mesmer suggested an invisible, universally distributed fluid that flowed continuously everywhere and served as a vehicle for the mutual influence among living creatures, including planet Earth as well as the heavenly bodies. He thought that problems arose when the natural flow of this energy was blocked and that he used his animal magnetism to free the blockages. Nowadays we know that there is no such invisible fluid, but we could use similar terminology to describe the interconnectivity of the quantum world. Mesmer was describing an energetic process and he had discovered a way to work with it.

Mesmer was a doctor who was able to charge high prices for his treatments, presumably because they were effective. He was not primarily in the business of growth and self-discovery; such matters were left to the Church in those days. It is assumed that Mesmer, like Charcot and Freud who followed in his footsteps, was working with hysterical patients who were highly suggestible and who suffered physical symptoms with no organic basis (medically unexplained symptoms).

There is an interesting relationship between hysteria and spirituality. Freud came to the conclusion that disorders of psycho-sexual development were responsible for hysteria, especially the unresolved Oedipus complex. According to Freudians, the classic hysteric tends to dissociate his or her developing sexuality into an idealized object, typically religion or some transcendent idea. Simply put, it is easier to find a psychic retreat in God rather than face the messy turbulent journey of sexuality.

The psychoanalyst Christopher Bollas offers a model of St. Francis as an ascetic hysteric. Francis was doted on by his parents until he disappointed his father by suffering a failure of nerve when he was on the verge of becoming a soldier and facing battle. The intention was that he would be welcomed home as a returning hero from a glorious war, but instead he was publically humiliated in the village square before disrobing and standing naked before everyone. He is said to have had a vision before embracing poverty, becoming an ascetic and forming his Franciscan order. Bollas suggests that his asceticism allowed him to refuse his sexuality and repudiate his father while joining his idealized father in the spiritual world and identifying with role of the mother infant dyad in the form of Mary and Jesus.[307] Bollas reminds us that the religion of Christianity has an inherently hysterical structure with a denial of parental intercourse and the Virgin birth.

These are points that need to be made, but psychoanalysis tends to be blind to numinous experience and most of us would find it an overly reductionist viewpoint to dismiss Francis as a hysteric without acknowledging that he developed other qualities of the highest order. Dissociative states may be sometimes associated with pathology but an ability to dissociate to some extent from everyday reality is a prerequisite to engage in a richer archetypal landscape. However, to be effective and helpful the dissociation needs to be completely reversible. If we return briefly to the allegory of Plato's cave, perhaps Mesmer and the Grofs discovered methods of allowing people to briefly detach themselves from their fixed position looking at the shadows allowing them some moments of exposure to sunlight. Providing the exposure is carefully managed, avoiding over exposure and managing the re-entry properly, the experience seems beneficial.

The Neptune Archetype

The theme of suggestibility, as a powerful factor in human behavior, needs further exploration. I have sometimes wondered if the transpersonal movement is a set of over-valued ideas that has developed a momentum supported by the coalescence of a group identity around certain valued ideas and experiences. Perhaps it is merely a fantasy of a group of creative and inspired veterans of the psychedelic era creating a New-Age paradigm that weaves Eastern mysticism with quantum physics as an alternative to the prevailing culture. The movement cross-fertilises itself as reputations are made, books are written and conferences are organised. There is an intriguing promise of revolutionary new paradigms that draws new recruits. There is a shared adventure, a feeling of closeness with fellow pioneers and a beguiling mystical flavour.

The British surgeon Wilfred Trotter brought us the concept of the 'herd instinct' where selected ideas become favoured. As people gather and subscribe to these ideas, a momentum develops and the ideas often crystallise into beliefs. The point that Trotter emphasised was that it is the accumulated social momentum that gives these ideas their gravitas and weight, but this does not necessarily mean that they are correct. Could the transpersonal movement be essentially the product of suggestion, perhaps even mass hysteria?

The archetype traditionally represented by Neptune, the Roman god of the sea, is associated with the yearning to go beyond the separate self and to become part of something greater. Neptune is the driving archetype of the transpersonal movement, although many other archetypal currents play a role. Neptune stands for that tantalising pull to the numinous, the spiritual ache and hunger for the sacred. Neptune dissolves ego boundaries and pulls towards an oceanic state of fusion. Indeed, Grof reports that many a fruitful collaboration was born as people relaxed in the hot springs on the Esalen estate, with a blurring of boundaries in a warm Neptunian bath full of spiritual promise.[308] There is a Neptunian flavour in the infant's wish to merge with the primary object and in our spiritual need to merge with the divine. High-intensity archetypal experiences with a Neptunian flavour have a numinous component that may help the ego function achieve a higher octave or may lead to spiritual confusion, delusion, or ego inflation.

Neptune has a tendency to dissolve the necessary structures of ideas and relationships; indeed, people in the grip of this archetype can rid themselves of more structure than is wise. One of the complications of a powerful spiritual opening can be the reckless jettison of structure, whether relationship, career or wealth. Real damage can result and the shadow side of the Neptune archetype is associated with broken families, alcoholism, substance abuse, codependence and other forms of escapism.[309]

The pull of the Neptune archetype draws people to retreats and to methods such as holotropic breathwork. The power of the yearning for the sacred predisposes to gullibility and it is easy to understand how this archetype combines with a person's psychological vulnerabilities and an intoxicating environment to produce a highly suggestible state of mind. People looking for a powerful message tend to find teachers ready and willing to deliver that message in authoritative style, which in turn shapes the seeker's experience of non-ordinary state of consciousness. These experiences are then fed back to the group as evidence in favour of the concept and the momentum of the movement accumulates. When ideas crystallise into beliefs supported by a community, it can become a new religious movement. Such movements tend to reflect the personality of the leader, which is often deeply pathological, so they often show authoritarian power structures, the use of splitting and the disowning and projection of shadow.

Grof cannot be faulted as a man of incomparable intellect and experience combined with impressive integrity, decency and compassion. But he is an enormously powerful transference figure and people attending his workshops and retreats often want to please him and be noticed by him. He speaks for long periods in his rich sonorous voice showing archetypally powerful images, often on the theme of the perinatal process. It is not surprising that many people report experiences in the holotropic breathwork sessions that mirror the material that he has been bringing them. In order to catch his attention, it would not be difficult to elaborate an experience that he would find of interest. This would not necessarily be done consciously or with intention but I have wondered if some of the detail of transpersonal experience described by Grof has been influenced by reports of sessions from suggestible breathers who want to interest and please him. The question inevitably arises as to whether holotropic breathwork is context dependent. Do the experiences that people report in holotropic breathwork flow from a herd instinct shaped by Grof's charisma and the power of his suggestion?

So I was particularly interested in the experiences of first timers in holotropic breathwork who have no prior expectations. They may have a polite interest and an open mind but are not inclined to a spiritual perspective and they have not heard Grof speak or read his books. The first timer may be an engineer or businessman perhaps, who comes to a holotropic breathwork session to accompany his wife. She may be a psychotherapist interested in potential new treatments. These are solid citizens who are experienced, grounded and highly functional in everyday life. I have found that it is often these people who have the most profound and surprising experiences. On one occasion, I was co-facilitating a holotropic breathwork workshop where all the people attending the workshop were first timers and had not had exposure to holotropic breathwork before. They listened to the usual introductory talk outlining the structure of the workshop and how to proceed in the breathwork sessions, but had no other instruction. I wondered how their experiences would compare with those of regular breathers who have developed a model and expectation.

I was surprised to find that the experiences these first timers reported had the same range that I had heard many times before in the training retreats reported by experienced breathers. Most of these people experienced a reliving of emotionally loaded events in their lives followed by a sense of relief and resolution and one person, much to his surprise, went through a classical perinatal sequence. A psychotherapist described a strong spiritual feeling followed by the revelation that the psyche was so much complex and multi layered than she had previously thought. The husband, the man who had come to keep his wife company, reported an experience of going to an inter-life zone before his birth and being reluctant to leave that serene place in order to join the gestating fetus and start his life. Another person reported an experience of being killed on a First World War battlefield with enormous reluctance and rage at leaving life behind only to find himself in a beautiful homeland where the physical and mental pain were replaced by a feeling that was beautiful beyond words. Such experiences are paradigm changing for those who undergo them and for those who hear about them.

What are we to make of such experiences and how should we approach them? Do these transpersonal experiences have an ontological reality, are they intrapsychic phenomena, or are they a mixture of the two domains? Are they cispersonal experiences, like a dream where biographical issues are amplified by archetype, or are they something from beyond the ego altogether? The participatory model articulated by Jorge Ferrer is perhaps the most helpful, suggesting that our individual psyche engages with the deeper collective energies in a co-operative, evolving, mutual engagement in consciousness. From this perspective, suggestion certainly plays a role in inducing and shaping the content, but we are participating in spheres of being and awareness that transcend the merely human and belong to an entirely different order.[310]

Pitfalls and Side Effects

There is an innate tension in any numinous encounter between regression and progression. Regression represents the gullible dissolution of ego structures, often to avoid some necessary developmental tasks. In psychiatric clinics I sometimes found that, when people profess to be 'spiritual', it really meant that they are abdicating from the responsibility to work and function like an independent adult. These are not people who have had a career or fulfilled social obligations, but people who are seeking a life of childlike dependency. For them, the term *spiritual* means a regressed state rather than a progressive state. In retreat settings people are not infrequently encountered who have emotional and interpersonal problems that I believe would be better addressed by more traditional psychotherapy to help them to develop more coherent ego structures. Essentially, in seeking a retreat, they are having the wrong psychological treatment. Sometimes they have the fantasy, which may be reinforced by the retreat leaders, that the spiritual path is all that is required and they do not need to do the gritty hard work of examining their problematic interpersonal and personality issues. This is unlikely to be correct; developmental problems are rarely be solved by numinous experience; indeed, the fragile ego structures may be further compromised.

The primary side effects of the transpersonal journey are narcissism and failures of integration. While we may all be subject to these pitfalls occasionally and to some extent; any regular participant in retreats will be familiar with a minority of self-absorbed people who believe others will share their fascination with their own internal processes, those who believe they have a special spiritual purpose, those who have built rigid belief systems onto their transpersonal experiences and those who become over-identified with their experiences.

Spiritual narcissism is a condition in which spiritual energies, practices or experiences are misused to bolster self-centred ways of being. There are three broad categories:

- Ego inflation—the aggrandizement of ego fuelled by spiritual energies
- Self absorption—over-preoccupation with one's spiritual status and achievement
- Spiritual materialism—the strengthening of egocentricity through spiritual techniques.[311]

Compassion and humility are the polar opposites of this type of narcissism. Any genuine spiritual growth will involve compassion and service as an integral component. What after all is the point of personal growth unless it has some use to other people too?[312]

Kansas Transformed

The final archetypal journey in this book will be with Dorothy in the classic movie *The Wizard of Oz*. I have chosen this film to illustrate the process that I believe occurs during the serious cumulative engagement with non-ordinary states of consciousness that would occur in a practice such as holotropic breathwork. *The Wizard of Oz* is above all a story of transformation, as a developing personal crisis in a traumatised child flows into a high archetypal penetrance state. There is an engagement with shadow in the form of the Wicked Witch, which becomes diminished and replaced by a positive energy. Previously disowned parts of personality — represented by the scarecrow, the tin man and the lion — are restored and the quality of life, after the return to ordinary reality, is greatly enhanced. This story, well known to all generations, is a version of the heroine's journey. Although we may identify with Dorothy as the primary character representing the ego, we should regard every character and scenario in the movie as representing an important aspect of us. The movie, taken in its totality, with all its various characters, represents the larger version of our psyche.

The story begins with Dorothy living on a farm in the bleak and featureless world of Kansas, depicted in black and white. Dorothy is an orphan, brought up by her uncle and aunt who never laugh; their humour has been baked out of them by the sun and the toil. It is a depressing place to be. There is not much love in her life and her main attachment figure is her dog Toto who has twinkly eyes. But she faces losing Toto and she is in a state of great distress. A sudden, unexpected, uncontrollable energy arrives in the shape of a tornado. She tries to take refuge in the cellar but she is hit on the head. The transformative journey begins with a dissociation from Kansas as she enters into a non-ordinary state.

Dorothy awakes to find herself in a Technicolor world of great beauty that is very different to the world she left behind. Her collapsing house has killed a wicked witch liberating a miniature people, the Munchkins, from her tyranny. This symbolises an end to repression for those little voices clamouring for freedom. But there is a long road ahead, which is sometimes pleasant but often frightening and dangerous. A good witch, an anima figure, offers support and magical help, but Dorothy has to make her own journey to see the great wizard of Oz, who is the only one who has the power to send her home. The way is clearly marked by the yellow brick road, which represents the golden path to individuation. Along the way she meets three allies who are damaged, but who want to be made whole: the scarecrow that wants a brain, the tin man who wants his heart, and the lion who wants to find courage.

The journey becomes dark and threatening as Dorothy and Toto are captured and face death by the wicked witch. This is the crucial encounter with the shadow and the challenge of ego death as the cast face many trials and dangers. But, eventually, the witch simply melts away when Dorothy finally confronts her and throws water over her. The Wizard of Oz, who stands for the overweening ego, refuses to grant them passage home but he is revealed by Toto to have little substance after all; he is a fraud. He is just an ordinary middle-aged man once he is stripped of his persona. He agrees to grant them their wishes and they are able to return home at last. Home.

Dorothy's transformative journey is completed. She is back in Kansas again, but this is now a Kansas with colour and vitality. It is not Kansas that has changed—it is her perception of it. As her traumas have healed, she is able to participate with Kansas in an entirely different way. There has been a positive transfiguration—even her aunt is smiling and loving. Moreover, her friends have found those gifts that they most desired and needed; they have become more whole versions of themselves. The scarecrow finds his brain, the tin man his heart and the lion his courage. The frightening figures that loomed large in the psyche have been faced and have lost their power. The shadow has been encountered and the cast has rediscovered those essential qualities that they were missing. A new balance has been found and they all live happily ever after.

Last Word

There is one thing that must never be forgotten.

If you were to forget everything else, but remember this, there is no cause to worry. While if you remember and attend to everything else but forget this one thing, you have in fact achieved nothing. It is if a king had sent you to a country to carry out one special specific task. You go to the country and do many things, good things but if you don't carry out the task which you were sent for, it as if you have achieved nothing at all. So man has come into the world for a particular task, and that is his purpose.

If he doesn't perform this he will have done nothing.

—Rumi

NOTES

1. I have chosen to omit a discussion of archetypal cosmology, which some would argue is an important aspect of the relationship between archetype and psyche. I refer interested readers to the seminal books by Tarnas (*Cosmos and Psyche)*, Le Grice (*The Archetypal Cosmos*) and Butler (*Pathways to Wholeness).*
2. Wolfe, *The Electric Kool Aid Acid Test.* 44
3. The Royal London Hospital at this time was the site of the specialist trauma unit serving greater London and was the base for the Helicopter Emergency Ambulance Service (HEMS).
4. This type of depression, which is more like an illness, is a constant unremitting depression with the loss of enjoyment (anhedonia) often with biological symptoms such as early waking and loss of appetite and libido as well as the cognitive symptoms of depression such as ideas of hopelessness, worthlessness and life not being worth living.
5. Bucke's cases include Jesus, Mohammed, Buddha, Loa Tzu, Dante, Blake, Tennyson and Bacon. Bucke himself had a similar experience as did some of his contemporaries. His book is striking for its tendency to hyperbole as well as its optimism—being written before the collective engagement in shadow of the 20th Century.
6. For example Isobel Clarke (ed) , *Psychosis and Spirituality*.
7. Catherine Lucas describes the lives of various saints who have passed through psychological crisis in her book *In Case of Spiritual Emergency*.
8. James, *The Varieties of Religious Experience.* 388.
9. I follow the lead of Stanislav Grof with the use of this terminology and the use of the abbreviation NOSC.
10. For example the mesolimbic system in the brain, mediated predominantly by dopamine.
11. Huxley, *The Doors of Perception.* 12–13
12. Oxford Dictionary.
13. Otto, *The Idea of the Holy*.
14. ibid 132

15. ibid 12–40
16. Whitehead, *Process and Reality.* 39
17. Armstrong, *The Great Transformation.*
18. Waterfield, Plato. The Republic. 335
19. Tarnas, *The Passion of the Western Mind.* 4
20. Waterfield, Plato. *The Republic.*
21. I will describe the views as belonging to Plato rather than Socrates although Plato uses Socrates as the narrator in his book
22. Since childhood, but not since birth. This implies that it is not their natural birthright but is imposed by conditioning.
23. Tarnas, *Cosmos and Psyche.* 81
24. I am indebted to Charles Tart for the term 'endarkenment'.
25. Jung, *Memories, Dreams, Reflections.* 217
26. David Cronenberg's film, *A Dangerous Method,* stars Keira Knightley as Sabina Spielrein, Viggo Mortensen as Freud and Michael Fassbender as Jung
27. Jung, Memories, Dreams, Reflections. 191
28. ibid 192
29. ibid 201
30. Harner, *The Way of the Shaman.*
31. The subtitle is 'seven exhortations to the dead, written by Basilides in Alexandria, the city where East and West meet'. See Stephen Hoeller's *The Gnostic Jung and the Seven Sermons of the Dead.*
32. Gnosis; the knowledge of transcendence arrived at by way of intuition.
33. McLynn, *Carl Gustav Jung: A Biography.* 242
34. ibid 243
35. Shamsadani. S. *Jung. C.G. Liber Novus: The Red Book.*
36. Jung, *Memories, Dreams, Reflections.* 218
37. I am guided by memories of regular monthly discussions with my Consultant Psychiatrist colleagues, in busy clinical practice in East London, where we brought our most complex cases for discussion. I consider these meetings to represent the best model of evidence-based, sensible and considered modern psychiatric opinion.
38. ICD10 and DSM4
39. The Mental Health Act in England and Wales allows for the compulsory admission to hospital if a person is deemed to be mentally ill in a manner that is potentially harmful to either themself or others.
40. Retreat at the Sacred Trust Centre. www.sacredtrust.org

41. ECT worked especially well for severe depression and less well for other psychotic illnesses. As there were no other treatments that had a specific effect on mental illness, it was over prescribed to avoid undertreating patients who may possibly have benefitted from it. Psychiatry has a long history of the inappropriate use of physical treatments, for example the use of insulin coma in the 1950s.
42. Strong hashish, often used for devotional purposes
43. Severe depressions are complex, highly charged, archetypal states with profound feelings of guilt, hopelessness and entrapment – so this classification has limitations.
44. Campbell, *The Hero with a Thousand Faces.* 2
45. Le Grice, *The Rebirth of the Hero.* 5
46. Richard Tarnas' seminal book *Cosmos and Psyche,* tracks archetypal currents through history, how they can dominate perspectives in groups of people, stimulate revolution, creativity and spirituality.
47. Alison, *Undergoing God: Dispatches from the Scene of a Break-In.* 33-49
48. It is less of a puzzle with bipolar disorder where there is increasing evidence of a link between creativity and a genetic susceptibility to mood disorders.
49. Laing, Transcendental experience in relation to religion and psychosis. 1965. Psychedelic Review 6: 7–15
50. Maslow, *Religion, Values and Peak Experiences.*
51. Schizoaffective disorder is a recurrent condition with mood disturbance combined with schizophrenic symptoms within the same episode of illness. It is considered to have features of both schizophrenia and bipolar disorder although sufferers do not develop the dementia praecox of chronic schizophrenia
52. Bion, W.R. Attacks on linking. International Journal of Psycho-Analysis 1959. 40: 308-315
53. Kammerer, *Das Gesetz der Serie. Versags-Anhalt.* This book was never translated into English.
54. Combs & Holland, *Synchronicity: Science, Myth and the Trickster.* 5
55. Von Franz, *C.G. Jung. His Myth in Our Time.* 247
56. Tarnas, *Cosmos and Psyche.* 53
57. Jung, *Synchronicity: An Acausal Connecting Principle.* 22
58. Grof, *When the Impossible Happens.* 8–10
59. St Augustine, *Confessions.* 177
60. Hillman, *Re - Visioning Psychology.* 194–198
61. Tarnas, *Cosmos and Psyche.* 52

62. Koestler, *Janus: A Summing Up.* 270

63. Russell, *The Global Brain.* 214

64. ibid 214

65. A Jungian friend suggested this woman represented an anima figure.

66. Wilber, (Ed) *Quantum Questions.* 51

67. Heisenberg, Schroedinger, Einstein, de Broglie, Jeans, Planck, Pauli and Eddington.

68. Jeans, *The Mysterious Universe.* 134

69. The classics of this genre are *The Tao of Physics* by Fritjof Capra and *The Dancing Wu-Li Masters* by Gary Zukav.

70. Bohm follows the tradition of panpsychism, considering that an element of mind is inherent in all physical material. Eminent philosophers such as Liebniz, Schopenhauer and Whitehead held a panpsychism perspective, but it is Bohm who puts it in a quantum physics framework and gives us a model of how physical and non physical domains may fit together.

71. Bohm and Krishnamurti, *The Ending of Time.*

72. Newton's universe was three-dimensional. Einstein's space-time universe was four-dimensional as all measurements depend on speed. Bohm's universe is five-dimensional adding meaning to space-time.

73. Bohm D and Weber R *The Search for Unity. Dialogues with Scientists and Sages.* 152. I am grateful to Mark Schroll for highlighting this.

74. There may even be states where consciousness is decoupled from the brain, such as the near death experience.

75. Schroll, Mark. 2013. Understanding Bohm's Holoflux. International Journal of Consciousness Studies. 32 (1) 140–163

76. Plotinus developed a more religious version of Plato's ideas. According to Plotinus, everything emanates from 'the One' with the primal energy dispersing through the cosmos as light disperses from a candle. Our material world is in the lower reaches of the hierarchy but man has the potential either to rise towards the One or to stay bound in the lower reaches of the spectrum of consciousness. Plotinus describes a participatory vision with a continuing outflow of this primal energy which permeates our material world and animates our bodies, followed by a gradual ascent of this energy back to the One as part of the philosopher's journey.

77. The psychoanalyst Melanie Klein termed this the 'paranoid schizoid' position.

78. This is a complicated and much debated area. Wilber has coined the phrase pre / trans fallacy to describe the manner in which the prepersonal may be mistaken for the transpersonal.
79. Foulkes, *Therapeutic Group Analysis*.
80. Bem, D. J., & Honorton, C. 1994. Does psi exist? Replicable evidence for an anomalous process of information transfer. Psychological Bulletin', 115, 4–18
81. Sheldrake, *The Science Delusion*. 239
82. Tart, *The End of Materialism*. 12
83. Dean Radin's books and website are good starting points for those who wish to make their own investigation of the research evidence.
84. See Dean Radin's google talk on youtube.
85. Ben Goldacre is highly informative on these subjects with his website, articles and books, *Bad Science* and *Bad Pharma*.
86. Sheldrake, *The Science Delusion*.
87. Kuhn, *The Structure of Scientific Revolutions*.
88. Turing, Alan. 1950. *Computing machinery and intelligence*. Mind 59. 433-460. Quoted by Dean Radin in *Entangled Minds* p73
89. http://www.huffingtonpost.com/ross-robertson/the-inner-life-nature-and_b_339016.html
90. A psychoanalytic perspective on climate change is put forward by Sally Weintrobe (editor) *Engaging with Climate Change*.
91. Anderton, *Christopher Lloyd: His Life at Great Dixter*.
92. Until 1967 when he was 46
93. Richard Bucke in his study of 50 cases of cosmic consciousness found that a disproportionate amount of these numinous moments occurred in spring or early summer.
94. These forces of constriction, stasis and suffocation are often associated with the Saturn archetype.
95. A Consultant position is the most senior medical rank in the hospital hierarchy in the UK. To become a Consultant it is necessary to qualify as a doctor of medicine and undergo general medical and surgical training followed by up to 10 years in postgraduate training in the chosen specialty. A Consultant Psychiatrist provides clinical leadership, supervision and training to the team, usually covering a specific geographical area and its inhabitants.
96. Those days are now gone. Although physical psychiatric treatments have not advanced much, the methods of engaging with patients and providing continuity of care have advanced enormously.
97. It was not uncommon for the psychiatrist in charge of clinical decision making to be an academic professor doing a token day or

so of clinical work a week. This professor may have done high quality research on dopamine receptors, brain imaging or some such, but would have poorly developed clinical skills and no great interest in therapeutic work. This scenario is much less common nowadays.

98. Winnicott, *Collected Papers: Hate in the Countertransference*
99. So called because the doctor would feel their heart sink when the patient walks into the consulting room. A classic example of a challenging countertransference.
100. Delusional mood is one of the 'first rank symptoms' described by Schneider as indicative of schizophrenia.
101. Dick Price was one of the founders of the Esalen Institute. This quote is from an interview conducted by Wade Hudson in April 1985.
102. Diagnostic and Statistical Manual (DSM) and International Classification of Disease (ICD)
103. Grof & Grof, (eds) *Spiritual Emergency.* 104
104. ibid 102
105. ibid 181
106. Sannella, *The Kundalini experience: Psychosis or Transcendence.*
107. Eastman, David T. 1985. Kundalini Demystified. Yoga Journal, 39, California Yoga Teachers Association.
108. Ritual postures in yoga.
109. Grof & Grof, *Spiritual Emergency.* 105
110. Kornfield, *A Path with a Heart. A Guide through the Perils and Promises of a Spiritual Life.* 129
111. Blackwell, *Am I Bipolar or Just Waking Up?* xi
112. http://www.spiritualcompetency.com/dsm4/dsmrsproblem.pdf
113. Grof & Grof, Spiritual Emergency. x–xi
114. ibid xiii
115. The classic version is Thomas Mallory's medieval 'La Morte d'Arthur', which is probably derived from various older sources.
116. Emma Jung, wife of C.G.Jung was a life long student of Arthurian mythology. Her book *The Grail Legend* was published after her death and was co authored by Marie-Louise Von Franz. It remains the definitive account of the symbolism of the Arthurian age.
117. Jung, *Collected Works Volume 8,* 414
118. Easwaran, *The Bhagavad Gita.* 24
119. ibid 24
120. For a comprehensive discussion of these issues see – Jorge Ferrer, *Revisioning Transpersonal Theory.*
121. Campbell, *The Hero of a Thousand Faces.*

122. Shakespeare, *Julius Caesar* Act 4, scene 3, 218–224
123. Bettelheim, *The Uses of Enchantment.*
124. A contemporary and much darker version of this is the phenomenon of the young Western Muslims flocking to the black banner of Is.
125. Kornfield, In Grof and Grof (eds). *Spiritual Emergency.* 140
126. Ovid. *Metamorphosis.* 109–116
127. Daniels, *Shadow, Self, Spirit.*
128. Steiner, *Psychic Retreats.*
129. Walach, Harold. Narcissism, the Shadow of Transpersonal Psychology. Transpersonal Psychology review. 2008. 12: 47–59
130. Glasser, *Some Aspects of the Role of Aggression in the Perversions. In Sexual Deviations.* (ed I Rosen) 278–305
131. Psychoanalytic theory would usually understand more mature spiritual yearnings in functional adults as a projection of the desire to merge with the breast.
132. Grof & Grof, Spiritual emergency. 34
133. ibid 36
134. This is the Kleinian psychoanalytic perspective.
135. The psychoanalyst Melanie Klein pioneered the psychoanalysis of children and developed the understanding of the infantile psyche. Her seminal work *'Our Adult World and Its Roots in Infancy'* is one of the most influential psychoanalytic papers.
136. I refer to the universal construct of evil rather than the relativist construct of evil where one man's freedom fighters are another man's terrorists. Michael Daniels in *Self, Shadow Spirit* and Grof in *The Cosmic Game* have both explored the concept of evil in detail.
137. Von Franz, *Projection and Re-collection in Jungian Psychology*: 19.
138. Para neoplastic syndrome is a condition where a primary cancer causes effects at a different bodily site due to hormones or cytokines rather than metastases. Neurological syndromes due to para neoplastic syndrome are very difficult to treat.
139. Although sometimes women collude with the abuse.
140. For Jung, the Self includes the dark side so the shadow does not oppose or compensate for the Self, but is an aspect of it.
141. Jung, *Collected Works of C. G. Jung.* 10, para. 19. This is apparently the only reference Jung makes to absolute evil and the only mention of absolute evil in the General Index to the Collected Works of C. G. Jung.
142. The ancient Greeks thought that such an inner voice or *daimon* was an entity somewhere between the gods and mortals.

143. Elenor Longden has given an excellent account of this process in a TED talk. http://www.ted.com/talks/eleanor_longden_the_voices_in_my_headwww.ted.com/talks/eleanor_longden_the_voices_in_my_head

144. There are some honorable exceptions where high quality psychological work of this nature is carried out in mental health units. Funding is always an issue.

145. In the same study, 77% did not have residual psychotic symptoms. Only 14% remained on disability allowance. These outcomes were achieved despite only 29% of clients using antipsychotic medication during this time.

146. Seikkula, J., Alakare, B., Haarakangas, K., Keränen, J., Lehtinen, K., & Aaltonen, J. Five years experiences of first-contact non-affective psychosis in open dialogue approach: Treatment principles, follow-up outcomes and two case studies. Psychotherapy Research, 2006. 16(2): 214–228.

147. Friedman, (Ed.). *The Reflecting Team in Action.*

148. Stein, *Jung's Map of the Soul.* 107

149. Julian Leff, Geoffrey Williams, Mark A. Huckvale, Maurice Arbuthnot, and Alex P. Leff. Computer-assisted therapy for medication-resistant auditory hallucinations: proof-of-concept study. BJP June 2013 202: 428–433;

150. Hill, *Confrontation with the Unconscious.* 74

151. ibid xiv

152. Keiron Le Grice gives a succinct outline of the alchemical process in *The Rebirth of the Hero.* 179–183.

153. Dean Radin gives an account of how these global archetypal events may be measurable. A dozen people in the USA and Europe who had random number generators (RNGs) ran them before, during and after Diana's state funeral. RNGs are programmed to give an equal amount of heads or tails or 0 or 1 but they found that the RNG had deviated significantly from the mean with odds against chance of 100 to 1. Stimulated by these anomalous results, the Global Consciousness Project was set up using RNGs around the world to test whether other high intensity events caused statistically significant deviations from the mean. The work can be viewed online and the results so far show that when a great event synchronises the feelings of millions of people, the network of RNGs becomes subtly structured.

154. There is some evidence that the severe form of anorexia is associated with some brain changes that may be a scarring effect flowing

from the illness or a possible predisposing factor. There may be some overlap with autistic spectrum disorder.

155. Lawrence Marilyn, Loving them to Death: Anorexia and her Objects. International Journal of Psychoanalysis. 2001. 82: 43–55.
156. This case in 2012 was widely reported n the press and divided opinion as to whether the Judge's intervention was appropriate.
157. Armstrong, *The Great Transformation.* 194
158. Pranayama is the name for controlled yogic breathing. There are many forms of this practice.
159. Groves, *Practical Buddhism.*
160. Catherine Lucas gives an account of the lives of Hildegard of Bingen and Teresa of Avila in her book *In Case of Spiritual Emergency.*
161. Lamb (tr), *Blessed Raymond of Capua, The Life of St. Catherine of Siena,* tr. Rockford, Illinois: TAN Books, 2003
162. I am greatly indebted to Alexandra Pittock for this perspective on anorexia. Her original paper on this subject, written when she was a medical student, was posted on the Psychiatry and Spirituality website of the Royal College of Psychiatrists. How are anorexia nervosa and spirituality connected, and what implications does this have for treatment? www.rcpsych.ac.uk.
163. I suspect that a deeper archetypal treatment such as holotropic breathwork could be a valuable adjunct to treatment for some people with anorexia nervosa. There has been no research in the use of HB for anorexia as yet.
164. Jung coined the terms *anima* and *animus* to describe the contra sexual principles that mediate to some extent between consciousness and the unconscious Self.
165. It seems to me that Jung's notion of the anima has to be considered within his personal context. He was a product of an age where gender roles were more stereotyped, society was more patriarchal and women were rarely permitted to vote. In Jung's native Switzerland, women's suffrage was not passed until after his death in 1971. Jung was a powerful man, an alpha male and a philanderer. On the other hand, his disciples were predominantly female and his work benefitted from the assistance of brilliant women such as his wife Emma, Toni Wolff, Marie-Louise von Franz and Aniela Jaffe. Any process of individuation for Jung was always going to involve the difficult breaking down of his patriarchal ego and an integration of a softer, more fertile and creative principle.

166. Le Grice explains how the shield of Perseus symbolises the clear reflective nature of consciousness illuminating the shadow. The myth does not represent the slaying of a feminine principle but the necessary slaying of the ego's domination by instincts so that a relationship can be developed with a higher feminine principle.
167. Washburn, *The Ego and the Dynamic Ground.*
168. Grof & Grof, *Spiritual Emergency.* 38
169. Readers who are psychiatrists may share my concern that Stefan had a mild form of bipolar disorder. I got to know Stefan well; he was quite happy to answer my questions and there was no evidence of the acceleration, elation or decreased need for sleep. I don't think he was bipolar.
170. Nelson, *Healing the Split.*
171. The Psychiatry and Spirituality Special Interest Group of the Royal College of Psychiatrists was founded by Dr Andrew Powell in 1999. Dr Paramabandhu Groves is the current chair. The group has a membership of over 1500 psychiatrists.
172. Andrew Powell. Love and the Near Life Experience. www.rcpsych. ac.uk
173. Wilber, *A Brief History of Everything.*
174. Huxley, *Visionary Experience in Moksha.*
175. Radin, *Supernormal.*
176. Nelson, *Healing the Split.* 312
177. The dismemberment motif occurs frequently in mythology, such as the death of Dionysus. It also occurs in shamanic journeying.
178. Wikman, *Pregnant Darkness.*
179. Bion Francesca. The days of our years. 1994. http://www.psycho-analysis.org.uk/days.htm
180. Vermote, R. On the value of 'late Bion' to analytic theory and practice. International Journal of Psychoanalysis 2011. vol 92 (5) 1089–1116
181. The same ideas could be applied to those mutative group events representing a mid life crisis of the nation state with revolutionary change birthed in the main squares of the great capital cities of sclerotic states where rebirth is required.
182. Job is often capitalized by police officers to denote the primacy and all consuming nature of the Police force in their lives. Capitalized Job is the big picture, with an archetypal quality, which is different from job, which is mundane.
183. This is a condition where people have physical symptoms that are not explained by physical pathology and the conclusion is that psychological issues are the main cause.

184. Freud, *Mourning and Melancholia* XVII
185. ibid 46
186. ibid 95
187. This is different to the stages of labour as described by obstetricians and midwives
188. Reprinted with permission of Stanislav Grof.
189. My birth was straightforward and quick. I suspect that I was able to retain these memories as the trauma was not overwhelming. It raises questions about the dreams and memories of trauma that babies and small children may suffer from. Perhaps babies do not wake up screaming at night just because they are hungry.
190. Nowadays modern SSRI and SNRI antidepressants are almost always successful in treating severe depression. ECT is very rarely used except in life threatening situations such as catatonic states or advanced malnutrition.
191. The place of deep unbearable pain as an archetypal quality is often compared to Chiron of Greek mythology, who used his pain to become a great healer.
192. Greene, *Relating: An Astrological Guide to Living with Others on a Small Planet.*
193. Grof, Personal Communication.
194. Grof, *Realms of the Human Unconscious.* 64
195. Huston Smith, *Tales of Wonder.* 47
196. Menzies Lyth, *Containing Anxiety in Institutions.*
197. Delirium tremens or DTs is a withdrawal state characterised by confusion and vivid frightening visual hallucinations. The DTs are associated with medical complications and can be fatal if not medically supported. Alcoholic hallucinosis is characterised by hallucinatory voices while intoxicated with alcohol, but the patient is not confused and the condition is not medically dangerous apart from the effects of the alcohol.
198. Grossman, *Life and Fate.* 825
199. Groves, *Practical Buddhism.* 28
200. British Medical Journal. 2013;347 f6192
201. Ballatt &Campling, *Intelligent Kindness.*
202. Healthcare Commission 2009. The Investigation into the Mid Staffordshire NHS Foundation Trust.
203. Ballatt &Campling. 189
204. Greene, *Saturn. A New Look at an Old Devil.* 10
205. Butler, *Pathways to Wholeness.*
206. *The Tempest*
207. Evans-Wentz, *The Tibetan Book of the Dead*

208. Sogyal Rinpoche, *The Tibetan Book of Living and Dying*, x

209. ibid, 7

210. The literature on NDEs begins with Plato's *Myth of Er*, but Moody's seminal book *Life after Life* in 1975 began the modern era. The Dutch cardiologist Pim van Lommel's *Consciousness Beyond Life* is recommended. The OBE literature includes the three books by Robert Monroe which paint a similar picture of an afterlife to that described by David Fontana in *Is There an Afterlife*. Michael Harner offers a shamanic perspective in *Cosmos and Cave*. Elizabeth Kubler Ross wrote the first book of the modern era examining the process of death in 1969. Sogyal Rinpoche's *The Tibetan Book of Living and Dying* emphasizes the importance of the mindset approaching death while Peter and Elizabeth Fenwick provide a Western perspective exploring the process of dying based on research in hospices.

211. Stevenson, *Children Who Remember Past Lives*. Tucker, *Life Before Life*.

212. ibid, 20.

213. ibid, 21.

214. Little James had three GI dolls who he named Billy, Leon and Walter, saying that they had met him in Heaven after he died. It turned out that these names belonged to three pilots from the Natoma Bay who had died before him. They were called Billy Peeler, Leon Connor and Walter Devlin.

215. Leininger, Andrea and Bruce, *Soul Survivor: The Reincarnation of a World War II Fighter Pilot*, 157

216. From Shelley's *Adonaïs: An Elegy on the Death of John Keats*

217. The book *Proof of Heaven* by the neurosurgeon Eben Alexander and the film *Heaven is for Real*, released in 2014, gives further impetus to the popular awareness of NDEs.

218. The Temple of the Tooth is the pre-eminent Buddhist temple in Sri Lanka, situated in the city of Kandy.

219. Jung, *Memories, Dreams, Reflections*, 320–329.

220. She wrote the original in German, which had become her first language and she translated it into her native English, which had become a third (after Spanish and German) and somewhat unfamiliar language.

221. The angel could also be understood as a symbol of Self.

222. The classical technique for the management of suffering was taught by the Buddha with the four noble truths and the eightfold path.

223. There is debate as to whether this innate tendency is mediated by brain alone or by a combination of brain and non-physical processes.

224. Ram Dass, *Still Here: Embracing Aging, Changing and Dying*.

225. This is not inevitable – meditation can be used to strengthen ego and promote repression – as always it depends on mindset, setting and integration.
226. Vipassana, meaning 'to see things as they really are'.
227. Washburn, *The Ego and the Dynamic Ground.* 167
228. Kabat-Zinn, *Wherever You Go, There You Are.* 4
229. See for an overview: Chris Mace, *Mindfulness and Mental Health.*
230. Developed by Dr Paramabandhu Groves http://www.breathing-spacelondon.org.uk
231. http://www.mindfulexperience.org/evidence-base.php
232. Albeniz, A. & Holmes, J. *Meditation: concepts, effects and uses in therapy.* International Journal of Psychotherapy, 2000. 5: 49–58
233. Kirk, Downer and Montague. Interoception drives increased rational decision making in meditators playing the ultimatum game. Frontiers in Neuroscience. 18.4.2011.
234. Chadwick, Paul. Mindfulness for Psychosis. British Journal of Psychiatry. 2014. 204, 333–334.
235. The retreat was organized by the Sacred Trust - www.sacredtrust.org
236. www.gurdjieff.com
237. Sparks, *Movie Yoga. How Every Film Can Change Your Life.* 34
238. Le Grice, *The Rebirth of the Hero.* 133.
239. The Scientific and Medical Network and the Psychiatry and Spirituality group at the Royal College of Psychiatrists were both helpful.
240. Many psychiatrists would take this view – eg Tom Burns. *Our Necessary Shadow.* 84
241. William James was the first person to use the word 'transpersonal' and the term was reintroduced in the 1960s by Maslow and Grof to define the enhanced model of mind that was emerging from quantum physics, the world's spiritual and wisdom traditions and contemporary LSD research. The prevailing paradigms at the time were behaviourism and psychoanalysis, which seemed inadequate for the understanding of higher qualities such as love, self-consciousness, self-determination, personal freedom, morality, art, philosophy, religion, and science.
242. A criticism of the transpersonal field is that definitions are lacking in clarity and there will be a range of opinion as to what these terms actually mean. This is inevitable given that archetypes are, by nature, ineffable and impossible to accurately describe. But we should nevertheless strive towards some operational definitions.
243. Beyond the Brain organized by the Scientific and Medical Network in Cambridge in the mid 1990s

244. Author of *Pregnant Darkness*.

245. Shamsadani, S. Jung. C.G. *Liber Novus: The Red Book*. 249

246. Harner, *Cave and Cosmos*. 135

247. Sonic drivers in a variety of forms are the usual induction methods for non-ordinary states of consciousness. Christian monks for example would chant together at intervals throughout the day although of course they did not engage in journeying practice.

248. Zoe Bran is a shamanic practitioner based in London: www.shaman.uk.net. Her first book on shamanism, *Where Shamans Go*, is in preparation.

249. Robert Monroe, *Journeys out of the body (1971)*. *Far Journeys* (1985) and *The Ultimate Journey* (1994).

250. Atwater. H Accessing anomalous states of consciousness using binaural technology. Journal of Scientific exploration. 1997. Volume 11 no. 3. article 1

251. For a succinct and comprehensive description of Monroe's model of a post mortem existence, see Christopher Bache, *Dark Night Early Dawn* 128–146

252. Fontana, *Is there an Afterlife?*

253. Huxley, *Moksha*. x

254. As the hydrosphere describes the earth's water and the geosphere the domain of inanimate matter, the noosphere derived from the Latin *nous* describes the zone of mind. The concept of noosphere was popularized by Teilhard de Chardin who considered that it emerged through and was constituted by the interaction of human minds.

255. Burkert, *The Anthropology of Ancient Greece Sacrificial Ritual and Myth*. 91

256. Armstrong, *The Great Transformation*. 185–187

257. Nutt was chair of the Advisory Council on the Misuse of Drugs until his dismissal in 2009. This was followed by resignations from other key personnel on the committee who supported Nutt's endeavor to classify drugs according to evidence of harmfulness. Nutt had commented that alcohol and tobacco were more harmful than LSD, ecstasy and cannabis.

258. Sessa, *The Psychedelic Renaissance*.

259. Hitherto psychoactive drugs had been divided into euphoriants like opiates, inebriants such as alcohol and a class of drugs such as mescal called phantastica.

260. Fadiman, *The Psychedelic Explorer's Guide*. 198

261. Cohen, S. Lysergic acid diethylamide: side effects and complications. Journal of Nervous and Mental Disease. 1960. 130, 30–40

262. Hofmann, *LSD, My Problem Child.* 50
263. Kast 1966, Pahnke et al 1969, Grof et al 1973.
264. See chapter 22 for further discussion.
265. R. R. Griffiths & W. A. Richards & U. McCann & R. Jesse 2006. Psilocybin can occasion mystical-type experiences having substantial and sustained personal meaning and spiritual significance. Psychopharmacology 187(3), 268–83, commentaries 284–292.
266. Side effects were minimal. 8 of the 36 subjects had some significant anxiety or low mood during the session but this did not last for long and was deemed of no lasting import.
267. Sessa, *The Psychedelic Renaissance.* 170
268. Peter Gasser, Dominique Holstein, Yvonne Michel, Rick Doblin, Berra Yazar-Klosinski, Torsten Passie, and Rudolf Brenneisen, 2014. Safety and Efficacy of Lysergic Acid Diethylamide-Assisted Psychotherapy for Anxiety Associated With Life-threatening Diseases. Journal of Nervous and Mental Disease. www.jonmd.com.
269. methylenedioxymethamphetamine. MDMA. Street name is ecstasy.
270. Sessa, The Psychedelic Renaissance. 41
271. I was present at the Symposium on psychedelic drug treatment, held by the Royal College of Psychiatrists in 2009. Dr Ben Sessa chaired the meeting and noted the historic moment as this was the first such symposium for psychiatrists in the UK for many years. Michael Mithoefer presented his findings. Was this a cure for PTSD? Yes, it's a cure, he said.
272. Tarnas spoke at the London group of the Scientific and Medical Network in Hampstead in October 2013. The meeting was organized and hosted by Claudia Neilson.
273. Grof, *Realms of the Human Unconscious.* 70
274. The transpersonal psychologist Steve Taylor has written extensively on such phenomena. Taylor, S. Temporary and Permanent Awakening: the Primary and Secondary Shift. Journal of Transpersonal Research, 2013, Vol. 5 (2), 41–48
275. Walsh and Grob, *Higher wisdom. Eminent elders explore the continuing impact of psychedelics.* 226
276. ibid 216
277. ibid 230
278. This does not apply to some psychiatric disorders which respond better to CBT or similar methods that do not involve the deep layers of psyche.
279. Meckel Fischer, *Therapy with Substance.* London: Muswell Hill Press. 2014.

280. Sessa, B and Meckel Fischer, F. Underground LSD, MDMA and 2-CB-assisted Individual and Group Psychotherapy in Zurich: Outcomes, Implications and Commentary. Journal of Psychopharmacology / Journal of Independent Scientific Committee on Drugs. (Accepted June 2011, Due in print in 2014/15)

281. Hill, *Confrontation with the Unconscious.* 63

282. Jung warned that allowing the images to arise without working on them or taking the trouble to understand them conjured the negative effect of the unconscious.

283. In 2011 in the UK, Peter Aziz, a self-proclaimed healer and shaman, was sentenced to 15 months in prison for producing and supplying a class A drug.

284. A recent example of ayahuasca research is the paper by Gerald Thomas. Philippe Lucas, N. Rielle Capler, Kenneth W. Tupper and Gina Martin. Ayahuasca-Assisted Therapy for Addiction: Results from a Preliminary Observational Study in Canada. Current Drug Abuse Reviews, 2013. 6. www.maps.org.

285. Tarnas, *The Passion of the Western Mind.* 426

286. Michael Harner introduced these terms in *The Way of the Shaman*

287. Abraham Maslow, Fritz Perls and Will Schutz were all prominent figures in the movement in the 1960s.

288. Grof & Grof, *Holotropic Breathwork.*

289. For a detailed description of the practice of holotropic breathwork, see the Grof's book *Holotropic Breathwork.*

290. The Grofs have provided a number of retreats of this nature with the Buddhist teacher Jack Kornfeld.

291. Grof & Grof, *Holotropic Breathwork.* 162

292. ibid. 36

293. There may be or experiences of the micro world such as an experience of cellular consciousness, DNA or subatomic particles. A transcendence of temporal boundaries may include foetal, ancestral or experiences of life in a different historic period.

294. Grof, *Beyond the Brain.* 131

295. Grof & Grof, *Holotropic Breathwork.* x

296. Some people with previous experience of psychedelics tend to just wait for the experience to happen rather than engaging with it and encouraging it, and sometimes they feel that nothing happens.

297. ibid 37–43. This is one of the more controversial aspects of HBW. In the traditional psychotherapies, touch is taboo.

298. Eyerman, James. 2013. A clinical report of holotropic breathwork in 11.000 psychiatric patients in a community hospital setting. www.jameseyerman.com

299. Tennyson, *The Works of Tennyson,* ed.Hallam Tennyson 940
300. Grof, *Beyond the Brain.* 366
301. An international program to train facilitators in holotropic breathwork. www.gtt.com
302. The future of breathwork is not assured. There is an established international program to train facilitators but the structures to support a developing movement have not been adequately developed, such as organizational coherence, international conferences, peer review journal, a body of research and adaptation of the model to suit different scenarios and client groups.
303. As well as the international training programme at www.holotropic.com, I recommend the retreats organized in Spain by Juanjo Segura and Sitara Blasco www.holotropica.org and in England by Holly Harman and Debbie Dunning; www.holotropicuk.co.uk.
304. I believe that holotropic breathwork could have great value in the training of health care workers, particularly mental health workers. Not only would they learn techniques for the optimal management of archetypal crises but their powers of compassion could be enhanced with less risk of burn out.
305. A conversion disorder is a psychiatric condition where the underlying problem is an unbearable anxiety that becomes 'converted' to a physical symptom such as paralysis.
306. Greene, *Neptune: The Quest for Redemption.* 114
307. Bollas, *Hysteria.* 80–81.
308. Personal communication.
309. Addicts will often recognize that their dependency is a perverse form of the need to fuse with a force that is transcendent and this may explain why spiritual approaches such as the twelve step program may work so well in the treatment of addictions.
310. Ferrer, *Revisioning Transpersonal Theory.* 117
311. ibid 35
312. The spoken induction at the beginning of a holotropic breathwork session invites us to dedicate the work that we are about to undertake to the benefit of all beings.

Bibliography

Alexander, Eben. *Proof of Heaven: A Neurosurgeon's Journey into the Afterlife.* New York: Simon & Schuster, 2012.

Alison, James. *Undergoing God: Dispatches from the Scene of a Break-in.* London: Continuum, 2006.

Anderton, Stephen. *Christopher Lloyd: His Life at Great Dixter.* London: Chatto & Windus, 2010.

Armstrong, Karen. *The Great Transformation.* London: Atlantic Books, 2006.

Bache, Christopher. *Dark Night, Early Dawn.* New York. SUNY Press, 2000.

Ballatt, John & Campling, Penelope. *Intelligent Kindness.* London: RCPsych publications, 2011.

Bettelheim, Bruno. *The Uses of Enchantment.* London: Vintage Books, 1975.

Blackwell Sean. *Am I Bipolar or Just Waking Up?* USA: Createspace, 2011.

Bohm, David and Krishnamurti. J. *The Ending of Time.* San Francisco: Harper, 1985.

Bohm, D. and Weber R. *The Search for Unity: Dialogues with Scientists and Sages.* London: Routledge and Kegan Paul, 1986.

Bollas, Christopher. *Hysteria.* Hove UK: Routledge, 2000.

Bucke, Richard. *Cosmic Consciousness: A Study in the Evolution of the Human Mind,* 2001. Mineola, New York: Dover Publications, 2009.

Burkert, Walter. *The Anthropology of Ancient Greece Sacrificial Ritual and Myth.* Berkeley. Plutarch fragment 168, 1983.

Burns, Tom. *Our Necessary Shadow.* London: Allen Lane, 2013.

Butler, Renn. *Pathways to Wholeness.* London: Muswell Hill Press, 2014.

Campbell, Joseph. *The Hero with a Thousand Faces.* 3rd edition. Novato, CA: New World Library, 2008.

Capra, Fritjof. *The Tao of Physics.* London: Wildwood House, 1975.

Clarke, Isabel. (ed) *Psychosis and Spirituality: Consolidating the New Paradigm.* Chichester: Wiley – Blackwell, 2010.

Combs, Allan, and Holland, Mark. *Synchronicity: Science, Myth and the Trickster.* New York: Paragon House, 1990.

Daniels, Michael. *Shadow, Self, Spirit.* Exeter, UK: Imprint Academic, 2005.

Dass, Ram. *Still Here: Embracing Aging, Changing and Dying.* New York: Riverhead Books, 2001.

Dufrechou, Jay. *Moving through Grief: Reconnecting with Nature.* London: Muswell Hill Press, 2014.

Easwaran, Ecknath. *The Bhagavad Gita.* Berkeley CA: Nilgiri, 1985.

Evans-Wentz, W.E. *The Tibetan Book of the Dead.* London: Oxford University Press, 1957.

Fadiman, James. *The Psychedelic Explorer's Guide.* Rochester VT: Park Street Press, 2011.

Fenwick, Peter & Fenwick, Elizabeth. *The Art of Dying.* London: Continuum Press, 2008.

Ferrer, Jorge. *Revisioning Transpersonal Theory.* New York: SUNY Press, 2002.

Fontana, David. *Is there an Afterlife?* Ropley UK: O Books, 2004.

Foulkes, S.H. *Therapeutic Group Analysis.* 1964. London: Allen and Unwin. Reprinted London: Karnac, 1984.

Freud, Sigmund. *Mourning and Melancholia* XVII (2nd ed.), Hogarth Press, 1955.

Friedman, S. (Ed.) *The Reflecting Team in Action.* New York, NY: The Guilford Press,1995.

Glasser, M. (1979) Some aspects of the role of aggression in the perversions'. In I. Rosen (ed.) *Sexual Deviation.* 2nd edition, Oxford: Oxford University Press, 1996.

Goldacre, Ben. *Bad Science.* London: HarperCollins, 2008.

Greene, Liz. *Saturn: A New Look at an Old Devil.* San Francisco: Red Wheel / Weiser, 1976.

——. *Relating: An Astrological Guide to Living with Others on a Small Planet.* York Beach, ME: Samuel Weiser, 1978.

——. *Neptune: And the Quest for Redemption.* York Beach ME. Samuel Weiser, 2000.

Grof Stanislav & Christina (eds). *Spiritual Emergency: When Personal Transformation Becomes a Crisis.* New York: Penguin Putnam, 1989.

——. *Holotropic Breathwork.* Albany: SUNY Press, 2010.

Grof. Stanislav. *Realms of the Human Unconscious.* New York: Viking, 1975

——. *Beyond the Brain.* Albany: SUNY, 1985.

——. *The Cosmic Game: Explorations of the Frontiers of Human Consciousness.* Albany, NY: State University of New York Press, 1998.

——. *Psychology of the Future: Lessons from Modern Consciousness Research.* Albany, NY: State University of New York Press, 2000

——. *When the Impossible Happens.* Boulder Co: Sounds True, 2006.

——. *The Ultimate Journey: Consciousness and the Mystery of Death.* Santa Cruz, CA: MAPS. 2nd Edition, 2010.

Grossman, Vasily. *Life and Fate.* Vintage Digital.

Groves, Paramabandhu. *Practical Buddhism.* London: Muswell Hill Press, 2013.

Harner, Michael. *The Way of the Shaman.* San Francisco: Harper, 1980.

——. *Cave and Cosmos.* Berkeley CA. North Atlantic Books, 2013.

Hill, Scott. *Confrontation with the Unconscious.* London: Muswell Hill Press, 2013.

Hillman, James. *Re-Visioning Psychology.* New York: Harper Perennial, 1975.

Hofmann, Albert. *LSD: My Problem Child.* Sarasota FL. MAPS. 1983.

Hoeller, Stephan. *The Gnostic Jung and the Seven Sermons of the Dead.* Wheaton II. Quest. 1982.

Huxley, Aldous. *The Doors of Perception.* London: Flamingo, 1954.

——. *Moksha.* 1961. Rochester VT: Park Street Press, 1977.

James, William. *The Varieties of Religious Experience.* 1902. Edited by William Marty. New York. Penguin, 1985.

Jeans,, James. *The Mysterious Universe.* Cambridge, 1930.

Jung, C.G. *Synchronicity: An Acausal Connecting Principle.* London: Routledge, 1955.

——. *Collected Works Volume 8.* Translated by R.F.C.Hull. London: Routledge and Kegan Paul, 1969.

——. *Memories Dreams Reflections.* 1963. Edited by Aniele Jaffe. Repr., London: Flamingo, 1983.

Jung, Emma, and von Franz, Marie – Louise. *The Grail Legend.* London: Coventure. 1960.

Kabat-Zinn, Jon. *Wherever You Go, There You Are.* New York: Hyperion, 1994.

Kammerer, Paul. *Das Gesetz der Serie.* Berlin: Deutsche Verlags-Anstalt, 1919.

Koestler, Arthur. *Janus: A Summing Up.* New York: Random House,1978.

Kornfield, Jack. *A Path with a Heart. A Guide through the Perils and Promises of a Spiritual Life.* New York: Bantam Books,1993.

Kuhn, Thomas. *The Structure of Scientific Revolutions.* Chicago: University of Chicago Press, 1970.

Lamb. George (tr). *Blessed Raymond of Capua, The Life of St. Catherine of Siena,* tr. Rockford, Illinois: TAN Books, 2003

Le Grice, Keiron. *The Archetypal Cosmos: Rediscovering the Gods in Myth, Science and Astrology.* Edinburgh: Floris Books, 2010.

Le Grice, Keiron. *The Rebirth of the Hero: Mythology as a Guide to Spiritual Transformation.* London: Muswell Hill Press, 2013.

Leininger Andrea and Bruce. *Soul Survivor: The Reincarnation of a World War II Fighter Pilot.* London: Hay House, 2009.

Lucas, Catherine. *In Case of Spiritual Emergency.* Scotland: Findhorn Press, 2011.

Mace, Chris. *Mindfulness and Mental Health.* Hove, UK: Routledge, 2008.

Maslow, Abraham. *Religion, Values and Peak Experiences.* New York: Viking, 1964.

McLynn, Frank. *Carl Gustav Jung: A Biography.* New York: St Martins Griffin, 1996.

McTaggart, Lynn. *The Field.* USA: HarperCollins, 2001.

Menzies Lyth, Isobel. *Containing Anxiety in Institutions.* London: Free Association Books, 1988.

Monroe, Robert. *Journeys Out of the Body.* New York: Broadway Books, 1971.

——. *Far Journeys.* Garden City: Doubleday, 1985.

——. *The Ultimate Journey.* Garden City: Doubleday, 1994.

Moody, Raymond. *Life after Life.* London: Random House, 1975.

Nelson, John. *Healing the Split.* Albany: State University New York Press, 1994.

Otto, Rudolf. *The Idea of the Holy.* 1923. Repr., London. Oxford University Press, 1958.

Ovid. *Metamorphosis.* London: Penguin Classics, 2004.

Radin, Dean. *The Noetic Universe.* USA: HarperCollins, 1997.

——. *Entangled Minds.* New York: Simon & Schuster, 2006.

——. *Supernormal.* New York: Deepak Chopra Books, 2013.

Russell Peter. *The Global Brain.* Los Angeles: J.P. Tarcher, 1983.

Sannella, Lee. *The Kundalini experience: Psychosis or Transcendence.* Lower Lake CA: Integral publishing, 1987.

Sessa Ben. *The Psychedelic Renaissance.* London: Muswell Hill Press, 2012.

Shamsadani. S. Jung. C.G. *Liber Novus: The Red Book.* Norton and Co. New York, 2009.

Sheldrake, Rupert. *The Science Delusion.* London: Coronet, 2012.

Smith, Huston. *Tales of Wonder. Adventures Chasing the Divine.* New York: Harper Collins, 2009.

Sogyal Rinpoche. *The Tibetan Book of Living and Dying.* San Francisco, Harper Collins. 2002.

Sparks, Tav. *Movie Yoga: How Every Film Can Change Your Life.* Santa Cruz CA: Hanford Mead, 2009.

St Augustine. *Confessions.* Translated by R.S. Pine – Coffin. Middlesex: Penguin Classics, 1961.

Stein, Murray. *Jung's Map of the Soul.* Peru. IL. Open Court,1998.

Steiner, John. *Psychic Retreats.* London: Routledge, 1993.

Stevenson, Ian. *Children Who Remember Past Lives.* Jefferson: NC: McFarland, 2001.

Tarnas, Richard. *Cosmos and Psyche: Intimations of a New World View.* New York: Viking, 2006.

———. *The Passion of the Western Mind: Understanding the Ideas That Have Shaped Our World View.* 1991. Repr., London Pimlico, 1993.

Tart, Charles. *The End of Materialism.* Oakland CA: New Harbinger Publications, 2009.

Tennyson, Alfred Lord, *The Works of Tennyson,* ed. Baron Hallam Tennyson London: Macmillan, 1913

Tiner, J.H. *Isaac Newton: Inventor, Scientist and Teacher.* Milford, Michigan, U.S.: Mott Media, 1975.

Tucker, Jim. *Life before Life.* New York: St Martins Griffin, 2005.

Van Lommel, Pim. *Consciousness Beyond Life.* New York: Harper Collins, 2007.

von Franz, Marie-Louise. *C.G. Jung. His Myth in Our Time.* Toronto: Inner City Books, 1975.

———. *Projection and Re-collection in Jungian Psychology.* La Salle, IL: Open Court, 1980.

Walsh, Roger & Grob, Charles. *Eminent Elders Explore the Continuing Impact of psychedelics.* Albany: SUNY Press, 2005.

Washburn, Michael. *The Ego and the Dynamic Ground: A Transpersonal View of Human Development.* 2nd Edition. Albany: State University of New York Press, 1995.

Waterfield, Robin. *Plato: The Republic.* London: Oxford University Press, 1993.

Weintrobe, S. *Engaging with Climate Change. Psychoanalytic and Interdisciplinary Perspectives.* London: Routledge, 2012.

Whitehead, Alfred North. *Process and Reality.* New York: Free Press, 1979.

Wikman, Monika. *Pregnant Darkness.* Berwick ME. Nicolas – Hays, 2004.

Wilber Ken. (ed) *Quantum Questions.* Boulder: Shambala,1984.

———. *A Brief History of Everything.* Dublin: Gateway,1996.

Winnicott, Donald. *Collected Papers: Hate in the Counter Transference.* London: Tavistock, 1954.

Wolfe, Tom. *The Electric Kool Aid Acid Test.* London: Black Swan Books, 1968.

Woolger, Roger. *Other Lives, Other Selves.* London: Thorsons, 1999.

Zukav, Gary. *The Dancing Wu Li Masters.* New York: William Morrow, 1979.

Index

Dr Tim Read is a psychiatrist in private practice in London, UK.